Digital Media and Technologies for Virtual Artistic Spaces

Dew Harrison
University of Wolverhampton, UK

Managing Director:	Lindsay Johnston
Editorial Director:	Joel Gamon
Book Production Manager:	Jennifer Yoder
Publishing Systems Analyst:	Adrienne Freeland
Development Editor:	Myla Merkel
Assistant Acquisitions Editor:	Kayla Wolfe
Typesetter:	Christina Henning
Cover Design:	Jason Mull

Published in the United States of America by
Information Science Reference (an imprint of IGI Global)
701 E. Chocolate Avenue
Hershey PA 17033
Tel: 717-533-8845
Fax: 717-533-8661
E-mail: cust@igi-global.com
Web site: http://www.igi-global.com

Library of Congress Cataloging-in-Publication Data

Digital media and technologies for virtual artistic spaces / Dew Harrison, editor.
     pages cm
 Includes bibliographical references and index.
 Summary: "This book brings together a variety of artistic practices in virtual spaces and the interest in variable media and online platforms for creative interplay, presenting frameworks and examples of current practices"--Provided by publisher.
 ISBN 978-1-4666-2961-5 (hardcover) -- ISBN 978-1-4666-2962-2 (ebook) -- ISBN 978-1-4666-2963-9 (print & perpetual access) 1. Art and the Internet. I. Harrison, Dew, 1952- editor of compilation.
 NX180.I57D54 2013
 776--dc23
                                          2012037378

British Cataloguing in Publication Data
A Cataloguing in Publication record for this book is available from the British Library.

All work contributed to this book is new, previously-unpublished material. The views expressed in this book are those of the authors, but not necessarily of the publisher.

Editorial Advisory Board

Table of Contents

Detailed Table of Contents

Chapter 1
The Re-Materialisation of the Art Object 1
> *Dew Harrison, University of Wolverhampton, UK*

The phenomena of the re-materialisation of the art object is presented through the shift in art-thinking since mid-last century, derived from the impact of earlier art. This shift is marked by Lippard's seminal book on the disappearance of the art object, as reflected in the title above, with reference to the Duchampian Readymade and Greenbergian Modernism. The chapter then reviews the current situation via contemporary understandings and the writings of Beech who challenges Lippard's view of immateriality within Conceptual art. This is followed by examples of recent practice where new technologies have allowed for a re-materialisation of the art object to include artists such as Intersculpt, Michael Eden, and those in the Second Life Kriti Island exhibition, where virtual objects solidified into physical forms. This re-positioning of the art object allows a return to the initial formative conceptual framework, and offers a way through to a cutting-edge form of postconceptual art practice.

Chapter 2
Data-Objects: Sharing the Attributes and Properties of Digital and Material Culture to Creatively
Interpret Complex Information 14
> *Ian Gwilt, Sheffield Hallam University, UK*

This chapter discusses a current shift away from thinking about ideas of virtual reality, towards a conversation around hybrid digital/physical constructs and the notions of mixed or augmented reality. In particular the chapter explores how physical artifacts that are based on data extracted from computer generated virtual spaces are being created as a way of challenging how we read, interpret, and respond to digital information. This emerging trend for the realization of data sets into three-dimensional (3D) physical objects is discussed from the perspective of creative practice and digital information visualization. In these new constructs, digital data sets are concretized into a physical form, remediated from information sources, such as mobile phone coverage records, crime statistics, and temperature patterns. Through a series of examples, the chapter will investigate how these tangible translations can change our relationship to screen-based digital content, in particular statistical data, and seeks to reveal how by encoding digital information into a physical object we can establish a way of reading this data through spatial, temporal, and material variations that sit outside of the computer-monitor and the digital environment. Rapid prototyping making techniques are discussed as a trigger for a conversation around the ontological and epistemological readings of these liminal physical/data objects.

Chapter 3

Martin Rieser, De Montfort University, UK

This chapter will examine and critically align a number of pioneering projects from around the world, using mobile and pervasive technologies, which have challenged the design and delivery of mobile artworks, as documented on the author's weblog and book The Mobile Audience (Rodopi, 2011). These will be presented together with examples from the artist's own research and practice, which have been concerned with the liminal nature of digital media and the intersection of the real and virtual, the physicality of place, and the immateriality of the imaginary in artistic spaces. Two projects in process are also referenced: The Prisoner—a motion-captured, emotionally responsive avatar in the round—and Secret Garden—a virtual reality digital opera. Lastly, this chapter considers the nature of digital materiality in the exhibition of miniature Internet transmitted sculptures: Inside Out: Sculpture in the Digital Age.

Chapter 4

Paul Sermon, University of Salford, UK
Charlotte Gould, University of Salford, UK

This chapter brings together the practice-based creative research of artists Charlotte Gould and Paul Sermon, culminating in collaborative interactive installations for urban screens that investigate new forms of social and/or political narratives in site-specific urban environments. The authors' current creative practice looks specifically at the concepts of social presence and performance and attempts to bridge two remote locations either virtually (using online virtual environments such as Second Life) or in the physical space through mixed reality techniques and interfaces that allow the public to direct the narrative and creative outcomes of the artwork.

Chapter 5

Denise Doyle, University of Wolverhampton, UK

This chapter interrogates the notion of the liminal in relation to the virtual and the imaginary through a consideration of the field of art and technology and current creative practices in virtual worlds and avatar-mediated space. In particular, the art project Meta-Dreamer (2009) is considered through the manifestation of the avatar as digital object. In its attempt to explore the experience of "living between worlds," it reflects the concerns of contemporary arts practice exploration of time and space relationships.

Chapter 6

Elif Ayiter, Sabancı University, Istanbul
Stefan Glasauer, Ludwig-Maximilian University, Munich
Max Moswitzer, University of Fine Arts, Zürich

This chapter will discuss the artistic processes involved in the creation of the three dimensional, virtual art installation La Plissure du Texte 2, which is the sequel to Roy Ascott's ground breaking telematically networked art work La Plissure du Texte, created in 1983 and shown in Paris at the Musée de l'Art Moderne de la Ville de Paris during that same year. While the underlying concepts of the original art work, as well as its capability of regenerating itself as an entirely novel manifestation based upon the concepts of distributed authorship, textual mobility, emergent semiosis, multiple identity, and participatory poesis will be underlined, the main focus of the text will be upon the creative strategies as well as the technological means through which the architecture was brought about in the contemporary creative environment of the metaverse. A further topic that will be covered is the challenge of exhibiting what is after all an art work that requires full virtual immersion to bring about a deep level experience and understanding of it, in the physical world, i.e. 'Real Life'5—in a gallery or museum space in which such a virtual immersion cannot be readily obtained.

Chapter 7

The chapter presents the trajectory of a collaborative art practice towards intuitive interaction for visitors accessing virtual spaces to achieve a shared holistic understanding of a complex system. From initial explorations into the efficacy of associative media for constructing conceptual-based artworks, in that hypermedia developed from the intent of augmenting human intellect, behaviours were applied to hypermedia data items. The rationale for this is explained through developments in the ongoing 'Deconstructing Duchamp' project, where 'flocking' behaviours have been applied to Duchampian digitised items to observe the familial relations within, and key to his work, at play. Following this project, a second work 'Shift-Life' has proceeded to further develop the idea of allotting animal-like behaviours to electronic data items giving them the appearance of possessing a basic intelligence. By then, observing their response to our physical interactions, we can glean a clearer understanding from their inter-relationships of a complex conceptual framework.

This chapter explores the philosophical notion of The Virtual in response to the writings of Gilles Deleuze and unfolds this thinking through its interdisciplinary and transformative affects upon contemporary fine art. The Virtual will be discussed in relation to forms of contemporary painting, yet provides a model for thinking through interdisciplinarity within, and from, other media. The Virtual acts as an instigator for change, which effectively destabilises the pre-formity2 attached to medium-specific practices. It is for this reason that The Virtual forces external relationships and connections to come to the fore in order to radically alter and transform the physical and conceptual constructs of different disciplines. This chapter will highlight these important ideas and present new ways to consider The Virtual in relation to contemporary fine art practice, with a particular focus upon current issues in Painting.

Drawing firstly on animation, this chapter will consider how applications of sound may demand new conceptual frameworks for animated work to develop. Making reference to audio-visual sound theory, the acousmatic and cinematic histories, the discussion surveys aspects of animation sound, and suggests the potential for exposing the sonic elements of the form to evaluation using means beyond current film-sound concepts. The application of recorded sound and the role it performs in the re-creation of synthetic life in new animated situations brings unconsidered possibilities for sound-image concepts. How sound functions and how it combines with an image on screen, in order to create a listening involvement in animation, is central to this consideration. Nevertheless, as the form transgresses, it is evolving from the structured sound space of the traditional screen; new spaces may present different challenges that motivate different sound to picture equations.

Chapter 10

Ian P. Stone, Independent, UK

Cinema remains current and saleable by constantly revolutionising the mode of its distribution. Film Auteurs are affected by these changes, using the contemporary "tools of their trade" to their advantage. This chapter focuses on two Auteurs' use of digital technologies. Jean Luc Godard, one of the most innovative filmmakers of the last fifty years is a recent convert to digital film, having denounced the medium previously. Mike Figgis has been an advocate of digital filmmaking until recently, when he has been more circumspect. These filmmakers employ techniques indebted to Sergei Eisenstein and Bertholt Brecht. The "active" variant of third text understandings applied represent a "para-formalistic discourse" where the audience is made aware of the film's artifice, projecting the audience into an ontological virtual space where they are compelled to confront conditions around them. A tentative advocacy of the digital as an aid to enhancing this experience is here advanced.

Chapter 11

Judith Aston, University of the West of England, UK

This chapter discusses ways in which the database narrative techniques of virtual media can be used to explore the relationship between real-world oral storytelling and embodied performance in the cultural transmission of memory. It is based on an ongoing collaboration between the author and the historical anthropologist, Wendy James, to develop a multilayered associative narrative, which considers relationships between experience, event, and memory among a displaced community. The work is based on a substantial living archive of photographs, audio, cine, and video recordings collected by Wendy James in the Sudan/Ethiopian borderlands from the mid-1960s to the present day. Its critical context relates to the 'sensory turn' in anthropology and to 'beyond text' debates within the arts and humanities regarding ways in which we can capture and represent the sensory experiences of the past.

Chapter 12

Rina Arya, University of Wolverhampton, UK

The transition from the real to the digital requires a shift of consciousness that can be theorised with recourse to the concept of liminality, which has multidisciplinary currency in psychology and other disciplines in the social sciences, cultural, and literary theory. In anthropology the notion of liminality was introduced by the ethnographer Arnold van Gennep in the context of the development of the rite of passage. Since van Gennep's discussion of the concept, the term has been used in a variety of contexts and disciplines that range from psychology, religion, sociology, and latterly in new media, where it has a renewed emphasis because of the transition from the real to the virtual space of the digital interface.

Chapter 13

The information society manufactures, manipulates, and commodifies information. Heritage is one such area that is undergoing digital transformation. Heritage is increasingly being transmuted through digitisation devices such as laser and structured light scans into multiple representations of information. The rich information of a heritage object or an environment can be restructured, transmitted, and recomposed into a mediated form both textual and non-textual. Once digitised, it becomes free from its physical predecessor; it enters another world that defies the physical laws of nature where the imagination of the maker is a limit. Such worlds accompanied by their objects are accessible in new yet intuitive ways via surface computers. The horizontal nature of the multitouch-multiuser surface computer then becomes the mirror that links both worlds, allowing access into a virtual space via the touch-table computing paradigm. This chapter explores 3D surface computing, its technology, capabilities, and limits with developments of two multitouch applications incorporating heritage objects and environments, and the observation of the reactions of initial users. It addresses new issues and challenges surrounding the use of surface computing and how the access and transmission of heritage information via multitouch-multiuser tables are able to contribute to the accessibility, teaching, and learning of heritage.

Artists who engage with the earth sciences have been able to explore all kinds of information about the natural environment, including information about the atmosphere, extremes of physical formations across immense dimensions of time and space, and increasingly 'invisible' realms of materials at the nanoscale. This is a rich area for identifying the relationship between digital and material cultures as many artists working with this subject are crossing boundaries and testing out the liminal spaces between the virtual and the real. After an overview of theoretical links between visualisation and geology, mineralogy and crystallography, this chapter explores four themes: (1) environment and experience, (2) code and pattern, (3) co-creation and participation, and (4) mining heritage.

This chapter explores the continuum between old and new media and presents the research area of Metaplastic Art and Design. The description of the Metaplastic Metaspace and its own methodology create interactive virtual spaces for Cyber Art between reality and virtual realities, from living code to software and vice versa through the Metaplastic Opencode Platform.

In Aristotelian philosophy, the process of change from a lower level of "potentiality" to the higher level of "actuality" is known as "becoming," or to become more and more of what one is, or capable of "becoming." For this process to take place, the dissolution of the normative values or understanding of one's self and context is necessary (Turner, 1968). Such dissolution, although initially destabilising, can create an environment conducive to the values and normal modes of behaviour being reflected upon and transformed. The chapter considers how selected context-responsive projects that use the Internet, develop and harness "communitas" (Turner, 1967) and function as "liminoid" (Turner, 1974) space, facilitating new understandings of place. The virtual manifestations of place highlighted are then reflected upon for their potential in the process of "place-making" to enable the process of "becoming," for people and the specific location.

Preface

Digital media and new technology is reconfiguring our relationship with the world and is also affecting how artists relate with their public. Current technologies can help to position art into the everyday of people's lives and activities, outside the gallery space. Digitally enabled new spaces have opened up where artists can engage with audiences in a participatory experience. Within the cityscapes of our urban environments, "Big Brother" media and CCTV surveillance allow for few informal, ungoverned social meeting places; therefore, it is the creation of interstices between the formal constructed and observed social spaces, where unorthodox art can happen and engage directly with its audience, that artists are interested in. Digital media provides such relational opportunities but as virtual platforms where accessing them means stepping from one world to the other, a conceptual moving from one state of being to another. Contrary to this human-to-avatar experience, virtual objects are being transformed into solid materiality by crossing this threshold between worlds. The threshold is then a magic alchemical space, an interstice between the real and the virtual, a moment of change, of becoming the other.

ISEA (Inter Society of the Electronic Arts) holds an annual seminal event for digital media art practice and research. For the two past ISEA conferences, I convened panels to discuss new work and ideas that cross the boundary between the analogue and the digital. For ISEA2009, a panel explored practice and curation across virtual and real spaces, while the ISEA2011 panel interrogated the varied forms of theory and practice apparent in approaching the liminal space positioned between the virtual and the real. Artists continue to explore the notion of the "liminal" that has arisen with the evolution of digital technology. The latter panel presented current contemporary understandings of this amorphous state of presence by generating discussion and argument around its nature. Considering the diverse determinations as to what the liminal means in our digitally driven culture this panel asked, "To what extent are artists digitally facilitating convivial spaces where participants can engage with and co-create an art work?" Different approaches were displayed within the panel expertise to interrogate digitally facilitated liminality as either a transformative space of creative transcendence or a convivial and social space where art occurs.

Although conference proceedings are published from these events, the panel talks are not included, and there exists a need for an edited collection of chapters in this area of digitally enabled transitional spaces for creative exploration. *Digital Media and Technologies for Virtual Artistic Spaces* brings the work of the panel speakers together and aims to provide relevant theoretical frameworks and examples of current practice in this area of variable media and virtual spaces for artists, theorists, and curators, as well as researchers working both in the field and beyond, to those working with new technologies, social media platforms, and digital/material culture. Digitally created and virtual platforms have emerged to become part of our everyday lives. We use them to socialize, play, and work. Artists have been experimenting within virtual spaces over the last decade with ongoing interests in identity, imagination, interactive play, and more recently, materializing code. The book displays expertise in varied forms of artistic practice in virtual spaces and shows the interest in variable media and online platforms for creative interplay. This specific synthesis of new technology and art practice, although centered on bridging the virtual to the real world offers an expansive take on creative digital practice and liminal spaces.

The first chapter, "The Re-Materialisaton of the Art Object," presents the shift in art-thinking since mid-last century derived from the impact of earlier art, and brings us to the phenomena of the re-materialisation of the art object. By giving examples of recent practice where new technologies have allowed for this re-materialisation, where virtual objects have solidified into physical forms, a re-positioning of the art object is undertaken. This then allows a return to the initial formative conceptual framework and offers a way through to a cutting-edge form of postconceptual art practice.

Ian Gwilt, in "Data-Objects: Sharing the Attributes and Properties of Digital and Material Culture to Creatively Interpret Complex Information," continues to explore the materialisation of virtual art objects by moving the discussion from virtual reality to that of hybrid digital/physical constructs and the notions of mixed reality.

Martin Rieser outlays his practice of moving between virtual and real worlds in "Mobility, Liminality, and Digital Materiality," where he critically aligns the use of mobile and pervasive technologies in a number of pioneering projects, with his own practice concerned with the liminal nature of digital media. His work lies at the intersection of the physicality of place and the immateriality of the imaginary in artistic spaces.

Paul Sermon and Charlotte Gould bring together their practice-based research in "Site-Specific Performance, Narrative, and Social Presence in Multi-User Virtual Environments and the Urban Landscape." They look at the concepts of social presence and performance and attempt to bridge two remote locations either virtually (using online virtual environments such as Second Life) or in the physical space through mixed reality techniques and interfaces that allow the public to direct the narrative and creative outcomes of the artworks.

Denise Doyle, in her chapter, "Living between Worlds: Imagination, Liminality, and Avatar-Mediated Presence," interrogates the notion of the liminal in relation to the virtual and the imaginary through a consideration of the field of art and technology, and current creative practices in virtual worlds and avatar-mediated space.

Elif Ayiter continues with the theme of virtual worlds and avatars in "LPDT2: La Plissure du Texte 2," where she discusses the artistic processes involved in the creation of the 3D virtual art installation La Plissure du Texte 2, a sequel to Roy Ascott's ground breaking telematically networked artwork La Plissure du Texte, 1983.

The next chapter, "Can Duchampian and Darwinian Virtual Objects Ever Behave Themselves?" follows with another exposition of a virtual world as creative space, this time not with avatars but with digital objects which are given human and animal-like behaviours. This chapter offers the trajectory of a collaborative art practice towards intuitive interaction for visitors in the real world accessing virtual spaces to achieve a shared holistic understanding of a complex system.

Alistair Payne explores the philosophical positioning of The Virtual in response to the writings of Giles Deleuze. In "The Virtual and Interdisciplinarity," he unfolds this thinking through its interdisciplinary and transformative affects upon contemporary fine art, specifically painting, but as an expanded practice engaging with other media.

Ross Winning, in "Behind the Sonic Veil: Considering Sound as the Mediator of Illusory Life in Variable and Screen-Based Media," draws on animation to examine how applications of sound may demand new conceptual frameworks for the traditional screen and enable new virtual moving image spaces to develop.

Ian Stone also explores traditional and digital screen space in his chapter "Para-Formalistic Discourse and Virtual Space in Film." He focuses on the use of digital technologies by two Auteurs' who use the "active" variant of the third text in their films to make the audience aware of a film's artifice, and project them into an ontological virtual space where they are compelled to confront the conditions around them.

Judith Aston considers screen space within her chapter calling for a "sensory turn" in anthropology in its meeting with new media. "Database Narrative, Spatial Montage, and the Cultural Transmission of Memory: A Case Study from the Sudan/Ethiopian Borderlands" looks at the potential of the Internet as a means through which real-world project materials can be made available to the wider diaspora as a basis to which others can add their own stories.

Rina Arya unpacks the term "liminal" or "liminality" and examines its applicability in a wider context beyond anthropology in her chapter "Exploring Liminality from an Anthropological Perspective".

Eugene Ch'ng considers Heritage as another area undergoing digital transformation in his chapter "The Mirror between Two Worlds: 3D Surface Computing for Objects and Environments." He sees heritage as increasingly being transmuted through digitisation devices such as laser and structure light scans into multiple representations of information. Once digitized, it becomes free from its physical predecessor and enters a world that defies the physical laws of nature where the imagination of the maker is the limit. The multi-touch table then becomes the mirror linking the real to the virtual world.

Suzette Worden, in "The Earth Sciences and Creative Practice: Exploring Boundaries between Digital and Material Culture," continues with the theme of heritage but only as it pertains to mining heritage. Her chapter concerns those artists who engage with the earth sciences and have been able to explore all kinds of information about the natural environment, including the atmosphere and extremes of physical formations across immense dimensions of time and space, and increasingly "invisible" realms of materials at the nanoscale.

Gianluca Mura, in "Metaplastic Cyber Opencode Art," explores the continuum between old and new media and presents the research area of Metaplastic Art and Design. Within this, he relates his own methodology for creating interactive virtual spaces for Cyber Art between reality and virtual realities.

Anita McKeown considers the process of "becoming" in her chapter, "Virtual Communitas, Digital 'Place-Making,' and the Process of 'Becoming,'" and how selected context-responsive projects that use the Internet can develop and harness communitas and function as liminoid space facilitating new understandings of place.

The chapters collected from the ISEA panel sessions together reflect the research and critical practice currently taking place in creatively exploring the space between the real and virtual worlds, and the conceptual approaches toward this. They include varied forms of practice, from avatars to film and animation, from heritage and anthropology to nanotechnology and from earth sciences to artificial intelligence. They move through painting, sculpture, and craft to conceptual art practice and social artwork in their scope, and offer insightful understandings of how the digital is offering new opportunities for the creation of virtual artistic spaces.

Dew Harrison
University of Wolverhampton, UK

Acknowledgment

I would like to gratefully thank all the Editorial Board members and reviewers, particularly Rina Arya, Gianluca Mura, Maggie Parker, Barbara Rauch, and Hal Thwaites.

I would also like to thank all the authors who have generously and patiently contributed to this book. With their important, innovative, and exciting work, they have made this book possible, particularly Elif Ayiter, Judith Aston, Eugene Ch'ng, Denise Doyle, Ian Gwilt, Anita McKeown, Alistair Payne, Martin Rieser, Paul Sermon, Ian Stone, Ross Winning, and Suzette Worden.

I wish to thank all at IGI Global for their kind and supportive help during the time taken to develop this book, with particular thanks to Myla Merkel. Her professional assistance and guidance have been much appreciated throughout this endeavour.

Thank you,

Dew Harrison
University of Wolverhampton, UK

Chapter 1
The Re–Materialisation of the Art Object

Dew Harrison
University of Wolverhampton, UK

ABSTRACT

The phenomena of the re-materialisation of the art object is presented through the shift in art-thinking since mid-last century, derived from the impact of earlier art. This shift is marked by Lippard's seminal book on the disappearance of the art object, as reflected in the title above, with reference to the Duchampian Readymade and Greenbergian Modernism. The chapter then reviews the current situation via contemporary understandings and the writings of Beech who challenges Lippard's view of immateriality within Conceptual art. This is followed by examples of recent practice where new technologies have allowed for a re-materialisation of the art object to include artists such as Intersculpt, Michael Eden, and those in the Second Life Kriti Island exhibition, where virtual objects solidified into physical forms. This re-positioning of the art object allows a return to the initial formative conceptual framework, and offers a way through to a cutting-edge form of postconceptual art practice.

INTRODUCTION

Within the Fine Art field, articulating the idea of the art object had made redundant the desire for the actual artifact by 1972 when text, language, and dialogue became the tools of a post-Duchampian Conceptual practice. The term 'postmodern' appeared in 1973, became current in the second half of the 1970s, and posited the end of art history as a linear narrative. Our considerations of art ideas were then contextualized without the need of anchorage to the history of object making. The second postmodern period, beginning at the end of the Cold War, was multiculturalist and global. Art became a form of social engagement concerned with social production, it allowed for multitemporality and syncretic identity. This era of the worldwide Web and global hypermobility

DOI: 10.4018/978-1-4666-2961-5.ch001

gave rise to new ways of perceiving human space and according to Nicholas Bourriaud, "The term 'postmodern' can be applied to art that is refractory to these two types of perspective: spatial and temporal." The virtual worlds of the new century are the playgrounds for artists to explore space, time, and identity, the digital objects created here are experienced by avatar, without the full range of sensory perceptions we use when confronting the real world. We cannot become truly digital so is it now time for those virtual art objects to materialize into physical solid form?

Artists, designers, and craft makers are currently exploring new materials and processes such as 'Accumulated Printing' within their practice to bring forth new forms and extend ideas. Often this is through a hybrid dialogic process of a maker's thoughts translated into code in the virtual world for production in the real world. Resulting in unique crafted objects created without the 'touch' of the hand-made, while encapsulating craft-thinking in the machine-made. This real-virtual-real approach is further streamlined, and without the craft signature, when working in shared virtual space. As artists are moving objects across the virtual from the real and back into solid form, so cyberspace gains a foothold in the real through materialisation and a return to the virtual. The second life platform is relatively new and still under development, but there are a number of artists beginning to explore the possibilities of this virtual world outside its commercial premise. For the Kritical Works in SL curation project artists were invited to the island to develop their practice with regard to bridging the virtual with the real world, and two of them created physical objects, which responded directly to their virtual counterparts. These materialised objects were exhibited in the Golden Thread Gallery, Belfast.

The solid, material art object was the central focus of Modernism derived from a history of making, skill, and craftsmanship through ages of different agendas dictated by patrons and the art market. In attempting to both circumnavigate the driving economic forces and to escape the restrictions of Greenbergian orthodox Modernism artists in the 1960s and 1970s re-visited the work of artists at the beginning of that century, such as Marcel Duchamp and the Dadaists. These early artists had moved away from the conventional object making of paintings and sculptures by weighting aesthetic values towards the 'idea' encapsulated in an artwork. The Conceptualists and proto-conceptualists then took this notion to the extreme point where the artwork had no material quality at all, no existence in the physical world. In the new century, we have virtual worlds and digital means of mass-production for manufacturing physical objects from code. We have craft-makers and artists re-investing in the exploration of materials, processes, and means of production, transferring ideas of the hand-made to machine production and formulating new approaches to making, skill, and craftsmanship. We also have social networks provided by the Internet and artists pursuing a social art practice, we have social virtual worlds in forms such as the Second Life (SL) platform on the Web, and the Web itself is in the process of development from Web 2.0 to Web 3.0 to become 'the internet of things.' Contemporary designers and engineers have now begun to explore the potential of rapid prototyping for manufacturing solid objects from code. The code can be taken from a virtual world or Internet site, which is where artists have been working for some time, and a growing number of them are beginning to experiment with the idea of the coded object. Are we then, on the verge of a re-materialisation of the art object?

The School of Art and Design at the University of Wolverhampton has a Second Life island for creative potential and experimentation. Dr. Denise Doyle, a SL artist and researcher, has curated two exhibitions on Kriti island for showing at ISEA2008 and ISEA2009 (Doyle, 2008, 2009). The first set of artists had a clear investment in the idea of bridging the virtual island to a real world space. For the second exhibition, Doyle specifically requested that this was to be the main agenda, which interestingly, resulted in two objects materialising from the virtual social platform for plinth display in the Golden Thread Gallery, Belfast.

This chapter therefore presents an exploration of the shift from object to idea, from the materially bound art of Modernism and the unleashing of the 'idea' by Marcel Duchamp, to the Conceptualist stance defined by Lucy Lippard in her seminal text *Six Years: The Dematerialization of the art object from 1966 to 1972:...*(Lippard, 1973). Almost 40 years later, her exposition of Conceptual practice is contested by David Beech and allows the chapter to move on through a voyage of post-Conceptual, postmodernist new media practice towards the digital virtual object and Relational Social Art with a view to Web 3.0. It then leads us to artists, designers and craft makers exploring processes within digital manufacture that transform ideas into solid form, and finally to the recent "Kritical Works in SL I and II" exhibitions (Doyle, 2008, 2009). The Kriti works are indicative of a return to the unique material-bound solid art work, complete with 'aura'—but perhaps only with the understanding that these pieces are acting in the 'new' position of 'transitional object,' intending to bridge the virtual platform with the real world for the visitor.

DE-MATERIALISING THE ART OBJECT

Marshall Berman's *All That is Solid Melts into Air* (Berman, 1982), written between 1971 and 1981, examines social and economic modernization and its conflicting relationship with Modernism. The title is a line from Karl Marx's *Communist Manifesto*, and in the second section, he uses Marxist texts to analyze the self-destructive nature of modernization. His intent was to show how

people from different walks of life were sharing "certain distinctively modern concerns... moved at once by the will to change—to transform both themselves and their world" (Berman, 1982, p. 13), Berman considered the living of modern life as a paradox and contradiction and stated that "It is to be overpowered by the immense bureaucratic organizations that have the power to control and often destroy all communities...; and yet to be undeterred in our determination to face these forces, to fight to change their world..." (Berman, 1982, p. 13). His book is largely declaring a move towards the Postmodern. Less than ten years earlier, Lippard had documented Conceptual Art from 1966 – 1972 as highly politicized in that artists were indeed sharing those 'distinctively modern concerns' and were in the process of facing the 'forces' in order to change their world. Lippard declared Conceptual Art as a product of the political ferment of the times, and states that her own version of Conceptual Art practice is "inevitably tempered by my feminist and left politics" (Lippard, 1973).

This politicised understanding of a Conceptual Art practice pertains to her own and others, but not to all artists, for example, contemporary to Lippard were Art and Language in the UK who centered their work on the internal dialogues of the group within the autonomy of art. Although, their documents could be read as the policies of the group's internalized art-political discourse affecting the larger art politics of the day.

In an article for Art International in 1968, she maintained that 'ideas were in the air' and that "the spontaneous appearance of similar work totally unknown to the artists that can be explained only as energy generated by (well known, common) sources and by the wholly unrelated art against which all potentially 'conceptual' artists were commonly reacting," (Chandler & Lippard, 1968, pp. 31-36). In order to escape the confines of culture and the patriarchal mythologies of the art world, art became immersed in counter-culture and transformed by the Conceptualists who attempted a tabula rasa for new forms as articulated by Joseph Beuys "Objects aren't very important for me any more…I am trying to reaffirm the concept of art and creativity in the face of Marxist doctrine… For me the formation of the thought is already sculpture" (Lippard, 1973). Lippard considered that as work was designed in the studio for professionally crafted execution elsewhere, the art object had become merely the end product. She saw that a number of artists were losing interest in the physical evolution of the work of art and that the studio was again becoming a study. To Lippard, this 'trend' appeared to be provoking a profound dematerialisation of art (Chandler & Lippard, 1968, p. 31). Seminal to her texts is the understanding that Conceptual Art means "work in which the idea is paramount and the material form is secondary, lightweight, ephemeral, cheap, unpretentious, and/or 'dematerialized'" (Chandler & Lippard, 1968, p. 31).

Interestingly, new technologies and social communication channels have allowed contemporary artists to consider a return to the studio and to the method of crafting objects outside it. A revision of the situation where the idea is still paramount, but now exists within an art object with extended reach contextualising it into the larger socio/political world. Thus, the material form can now be placed on equal footing with the idea. This reviewed position is discussed in more detail, later in the chapter.

To support her understanding of Conceptual Art, Lippard identifies the historical source for this form of dematerialised practice as Marcel Duchamp and the re-reading of Duchamp's work undertaken by practitioners in the 1960s ensured that Duchamp was a major catalyst in the turning of the Modern to the Postmodern. Duchamp was a Modernist artist who remained highly influential in the Postmodern climate through his practice of promoting the 'ideas' and 'concepts' within his work to a higher value than, and taking precedence over, the traditional visual aesthetic. According to art historian Amelia Jones (1994),

Duchamp is consistently featured in Postmodern discourse as the origin of radical Postmodern practices. "Duchamp, with his ironic readymade gesture, is seen as having inspired younger artists in their critique of Greenbergian Modernism and the modernist institutions of art" (Jones, 1994, p. 56). Jones understands Postmodernism as both challenging and in succession to Modernism, she argues that the term Postmodernism is applied to those contemporary art practices which she defines as progressive or radical and that it is therefore in direct conflict with—has an inherent resistance to—Modernism as defined by Clement Greenberg in his theories of modernist art.

THE RE-DEFINITION OF THE ART OBJECT

The reappraisal of the Duchamp's 'Readymade' art objects in the 1960s situated them in direct opposition to the then dominant orthodox view of 'Modernism' within the field of fine art, most clearly articulated by the critic Clement Greenberg. Greenberg understood art as a 'pure' practice concerned with medium specificity for visual aesthetics, whereas the Readymade epitomized Duchamp's premise that it was the 'idea' underlying the artwork that was paramount to a variety of practices within the domain of art. Greenberg's Modernism was an attempt to provide an historical and critical framework within which most modern art could be conventionally understood. His 1965 paper "Modernist Painting" gave a retrospective account of the development of painting since Edouard Manet, moving through the work of Paul Cezanne, the Cubists, and Piet Mondrian to the contemporary paintings of the American Abstract Expressionists. In these paintings, Greenberg recognised the inherent qualities of the medium identified as colour, flatness, edge, and scale seeing the attainment of high quality in painting as determined by self-definition, self-criticism, and the elimination of elements from other disciplines.

"The essence of modernism lies, as I see it, in the use of the characteristic methods of a discipline to criticize the discipline itself – not in order to subvert it, but to entrench it more firmly in its area of competence" (Greenberg, 1965, p. 194).

In this sense, Greenberg saw Modernism as the natural successor of the Enlightenment and conceived of Immanuel Kant as the first real Modernist, "because he was the first to criticize the means itself of criticism" (Greenberg, 1965, p. 193). Greenbergian Modernism was concerned with art's 'purity,' visual aesthetics, and the idea of a progressive 'orientation to flatness' in painting. His account of the 'continuity' in art through a lineage of great masters enabled him to maintain that the quality found in these works was the consequence of:

- Submission to the inescapable demands of the medium;
- Attaining parity with the standards of the art of the past;
- Ensuring the continuation of such standards.

The outcome of this emphasis on the autonomy and purity of art was a restrictive code of practice found wanting by many artists of the time searching for an adequate language with which to articulate new modern concerns. Alternatives to these three positions where then considered which contested their validity.

The priority given to visual aesthetic quality over social, political, or economic relevance in deciding the function of art restricted the artist from pursuing an expanded range of concerns. The range included the political and economic causes ascribed to the operation of capitalism, the imbalances of gender in a capitalist society in turn ascribed to the operation of patriarchy, and to the oppression of certain ethnic groups by others, in turn ascribed to the operation of imperialism. The modernist preoccupation with art's aesthetic effects was anathema to the socially conscious

artist, particularly when new communication channels enabled the media to keep the world (and therefore the artist) well informed.

The belief in the autonomy of the aesthetic upheld by a lineage of great European masters failed to account for female and non-western artists who, because of their omission from the list of great artists, could only be understood as inferior. Women artists allied to feminism saw Modernism as discriminating, seeing its concepts of 'genius,' 'mastery,' and 'talent' as being devised by men to apply to men.

From the understanding that painting and sculpture belonged to the realm of 'high art'—which was to continue to be an absolutely defensible aim—Modernism refused to acknowledge the wide field of popular culture which Greenberg dismissively labeled as 'kitsch.'

In the aftermath of the Second World War the centre of gravity for modern art shifted from Paris to New York. During the 1960s the new technological advances in communication channels, in particular the television set, made social concerns such as the campaign for civil rights, the Vietnam War, and the demands of the women's movement, highly visible. The work of the Abstract Expressionists was not concerned with social issues and had no interest in capturing these experiences of modern life. It was at this point, when Greenbergian Modernism was at its zenith, that art and art criticism began the dismantling of the authority of Modernism and the dissolution of its oppressive progression of 'purity' and great masters. The new anti-Greenbergian position stimulated a retrospective view of the art practices excluded from his art history line and so to a reappraisal of Dada activities and Duchampian objects. Duchamp's work was excluded from the highly selective Greenbergian view of continuity in art practice. The Readymade refocused art from concern with the predominant visual aesthetic to the idea or concept underlying the artwork. Jones, 1994, explains this refocusing through the cultural practices of avant-garde Postmodernism which "opposes itself to Greenberg's dramatically in its choice of object, shifting Greenberg's (located in the trajectory from Manet to Courbet through Cézanne and Picasso to Jackson Pollock) to a Dadaist-Surrealist lineage epitomized, in the visual arts, by Duchamp and his Readymades" (Jones, 1994, pp. 12-13).

Jones substantiates her view through Peter Bürger's definition of the 'historic avant-garde' through its specific association with the practices of Duchamp and his fellow Dadaists and Surrealists who concerned themselves with the break-down of Modernism's rigid separation of high (elitist) and low art (mass culture) (Bürger, 1972). The outcome of this shift in historical perspective has been a revaluation of the artists marginalised in Greenbergian Modernism. Duchamp's 'Readymades,' always seen as enigmatic, idiosyncratic works, were now reconsidered and accordingly emphasis was placed on the choosing of the existing objects and phenomena, at the same time elevating the idea-structure of art at the expense of the visual alone. Between the mid-1970s and early-1990s an unusual quantity of aesthetic energy was invested in the concept of the 'Readymade.' The 'Readymades' (assisted or plain) allowed Duchamp to reduce the idea of aesthetic consideration to the choice of the mind, not to the ability or cleverness of the hand which he objected to in many paintings. Duchamp's practice had been concerned with putting art 'at the service of the mind' since 1912 when he abandoned painting as offering only 'retinian' pleasure.

THE DUCHAMPIAN OBJECT

Duchamp became a significant figure for artists and theorists searching for an alternative to Greenbergian Modernism. Calvin Tomkins, art writer for the New Yorker and essayist about Duchamp and his American neo-Dada and Pop followers, states that, "Entire careers in art were being devoted to colonizing territories that Duchamp opened up" (Tomkins, 1980, pp. 272-273). Throughout his life as a practicing artist, Duchamp had taken a questioning or 'anti-art' position and considered the painters of his time to be in opposition to his own understanding of art as an 'intellectual expression.' He extended his own work by using alternatives to paint and canvas focusing instead on analysis and criticism, which he perceived to be the major preoccupations of the century. For his art materials, he looked at machinery, everyday objects, and language. His adaptation of a female alter ego, Rrose Sélavy, questioned notions of female identity with respect to the reception of art works from female artists and his Readymades undermined the elitism of the notion of 'high' art as superior to the social values within mass culture. The Readymades were realised from mass-produced everyday objects and as such were representative of their (low) culture. Greenberg recognised the threat the Readymades posed to his aesthetic: "Duchamp's 'theoretical' feat (with the Readymades) was to show that 'raw' art could be formalized, made public, simply by setting it in a formalized art situation…Since Duchamp this formalizing of 'raw' art by fiat has become a stereotype of avant-gardist practice" (Greenberg, 1971, pp. 16-19). He then continued to describe the work following on from the Readymade model as "Bad formalized art" in that it "sinks to the level of…sub-academic, sub-kitschig art—that sub-art that is yet art" (Greenberg, 1971, p. 19).

The Readymades, industrial objects reclassified as artworks, challenged the traditional concepts of beauty, creativity, originality, and autonomy in 1917 when Duchamp declared as a work of art an object designed for reproduction—a urinal, which he entitled Fountain and signed with the pseudonym R. Mutt. This object only became a work of art by virtue of the fact that an artist had submitted it for exhibition. By declaring a mass-produced urinal as a fountain sculpture, he succeeded in destroying what Walter Benjamin had called the traditional art work's 'aura'—that aura of authenticity and uniqueness that constituted the work's distance from everyday life. Benjamin (1936) argues in the text, *The Work of Art in the*

Age of Mechanical Reproduction (Benjamin, 1936, pp. 219-253), that the loss of the 'pure' art object's aura to reproducibility is positive in that it opens up progressive possibilities for art and society. In *The Author as Producer* (Benjamin, 1934), Benjamin himself acknowledged that the intention to destroy this aura was already inherent in the artistic practices of Dada and therefore, by association, in the work of Duchamp. With the introduction of the Readymade Duchamp challenged the conventional concepts of artistic skill and aesthetic value leading to a redefinition of the art object. By taking an everyday manufactured object and exhibiting it in an art gallery, the object became an art object because the artist said it was. This led to the practice of not making objects for critical assessment but applying critical assessment to a chosen object. Duchamp had proposed "a new thought for that object" (Duchamp, 1917). It is arguable whether or not the 'aura' of the object had been negated through this activity.

Following the Duchampian appropriation and claiming of the Readymades, the Conceptualists invested concern with the idea-structure in art, and non-object art emerged as information, systems, and actions. A prime example of non-object art was the huge column of air hovering over Oxfordshire in 1968 taken as a hypothetical object for critical discussion by the Art and Language collective (Atkinson & Baldwin, 1968, pp. 868-873). Text and language became prominent forms for displaying idea, text being inserted into the field of the art object, and also text presented as art. In his paper "Words and Objects after Conceptualism" (Beech, 2009), David Beech suggests that art objects are 'inert without their texts,' inertia in this case, being a social characteristic of art and not a physical one. He refers here to the various forms of dissemination, which are part of the art piece reaching out as multiples, invites, publications, etc. "To rearticulate the relationship between art objects and their texts is, therefore, to reinsert art into its social context." Beech argues that Lippard's 'dematerialization' wrongly characterises Conceptualism in that it never fully escaped materiality,

and that this could now be remedied if we consider the Conceptualists as re-contextualising the inert traditional art object. He aligns this position with Benjamin's concept of aura as the supernatural activity, which rescues art objects from deathliness, and asserts that without that aura, "the life of objects is given back to them through the social processes in which they participate" (Beech, 2009, p. 3). Postconceptualism therefore redeploys art's social relations.

Although this redeployment is affective within current social art forms, this is also evident in the new craft-thinking currently emerging (Adamson, 2010; Buszek, 2011; Veiteberg, 2011) and exampled by makers such as Michael Eden who is creating machine-produced digitally-enabled designed objects with RDIF codes patterned into them, which connect to websites of information.

MOVING THE ART OBJECT THROUGH MODERNISMS

Modernism has been retrospective as a general term since the middle of the last century when Western Culture moved into the Postmodern. Although according to Heinrich Klotz (1997), the Director of ZKM through the 1990s, there has not been an end to Modernism and it is by no means exhausted, it no longer exists in the form it took at the beginning of the twentieth century, but there is a clear connection between this and the art of today. Klotz collected for the contemporary art museum based upon his theory of the "Second Modernity" and argued that the modernist 'project' had not lost momentum, nor had it been fatally undermined by the Postmodern to the point where it exists only as a nostalgic Historicism. He perceived that the Postmodern period is actually the second phase of Modernism, the first phase being the 'Classical Modernism' of painting, sculpture, drawing, architecture, and design, constituting a revolution in artistic styles. The second phase, from the 1960s onward, being 'Second Modernism'—which concerns a revolution of artistic categories. Koltz understood 'Second Modernism' at the end of the twentieth century as having an investment in the 'noisy image' initially central to electronic technology and now central to the visual arts. He argued that this 'electronic revolution' (digital) which was transforming society was simultaneously transforming the world of fine art. Koltz's 'Classical Modernism' can be read as 'Modernism' and his 'Second Modernism' is synonymous with 'Postmodernism,' where the anti-modernist practice of non-medium specificity led to a plethora of media being used in a wide range of art activities towards the end of the century, the media being predominantly digital.

Digital art works were the epitome of dematerialized art objects in that they were ephemeral, interactive, playful, non-linear, and difficult to exhibit in traditional gallery spaces. Many existed solely online across the Internet; they were constructed of electric impulses in the coded forms of bits and bytes and as such were immaterial and ethereal. Others tended to be screen-based or projected as installations, works of pure sound, or immersive environments to be experienced physically. They invited the viewer to participate in the work to make the work happen and they extended across the globe in multinational occurrences that sliced across time zones and cultural differences. Towards the end of the century art came to be understood as a 'Relational,' social practice, according to Nicholas Bourriaud, "Artistic activity is a game, whose forms, patterns, and functions develop and evolve according to periods and social contexts" (Bourriaud, 1998, p. 11). For Bourriaud, Relational Aesthetics is part of a materialistic tradition, not in the sense of a work's economic worth but as allowing for a 'materialism of encounter.' He acknowledges that the principal argument held against relational art is that it can be seen as representing "a watered-down form of social critique" (Bourriaud, 1998, p. 82), and he is well aware of his critics, such as Claire Bishop, who argue that relational aesthetics is not politically engaged enough to be a form of social activism. However, as a curator he identi-

fied a similarity of concern among his selected artists for providing convivial social spaces for participants to meet and where art could happen. These exhibitions were initially confined to gallery spaces but the idea of Relational Art has spread beyond and into a diversity of social arenas and public settings.

For the new century, Bourriaud curated the fourth installment of the Tate Triennial, "Altermodern," Spring 2009, and in so doing, declared the end of the Postmodern. "The term 'altermodern,' which serves both as the title of the present exhibition and to delimit the void beyond the postmodern, has its roots in the idea of 'otherness' and suggests a multitude of possibilities" (Bourriaud, 2009, p. 12). He argues that although the postmodern has an inherent value, it is no longer necessarily relevant in today's world, that within the theory of the Altermodern, we start from a globalised state of culture where artists are viewed from a macrocosmic perspective, and are appreciated for how they function and interrelate within the world. In these terms, the Altermodern is an extension of the materialistic tradition of the Relational to include the digital and new technologies, which network the world and uphold social participation creating new pathways from which to explore culture and tradition. "Artists are building, what I call, journey-forms, which is a combination of, a way to exchange, time, and space values" (Bourriaud, 2009, p. 15).

Exchanging the term 'globalised' for an 'In-World' state of culture and artists using journey-form are not only evident, but prevalent within Second Life creative practice. Doyle's avatar is named Wanderingfictions Story and her piece for Kritical Works in SL I, "Map to Grid," was made in collaboration with Taey Kim (Doyle, 2008). Kim's avatar Lime Galsworthy and Wanderingfictions Story play with their narrative exchanges and question what it means to map virtual space. Within their work, they are locatable by definition over form and exist as non-human metadata describing the virtual world through digital narrative. For Map to Grid, Kim used a real doll 'Dongdong' to exchange stories and conversations with the virtual avatar Wanderingfictions. Using psychogeography they proceeded to map the grid so that their states of mind, or physical bodies, were forced to confront both physical and virtual spaces. They were situated, yet still struggled to determine that exact position, their dwelling place. The artists' statement for the work gives a clearer rationale, "One discovery: understanding our geographical position in this digital era is absolutely essential as we are able to live in, and embody, multiple realities. Our 'I's travel through multiple spaces and times" (Doyle, 2008, p. 24). Within Map to Grid, they re-present their conversations as actual snapshots of the maps created.

Joseph DeLappe's reenactment, The Salt Satyagraha Online, is another example of an SL artist using journey-form in a mixed reality performance. This was of Gandhi's march to Dandi but in SL from Eyebeam, New York City, March 12 – April 6, 2008. Over the course of 26 days DeLappe used a treadmill, customized to affect cyberspace in real-time, to re-walk Mahatma Gandhi's famous 1930 Salt March. The original 240-mile walk was made in protest of the British salt tax, for this performance, DeLappe walked the entire 240 miles of the original march where his steps on the treadmill controlled the forward movement of his avatar, 'MGandhi Chakrabarti,' enabling the live and virtual reenactment of the march across the islands of the virtual world platform meeting other avatars on the way.

RE-MATERIALISING THE ART OBJECT

The new social platforms evolving across the Internet through mass participation and cultural trends are moving the public interconnectivity of Web 2.0 towards the 'Internet of things' and Web 3.0. The relationships of these virtual dialogues is extending out to include the material, physical real world and the virtual now includes the Second Life world, (SL) created by Linden Labs 6 years ago. SL is easily accessible and not too complicated for building on and customizing spaces allowing for a high level of control when creating a virtual environment, and the SL community now has a large number of artists experimenting with this new Internet platform. Two exhibitions were curated on the SL island of Kriti, to explore the diversity of practice unfolding across this global virtual space. The first Kritical Works in SL show was screened at ISEA2008 in Singapore, the artists were SL practitioners familiar with, but intent on pushing the creative possibilities of the platform itself. The second exhibition "Kritical Works in SL II" for ISEA2009 included real-world artists, such as the Conceptualist Lynn Hershman-Leeson, now beginning to explore SL, and exampled the relatively recent interest in bridging the virtual to the real-world. Two of the artists from the second exhibition, Doyle and DeLappe not only worked in 'journey-form' but materialized objects into the physical gallery-space from the SL Island (Doyle, 2009).

There are a number of ways of materialising objects from code within industrial manufacturing technologies and designers continue to develop working practices in 3D imaging, object scanning, 3D printing, and rapid prototyping. Using 3D imaging hardware, optical geometry processing software: the spatial, colour, and textual information of objects can be scanned, digitized, sampled, and archived. There are two broad methods of production processes available within manufacturing, Additive and Subtractive. Subtractive is a solid block of hard material such as wood or granite is 'sculpted' (as by hand) with digitally controlled machines, for example, using laser or water-jet cutting. Additive manufacturing processes are more interesting as a new form of production in that there is no dense mass of resistant material to start with; no stone to carve, instead new powdered materials are deposited (added) in fine layers to gradually build up a flawless, seamless, object from seemingly nothing. These new modes of production and reproduction afforded by reverse engineering and rapid prototyping technologies are generally considered as being for mass production. However, experimentation with new materials and processes is also apparent within contemporary fine art, design, and crafts where, for artists and craftspeople, the uniqueness of the formed object is paramount and purposefully made without regard for mass production.

Compared to the analogue material world, the digital is determined by its potential for multiplicity, reproduction, and dissemination. However, artists such as Brit Bunkley, Ian Gwilt, and Michael Rees exhibit at "Intersculpt," a biennial 3D digital event that opens simultaneously in 8 – 10 cities worldwide utilising rapid prototyping as both a tool and as a component of the content, prints of 3D stills, and 3D animation. These artists produce materialised objects as single, unique, sculptures by using 3D printing (additive manufacturing) to calculate the thin cross sections of the virtual model and building the layers together out of extruded plastic, metals, bonded plaster, or cut and glued paper.

Michael Eden, a highly successful potter for over twenty years, has recently shifted the focus of his work to engage with digital technology and understands that craft ideas for 'making' are transferrable to current methods of mechanised production; even though the finished product is not 'hand-made' Eden still considers himself a 'maker.' He creates unique pieces in new materials through additive manufacturing methods, in direct response to classical craftware, but with RFID codes built in to the new objects as both pattern and structure. The entire object can be scanned with a mobile phone and connected with its accompanying website/s (Eden, 2012) (see Figure 1).

These digitally engaged forms of contemporary practice, where the creation of new unique objects

Figure 1. The Mnemosyne: a box of memories, to be scanned with a barcode reader app (©2011, Michael Eden. Used with permission)

can take place long-distance across the World via the Internet, returns the 'aura' to the art object. The perfectly manufactured objects can be networked into related current readings, whether social, cultural, or political, and so negate the otherwise discrete object's 'inertia' through connecting the digital communication channel of cyberspace to their material form, and this is specifically evident in the Kritical Works pieces where their virtual world is a social platform. The form of production for the Intersculpt artists and for Eden is not absolutely about new manufacturing processes, or whether tacit knowledge and hands-on sensitivities can be transferred to digital tools to refine existing craft skills, but also investigates the materialisation of ideas made solid. As Eden says, 'It's the idea that should be at the forefront of the maker's mind, not the tool' (Eden, 2012). For the Kriti Island artists the agenda was slightly different in that it was inherently connected to the social conditions of the virtual platform itself. They were concerned with relating the avatar activity in SL to the real world gallery space in Belfast, avatars rarely travel islands to meet others and never cross the boundary into the real world. Doyle's avatar Wanderingfictions Story was materialised into solid form from the SL grid to stand on a pedestal in the Golden Thread Gallery as an inanimate being, frozen from the 'real' life she had in SL. Joseph deLappe's Gandhi figure had traveled the islands reenacting the 26 day 1930s Salt March on the SL grid meeting the public in this social domain, before materialising in giant glued cardboard form in one Belfast gallery, and also as a small 8" figurine in another.

For "Kritical Works in SL II" both DeLappe and Doyle materializsed their avatars as signifiers of their true animated Second Life forms. By bringing their avatars into the real-world to meet their viewers, as solid and tangible objects prior to online access, DeLappe and Doyle had reached out to help the virtual become more familiar to their viewers, and therefore closer and easier to connect with. The gallery viewer would meet the figurines before they sat at the computer and logged on to the SL platform to engage with the avatars, many of these gallery-goers were unfamiliar with accessing a virtual world and so used these statues as transitional objects to, conceptually, move them across and into the cyberworld of SL. The material presence of Doyle and DeLappes's avatars as art objects allowed them to ease their viewers into their natural environment of social cyberworld as a way of bringing audiences across the divide between the real and the virtual.

It would seem that the art object is now about to become part of a re-materialising process (post Lippard), to create impossible objects that couldn't be hand-crafted, to create objects which directly communicate with the social Internet platforms, and to contribute to ways of bridging the virtual to the real evident in our current digital social culture, a possible element of the forthcoming Web 3.0 (see Figure 2).

Figure 2. MGandhi1 and Wanderingfictions'– digitally materialised art objects golden thread gallery (©2009, Denise Doyle. Used with permission)

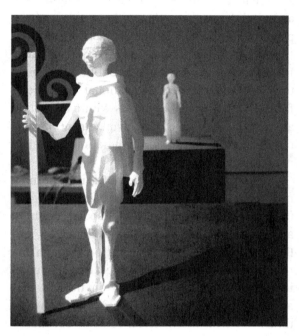

CONCLUSION

The material, physical, solidity of the art object, held in high regard since the first human mark was brought under inspection at the beginning of last century and found wanting. By mid-century, it had undergone a disappearance and had transformed into process and immateriality. According to Lippard, the then contemporary art practice of Conceptual Art was not concerned with the materiality of object making but with disseminating social, cultural, and especially political information to the art world and general public. Many artists, Lippard included, then reviewed the work of earlier non-artifact artists moving forward from Duchamp. Beech argues that this understanding was misguided in that Conceptual practice had an ongoing investment in the material and proposes that materialised forms of dissemination can emanate from the art object keeping it alive and vital, he suggests that without its periphery paper, texts, and events the artifact suffers from 'inertia' and loses its unique Benjaminian 'aura.' In the new century, art practice follows on from the Conceptual Art era as relational, with social forms of engagement as events within the public arena, but also, due to the advancement of digital technology, allows for explorations into new materials and new processes.

Sculptors, craftspeople, and artists are now making artifacts, which can reach out beyond their pedestal and impact upon social, cultural, and political concerns, as well as dialogues into their own identity as art objects. It is through this re-materialisation of the art object that Lippard's initial understandings derived from the artworks and ideas corralled into her 1972 book, can continue, not with the material form as secondary to the idea, and therefore unnecessary, but as an integral part of it then expanded through digital affordances, such as the Internet and Second Life, to reach the public sphere.

REFERENCES

Adamson, G. (2007). *Thinking through craft.* London, UK: Berg Publishers.

Atkinson, T., & Baldwin, M. (2003). Air show. In C. Harrison & P. Wood (Eds.), *1900-2000: An Anthology of Changing Ideas*, (pp. 868-873). Oxford, UK: Wiley-Blackwell.

Beech, D. (2009). *Words and objects after conceptualism.* Retrieved from http://www.art-omma.org/NEW/issue%2011/pages/dave_beech.pdf

Benjamin, W. (1973). The work of art in the age of mechanical reproduction. In Arendt, H., & Benjamin, W. (Eds.), *Illuminations* (pp. 219–253). London, UK: Fontana.

Benjamin, W. (1978). The author as producer. In *Reflections*. New York, NY: Harcourt Brace Jovanovich.

Berman, M. (1982). *All that is solid melts into air: The experience of modernity.* New York, NY: Simon and Schuster.

Bourriaud, N. (1998). *Relational aesthetics.* Paris, France: Les Presses du Réel.

Bourriaud, N. (2009). *Altermodern.* London, UK: Tate Publishing.

Bürger, P. (1972). *Theory of the avant-garde* (Shaw, M., Trans.). Minneapolis, MN: University of Minnesota Press.

Buszek, M. E. (2011). *Extra/ordinary: Craft and contemporary art.* Chapel Hill, NC: Duke University Press.

Chandler, J., & Lippard, L. (1968). The dematerialization of art. *Art International, 12*(2), 31–36.

Doyle, D. (2008). *Kritical works in SL. Exhibition Catalogue.* Morrisville, NC: Lulu Publishing.

Doyle, D. (2009). *Kritical works in SL ii. Exhibition Catalogue.* Wolverhampton, UK: CADRE Publications.

Duchamp, M. (1917). The Richard Mutt case. *The Blind Man, 2*(5).

Eden, M. (2012). *Website.* Retrieved from http://www.edenceramics.co.uk/diary.html

Greenberg, C. (1965). Modernist painting. *Art & Literature, 4.*

Greenberg, C. (1971). Counter avant-garde. *Art International, 15*(5), 16–19.

Jones, A. (1994). *Postmodernism and the engendering of Marcel Duchamp.* Cambridge, UK: Cambridge University Press.

Klotz, H. (1997). *Contemporary art: The collection of the ZKM/center for art and media, Karlsruhe.* New York, NY: Prestel.

Lippard, L. (1997). *Six Years: The dematerialization of the art object from 1966 to 1972: A cross-reference book of information on some esthetic boundaries: consisting of a bibliography into which are inserted a fragmented text, art works, documents, interviews, and symposia, arranged chronologically and focused on so-called conceptual or information or idea art with mentions of a such vaguely designated areas as minimal, anti-form, systems, earth, or process art, occurring now in the Americas, Europe, England, Australia, and Asia (with occasional political overtones).* Berkeley, CA: University of California Press.

Tomkins, C. (1980). *Off the wall: Robert Rauschenberg and the art world of our times.* Harmondsworth, UK: Penguin.

Veiteberg, J. (2005). *Craft in transition.* Bergen, Norway: National Academy of the Arts.

KEY TERMS AND DEFINITIONS

Art Object: A physical, material item of artistic creation.

Conceptual Art: Type of modern art in which the idea or ideas that a work expresses are considered its essential point, with its visual appearance being of secondary (often negligible) importance.

Dematerialisation: The process by which objects in the art world tend towards intangibility.

Digital Technologies: Social media platforms, the Internet, smartphones, gadgets, Web 2.0/3.0, computerised manufacturing.

Readymades: Ordinary manufactured objects that the artist selects, modifies, and exhibits as art objects.

Real: The physical world of tangible objects. Not to be confused with the Lacanian relation of the real to the self.

Rematerialisation: The process by which art objects in intangible form are converted into physical form.

Virtual: The virtual here refers simply to digitally bound objects and computer supported spaces such as Second Life. Not to be confused with Deleuze's take on the virtual as the main characteristic of a state of being that exists along with reality. Nor with Pierre Lévy's extension of this understanding where virtuality opposes the actual, in that virtuality is a creative approach to solving problems, which will be actualised (materialised) before the relaunch of another problem.

Chapter 2
Data–Objects:
Sharing the Attributes and Properties of Digital and Material Culture to Creatively Interpret Complex Information

Ian Gwilt
Sheffield Hallam University, UK

ABSTRACT

This chapter discusses a current shift away from thinking about ideas of virtual reality, towards a conversation around hybrid digital/physical constructs and the notions of mixed or augmented reality. In particular the chapter explores how physical artifacts that are based on data extracted from computer generated virtual spaces are being created as a way of challenging how we read, interpret, and respond to digital information. This emerging trend for the realization of data sets into three-dimensional (3D) physical objects is discussed from the perspective of creative practice and digital information visualization. In these new constructs, digital data sets are concretized into a physical form, remediated from information sources, such as mobile phone coverage records, crime statistics, and temperature patterns. Through a series of examples, the chapter will investigate how these tangible translations can change our relationship to screen-based digital content, in particular statistical data, and seeks to reveal how by encoding digital information into a physical object we can establish a way of reading this data through spatial, temporal, and material variations that sit outside of the computer-monitor and the digital environment. Rapid prototyping making techniques are discussed as a trigger for a conversation around the ontological and epistemological readings of these liminal physical/data objects.

DOI: 10.4018/978-1-4666-2961-5.ch002

INTRODUCTION

In the 1990s, the arrival of domestic computing and mainstream digital technologies signaled the start of what seemed to be a concerted effort to digitize all forms of creative, cultural, and scientific content. Since this time, we have seen the creation of all manner of digital archives, and the platforms and interfaces with which to explore this digital content, either as an individual or part of a distributed and networked community. Some ten years on the digital is now a fully integrated meta-form that plays out across much of our communication, social and work practices (Gwilt, 2010). However, after this initial rush of digital migration we are beginning to witness more consideration for the importance of locating our relationship with the digital in respect to our environmental surroundings, material artifacts, and physical bodies. In addition, in the last few years we have seen a marked increase in interest in how we can build stronger relationships between digital and physical practices and experiences. Whether through biological necessities or a long established hardwiring into Euclidian space, it appears that we are beginning to question the singularity of digital culture.

At a time when the promise of a transcendent digital virtual reality has failed to live up to populist expectations, a new way of thinking about and interacting with the digital is beginning to unfold. In the computer games world immersive virtual reality constructs have been combined with gestural interfaces, where players can see the unmediated expressions of their competitors and physical actions become critical to the navigation and interaction with new digital game formats. Biomorphic forms in architecture and product design signal a new urban zeitgeist as digital technologies develop the processing power to visualize and model the complex curvilinear shapes and patterns found in nature. Everyday objects such as domestic appliances, furniture, and automobiles are increasingly enabled with sensor and user-feedback technologies that can respond to and even preempt our individual needs in the physical world. Mobile technologies are moving the capabilities of the digital computer into the street and the public arena where their use is becoming increasingly commonplace, connecting the digital with real-world events, and locating our engagement with computing technologies into real-time social, cultural, and political contexts. The terms augmented and mixed reality are now appearing in mainstream media and entering the public psyche to sit alongside the established technological and perceptual ideas of virtual reality. These emergent constructs allow us to play in and explore the liminal spaces where the digital and material paradigms overlap and interplay.

Consequently, the technological and perceptual dispersal of the digital computer from something that sits on the office desk, to an increasingly distributed and embedded set of multiform devices helps to disarm the established idea that the digital and the physical are in binary opposition to each other. And as computing technologies, and our experience and interaction with these technologies becomes increasingly more located—related to place and social contexts—the potential for the digital to augment and interact with material culture become ever more opportune. The cultural theorist Pierre Levy (1998) refers to this rapid and diverse range of digital integrations as accelerated techno-cultural heterogenesis. This shift in emphasis (back) toward privileging the physical however does not mean that we are about to relinquish the potentials of the digital as accessed through a variety of screen-based forms of interaction, and although the experiences promised by immersive virtual reality have yet to find a place in mainstream engagement with digital technologies, the types of informed digital/material constructs described in this paper are beginning to gain wide spread recognition. Terms like augmented, and mixed reality are increasingly being used to describe a set of relationships, technologies and expectations for a variety of combined digital/material constructs.

These neologisms are quickly becoming part of the public and broadband media vocabulary, in a reflection of an increasingly technologized society.

As part of this technologized society, we are increasingly exposed to digital information in the form of complex data sets, statistics, and other forms of visualizations. The movement towards the materialization of the digital is also occurring in the area of computer-based information visualization, which is in itself a relatively new phenomenon. In respect to information visualization this closer relationship between digital/material constructs does two things: first, it provides new opportunities for the generation of content; and second, it drives the desire for the design of data visualizations that speak to or reference both our real-world and digital connections, activities and experiences. This data materialization is being facilitated through the use of a number of developing manufacturing technologies such as computer controlled laser cutting, 3D printing and rapid prototyping (as well as other traditional fabrication techniques that allow for the translation of digital data back into physical forms). I will discuss some of these techniques later in the chapter, but first it is important to establish an overview of digital information visualization, as a grounding for a discussion on how the shift towards materializing data is impacting on this field.

DATA VISUALIZATION

In the last 8 to 10 years, we have witnessed a phenomenal growth in digital information visualization and information design (Card, et al., 1999; Klanten, et al., 2010; Ware, 2004). As digital data and statistical data sets have become more accessible, designers, computer scientists, and social commentators have taken to the task of visually interpreting this data with gusto. The bread and butter content of convention data visualizations, stocks and shares analysis, scientific findings and other social, political, and economic statistics are now accompanied by visualizations of our real-world comings and goings, which utilize regional or demographically specific data on such things as visits to fast food outlets, coffee consumption, use of cycle lanes, etc. These visualizations also vie for space in the public data arena alongside measurements of our use of the digital, such as social networking patterns, Internet distribution arrays and mobile phone networks. A huge range of visual representation techniques are employed to communicate this content, including; bar charts, graphs, diagrams, illustrations, information graphics, 3D models, maps, animations, motion graphics and generative designs based on the use of computer algorithms and visualization software. This assortment of informatics can be privately and publically accessed and is distributed through a range of screen-based interfaces in a variety of locations and in a number of different scales and formats. This data is available not only on the 'conventional' computer-monitor but can increasingly be consumed through mobile devices such as smart phones, public screens, games, and social media interfaces, and digital broadcast media, as well as emergent technologies such as heads-up displays, 'smart surfaces,' and augmented reality technologies which allow digital content to be mapped into and onto physical objects and locations.

However, information design has a long history prior to the invention of the digital computer, and we can trace the desire to visualize information back to the earliest forms of mark making and symbolic languages. Edward Tufte (1993) a leading authority in information design argues that the abstract visualization of quantitative, statistical data began in the mid 18th Century, when tabular data was first replaced by charts and graphics. These early 'interpretive' graphics introduced another way of reading quantitative data using a visual language based on graphical elements such as lines, arrows, symbols, coloured elements and forms of illustrative material. These graphic interpretations came with their own issues of cognition and understanding. Tufte suggests that data visualizations perform a dual purpose, to carry information and to communicate something about that information (Tufte, 1993, p. 139). Moreover, Tufte advocates a minimal use of visual elements, which should be used to communicate as much data as possible, advice that often seems to be overlooked thanks to the visualization capabilities of the modern day computer. However, although many of the data visualizations of today are still primarily concerned with the interpretation of quantitative data, Manuel Lima (2009), in his *Information Visualization Manifesto* suggests that unlike design in the material world, where form is regarded to follow function, form does not necessarily follow data.

The concept of data, which can be dislocated from an associative visual metaphor, incongruent data, progresses the idea that any number of abstract or metaphoric visualizations of data can be made from the same data set, and that any visualization might make an equal claim in terms of veracity or appropriateness. This dislocate between form and function goes some way to explaining the plethora of styles and forms in which computer-based data visualizations are beginning to appear; some of which attract criticism for being unnecessarily complex, meaningless and at worst unintelligible. Freed from the design parameters that are usually associated with form and functionality, data can be visualized in any shape, from a simple bar graph to a dynamic info graphic, following any number of aesthetic conventions or metaphors. However, Lima and others, in a note of caution, suggest that information visualizations should at their core be used to provide insight or clarity, and that this precedent is a way of legitimizing design decision-making processes. Furthermore, Card, Mackinlay and Shneiderman declare that the practice of information visualization can be defined as "the use of computer-supported interactive, visual representations of abstract data to amplify cognition" (Card, et al., 1999, p. 7). Similarly, the champion of digitally

enabled information aesthetics, Andrew Vande Moere foregrounds the democratizing potential that information visualization tools can have as an inclusive communication device (Klanten, et al., 2010). In summary, effective and insightful information visualizations can be created if some effort in achieving contextual or sympathetic connectivity between data content, data visualization techniques, and the design/visual language used to communicate the content is undertaken.

In the following section, I will examine in some detail how the property norms of digital and material culture can be considered in relation to how we might read information visualizations, and suggest a way in which we might begin to consider the inherent qualities of these two paradigms employed together, to 'amplify cognition,' by building a relationship between data and material form.

ATTRIBUTES AND PROPERTIES OF DIGITAL AND MATERIAL FORMS

On the face of it transforming a digital data set into a physical object might seem to be a strange almost counterproductive thing to do. However, by crossing the digital/material border we can begin to consider and describe the different attributes and properties, which are typically assigned to information and objects in both cultures and start to look at ways in which we might make links between the two. In the digital realm attributes including, networkability, replicability, morphology, complexity, responsiveness, shared or democratic ownership and so on are seen as conventional, expected, and desirable traits that we commonly associate with digital content. On the other hand, in terms of the physical and perceptual properties we commonly ascribe to objects in the material world notions around such things as tangibility, uniqueness, preciousness, durability, history, and value, in both economic and socio-cultural terms often come to mind.

As suggested the act of actualizing digital information into a physical object may initially seem paradoxical and nonsensical, since by fixing a data set in time and physical space we appear to disable much of the dynamic potential inherent in the digital. The interesting question here is can these concertized data sets retain the echoes of their digital origins and capabilities, such as dynamism, complexity, interconnectivity, mutability and so on. Certainly, as we will see in the following examples these digital heritages will often inform the look and feel of the physical data-object. However, importantly, by creating a data-object, we can begin to describe a set of possible relationships between the digital traits described above and the material properties inherent in the physical object (see Table 1). In these data-objects, the ontological qualities we typically assign to the material such as economic, social, and cultural value, originality, tactility, textural quality, and other sensorial associations can be hybridized with attributes and drivers of digital technologies. In this fused form the properties and conventions, which typically convey the different cultural values we ascribe to the digital and the material, can be bridged, and become open to discussion. In terms of the representation of statistical data, this fusion opens up the possibility to explore a number of experientially located insights and readings to the original data.

To fuse properties from both paradigms into a single data-object might then appear to compromise the expectations or benefits we associate with the discrete digital or material article. However, the dialogic exchange between digital information and material form engendered in the shape of the data-object can equally establish new potentials for reading and interacting with content and form. Nevertheless, we should not understate the fundamentally ontological and epistemological differences that frame our understanding of digital and material cultures. Reconciling these differences is a difficult task, but what the data-object offers is a confluence where those differences can be challenged or explored.

Table 1. Epistemologies of the data-object (© 2010 Ian Gwilt. Used with permission)

Epistemologies of the data-object	
Material properties/traits	**Digital attributes/traits**
Tangible	Virtual
Unique	Multiple
Stable	Responsive
Precious	Replicable
Located	Dynamic
Fixed	Morphological
Historic	New
Patina	Networked

In this respect, let us briefly examine some fundamental concepts that could be argued to have particular and different associations/connotations in both the digital and material realm. Within the digital for example, the Euclidean and quantifiable notions of size is abstracted, we talk about large and small file sizes that take up space in computer memory, sizes of disc space, etc. but these sizes/amounts are hard to visualize. Whereas in terms of how we quantify size in the material world, the physicality of an object is often seen as an indexical indicator of size. The 'physical' perception of scale, as opposed to the 'digital' perception of scale is something we are much more attuned to and is a property that can be explored in the creation of a data artifact. Equally, notions of time can be seen to have particular connotations in digital and material cultures. When we think of time in relation to the digital, it is often in terms of the immediate present, where synchronous feedback across space, data, and community is the usual expectation. In the digital, time or time based media can also be replayed or visualized at different speeds, increments and scales, it can be archived for viewing at some other date, we can even 'undo' an action or sequence of events. In contrast, our perception of time in relation to material objects often has a fixed connection with the way we understand/experience the physical world. Physical objects cannot be scrolled backwards or forwards, out of sync with the time continuum, and are very finely linked into cultural notions of age, newness, or oldness. There is often a tacit sense of time and value accrued with age, embedded in the way we read physical objects. This sense of time: how old an object is; how long it took to make; how long it took to acquire; or even physically reach, is an important factor in the way we attribute value to material artifacts. In terms of the digital however, 'newness' is more frequently used as a measure of value. One implication for the data-artifact therefore, might be that physical notions (and values) of time and time scale may be gained at the expense of digital immediacy or temporal non-linearity.

Consider the work entitled iForm (2010) by the New Zealand artist James Charlton. In this work, GPS tracks of iPhone users were recorded over a set period of time and location. This information was then used to create a physical sculpture which transcoded the digital representations of time and space into a physical form (Figure 1). Charlton (2010) notes that the representation of time and movement (as recorded in the GPS data) when translated into a physical object challenges the assumptions we make on the meaning of an object's form. As we saw earlier, objects that are derived from the visualization of digital data do not need to conform to the representational mores of objects that draw a reference to material culture. In this case, the surfaces and angles in the work represent spatial and temporal variations of a digital data set, which are used to inform the shape of the object. Charlton's data driven object concretizes and recodes digital concepts of space, time, and movement.

Other fine grain readings of time and use/age often come in to play around material form and the signifiers of such can influence how we might ascribe authenticity to the information encapsulated in the form of a data-object. Physical objects collect dust, become dirty, worn or broken, and accrue 'character' via our interaction with them, and being in the world. This patina can be hard to fabricate in the digital but is something that in material culture can implicitly denote age, value, and frequency of use or popularity; these last two

being strong signifiers in the digital domain too. Moreover, physical objects decay with time (although perceptions of age can often increase the value of an object), whereas, at least in theory, digital data can indefinitely be stored without loss of fidelity. This distinction informs differences in the notion of 'history,' between the digital and material. Digital content is intrinsically iterative, multiple and variable. Think of the 'save' and 'save as' functions in computer software and the different results which arise from using these two options—the 'save as' option allows for multiple variations or histories, whereas the 'save' function replaces one history with another. Equally, the concept of non-linearity is often ascribed to the digital as one of its key attributes. Similarly, the history and story of a physical object is told through a complex assemblage of relationships, which takes into account an object's age, use, ownership, geographical location, material composition and so on, and the changes in these aspects that occur

Figure 1. iForm rapid prototype sculpture (© 2010 artist James Charlton. Used with permission)

over time (Riggins, 1994). However, the flexibility with which digital data can be manipulated, reproduced, and rearranged does not necessarily lead to a perceived lack of authenticity as it might with a physical object. Indeed, in the digital, updates that replace older versions are seen to be most desirable. Although real-world oral, written, and material histories are also open to interpretation, the authenticity of a physical object is often gauged through a validated history, and even 'fake' physical objects can accrue cultural and economic value. In the digital realm notions of truth or authenticity can often be assigned by popularity as much as by provenance and the idea of an altered or adapted history is not an issue, being 'out of date,' corrupt or simply unpopular is perhaps more a critical allegation.

The capacity of the digital to easily create multiple versions of the same artifact is to some extent reflected in material culture through mechanical mass-production methods. As Walter Benjamin commented, these production processes have an important perceptual impact on our notion of a physical object's originality (1968). However, in terms of the digital the importance of the original is intrinsically diminished. As we move into an era of new forms of advanced manufacturing, the idea of mass customisation and the individually specified object is increasingly taken precedent. This has largely been enabled by digital technologies. New adaptive and programmable digital production processes are increasingly making the fabrication of the bespoke physical object possible. I will discuss some of these fabrication techniques in the following section.

Putting production processes aside for a moment, it is generally accepted that physical artefacts become imbued with a social cultural narrative by way of our interactions with them (Miller, 2010). Moreover, interaction with a specific object can bring cultural and individual value to even a mass-produced item. This notion of interaction is quite different from the functional goal orientated interaction, which is often associated with digital technologies. These different notions of interaction in the digital and material/physical represent another touch point for consideration in terms of migrating digital data into form. Data on the computer screen can easily facilitate a variety of individual and shared spaces across a broad spectrum of communities. However, this distributed experience is harder to recreate in the physical world and is something that the social networked space of the digital is very adept at. Although the 'first-hand' tangible experience of the physical object might be lost in the mediated channels of the digital, this loss of the empiric is made up for through the potential of multiple sharing, commentary and reinterpretation. On the one hand, we have the democratic possibilities of the digital to give widespread access to information and knowledge, which is often beyond the reach of a physical object. On the other, the inherent cultural notions of authenticity that can be ascribed to the experience and interaction with a singular physical object can provide an unmediated and often richly contextualised experience (Riggins, 1994). In the best case scenario the manifestation of digital information into a material form should play to the strengths of both of these two paradigms, in the worst case, it would fail to capitalise on either.

I have talked about some of the differences and similarities between the socio-cultural perception of physical objects and digital data. However, another obvious point of difference between the physical object and its digital counterpart is the molecular composition of the object. The material properties of wood, metal, plastic and so on, all have a set of cultural resonances and fine-grained readings that prefigure how we think of a particular object. For example, the clean, smooth lines of melamine (plastic) furniture point to the conceit of 'modernist' aesthetics (Shove, et al., 2007). Whereas, the high-tech finish of carbon fibre hints at the composition of future worlds and artifacts. Each material form has its own set of cultural readings, which may be complex and subtly interwoven within the use of the object and the context or setting in which the object is found. For instance in many circumstances, wood is associated with natural materials/nature and may bring to mind a set of attendant attributes which support this assumption. However, it can also be perceived as a sophisticated urban form, which is used in contemporary architectural environments as a part of a design language far removed from an association with trees and natural spaces. Just as the general characteristics of different physical materials can prefigure the reading of an object, the 'finish' of a particular material can also be very important. Returning to the example of the wooded artifact, a table top roughly cut from a tree might retain pieces of bark and the inconsistencies of natural growth, a finish that has very different set of associated cultural values from that of a wooden table top carefully cut, geometrically shaped, sanded and varnished. These finishes have their parallel in the digital domain where the visualization and presentation of data can prefigure expectations and attendant uses, for example low resolution digital images (rough cut), and high pixel count images (refined), have different value/quality associations. Just as the use of colour, composition, line-weight and typography in digital information visualization can set up a way of reading content, the material choices and finishes of a material based data-object can equally influence how the object is interpreted. For the hybrid data-object that draws on digital data, choices need to be made in both aspects of the digital to material making process.

MAKING TECHNOLOGIES

In this 'first generation' of data-objects, many of the objects are created utilizing a variety of fabrication technologies that sit under the broad category of rapid prototyping. These technologies include; computer controlled milling or CNC machines, laser cutters, and three-dimensional printers, often referred to as Rapid Prototype (RP)

machines. RP machines can fabricate objects in a variety of materials, and use a number of different processes to make objects. Models designed in 3D modeling software are used as a template for the creation of material artifacts (Noorani, 2006). Within this set of fabrication processes, there are a number of material options to choose from, ranging from paper, to different types of plastic, waxy materials and precious metals. One of the more unconventional RP techniques is Laminated Object Manufacturing or LOM. In this process sheets of paper are glued together one layer at a time, a computer-controlled laser is used to trace out the required form and to 'cube' unwanted material ready for removal. This process requires much hand finishing—the removal of unwanted material and the sanding down and treating of the finished object. The LOM process effectively turns paper *back* into a wood-like material and the burnt laser cut edges of the laminated paper give the object an unusual low-tech feel. The slightly rough, handmade look of the object, as well as its heavy weight, gives it a set of qualities that echo pre-industrial revolution manufacturing/making processes that do not exhibit the typical look and feel we might expect to see from a computer-controlled manufacturing processes. The artist Brit Bunkley (2009) has effectively used the LOM fabrication process in a number of his sculptural works (see Figure 2). Although not using digital data in an informatics sense the cuboid manufacturing method used in Bunkley's work hints at the underlying mathematical processes.

Computer controlled laser-cutting technologies for shaping Two-Dimensional (2D) materials are another popular technique for producing data artifacts. In Abigail Reynolds (2002) work, *Mount Fear: Statistics for Crimes with Offensive Weapon South London 2001-2002*, sheets of laser cut corrugated cardboard are cut out and stuck together to create a room sized three-dimensional bar chart of crime statistics in London, England. The sheer physical presence of the object—roughly constructed and finished—creates an

Figure 2. Trophy laminated object manufacturing (LOM) detail (© 2006 artist Brit Bunkley. Used with permission)

intimidating presence in the gallery, particularly when the form is associated with the nature of the data content. Both the LOM manufacture process and laser cut cardboard techniques described above seem strangely at odds with the computer fabricated making and finishing technologies, where hard, precise surfaces and bright white plastics are the norm. Yet what these examples begin to reveal is the complexity of material culture wherein an ecology of readings can surround even the simplest of objects, prefigured by making technologies and choice of material. Further levels of interpretation are introduced when the object itself is a representation of a digital data set. Daniel Miller (2010) comments on the importance of objects in society not just as things that affect our behavior and sense of self, but also as scene setting agents which move in and out of our attention and focus. In this respect, our relationship to material objects might be seen to parallel our relationship to the computer desktop interface, which according to Bolter and Grussin (1999) operates as both window and a mirror, something you can look through and look at; at times content, at times form, and at times both. Similarly, data-objects read on a number of inter-linked levels as form and content, physical and digital.

DATA AND METAPHOR

As discussed, the manifestation of digital data into material objects is increasingly taking place across the practice of information visualization. These data driven artifacts are based on a diverse assortment of data sets, many of which are generated through our engagement with natural and man-made phenomena, from the micro to macro, we are feverishly collecting data from the analogue world on an individual, communal and global level. It is an interesting feedback loop that brings these statistics back into the material world, having often being collected, processed, and analyzed in the digital realm. Although, as discussed earlier, Lima (2009) claims that when it comes to information visualization, form does not necessarily follow function; Lakoff and Johnson (1980) suggest that we frequently use spatial metaphors to help us understand complex concepts. It follows that information visualization often uses metaphor to create relationships and understanding, based on the use of objects, spaces and experiences in the material world. Within computer-based data visualization metaphor is often used to aid understanding by association with physical phenomena (Anders, 1999). These metaphors can literally be given material weight when data sets are materialized as physical objects. In Nadeem Haidary's (2009) work, *Caloric Consumption*, statistics commenting on the average calorific intake per capita in different countries are visualized as the prongs of a real/physical fork. The various prongs lengths on the folk represent the data from four different countries (Haidary, 2009). This data-object uses the fork as a metaphor for personal and global consumption. Because of the different lengths in the prongs, the fork is not fully functional but it is still usable and operates as a symbol for differences in food consumption around the world. The fork, as object and information has multiple readings as data and form, seen through the lens of the cultural artifact. As Latour and Weibel (2002) suggest there are any number of possible readings and multiple encodings for a cultural symbol and the notion of the data-object adds further dimensionality.

The visual language of data visualization is also well served with biological metaphors. From the use of molecular and cell structures, to tree flow charts, growth rings, cloud patterns and particle diagrams. These organic reference points are commonly used to aid understanding of statistical data and to give some form of material world context to data. Importantly, Tufte (1997) comments on the relationship between visual and statistical thinking and how the application of visual language to data can aid or detract from the understanding of data. The use of metaphor becomes more malleable when we combine data with the material language of physical form, as we will see in the examples from the following section.

MAKING FROM THE DIGITAL

As touched upon earlier there are a number of enabling fabrication technologies that have facilitated the production of data artifacts. As these technologies have become cheaper and more readily available, the creative community has begun to take advantage of these new production processes. An interesting example of creative practitioners experimenting with these technologies can be seen in the *Inside Out* (2010) rapid prototype exhibition. In this exhibition, over 40 miniature sculptures were produced using rapid prototype technologies. The show was the result of a collaboration between artists and designers in the UK and Australia, drawn from a variety of creative disciplines including, fine art, graphic design, sculpture, architecture, and textile design; each person contributing one RP sculpture to the show. The sculptures were initially designed on the computer and output in resin for exhibition in both countries. The *Inside Out* show, in name and theme, explored the making potentials and perceptions of creative practice in physical and digital environments, and allowed artists from

different disciplines to consider how these new fabricating methods could inform their work and making processes (Smith & Rieser, 2010).

In particular, two of the works included in the show demonstrate how data recorded from natural phenomena and biological processes could be used in the creation of a data-driven object. In the work by Mitchell Whitelaw (2010) entitled *Measuring Cup (Sydney 1859-2009)*, we see a materialization of temperature statistics for Sydney, Australia over 150 years. In Whitelaw's work this data is used to form the shape of a resin beaker (see Figure 3). Each layer of the beaker represents a year's statistics and placed one on top of another, the rings of data build up the sides of the container. Like the growth rings of a tree, the annual rings of temperature data give a tangible suggestion of growth and flux. Interestingly the ergonomic affordance of a flared lip, usually introduced to aid drinking, is reflected by the recent upward (outward) trend in overall temperatures (Whitelaw, 2010).

Figure 3. Measuring cup (Sydney 1859-2009) rapid prototype sculpture (© 2010 artist Mitchell Whitelaw. Used with permission)

While Whitelaw's piece is a representation of data analysis from the natural environment, Michele Barker and Anna Munster's piece in the exhibition utilized a data set of a much more personal, and intangible nature. In the work, *The Brainwave of a Monk Meditating on Unconditional Loving-Kindness and Compassion*, Barker and Munster (2010) materialize the act of thought; something often considered as abstract and non-representational. Using neuroscientific data of brain activity, the recorded differences in electromagnetic energy emitted during meditation were used to form the basis of the rapid prototype sculpture. Tipping a hat to the discipline of bioinformatics the 3D sculptural form of a data trace is both informative and fragile, the qualities of the physical object portraying an intimacy, which is missing in a conventional 2D diagram.

In a similarly intimate fashion, the singularity of our individual physiology is the inspiration for a series of works by the jewelry maker/conceptual artist Christoph Zellweger. In Zellweger's (2006) *Data Jewels*, wearable rapid prototypes and other computer controlled manufacturing processes are used to create jewelry based on an individual's genetic code (Zellweger, 2007). Zellweger's jewelry reveals the hidden codes and data of our physical being, and exploits the trend in advanced manufacturing where individual items can be fabricated to exact personal taste or requirement (see Figure 4). This flexibility in physical making echoes the type of adaptive morphological attributes we normally ascribe to the digital, yet still allows us to benefit from the tangible properties we gain from material culture. In their own way, the three examples mentioned above all explore and combine attributes and properties that we commonly associate with either digital data or material objects. Each work combines these attributes in a different way to create a hybrid, data-object that is conceptually and formally challenging.

Figure 4. Data jewel rapid prototype jewelry (© 2006, artist Christoph Zellweger. Used with permission)

CONCLUSION

In this chapter, we have looked at the recent trend for making objects from digital data as a form of creative practice. This activity is being enabled through increasing access to new fabrication technologies, which are opening up opportunities for artists and designers. From a philosophical perspective, the creation of these digitally informed objects brings into question the value systems we typically ascribe to digital and material artifacts and allows for a softening of the classic binary opposition in which these two paradigms are traditionally aligned. These data-objects, which incorporate properties and traits from both material and digital cultures sit on the border between both spaces and can play to the expectations of each.

Furthermore, the data driven object should be considered in respect to existing issues and ongoing conversations around contemporary art/design practices, information visualization, and digital inclusion. Yet their creation is in a sense a new media form, open to a complex set of readings in a technologically enabled society, which is still grounded however, in material culture and the embodied experience. These dialogic objects have the ability to capitalize on the inherit traits found in both the digital and the material, and if successful can combine these attributes into a hybridized form, which can offer a new way of looking at the digital/material relationship. How we might then begin to communicate ideas and concepts though these constructs is only now beginning to emerge. These new synthesized data-objects populated with the attributes of both digital and material culture invite us to apply a new typology to a variety of social cultural contexts and take advantage of the potentials of the liminal space from which they are conceived.

REFERENCES

Anders, P. (1999). *Envisioning cyberspace.* New York, NY: McGraw-Hill.

Barker, M., & Munster, A. (2010). *The brainwave of a monk meditating on unconditional loving-kindness and compassion.* Retrieved April 20, 2011, from http://www.insideoutexhibition.com/

Benjamin, W. (1968). *Illuminations: The work of art in the age of mechanical reproduction.* New York, NY: Schocken Books.

Bolter, J. D., & Grusin, R. (1999). *Remediation: Understanding new media.* Cambridge, MA: MIT Press.

Bunkley, B. (2009). *Displaced animals 2004-2006.* Retrieved April 30, 2011, from http://www.britbunkley.com/

Card, S., Mackinlay, J., & Shneiderman, B. (1999). *Readings in information visualization: Using vision to think.* San Francisco, CA: Morgan Kaufmann Publishers.

Charlton, J. (2010). *iForm.* Retrieved April 20, 2011, from http://www.mic.org.nz/artists/james-charlton/

Gwilt, I. (2010). Compumorphic art-The computer as muse. In S. Baker & P. Thomas (Ed.), *The First International Conference on Transdisciplinary Imaging at the Intersections between Art, Science and Culture: New Imaging: Transdisciplinary Strategies for Art beyond the New Media,* (pp. 72-76). Sydney, Australia: Artspace. Retrieved from http://blogs.unsw.edu.au/tiic/

Haidary, N. (2009). *In-formed.* Retrieved April 23, 2011, from http://nadeemhaidary.com/informed.html#Lima, M. (2009). *Information visualization manifesto.* Retrieved April 11, 2011, from http://www.visualcomplexity.com/vc/blog/?p=644

Klanten, R., Ehmann, S., Tissot, T., & Bourquin, N. (Eds.). (2010). *Data flow 2: Visualizing information in graphic design.* Berlin, Germany: Gestalten.

Lakoff, G., & Johnson, M. (1980). *Metaphors we live by.* Chicago, IL: University of Chicago Press.

Latour, B., & Weibel, P. (2002). *Iconoclash: Beyond the image wars in science, religion and art.* Cambridge, MA: MIT Press.

Levy, P. (1998). *Becoming virtual-Reality in the virtual age.* New York, NY: Plenum.

Miller, D. (2010). *Stuff.* Cambridge, UK: Polity.

Noorani, R. (2006). *Rapid prototyping principles and applications.* Hoboken, NJ: John Wiley and Sons.

Reynolds, A. (2002). *Mount fear: Statistics for crimes with offensive weapon South London 2001-2002.* Retrieved April 20, 2011, from http://www.abigailreynolds.com/mntF/mntFSth.html

Riggins, S. (Ed.). (1994). *The socialness of things: Essays on the socio-semiotics of objects*. Berlin, Germany: Mouton de Gruyter. doi:10.1515/9783110882469

Shove, E., Watson, M., Hand, M., & Ingram, J. (2007). *The design of everyday life*. Oxford, UK: Berg.

Smith, C., & Rieser, M. (2010). *Inside out rapid prototype exhibition*. Retrieved April 20, 2011, from http://www.insideoutexhibition.com/

Tufte, E. (1993). *The visual display of quantitative information*. Cheshire, CT: Graphics Press.

Tufte, E. (1997). *Visual explanations: Images and quantities, evidence and narrative*. Cheshire, CT: Graphics Press. doi:10.1063/1.168637

Ware, C. (2004). *Information visualization: Perception for design*. San Francisco, CA: Morgan Kaufmann.

Whitelaw, M. (2010). *Measuring cup (Sydney, 1859-2009)*. Retrieved April 20, 2011, from http://www.insideoutexhibition.com/

Zellweger, C. (2007). *Journal of modern craft review*. Retrieved April 20, 2011, from http://www.christophzellweger.com/about/

Chapter 3
Mobility, Liminality, and Digital Materiality

Martin Rieser
De Montfort University, UK

ABSTRACT

This chapter will examine and critically align a number of pioneering projects from around the world, using mobile and pervasive technologies, which have challenged the design and delivery of mobile artworks, as documented on the author's weblog and book The Mobile Audience (Rodopi, 2011). These will be presented together with examples from the artist's own research and practice, which have been concerned with the liminal nature of digital media and the intersection of the real and virtual, the physicality of place, and the immateriality of the imaginary in artistic spaces. Two projects in process are also referenced: The Prisoner—a motion-captured, emotionally responsive avatar in the round—and Secret Garden—a virtual reality digital opera. Lastly, this chapter considers the nature of digital materiality in the exhibition of miniature Internet transmitted sculptures: Inside Out: Sculpture in the Digital Age.

THE PARADIGM

As computing leaves the desktop and spills out onto the pavements, streets and public spaces of the city, we increasingly find information-processing capacity embedded within, and distributed throughout the material fabric of everyday urban space. Ubiquitous computing evangelists have heralded a coming age of an urban infra-structure, capable of sensing and responding to the events and activities transpiring around them. Imbued with the capacity to remember, correlate, and anticipate, this near-future "sentient" city is envisioned as being capable of reflexively monitoring its environment and our behaviours within it—becoming an active agent in the organization of everyday life in urban public space. However, beyond such techno-utopianism, the use of mobile

DOI: 10.4018/978-1-4666-2961-5.ch003

code-based technologies can give new agency to the public, and create a distinctive meld of embedded history and imagination, which in the urban projects described in this chapter, represents a very different form of 'sentience.'

Our mental representations of cities are necessarily complex, and to me it seems problematic for artists to merely map literal representations back onto space using locative technologies, but this appears to have been the predominant practice of many early projects, such as the first Locative Media workshop1 and Urban Tapestries2. Research into spatial representation shows how mental maps create subjective distortion, describing not space, but the objects or nodes in it, and so our inner representations appear to be a direct contradiction to the continuous Euclidian 'space between' of a (Google) map, which is the dominant trope of the age of GPS (Tversky, Kim, & Cohen, 1999). Many of my own and the other projects considered here are an attempt to view the city as a series of social markers, landmarks and imagined human presences, rather than as simply abstract representations of space.

In current artistic interventions deploying locative technologies, there exist two distinct domains of practice—one that engages the "digital tame" of social media, online consumer culture and easy post-Situationist urban interventions, and another, which critically interrogates the digital "wild" by considering the liminal: the marginal and the excluded, both in fact and imagination.

While media arts using locative tools have naturally gravitated towards urban environments and have been drawn from either game or Situationist strategies, this chapter will develop a theory and practice of situated and embodied arts related to a broader spectrum of ambulant and location-based practice making use of the new digital affordances. This chapter will discuss how particular artworks that use technologies such as GPS have transformed landscape from a "picture" to a multi-layered, multi-channel experience, often incorporating multiple sense

modalities and extending beyond the instant into a highly durational, expanded spatio-temporal field. This field may reconnect the human experience of landscape, through the newer opportunities provided by mobile technology, to its very long artistic and cultural traditions. My use of Liminality also refers to the increasingly shaded edge area between virtual and physical experience, as well as the sense of 'otherness' or the uncanny, engendered by technologies of this kind.

LOCATIVE ART

Karlis Kalnins coined the phrase 'locative media' as the title for a workshop hosted by RIXC, an electronic art and media centre in Latvia during 2002. Whilst locative media is closely related to augmented reality (reality overlaid with virtual reality) and to pervasive computing; locative media concentrates on social interaction with a specific place through mobile technology. Hence, many locative media projects have a background in social, critical, or personal memory. In this chapter, I will describe attempts to use location-specific media in narratised contexts, both as a researcher's tool and a way to bring contemporary stories alive for the new technologically driven public.

Much reflection on Locative media art has been premature, for as Drew Hemment observes:

It is too early to offer a topology of locative media arts, however, or to tie the field down with strict definitions or borders... We have not yet reached the point at which the technology disappears-all too often the tendency is to focus on the technology and tools rather than the art or content. [3]

The waters have been further muddied by the convenient way in which artist's projects have often aligned with the consumer research interests of the mobile phone companies, where yesterday's locative project becomes tomorrow's "killer app." Mike Liebhold of the Institute for the Future (IFF) regards "geohackers, locative media artists, and psychogeographers" as key players in developing the "geospatial Web," in where the Web becomes tagged with geospatial information, a development that he sees as having "enormous unharvested business opportunities." and believes that this context-aware computing will emerge as the "third great wave of modern digital technology."[4]

Locative art, by its very nature, trespasses into the realm of Public Art, but by its interaction with the public, transforms our notions of site-specific and ambulant practices, defined over the last few decades by artists such as Richard Long, Robert Smithson, Hamish Fulton, Vito Acconci and Sophie Calle. The history of located and nomadic art is indeed a very long one-stretching back to Aboriginal Songlines and spatialised religious rituals. I pose here the question whether, by similarly rooting locative practice in profound cultural and psychological structures, locative work can gain greater artistic resonance. The exploration of the syntax of spatial language and its relevance to current practice is the subject of this essay. Respect for place and space has long gone from our social uses of location-based technologies, but may still perhaps be reclaimed by artists.

Which brings me to a further issue relating to the art practice in this new medium. Much of what is named 'Locative Art' is not really art, but rather games-based work or spatialised documentary or simply advanced toolsets that happen to use this technology. I think the potential is there, but art has a different function to these uses, and when it is truly present, you can sense it from afar. To illuminate further we must ask a central question: what are the pleasures and modes of mobile user experience and how we can distinguish these from other media art forms or genres of work?

This extension of interactive technology from fixed installation to real urban geographies is radically altering the modes of audience participation and reception. When the physical space overlaps the space of diegesis, the emergent space for art and performance appears to open new perceptions of space and place in the audience. We need a redefinition of the concept of physical space (including hybrid environments), since through such technologies a new form of urban space seems to be emerging, which is not primarily visual, but in essence, conceptual.

Understanding emergent forms and visual and auditory artistic strategies of locative and pervasive media, which may enhance interactive narrative in urban and site-specific environments—is still a huge challenge. But only through such an understanding of these new and radical forms of experiment, can we attempt to both map changes in sociability and communication patterns and to understand these new forms of collaborative art.

In defining the pleasures of the medium, the Mobile Bristol[5] project made an attempt to identify these through a seminar series in 2005, where for example, it was discovered that the accidental overlapping of ambient environmental sound and augmented sound with in a locative work created a delicious ambiguity and a sense of extra resonance for an audience, a phenomenon termed "Magic Moments." Now what is needed most is to not only the pleasures of reception and use in this medium, but also to understand the social and physical context of these new artworks. These are increasingly dependent on haptic and spatial senses such as proprioception, which are little understood by artists, but are within the affordances of the emerging technologies.

HOSTS AND STARSHED: UNCANNY SPACES

In 2006 I developed Hosts[6] for display in Bath Abbey, in an attempt to create an experimental ubiquitous artwork, sensitive to a specific location, by adapting new technologies to give a fully realized and embodied audio-visual user experience which touched on some universal thematics in art, in both its ancient and modern incarnations and explored the sense of uncanny associated with such technology. The piece was designed as a reflection on human life and death, presence and absence. Vertical screens were placed at strategic points of the space. A visitor triggered the presence of a variety of unfocused and evanescent video characters through the use of positional detection microphones, ultrasound emitting badges or 'Chirpers,' and interpretative software. Individual characters appeared seemingly at random, but then spoke to an individual visitor and accompanied them from screen to screen. These "Hosts" were of a wide range of ages and of different gender, but always appeared singly to the particular participant wearing the unique ultrasound-code (see Figure 1).

The "Hosts" could be taken to represent a variety of presences: from the angels of the Jacobs Ladder, sculpted on the building's exterior, to the spirit of people who had inhabited the same spaces, or seen as fragments of an individual psyche. The emotional mood was deliberately variable and the encounters changed depending on a randomised selection sequence for the video sprite characters and sounds. A 3D audio landscape of acapella tonal voices accompanied the visitor between the screens, accessible on wireless headphones, and formed a tangible changing audio landscape. I worked with singers, musicians, and sound designers in Bristol/Bath on this aspect of the piece.

If a visitor stood for more than a few seconds in front of a particular screen, the figure turned in the direction of the viewer and returned the visitor's stare. The video sprite looked the visitor up and down, or turned away in distraction and then spoke a series of poetic aphorisms, also seen as animated text on the screen. On a separate screen evanescent figures were continually climbing up and down two ladders mirroring the motif carved on the Abbey. It was out of this initial project that I developed a series of mobile art experiments to answer some of the research questions emerging in this new field. Simultaneously, I was research-

Figure 1. Hosts in Bath abbey (© 2006 Martin Rieser. Used with permission)

ing a book on the subject: The Mobile Audience7. One of the first tasks was to gain an overview of the phenomenon of artworks in this domain of embodied experience, an emerging arena for self-performance.

Hewlett Packard has coined the term for mobile interaction spaces as "mediascapes"; and this hybrid media space is an in between, threshold place, an amalgam of imagination and the physical. De Certeau understood space as something that is produced through social practices (Lefebvre, 1991; Certeau, 2002). With new social behaviours, emerge new spatial possibilities, so if Locative Media is to move beyond the production of novel experiences for extremely limited (art) audiences, it has to realize its potential by also addressing cultural, social and political contexts, and its practices need to be evaluated against the larger social framework of urban public space, critically engaging with the social and political realities of contemporary cities.

This project was followed by a collaborative commission for the Electric Pavilion event at the Watershed Media Centre by the Ship of Fools[8] artist group, where we constructed an interactive map of Bristol, correlated a starry map of the heavens. Stories were aligned star by star with real locations in the city. Participants were able to log sites and add rich-media stories of uncanny happenings and encounters across the city. As the first serious attempt to use mobile media for this purpose, it was a unique piece and opened out in graphic form, the liminal and uncanny nature of the medium and how metaphoric mapping could elide the physical and the imagined into a single metaphoric interface (see Figure 2).

A GENDERED FORM

The political and economic shape of society ultimately forms contemporary modes of narrative. The contradictory pressures of neo-liberal economics, which drive the growth of personalised and peer-to-peer media and the inter-penetration of workspace and private space, also seem to offer a unique opportunity to break Laura Mulvey's determinist "male" control of narrative vision, which dominated narrative in the 19th and 20th centuries and therefore to promote a more de-centered and subtle mapping.

Feminist critics have often raised alternative strategies to break the negatives of a culture of male "control". Not surprisingly, some interesting female locative practice explores precisely this area. Teri Rueb's Drift9, for example, tied a sound landscape to the movements of the tide on a north European beach. The installation covered a 2 km x 2 km region on the Wadden sea that was filled with areas of interactive sound. The piece creates a space of flows consisting of sounds and words that travel like particles on simulated air and water currents loosely based on actual oceanographic and meteorological data. The audience had either to open itself up to these primal cycles of nature or risk confusion and data loss.

PERFORMANCE OR GAME-PLAY?

Mobile devices already appear performative in their nature, with public space interpenetrating our private concerns, so that any conversation has its willing or unwilling eavesdroppers. Add to this the potential for social interaction, crudely

Figure 2. The starshed interface (© 2006 Martin Rieser. Used with permission)

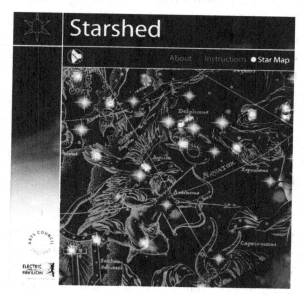

demonstrated by Flashmobs and in more sophisticated ways by mobile gaming and you have a case of new technology creating adaptive social behaviours, which contain strong performative elements. Demanding games are already being played using mobile technologies such as Catchbob and Blast Theory's Uncle Roy All Around You10, which combine Internet and mobile technologies, where the city and the Internet were regarded as related stages on which we play, regardless of the specific context. Steve Benford of Nottingham University now talks of "seamful" media where players have learnt to exploit GPS "shadows" (where tall buildings block satellite triangulation) to their own advantage during game play, describing how such unforeseen effects of the technology encouraged new kinds of movement through the city.

The failure of such works is often in terms of misapplied contextual practice: I once tested Valentina Niisi's Media Portrait of the Liberties11 in Dublin before the demise of MIT's Eurolab. We had gone about a block when the local youths began stoning us. The technology was certainly impressive, but this new form of public art was alien even to the children of the local contributors to the artwork. When participating in Blast Theory's Uncle Roy All Around You, I reflected on how the game's format had reduced the richness of the city to a few textual clues and a dangerous process of frantic searching, with users crossing roads with even less awareness than the average iPod listener.

SPATIAL ANNOTATION AND COLLABORATIVE MAPPING

Spatial annotation has emerged in the last few years as a major Internet phenomenon, particularly with the growth of Google Maps and social photo-sharing sites such as Flickr. In spatial annotation projects like Yellow Arrow12 and Neighbornode13 and in my own Starshed14 for Electric Pavilion, cities are increasingly being treated as surfaces on which individuals can inscribe annotation, and which will ultimately become repositories of collective memory. Such story-telling projects allow for new social and cultural readings of space, allowing private narratives to become public and subject to reinterpretation.

One of my current projects—Songlines[15]—is a collaboration between the University of Bath, De Montfort University's Institute of Creative Technologies, Sustrans, and two media design companies. The project is an exemplar of subjective mapping, and will work by upgrading current Internet wiki-mapping technologies, combined with public databases to create mobile cycling/walker maps, responsive to changes in the road environment using updates from end-user and public knowledge bases. A combination of innovative mobile phone-based sensing software will encourage and enhance the experience of cycling or walking in urban environments through the use of reliable location-specific mobile info-services (updateable maps and audio and rich media stream services) giving convenient infield access to better customised traveller information and to provide intelligent support with context-awareness to individual travellers. On the basis of this investigation, Sustrans will commission virtual located artworks for the city for walkers and cyclists, which will be delivered by the location-sensing test infrastructure as rich-media audio-visuals. These artworks/information layers will all be relevant to specific landmarks and locations on proposed routes. The mobile phone based location-detection features will be used to update user's positional information. Automated audiovisual casts of route directions and art/information would be uploaded in advance of the journey and be tagged to correlate against positions along the route and be triggered by positional data. Thus, it is envisaged that both directional instructions and the rich media streams could be delivered to mobiles according to route progress (see Figure 3).

THE CITY AS STORY TRAJECTORY

The collective project The Third Woman[16] is relevant to this mapping of imagined worlds onto the physical city. It was an interactive mobile film, part of the European emobilArt initiative, which combined mobile game and performance based on a contemporary Vienna, revisiting the familiar territory of the post-war film noir The Third

Figure 3. Songlines: postcard advertising the project (© 2012 Martin Rieser. Used with permission)

Man and re-imagined it for the 21st Century. The public participated in a guided performance game in the Viennese U-Bahn system, using QR codes as triggers for film-noir fragments and text messages, which moved them through a scenario that varied, depending on location or choice; driven by an intelligent film engine derived from Pia Tikka's Enactive cinema research[17]. The film itself was structured into three parallel dramas, where the same scene was available in three different emotional moods.

The work toured internationally and was re-worked substantially for each succeeding venue. Latterly, The Third Woman film-game explored a theme of pervasive global threats to use bio-engineered terrorism in the 21st century. The film was the central element in a more complex interactive event. Using smart phone technology, participants could interact with media by responding to questions derived from ethical, moral, and social perspectives embedded in the content of the film (see Figure 4).

In New York, performers on stage, wore fashion items made of QR images, used their bodies to demonstrate how to scan the codes and link to The Third Woman media. Spilling off stage into the audience, they invited people to play the film-game. Participants playing the game became part of The Third Woman interactive performance and could choose routes through the multi-stranded

Figure 4. The third woman showing Margarete Jahrmann's interactive clothing for QR codes (© 2011 Martin Rieser. Used with permission)

narrative by selecting subtle statements on their smartphones, related to character behaviours. Their choices could be examined individually or form a 'vote' for the preferred version which would then appear on a larger communal screen. As an experiment in hybrid mobile film and performance the project broke new ground, particular by envisaging the narrative as a story space which could connect with audiences in a variety of ways both online and through live performance and installation, and offer unique story routes to each individual depending on their interaction and conscious choices (see Figure 5).

It was invaluable as a crucible for refining hybrid mobile experiences for new audiences, equipped with smartphones, and was instrumental in finding the simplest and most inclusive method for singular and collaborative engagement with mobile-based narratives.

MAPPING AND HISTORY

Satnav systems tend to reduce our world to roads between A and B. The specific tagging potential of the locative can certainly overlay this reductive idea of space with all the richness of personal experience, but that depends on the framework provided and the context set by the artist, and in many projects, this is so loosely drawn that we simply achieve a kind of public palimpsest.

In their project 34n 118w[18], Jeffrey Knowlton, Naomi Spellman, and Jeremy Hight had users take Tablet PCs with Global Positioning Devices and headphones onto a former railway yard in downtown Los Angeles. As participants walked around the site, they could hear fictional statements recounting the history of the place. To quote Hight: "The story world becomes one of juxtaposition, of overlap, of layers appearing and falling away. Place becomes a multi-tiered and malleable concept."

There are other contemporary narratives resonant with the reinforcement of site and story.

Figure 5. The third woman performance in Galapagos, Brooklyn, NY (© 2011 Martin Rieser. Used with permission)

Riot1831![19] from Mobile Bristol depicted the Bristol Riots of 1831. This first GPS-enabled locative drama was an immersive and powerful experience, engaging with the immediate spaces of history, mapped onto a Georgian square where the original events took place. At first sight, it seems contradictory that such engaging locative works tend to deal with an historical past rather than the lived present. After all Paul Virilio identified new media as promoting the change from considered diegesis to continuous and automatic present; the user creating the narratives both as subject and object. The visual subject becoming transferred to a mere technical effect, which forms a sort of 'pan-cinema,' turning our most ordinary acts into movie action (Virilio, 1989). However where these locative works succeed, they seem to overlap the user's enactment of a continuous present with the user's immediate perception of a contiguous past.

The ever increasing technologising and enclosure of urban and public spaces is a phenomenon associated with the growth of 'Herzian' Space and what Mark Augé[20] has termed to growth of "no place" (The anonymous motorway or mall). Stephen Graham points to how: "places [are] becoming increasingly constructed through consumer decisions which, in turn, are influenced through the… surveillance, and sorting, of cities" (Graham, 2004).

Such cities, increasingly "sorted" through the software and networking, point up a related political question about the embedding of previous relations of power, class and ownership in the new infrastructures and whether this perpetuates ancient divisions or raises further questions related to the potential for community and individual empowerment.

A project of mine used the city as both metaphor and as a respectful multilayered repository of meaning. Riverains[21] was developed for the B.Tween festival in Manchester and was predicated on the idea of underground presences derived from the city's past, which lingered in the underground spaces riddling our cities. These presences could both be detected and unlocked by the public, using mobile devices in the manner of a water douser. It was planned to later add user contributions in the form of avatars to create an ever-growing layer-cake of histories and narratives. It was further developed for the Illumini Festival in Shoreditch, where multiple histories were layered along Shoreditch High Street and Old Street.

Both Manchester and London have rich underground worlds of hidden or "lost" rivers, nuclear fallout facilities and command centres and Second World War bunkers, in addition to Victorian sewers and underground railway systems. They also have an archaeology going back through medieval to Roman times. The Riverains were drawn from this rich history of poverty, industrial revolution, immigration, political protest, commerce and innovation, gang warfare and crime. The project is planned to map video and photo-stories across central areas of other cities (see Figure 6).

Riverains was run in Pilot form at the Illumini Festival in September 2010 tracing a portion of Old Street and Shoreditch High Street. Secret Subterranean London was the third Illumini event, curated by Jane Webb, and located in the basement of Shoreditch Town Hall. Over 50 artists/artist

Figure 6. Riverains: screen interaction (© 2010 Martin Rieser. Used with permission)

groups exhibited and performed during the week-long festival, which also included guided underground tours, artist talks and workshops. Over 3300 people attended the opening evening, Thursday 9th September 2010, and 9247 people in total visited Illumini during the whole week's event.

Riverains at Illumini was designed to comprise four elements, offering interaction to users with varying levels of technical requirement (users are expected to provide their own mobile phone). The work built on the Riverains development for Manchester's B'tween festival, extending it through collaboration with artists Ximena Alarcon and Kasia Molga, with technical development by Sean Clark and Phil Sparks (Empedia by Cuttlefish Multimedia) and Gareth Howell (using Layar). Two 'guided walks' followed in which participants were supported in using the QR code reader version, and Layar (for those with suitable phones), as they followed the trail along Old Street and Shoreditch High Street. Those without appropriate phones were able to share the experience using spare iphones during the walks. Riverains was aimed at the broad spectrum Illumini audience.

The video pieces by Alarcon and myself were either triggered by photographing QR codes distributed on stickers along the route, carrying visual clues as to locations associated with the video content. While encouraging audiences to download in advance in areas of free WiFi; the 3G downloads took no more than a minute and in fact began streaming almost instantly. The Layar version was equally successful and it is hoped that the next incarnation will fully develop all the intended game elements and the user software to upload further stories.

As it was, the rich history of Shoreditch was explored with pieces on early Shakespeare, using imagined voices of characters or actors from the plays "Henry IV" and "Romeo and Juliet"; verbatim readings from the coroner's report of the "Ripper" murder of Mary Kelly: held in the Town Hall site of the exhibition, with interjections by the Ripper's imagined persona; immigrant voices from Jewish, Huguenot, and contemporary narratives were available, as were reflections on the Plague in London, creating dramatised monologues based on Daniel Defoe's Journal of the Plague Year. Suffragette histories became audio-visual sound-image montages echoing their dire treatment in Holloway Prison. Finally, there were reflections on the early history of underground rivers that criss-cross the area and notionally held the historical presences, which are the Riverains.

MAPPING AS CRITIQUE

Apart from the arguments that the technology is intrusive and very commercial and is being "sold" to us via arts projects, there are those about the role of Situationist ideology in locative media (something about which I am personally deeply sceptical, mainly because so few artworks succeed in the 'Detournment' of the original movement). The GPS mapping practice of modern psychogeographers[22] are seemingly related to the writings of Guy Debord and his practice of the 'Dérive'[23], but in reality seldom appear to achieve anything identifiably subversive. To quote one cultural critic:

Locative media is: Psychogeography without the critique. Algorithmic psychogeography, the term used by http://socialfiction.org to describe their rule-based derives through the city, is not just a development, but actually a fundamental reversal of the critical use of this Situationist tool. [24]

The "Dérive" or 'drift' was a method for subversion, of remapping the world with 'uncontrolled' clarity, for identifying the secret flows of money and power below the surface of the city. However, one strategy Debord does cite: "the introduction of alterations such as more or less arbitrarily transposing maps of two different regions," has been successfully adapted in several locative works. Jen Hamilton in Distance Made Good (Southern & Hamilton, 2003), used parallel mirrored journeys on two continents; in Shadows from Another Place[25], Paula Levine creates a hybrid space between Baghdad and San Francisco composed of the superimposition of their city centres. A mapping of the initial US attack on Baghdad is superimposed upon downtown San Francisco. The longitude and latitude of each bombsite is marked in San Francisco using a GPS device. C5 in The Other Path[26] set out on a month long Great Wall trek, starting in the northwest desert of China and following the Wall eastward to where it runs to the edge of the Yellow Sea. GPS data collected during this trek was used to develop a pattern matching search procedure for locating the most similar data model in the most similar terrain in California.

Mark Tuters has perceptively identified how such annotation and tracing fits into the legacy of Situationism, which Locative Media has claimed as a philosophical base from its inception.

Roughly, these two types of locative media, Annotative and Tracing, correspond to two archetypal poles winding their way through late 20th century art, critical art and phenomenology, perhaps otherwise figured as the twin Situationist practices of detournement and the derive.[27]

Situationism in Locative media resists easy definition, but may best be represented says Tuters, by one of Deleuze and Guattari's maps, which distinguish between annotation and tracing:

The map is open, connectable in all its dimensions, and capable of being dismantled; it is reversible, and susceptible to constant modification. It can be torn, reversed, adapted to montages of every kind, taken in hand by an individual, a group, or a social formation. It can be drawn on a wall, conceived of as a work of art, constructed as a political action or as a meditation...Contrary to a tracing, which always returns to the 'same,' a map has multiple entrances.[28]

An early locative project, which epitomized such emergent qualities was MILK[29], winner of a Golden Nica at Ars Electronica. With MILK, the artists, Esther Polak and Leva Auzina, used GPS to trace routes to create a form of landscape art for a network society. MILK was based in part on a project by Polak and the Waag Society, Real Time Amsterdam, in which GPS transponders mapped cyclists in Amsterdam on their traffic routes by the aggregation of their travel measured over a period of weeks. MILK suggested a god-like vision of locative technologies that allowed the tracking of freighted foodstuffs. In this case with heavy irony, since the dairy-rich Netherlands import their milk from Latvia making visible the contradictions and excess of a networked society.

The increasing importance of maps in defining space within these projects should not blind us to the fact that mapping itself is not a neutral process, but always has been a highly selective and subjective one, in which can be embedded various (invisible) ideological assumptions. Many GPS mapping projects tend to forget this and even revel in the act of remapping without context.

Media artist Coco Fusco also launched a headlong attack on new media practices associated with networks and mapping, declaring:

It is as if more than four decades of postmodern critique of the Cartesian subject had suddenly evaporated...In the name of a politics of global connectedness, artists and activists too often substitute an abstract 'connectedness' for any real engagement with people in other places or even in their own locale.[30]

SURVEILLANCE AND SOUSVEILLANCE[31]

In a C-Theory article entitled 'Operational Media'[32], Jordan Crandall spoke of the "resurgence of temporal and locational specificity witnessed in new surveillance and location-aware navigational technologies" and Stephen Graham has warned of the invisibility of such tools and the embedding of discriminatory and selective process in such things as network server logic. Steve Mann caught on to this process very early in 1998 and labelled its subversion as "Souveillance" or 'Surveilling the Surveillers.' Specifically he refers to Reflectionism as being especially related to "detournement": the tactic of appropriating tools of social controllers and resituating these tools in a disorienting manner.

Fears of surveillance are undoubtedly real and relate to the imperative of the State in an age of counter-terrorism, to quote Manovitch[33] "to make the map equal the territory." Of course this technology is a double-edged sword, but then it is also made democratic by its distributive nature and is now in many hands. Artists who have questioned the vulnerability of the individual to tracking include Drew Hemment through his Loca project[34], and Jonah Brucker Cohen with his WiFi Hog[35] has challenged the enclosure of Hertzian space.

In the face of new enclosures of public electronic space, through surveillance and border control, biometrics, and consumer tracking technologies, as Crandell puts it:

The challenge is not only to endeavor to understand this operational construct, but to understand the forms of opposition to it that are emerging in the globalized world. For the operational is only one "window" onto reality. There are other orientations that counter it, and for which, by its very nature, it is unable to account. It is powerless to envision terms of engagement that do not operate according to its logics. It can only assign them to the realm of the barbaric or irrational: that which lies outside of its license on reason.[36]

The compromised publics can choose to respond through collective action, violence or the through the 'reflective' intelligence of these new forms of media art.

MAPPING THE CRISIS

The aim of my 2011 Athens-based workshop Codes of Disobedience and Dysfunctionality[37], was to study elements of the urban environment, and to form new locative trails in the form of a structured collaborative narrative, enriching the city through interactive content, which reflected its contemporary transformations. Codes of Disobedience and Dysfunctionality was part of the Hybrid City Conference initiative, sponsored by Global Gateway. Inspired by the numerous posters and the dense graffiti encountered in the city centre, the workshop connected the urban surroundings of Athens to opinions and statements of its inhabitants towards the challenges imposed by current social, political, and financial circumstances, namely: anger, disobedience, opposition, dysfunctionality. The features of the contemporary metropolis in the midst of a period of crisis were the main focus of the project, posing at the same time questions about the role of and scale of mediation by technology in urban everyday life (see Figure 7).

Figure 7. Codes of disobedience, empedia map (© 2011 Martin Rieser. Used with permission)

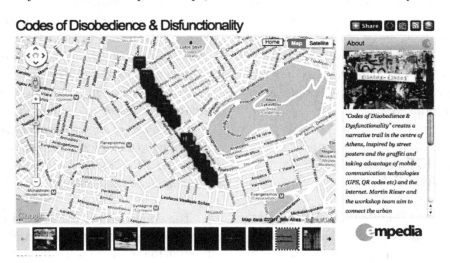

The work formed after the completion of the workshop was presented at the premises of the National Museum of Contemporary Art in Athens, on the Internet and in the centre of the city (on the streets Skoufa – Navarinou – Tzavela). QR coded stickers, carrying imagery from the immediate environment, were placed in selected locations and by scanning them with a mobile phone, access to the audiovisual material, created during the workshop, was accessible to the public. Combining elements of installation art, urban intervention, gaming and performance, Codes of Disobedience and Dysfunctionality reflected my long-term practice using art and technology.

A couple of months later, Urban Digital Narratives looked at the crisis of immigration and gentrification in the Gazi area and the impacts of neo-liberal economic processes on the locally diverse social and ethnic groups. Funded by the British Council, the project explored the new possibilities offered by technology and attempted to ask whether one could really capture the social needs and attitudes of a city like Athens, and whether the patterns and characteristics of urban life could be identified by adapting the uses of these communication systems. Working with such groups at the extreme margins of the neo-liberal European project was illuminating and gave a new voice to these liminal and forgotten lives through technology.

AN EMOTIONAL AUGMENTED REALITY

In the Prisoner project, we motioncaptured real movements to create a animated avatar figure, seen in the round, which exhibited a number of alternative emotional behaviours in reponse to an individual audience member's audio input. The Prisoner "cube" could be regarded as a bounded piece of virtual space, within which the "Prisoner" is forced to live. Loud noise or sudden close movements will drive the figure into a fetal position in the furthest corner away from the responsible audience member. Quiet oral comments will coax the figure forward in an attentive or searching movement mode. The attribution of behaviours to the figure, through audience interaction, personalizes the material and adds a compassionate or curious aspect to the interaction. The piece is intended to explore to boundary between that mysterious boundary between virtuality and the real, as well as generating questions about our social complicity in societies of imprisonment, punishment, containment and the modern panopticon of surveillance. By its nature, the rig has affinities with the cages at Guantanamo and draws on the experience of the Stanford Prisoner Experiment[38].

A microphone mounted above the centre point of the gallery feeds to a multi-channel input. Sound triggers are prioritised and localized by software to one of the four cube front surface areas. Overhead infrared tracking will allow precise calibration of audience position and allow for the development of mirroring behaviours, in terms of the avatar pacing up and down in synch with individual audience members, or having forward and allow matching backward movement inside the cube volume. The motion capture allowed for natural movements and was translated into multi-directional animated segments, which can be concatenated according to audience behaviour. A priority system will operate on a first-come-first-served basis, and interaction continues for a fixed period and then lapses into an idle state to pick up the next interactor.

The project used a female dancer in a body suit with multiple control points to interpret 27 different emotional states, ranging from panic to hope, from fear to jubilation. These movement sequences were motion-captured in full 3D on a Viacom system and the data was converted into movement trajectories for an avatar model, which can be animated in real time. The four facing screens of the rig allowed an illusion of cubic dimensionality within which the avatar exists and reacts to audience. An individual audience member can either operate by voice only (the volume, attack and language keywords will all be interpreted to control the particular reaction of the avatar).

An Emotion Grid of emotional states was worked out in conjunction with the participating dancers and whilst some are obvious, others in-

clude obsessive behaviours, communication with an "imaginary friend," and close observation of vermin in the cell.

AUGMENTED REALITY AS MYTHOLOGY

Secret Garden is an attempt to recreate a contemporary version of the Eden myth in the midst of an urban environment. It is also one of the first located mobile digital operas. A collaborative work between Andrew Hugill, composer, and myself will be available in two versions—a physical installation and as a virtual mobile experience linked to selected site locations. In its installation aspect, it will have eleven iPad viewports distributed around the circumference of a circle. Peering into one of the viewports triggers a view of an idyllic three-dimensional scene in the 'Secret Garden' and tells part of the mythical story of the Fall, through words, music, and actions. This same content will also be made available using Augment Reality software to any visitor with a smartphone.

The Fall story is common to many of the world's religions, including Judaism, Christianity and Islam. The structure of Secret Garden is loosely modelled on the ten paths of the Sephirot in the Jewish telling of the story, which is itself also a symbol of the Tree of Life and the oldest extant version. Two contemporary human figures dressed in traditional iconic colours of blue (Male) and red (Female), will enact the story of the Fall, combining sung poetry and video vignettes within 3D generated environments, each scene distributed to a different one of the eleven viewports. The viewer's presence triggers both music and action.

The texts comprise original poems that tell this classic story in a timeless and relevant way, examining choices in a fallen world. The musical composition is adaptive and features vocal settings and digitally treated percussion. The virtual scenography consists of 3D designs based on an idealised garden space, inspired by the 19th century Mezzotints for Milton's Paradise Lost by John Martin. Viewing the eleven viewports gradually assembles the elements of a story in the user's mind. The story makes reference to the four elements (earth, air, fire, water) and to natural disasters, which might overwhelm the garden. While the story is mysterious and mythical in nature, one of the viewports will provide a climactic coming-together of all the elements. However, it is not necessary to see the viewports in any particular order, and a partial viewing will also provide a complete experience in itself.

The installation is a unique virtual reality amalgam of poetry, music, and 3D panoramic images. It plays with sound narrative and myth, transposed into a modern context, using technology both in production and delivery in a synthesised and holistic capacity. Audience movement from viewport to viewport triggers vocal settings of authored verse. An especially designed circular exhibition installation will be created. This will contain iPad computers and earphones, which can be sited in any gallery. By using 11 small screens, an audience will see true 3D vision, with the parallax shift tied to screen movements. The software will detect iPad movements and adjust the scene's parallax in real-time. Viewers will not be required to wear any other special headgear or glasses: they simply need to touch the iPads to trigger the scene.

We further propose to build a mobile phone version for iPhone and Android smartphone platforms, with a mixture of Augmented Reality and GPS location technology. This will build on the Empedia Platform[39] developed with Cuttlefish Multimedia as a KTP project with the IOCT. We will port the Layar AR api into the Empedia software allowing the user to experience a locative trail where the 11 scenes are linked to 11 key locations in the area. The polyphonic aspects of the original design will be preserved and it will embody the first AR opera ever designed for mobile technologies. The Eden scenes will grow

around a user in 360 degree 3D panoramas tied to the GPS nodes selected and will be triggered by location automatically.

The musical composition involves highly complex counterpoint, since at any one moment there is a possibility of up to twenty-two vocal lines unfolding from any point around the installation. In other words, this is 'adaptive' music, a term derived from computer game composition. The music is harmonically restricted to a hexatonic gamut. The vocal lines illustrate the words, with gong/crotale strokes acting as punctuation. The composition uses the number symbology that lies behind the Ten-branched Sephirot as an organising principle.

By aligning locative technologies with the oldest of mythologies, we are building on the notion of the technology offering not simply a portal into the past, but one into the deeper layers of collective cultural myths, revivified for a contemporary audience.

EXPLORATION OF TANGIBLE OBJECTS

We are entering into a society based on ubiquitous networked objects or Bruce Sterling's Spimes[40]. Soon, objects will be the most frequent users of the Internet, as fridge talks to oven and RFID tags note the progress of stock to central computers. But what the ITU has termed the "Internet of Things" means far more than just tracked objects, as Tuters observes:

'Things' are controversial assemblages of entangled issues, and not simply objects sitting apart from our political passions. The entanglements of things and politics engage activists, artists, politicians, and intellectuals. To assemble this parliament, rhetoric is not enough and nor is eloquence; it requires the use of all the technologies, especially information technology, and the possibility for the arts to re-present anew what are the common stakes.[41]

The pervasive and context aware object will partner a far more physical engagement with mobile devices. The Wii has fomented a revolution in indoor gaming. Devices such as that of the US firm Gesturetek, which has developed software to use a phone's camera to interpret how the phone is being moved; translating gestures into action will promote the use of body actions in street level mobile gaming, but as John Vincent, president and founder of the firm, said: "Being able to do natural movements, not just hand but also full body movement is the way forward."

The technology is embedded in phones released by NTT Docomo in Japan and allows gamers to move the phone, forward and backward, shake it, and roll the device to control action on the screen.

THE MATERIALITY OF THE DIGITAL

In Solaris, Stanislav Lem imagines a planet that is both alive and sentient, which can materialise simulacra of thoughts drawn from human minds into living objects and landscapes. As in so much Science Fiction, an eerie prescience points towards a new definition of materiality, which is emerging in our world where technologies are blurring the boundaries between our notions of 'virtual' and 'real.' These technologies are not confined to those underpinning this exhibition[42] (jointly curated with Claire Smith), but are now extending into haptic interfaces, touchable holograms and responsive 3D environments.

Furthermore, what we perceive to be 'materiality,' is seemingly determined by the infantile hardwiring of our brains, which in turn determines our consequent ability to interpret our sensory inputs. The blind from birth, when given sight, cannot make real sense of what they see- since context is as crucial as content (Gregory & Wallace, 1963).

This redefinition of the "real" can only lead us to conclude that materiality is not simply about physical objects, but about the processes and relations which give rise to materiality. In this sense, the world is full of potentials, which can at any time result in instantiation. "The artist is the origin of the work. The work is the origin of the artist. Neither is without the other" (Heidegger, 143). Materiality is not only about tangibility-for example software, while being immaterial in the strictest sense, impacts hugely on our world through its affordances and organising properties, it depends on material artefacts and has material effects; so perhaps the relationship between virtual and real is more nuanced than we readily allow.

This exhibition therefore attempted to explore a new boundary between the digital artefact and its instantiation. The project's removal of the normal intuitive and iterative processes of creative production, and (in such a long distance exchange) the necessary substitution of a more industrial model, was a singularly extreme approach. Particularly where the CAD modeling embodied the totality of the artists' spatial and creative knowledge, but was only revealed and tested in a single prototype. Nevertheless, it was a process one, which we hope stimulated, rather than restricted the practitioners. With Rapid Prototyping (RP) for sculptures, there are other points grading between an extreme craft and extreme industrial strategy, but while others have already explored these gradations: we deliberately chose to expose a mix of traditional artists and crafts people to this uncompromising experiment, in order to preserve that almost magical sense of materialisation offered by the technology.

The last two decades' debates about the nature of computer art, and the necessity of creative code as an integral aspect of it as a distinct form need, not be rehearsed again here, but it is cogent to consider the difference conceptually between using the computer as the original medium rather than merely as an assistive tool. I think this was always our intention: to force people to inhabit the process and the medium entirely, to ignore past notions of materiality, truth to materials etc and to consider the affordances of RP: the ability to fully describe and realise the intricate delicacy of internal as well as external surfaces, hence the title and theme of the exhibition. It is not, I think entirely coincidental that some of the forms in the show exhibited organic and micro-organic affinities with diatoms; pollen grains; and complex crystals, for these are also forms that grow, as it were, algorithmically or parametrically.

The intrinsic limitations and costs of practical production led us to choose the miniature as a format, but as curators, I think we unconsciously had in mind antecedent forms of display such as the Cabinet of Curiosities and the exquisite drawers of objects in the Pitt River's Museum, Oxford, and The Natural History Museum in London. This sense of the fruits of exotic travel, the trawling of riches from around the globe, for all its colonial taint, has immense appeal and forms a valid iconography for these objects dredged from the depths of an emergent technology.

The fascinating range and variety of submissions is of a particular satisfaction to us both. Even dealing as we were with two related but widely separated artistic milieus, the final objects run giddily from the ironic to the platonic, from the deeply serious to the playfully superficial. This protean gamut is really the point of the exercise-to show how little barriers exist to the imagination, in this particular process of realisation; the constraints of gravity and durability, so familiar to the sculptor, can for once be largely set aside to give free rein to the creative concept. In a sense, many artists have chosen to revisit the purity of the modernist and constructivist ethos, alongside the post-modern knowingness of our era. It is important not to treat these objects not as maquettes for larger works, but as celebrations of the small, but perfectly formed!

CONCLUSION

The advent of mobile technologies has placed powerful computers in the pockets of more people than have ever possessed a desktop PC. It has created new affordances for artists out in real space, dissolving the traditional gallery walls and has allowed new audiences to relate to the spaces of their urban worlds by turning them both into places and spaces of liminal possibility, where inner and outer spaces, histories and narratives can be interlocked and explored. It has allowed the user the privilege of co-authorship via social media and other two-way interventions. I hope through my examination of a broad range of projects the common thematics have been illuminated: that mobile and digital media can create a portal to a space where social, physical and virtual worlds can collide and cross-fertilize; enriching our experience of the city as a space of possibility by our augmenting our sense of the present and past. It could be said that we are looking at the very beginning of a new art form, one that happily exists in both the hybrid world of the new "Hertzian" spaces and in the imagination of the new audiences.

REFERENCES

Augé, M. (1995). *Non-places: Introduction to an anthropology of supermodernity*. Paris, France: Verso.

Codes of Disobedience and Disfunctionality. (2012). Website. *Retrieved from* http://empedia. info/maps/41

Deleuze, G., & Guattari, F. (1983). *On the line*. New York, NY: Semiotext(e).

Graham, S. (2004). The software-sorted city: Rethinking the digital divide. In Graham, S. (Ed.), *The Cybercities Reader* (pp. 324–331). London, UK: Routledge.

Gregory, R. L., & Wallace, J. (1974). Recovery from early blindness: A case study. In Gregory, R. L. (Ed.), *Concepts and Mechanisms of Perception*. London, UK: Duckworth.

Inside Out. (2012a). Website. *Retrieved from* http://insideout.digitalalchemist.com.au/artists/

Inside Out. (2012b). Website. *Retrieved from* http://www.insideoutexhibition.com/

Lem, S., Kilmartin, J., & Cox, S. (1970). *Solaris.* New York, NY: Harcourt Brace Jovanovich.

Mann, S., Nolan, J., & Wellman, B. (2003). Sousveillance: Inventing and using wearable computing devices for data collection in surveillance environments. *Surveillance & Society, 1*(3), 331–355.

Martin Reiser. (2012). Wikipedia. *Retrieved from* http://en.wikipedia.org/wiki/Martin_Rieser

3rd Woman. (2012). Website. *Retrieved from* http://thirdwoman.com/index.html

Reiser, M. (2012). Website. *Retrieved from* http://www.martinrieser.com

Ship of Fools. (2012). Website. *Retrieved from* http://www.shipoffools.pwp.blueyonder.co.uk/artists/martin_home.htm

Songlines. (2012). Website. *Retrieved from* http://www.hollandalexander.com/?attachment_id=615

Southern, J., & Hamilton, J. (2003, October). Unfeasible symmetry. *Artists Newsletter Magazine.* Retrieved from http://www.theportable.tv/dmg/index.html

Starshed. (2012). Website. *Retrieved from* http://www.electricpavilion.com/starshed.html

Sterling, B. (2007). *Ascendancies: The best of Bruce Sterling.* Burton, MI: Subterranean Press.

Tikka, P. (2008). *Enactive cinema—Simulatorium eisensteinense.* Helsinki, Finland: University of Art and Design Helsinki.

Tuters, M., & Varnelis, K. (2006). Beyond locative media. *Leonardo, 39*(4), 357–363. doi:10.1162/leon.2006.39.4.357

Tversky, B., Kim, J., & Cohen, A. (1999). *Mental models of spatial relations and transformations from language.* Palo Alto, CA: Stanford University/Indiana University. doi:10.1016/S0166-4115(99)80055-7

Virilio, P. (1989). *War and cinema: The logistics of perception* (Miller, P., Trans.). London, UK: Verso.

ENDNOTES

[1] Locative Media Workshop: The international workshop entitled "Locative media" focusing on GPS, mapping, and positioning technologies took place from July 16 – 26, 2003, at the K@2 Culture and Information Centre on an abandoned military installation in Liepaja on the coast of the Baltic Sea http://locative.x-i.net/(July2005).

[2] UrbanTapestries <http://urbantapestries.net/>Proboscis: Urban Tapestries (2002-2004). The Urban Tapestries software platform allows people to author their own virtual annotations of the city, enabling a community's collective memory to grow organically, allowing ordinary citizens to embed social knowledge in the new wireless landscape of the city.

[3] See http://www.drewhemment.com/2004/locative_arts.html.

[4] Quoted in Beyond Locative Media by Marc Tuters and Kazys Varnelis. See also The Geospatial Web: A Call to Action- What We Still Need to Build for an Insanely Cool Open Geospatial Web by Mike Liebhold, Senior Researcher, The Institute for the Future http://lists.burri.to/pipermail/geowanking/2005-May/001536.html>accessed>12/03/08.

5   A series of locative artwork experiments by Hewlett Packard, Watershed Media Centre, and Bristol University 2004-2005.

6   See http://www.martinrieser.com/Hosts.htm.

7   See http://www.digicult.it/en/2011/TheMobileAudience.asp.

8   See http://www.shipoffools.pwp.blueyonder.co.uk.

9   See http://www.terirueb.net/drift/index.html.

10   See http://www.blasttheory.co.uk/bt/work_uncleroy.html.

11   See http://www.valentinanisi.com/liberties.html.

12   See http://yellowarrow.net/index2.php.

13   See http://www.neighbornode.net/.

14   See http://www.electricpavilion.org/content/roots/starshed/index.html.

15   See http://www.pervasive.org.uk/projects/songlines.

16   See www.thirdwoman.com.

17   Tikka, Pia; Enactive Cinema—Simulatorium Eisensteinense. University of Art and Design Helsinki, 2008.

18   See http://34n118w.net/.

19   See sal.cs.bris.ac.uk/Publications/Papers/2000261.pdf.

20   3 Augé, Marc, Non-Places: Introduction to an anthropology of supermodernity, Verso, 1995.

21   See http://empedia.info/maps/20?resource=resource%2F557.

22   See http://www.gpsdrawing.com and http://socialfiction.org.

23   "The Dérive (with its flow of acts, its gestures, its strolls, its encounters) was to the totality exactly what psychoanalysis (in the best sense) is to language. Let yourself go with the flow of words, says the psychoanalyst. He listens until the moment when he rejects or modifies (one could say detourns) a word, an expression, or a definition. The dérive is certainly a technique, almost a therapeutic one. However, just as analysis unaccompanied with anything else is almost always contraindicated, so continual dériving is dangerous to the extent that the individual, having gone too far (not without bases, but...) without defenses, is threatened with explosion, dissolution, dissociation, disintegration. In addition, thence the relapse into what is termed 'ordinary life,' that is to say, in reality, into 'petrified life.' In this regard, I now repudiate my Formulary's propaganda for a continuous dérive. It could be continuous like the poker game in Las Vegas, but only for a certain period, limited to a weekend for some people, to a week as a good average; a month is really pushing it. In 1953-1954, we dérived for three or four months straight. That's the extreme limit. It's a miracle it didn't kill us" (Ivan Chtcheglov, excerpt from a 1963 letter to Michèle Bernstein and Guy Debord, reprinted in Internationale Situationniste #9, p. 38).

24   Saul Albert www.twenteenthcentury.com (message dated Tue Apr 27 2004).

25   Paula Levine, Shadows from Another Place (2003). Levine builds upon this link, creating Hybrid space between Baghdad and San Francisco composed of the transposition of Baghdad and San Francisco. A mapping of the first US attack on Baghdad is superimposed upon San Francisco. The longitude and latitude of each bombsite is marked in San Francisco using a GPS device.

26   C5: The Other Path (April 2004) http://www.c5corp.com/projects/otherpath/index.shtml. In April of 2004, C5 set out on a month long Great Wall trek, starting in the northwest desert of China and following the Wall eastward to where it runs to the edge of the Yellow Sea. GPS data collected during this trek is being used to develop a pattern matching search procedure for locating the most similar data model in the most similar terrain in California.

27   Beyond Locative Media by Marc Tuters and Kazys Varnelis.

28   *G. Deleuze and F. Guattari, On the Line, New York: Semiotext(e), (1983) pp. 25-26.*

29   See http://milkproject.net.

30   Coco Fusco, Questioning the Frame: Thoughts about maps and spatial logic in the global present http://www.inthesetimes.com/article/1750/.

31   Steve Mann, Jason Nolan, and Barry Wellman, Sousveillance: Inventing and Using Wearable Computing Devices for Data Collection in Surveillance Environments in Surveillance & Society 1(3): 331-355 http://www.surveillance-and-society.org.

32   Crandall, Jacob. 'Operational Media' CTheory Articles: a148 Date Published: 1/6/2005 http://www.ctheory.net/articles.aspx?id=441.

33   See manovich.net/DOCS/Augmented_2005.doc.

34   See http://leoalmanac.org/gallery/locative/loca/index.htm.

35   See http://www.coin-operated.com/projects/wifihog.html.

36   Ibid CTheory.

37   Curator Daphne Dragona and participating organizer Dimitris Charitos (University of Athens), technical support from Phil Sparks (Cuttlefish Multimedia) and Jackie Calderwood (PhD Candidate De Montfort University), additional technical support Ha-

ris Rizopoulos, Aris Tsakoumis (University of Athens) see: empedia.info/maps/41 and http://globalgatewayproject.eu/codes-of-disobedience-disfunctionality/.

38   The Stanford prison experiment was a study of the psychological effects of becoming a prisoner or prison guard. The experiment was conducted from Aug. 14-20, 1971 by a team of researchers led by Psychology professor Philip Zimbardo at Stanford University. Twenty-four students were selected out of 75 to play the prisoners and live in a mock prison in the basement of the Stanford psychology building. Roles were assigned randomly. The participants adapted to their roles well beyond what even Zimbardo himself expected, leading the "Officers" to display authoritarian measures and ultimately to subject some of the prisoners to torture (Wikipedia).

39   See www.empedia.info.

40   Ascendancies: The Best of Bruce Sterling by Bruce Sterling (Author), Jonathan Strahan (Editor) and also http://www.wordspy.com/words/spime.asp.

41   See http://vagueterrain.net/journal06/marc-tuters/01.

42   Inside Out was jointly curated with Claire Smith in Melbourne 2010-2011 and involved universities and artist groups in both Australia and UK.

Chapter 4

Site–Specific Performance, Narrative, and Social Presence in Multi–User Virtual Environments and the Urban Landscape

Paul Sermon
University of Salford, UK

Charlotte Gould
University of Salford, UK

ABSTRACT

This chapter brings together the practice-based creative research of artists Charlotte Gould and Paul Sermon, culminating in collaborative interactive installations for urban screens that investigate new forms of social and/or political narratives in site-specific urban environments. The authors' current creative practice looks specifically at the concepts of social presence and performance and attempts to bridge two remote locations either virtually (using online virtual environments such as Second Life) or in the physical space through mixed reality techniques and interfaces that allow the public to direct the narrative and creative outcomes of the artwork.

INTRODUCTION

Through practical accounts of four recent projects by the authors, "Urban Intersections," "Liberate Your Avatar," "Picnic on the Screen," and "Zombie Nation," presented by "Hub"; an innovation space and pop up gallery, which aimed to support the regeneration of the City of Salford funded by the University of Salford, Arts Council England, and social enterprise fund Unltd.

The authors will explore the impact of interactive works for urban screens on our communities and our environment and evaluate how these works can contribute to a sense of citizenship,

DOI: 10.4018/978-1-4666-2961-5.ch004

in our globally networked, multi-ethnic cities. In our urban environment, we are surrounded by strangers, observed via surveillance cameras, and linked through the digital infrastructure to cities across the world. We project multiple identities in real and virtual space. Can interactive works promote civic responsibility, collectivism, creativity, and responsiveness, as well as new ways of engaging with each other and public space, or do these urban screens merely contribute to the Orwellian dystopia of societal control?

In 1974, Richard Sennett argues in the *The Fall of Public Man* that the city of the late Twentieth Century promoted individualism and blurred our view of our economic and social conditions (Sennett, 2002). Paul Virilo described television as one of the biggest promoter of individualism and suburbanism (Virilio, 1997). The first large-scale urban screens in New York functioned purely as advertising space and there has been much discussion of our media withdrawing us from our communities and promoting insular behaviour. With the development of social networking has this all changed? Does the new generation of public urban screens and digital networks offer a new egalitarianism for the twenty first century? Scott McQuire (2009) argues that digital media networks have decentralised traditional media hierarchies in that the majority now have access to instant media production, our mobile phones give us access to mobile Internet, photographs and filmmaking so that the public can film key events on their phone and upload content for professional broadcast, competing with Reuters. In this way, as Scott McQuire describes, we are experiencing a new relationship to time, space and identity and he states that "dimensions, boundaries, scales and borders have become increasingly contested" (McQuire, 2009, p. 48).

The first part of this chapter will look at how new communities are being developed and through social networking people are communicating across the globe, real time, and at regular intervals. Asking if the new digital networks and

public screens offer a heightened collectivism, is this empowering, or is it merely creating a greater sense of alienation? What does this mean in an environment and culture where the virtual and real merge and how do we construct a sense of community, place, and identity in this state of 'co-presence' as described by McQuire? Does this merging of physical and virtual lead to a greater state of connectedness?

In the second part of this chapter, we will reflect on the discourse on ludic interfaces and the discussion on urban play introduced by Gunalan Nadarajan at ISEA 2008 as a panel in the conference proceedings. Here the discussion was centred on the importance of play to engage and give multi-ethnic communities a sense of commonality. Richard Sennett talks of the importance of ritual and play in the formation of public culture and argues that sociability is nether predefined or natural. How then can we offer a framework to promote this (Sennett, 2002)? The authors will look at how interactive artworks offer the public a framework to contribute to cultural content through the creation of the participant's own individual narrative.

Urban screens have been installed across the world and in eighteen cities in the UK, funded by the BBC and Local Authorities; aiming to address local communities so that the screens reflect something of their respective location and community. These systems are governed by civic control and regulations so in this context how far can the public shape their content? The majority of the programming on the BBC Big Screens is news and sports related and some of these screens have now been taken over by private corporations with much of the content focusing on advertising.

Andreas Broeckmann argues that any medium can be used as a tool for propaganda and stresses the importance of using the Urban screens in a democratic way, offering access to content development by the public and not merely using the screens as advertising space (Broeckmann, 2009).

The issue of public access to the creative use of the public space both digital and physical is political, who controls these large public screens? Who has access and is the process of co-production of culture empowering? Diversification of content through input by a range of users can as Audrey Yue describes, 'add value to public spaces' (Yue, 2009, p. 264) and interactive works offer an opportunity for this, as Richard Sennett argues, it is important to offer a framework to promote sociability as it is not a pre-given (Sennett, 2002). Without public engagement in the content the screens potentially could become just another form of passive consumption.

IDENTITY, COMMUNITY, AND POLITICAL ENGAGEMENT

With the development of social networking, any discussion about community must also include virtual online spaces. The ontological questions associated with identity in virtual reality, be it online or offline, have been at the centre of the contemporary media arts and science debate for the past three decades, and this discourse continues to dominate the annual conference themes of Ars Electronica Linz, the Transmediale Berlin and SIGGRAPH USA. The recent rapid increase in users of multi-user virtual environments has now brought them under this microscope, noticeably by inclusion at Ars Electronic 2007 in 'Second City,' a festival strand that paralleled first and Second Life in mixed-reality artworks, scientific experiments, and theoretical debate. This creative practice and debate is firmly rooted in the discourse of semiotics, reflecting a poststructuralist debate from the linguistic origins of F. de Saussure's notion of reality as a construct of language to Jacques Lacan's construction of Freudian identity through the mirror image of the self and Jean Baudrillard's 'Simulacra' of reality itself.

So as to explore this emerging relationship between the virtual and physical, Paul Sermon and Charlotte Gould have developed a number of inter-active installations using "Second Life" that focus on the interaction and exchange between online and offline identities through social practices, such as performance, narrative, embodiment, activism, place, and identity construction. Their collaborative experiments seek to question whether Second Life is a platform for potential social and cultural change—appropriated as a mirror image of first life. By consciously deciding to refer to this image that is mirrored as 'first' life rather than 'real' life, the authors' central question poses a paradox in Second Life when we consider Jacques Lacan's proposition that the 'self' (or ego) is a formulation of our own body image reflected in the 'mirror stage' (Lacan, 1949). However, there is no 'mirror stage' in Second Life. This would suggest that the computer screen itself is the very mirror we are looking for, one that allows the user to formulate her/his 'second self.' Although an 'alter ego,' this is nonetheless a self that can have an engaged social identity.

In Second Life, the user can create an avatar that lives out an online existence. There are no set objectives, one can buy property, clothing, accessories, furnish one's home, modify one's identity, and interact with other users. This online community has grown to seventeen million residents since launching in 2003, generating a thriving economy. However, based our own observations through developing works in Second Life, while the virtual shopping malls, nightclubs, bars and beaches often reach their user capacity, there are noticeably fewer creative and sociological modes of attraction. Consequently, there is an increasing need to identify new forms of interaction, creativity, cultural production, and sociability.

However, when the 'Front National,' the far right French political party of Jean-Marie Le Pen opened their Second Life headquarters in January 2007, the Second Life residents reacted in a way that would suggest they are far from complacent avatars wandering around a virtual landscape, and that they possess a far greater degree of social conscience than the consumerist aesthetics of Second Life suggest. Through prolonged mass virtual protest, the centre was razed to the ground in the space of a week and has not returned since. The reaction to the Le Pen Second Life office suggests that Second Life is indeed a platform for potential social and cultural change. In addition, there is a hidden desire and ambition to interact and engage with this online community at an intellectual and creative level that transcends the collective 'I shop therefore I am'[1] apparentness of its community. Moreover, Second Life could then influence our first lives. As the landmass and population of Second Life expands at an ever-increasing rate it is clear that the essential research by Tom Boellstorff into the intersection and interplay between first and Second Life, and both new and old patterns of consumption, cultural production and sociability (Boellstorff, 2008) is urgently needed.

Urban Intersections

"Urban Intersections" focused on contested virtual spaces that mirror the social and political history of Belfast as a divided city, and was presented at ISEA09 (International Symposium of Electronic Arts 2009). This collaborative project specifically reflected on the ironies of contested spaces, and stereotypes in multi-user virtual environments, exposing an absurd online world that consists of perimeter fences, public surveillance, and national identity. These futile efforts to divide and deny movement and social interaction were an uncanny reflection of the first life urban and social landscape of Belfast. So whilst it is possible to defy and transcend these restrictions in Second Life where we can fly, teleport and communicate without political constraint and national identity, we can question the need for such social and political boundaries enforced in first life and consider the opportunity to initiate social change in first life through our Second Life experience (see Figure 1).

The installation was located on the regenerated landscape of the Waterfront Plaza Belfast, directly outside the newly developed concert hall

Figure 1. Urban intersections Sermon and Gould at ISEA09, Belfast (© 2009 Paul Sermon & Charlotte Gould. Used with permission)

building. This utilitarian environment was used as a stage set to represent an augmented garden that explored the concept of boundaries and territories, a virtual plaza encapsulated by the ironies, contradictions, and obscurities of a divided city, and a metaphor of Belfast's social history. As the participants walked through this urban landscape, both first and second life inhabitants came 'face-to-face' on screen, in the form of a live digital mural projected on the façade of the Waterfront building. This mural formed the central focus of the installation and immediately spoke of the infamous painted murals on houses across West Belfast. Those depict a deep political divide, but post-conflict society now refers to them as a stark reminder of recent troubles, and thereby maintaining the peace that now prevails. In a city such as Belfast, it would be impossible to evade such references when projecting images onto a building, as though the project itself were projected onto the gable end wall of a house on the Falls Road or the Shankhill Estate (see Figure 2).

The local audience formed an integral part of this installation that relied on user interaction and aimed to transcend boundaries through user-generated storytelling and memory building in a post-conflict society. The complete installation utilised three interface techniques. Charlotte

Figure 2. Motion tracking movement of avatar, Charlotte Gould ISEA09, Belfast (© 2009 Paul Sermon & Charlotte Gould. Used with permission)

Gould's motion tracking interface allowed visitors in Belfast to wear a large puppet-like copy of her unique avatar head. Covered in an array of LED lights that were tracked, participants could then control the movements of the Second Life avatar as a means of alternative navigation through a maze of chain-link garden fences. Paul Sermon's interface combined first life visitors and Second Life avatars within the same live video stream. By constructing a blue chroma-key studio in Second Life, it was possible to mix live video images of online avatars with the audience in Belfast, enabling these participants to play and converse on a collaborative video stream simultaneously displayed in both first and second life situations. The third interface was developed by sound and media artist Peter Appleton, whose contribution included a barbecue on the Waterfront plaza that simultaneously controlled the conditions of an identical Second Life barbecue. Through a series of light and heat sensors, it was possible to relay commands to the online situation, so that when the first life barbecue was lit so too was the Second Life barbecue and as food started to cook and brown so did its online duplicate. All these

interfaces referred to the domestic garden and the infamous Belfast perimeter fences and aimed to break down these boundaries through social interaction that prevailed, be it through a video portal, a didactic maze or over a grilled sausage (see Figure 3).

The conference participants made up a large part of the audience, though there were also local Belfast residents who took part and the barbeque was a successful way to draw them into the installation. The connection of the simultaneous lighting of the barbeque in first Life and Second Life effectively connected the audience to the virtual environment on screen. One of the visitors remarked that the use of props such as the head, effectively connected the user to the Second Life space on screen, and did so literally as the first life body became the interface to the second life avatar and this supports Patrick Allen's assertion that focus on the body in virtual space helps us to locate ourselves in that space (Allen, 2008).

It was interesting that one of the Belfast visitors said that the culture of the curfew was still prevalent and this area was notoriously quiet at night except for some groups of youths who participated with unbridled enthusiasm. Their

Figure 3. Barbecue in first life controlling Second Life barbecue, Peter Appleton ISEA09, Belfast (© 2009 Paul Sermon & Charlotte Gould. Used with permission)

arrival on the scene prompted a quick response from security, who were able to manage the kids with a light hearted banter and at the same time reaffirming their authority over the situation and moving them on fairly quickly. This also brings about questions around the audience, whether there is an undesirable and desirable audience, and who decides on this? In this case study, it was the security guards at the Waterfront Building who were employed to protect the facilities as well as the other members of the audience, who managed the situation and moved the gang on amicably. However, there have been examples of social disobedience which have developed around urban screens, such as the recent riots in Vancouver (15th June 2011) after the local ice hockey team (the Vancouver Canucks) lost to Boston in the Stanley Cup finals and this has instigated much discussion by Canadian local government about urban design and the social need for urban gathering spaces and on how social order can be maintained. Alcohol and boredom have been blamed for the riot and it has been reported that social networking provoked and ignited it. This demonstrates the way that the digital infrastructure connects us to time and space and our communities and how social networking can be used as a promoter of action, which can of course be used to a positive or negative end. The nature of the event will attract different audiences, whether it is a sporting, music or cultural event and this can indicate the demographic as well as the size and nature of the audience (the authors will address this below though other case studies).

Urban Screens have also been used in the past towards the social good as a platform to promote social harmony, and in 2008, the Federal Government of Australia used the big screen in Sydney to stage a public apology to the Stolen Generations. Mirjam Struppek, an instigator of the Urban Screens 07 conference in Manchester, has highlighted the importance of consultation with the local community and has identified a number of proposed screens, which met with antagonism, due to the public's resistance around the idea of public engagement projects as a precursor to re-

generation. "Placemaking" through a process of gentrification can have negative repercussions on existing communities, moving them into the outskirts and away from the upwardly socially mobile areas. Struppek talks of the uncomfortable role that art can play in this process (Struppek, 2006).

"Urban Intersections" was commissioned by ISEA and the University of Ulster with support from the Waterfront Hall Belfast. This is a large bi-annual international festival, which attracts a regular international audience of academics and media artists so this had a considerable impact on the nature of participants. There had been little advertising to attract a local audience outside the University, so most of the local participants were coincidental passersby. The random nature of this results in participants who are representative of a broad cross-section of society, a large portion of whom on interview stated that they would not usually visit a traditional art gallery but were enthusiastic to get involved and many remarked on how much they enjoyed the experience. The use of the large urban screen and the virtual environment signifies the idea of a game and passersby often enquire as to which game engine we are using. People also identify gaming as a socially acceptable form of adult play and so in varying degrees are interested in getting involved or watching others interact with the piece. In this way, it opens up the lines of communication, the audience are engaging both with their environment and with total strangers who they may not have otherwise met.

The design of public meeting places is an important consideration for urban planners when developing new urban areas as well as consideration of spaces where cultural events can take place. Urban spaces left vacant or disused can lead to crime, which can lead to public fear and further avoidance. It is as much a consideration for modern urban designers to consider the use of lighting to counter crime, as the development of cultural spaces, breathing life into a place and developing a sense of community. At the project planning stage of "Urban Intersections," it was evident that the Waterfront Building staff, as well as neighbouring hoteliers, were very keen to support the project. They are used to seeing visitors to the music events held in the concert hall but not in the square outside. The programming of outdoors events will bring new audiences into that space, drawing in life and activity and thereby adding value as described by Audrey Yue (2009). Works such as "Urban Intersections" as well as bringing an international audience encouraged them to reflect on social and political issues and on the history of Belfast. They were invited into a virtual garden superimposed on the space with all of the contradictions that the garden offers as a place to share a barbeque with neighbours and friends but also with fences and gates and the potential restrictions and disputes that can arise. The murals from both political sides remain in Belfast as a historical reminder of the past troubles and a keeper of the peace. "Urban Intersections" represented a life size interactive mural on the building, into which the audience could enter, in the form of an avatar, and this aimed to encourage further reflection reinforcing a pride in the progress made and offering a framework which Richard Sennett argues is essential for social engagement as this does not come naturally (Sennett, 2002).

Liberate Your Avatar

Another case study, which sought to make a political connection to the history of a specific location through the virtual world of "Second Life," was Paul Sermon's "Liberate Your Avatar." This was an interactive public video art installation incorporating Second Life users in a real life environment, located on All Saints Gardens, Oxford Road, Manchester, for the Urban Screens Festival 2007. This is where Emmeline Pankhurst, a century before, had chained herself to the railings in a suffragette protest, and in this installation her avatar was again chained to the railings. The merged realities of 'All Saints Gardens' on Oxford Road, and its online three-dimensional counterpart in 'Second Life' allowed 'first life' visitors and 'second life' avatars to coexist and share the same park bench in a live interactive public video installation. Entering into this feedback loop through a portal between these two parallel worlds this event exposes the identity paradox in Second Life.

The participants comprised of a broad spectrum of visitors from conference attendees to the local homeless, and one man on interview remarked with enthusiasm that it was like having a big television in his front room. Another visitor was delighted to undertake an arranged meeting on screen with the avatar of a friend in Australia! This demonstrates the way that social networking and online virtual environments can be used to draw people together from across the world, sharing spaces and opening the channels of communication and in this way making us more connected. The site specific nature of the installations reaffirm that sense of place and both of these case studies use the local history as a framework from which the audience is asked to develop a narrative and in this way the participants develop a stronger sense of "placeness" as described by Saskia Sassen (2009) (see Figure 4).

Figure 4. Liberate your avatar, Paul Sermon urban screens 07, Manchester (© 2007 Paul Sermon & Charlotte Gould. Used with permission)

LUDIC NARRATIVES

Picnic on the Screen

Another site specific work developed by the authors was "Picnic on the Screen" an interactive ludic narrative, which was first developed for the 'Village Screen,' a public urban screen at the Glastonbury Performing Arts Festival in 2009, an annual three day open air music festival in south west England. This work explores the creative potential of the Glastonbury audience as performers that have the capacity to create improvised narrative sequence through the 'Village Screen' as a communications portal. This work was designed for large format public video screens and was commissioned as an interactive work to explore the screens creative and cultural potential. It offered an opportunity to be involved in the development of innovative ways of engaging with the pubic in a festival context using digital technology. Through the augmentation of the virtual and the real, users could explore alternative telepresent spaces and develop unique playful narrative events. 'Picnic on the Screen' explores social play and the way that we derive pleasure from interaction with new technologies and digital media, through its design, creative development, application, and resulting dialogue.

The installation consisted of two blue picnic blankets in front of the BBC Big Screen. The audience groups sitting on these blankets were captured on camera and brought together through a system of live chroma-keying, and placed on a computer illustrated background, and behind computer animated elements that were triggered and controlled by the audience through a unique motion-tracking interface that was integrated in the installation. The two blankets were placed as far apart as possible not to disclose the location of the two groups and encourage the audience to explore the telepresent communication. When the audience member discovers their image on screen, they immediately enter the telepresent

space, watching a live image of themselves sitting on picnic rug next to another person. They soon start to explore the space and understand they are now in complete physical control of a telepresent body that can interact with another person in an illustrated enchanted ludic scene, complete with animated characters that respond to the their movement and actions.

People of all ages enjoyed using the piece, and often learned from each other how to make the most of the installations. There was an assumption from the programmers, initially, that children would be particularly drawn to the work but people of all ages enjoyed taking part. When each programmed event started it took a few minutes for people to build up the confidence, or perhaps feel reassured that it was acceptable to enter the telepresent space. This is possibly because adults are rarely encouraged to play and seek validation from other adults to reassure them.

It was interesting to see how the personality of the audience changed with the environmental factors and the audience at Glastonbury is likely to be fairly unique, a wide age range but predominantly those in their 20s to 30s with a keen interest in music, performing arts. The bands or other events happening on the screen (for example a live international Rugby Union match shown on the BBC Big Screen during the festival) influenced the people and the mood of those who were congregating and this had to be taken into consideration when programming the piece.

The location of the screen was central and could be seen from three of the main artery roads including that to the main Pyramid music stage, so the works were able to draw a wide audience. The feedback from the audience was extremely positive one visitor said they never expected to find something like this at Glastonbury; they expected to watch the bands but did not expect to see themselves on the big screen. Another commented on how different things are revealed to the participants as they sat on the rug, and described different layers of discovery, 'you find that you are next to someone that you are not physically next to who you can interact with and then there are the animated elements which you can play with' (see Figure 5).

This work locates itself in the telematics discourse and has continually drawn on the concepts of user-generated content and communication. The audiences form an integral part within these telematic experiments, which simply would not function without their presence and participation.

Initially the viewers seem to enter a passive space, but they are instantly thrown into the performer role by discovering their own body-double in communication with another physically remote user on video monitors in front of them. They usually adapt to the situation quickly and start controlling and choreographing their human avatar. Nevertheless, because the installation is set up in the form of an open accessible platform, it offers a second choice of engagement: the passive mode of just observing the public action, which often appears to be a well-rehearsed piece of drama confidently played out by actors. Compelling to watch, it can be a complex issue to discover that the performers are also part of the audience and are merely engaging in a role.

The entire installation space then represents two dynamic dramatic functions: the players, controllers, or puppeteers of their own avatar, absorbed by the performing role; and the off-camera members of the audience, who are themselves awaiting the next available slot on the telematic stage, soon to be sharing this split dynamic. However, the episodes that unfold are not only determined by the participants, but by the given dramatic context. As artistic creators, Paul Sermon and Charlotte Gould are then designers of the environment and, consequently, 'directors' of the narrative, which is determined through the social and political milieu that they choose to play out in the telepresent encounter. Different versions of Picnic on the Screen have since been developed between Bluecoat Liverpool and Shanghai University for the Liverpool Biennale in 2010 and between the

Figure 5. "Picnic on the Screen," Paul Sermon and Charlotte Gould BBC big screen, Glastonbury 2009 (© 2009 Paul Sermon & Charlotte Gould. Used with permission)

Lowry Salford and Ningbo University, China in 2011, with specific reference to the place they are installed. Each time the audience has responded in a different way, depending on culture and demographic and it is this exchange between the artists, the audience and the location, which is key to the development of the narrative.

Zombie Nation

Another site-specific piece developed by Lets Go Global and supported by Hub was "Zombie Nation," a pervasive game that took place in Eccles Shopping Centre in Salford. The Hub project concerns the City of Salford City through cultural and economic intervention, bringing about a closer relationship between the arts and the local community, by using creative arts practice as vehicle for potential social and economic relief during a period of downturn and recession. The proposal was to generate a series of arts projects each with a digital theme to be supported by 'Hub' a gallery and innovation space utilising a disused retail space within the heart of Salford, left empty as a result of the current recession. By attracting an audience to an otherwise empty row of retail units, this project aimed to support the regeneration of the City and further create links between its local community and the creative industries that surround it. It aimed to facilitate the incubation and showcase for ideas and creative outputs through a series of curated shows and events by the partners involved. Each of the projects aimed to be collaborative involving the community and the creative industries. Partners included Central Salford Urban Regeneration Company, BBC21CC, Lets go Global, and Soup Collective to further secure cultural and industry links within the community.

The interdisciplinary nature of this project aimed at enabling knowledge transfer between its partners from the cultural industry as well as the local community. Hub facilitated the dissemination of creative outputs directly into the community, drawing an audience from further afield into the heart of Salford and in this way attempted to drive cultural activities as a mechanism of social and economic intervention.

The collaborative objective of Hub covered a range of outcomes relevant to the different projects showcased, focusing upon creative outputs. Although all the projects presented at Hub used new media technologies in some way, they were interdisciplinary in nature, with each show having fundamental consequences for a broad range of artistic and technological disciplines involved, whilst aiming to push boundaries within their field.

Our collaborative approach covered a range of methodologies relevant to the different disciplines and projects to be showcased but focused on creative practice-based methods. The Hub projects were interdisciplinary and collaborative, and the activities involved within each of the shows have had fundamental consequences for the broad range of scientific and artistic disciplines involved in the programme. Through this project, we aimed to explore the potential for regeneration through cultural and social intervention, to be measured through audience response, interviews, and evaluations. Mary Oliver and Lois Klassen a Canadian artist undertook research directly on this subject,

looking at the idea of the Arts Centre as a means of "gentrification" of an Urban area. They developed an installation and held a series of events entitled, 'Conversations' which the local community artists, university academics, planners and partners from the Salford City Council and Regeneration company were invited. Through a series of performances and recorded conversations, they explored the idea of regeneration through arts intervention. The public were interested to see a gallery space in this area and many were surprised by the images placed in the windows, which looked similar at first glance to an estate agents window. When the viewer looked closer, they were set 'off kilter' as the images were of partially demolished buildings in the area. Through public intervention, this project aimed to bring new ideas and creativity into the community that acted as an incubator for future creative industries.

For the purposes of this chapter, the authors will focus on one project 'Zombie Nation,' a pervasive game devised by Lets Go Global, a community online TV production company who work with community groups to deliver digital media projects. The event took place in Eccles Shopping Centre as part of the Eccles Festival (a local community festival complete with farmer's market). This is an area which was once made wealthy by the textile industry, badly hit initially from the decline of the industry, then from the opening just outside of the town, of two huge retail centres, also from a large supermarket moving into the town and then further from the recession, with many shops in the shopping centre left empty. Eccles is only a few miles away from MediaCityUK, a new large scale Salford Quays business and residential development becoming home to the BBC, ITV and the University of Salford, which lies in stark contrast to its neighbour. The Eccles shopping centre was built in the seventies and viewed by many at the time as progressive but like so many other public buildings in the UK built in that decade, it has not lived up to the ravages of time and many of the shopping units remain empty.

Zombie Nation was developed as a site-specific piece to explore new ways of engaging with the urban public environment and raise morale. It combined creative technology, gaming and performance and involved local youth groups who through playing the game experienced digital media training, with 'mash up' edits of the film captured on their hand held digital video cameras as part of the game as they moved through the shopping centre to solve the clues. Karen Shannon of Lets Go Global said that it is important to provide a framework through which people can engage. Projects such as this 'transform ordinary spaces into extraordinary spaces' and people who would not usually meet, are able to interact. Let's go Global used a number of the empty retail units as well as the farmers market, some of the shops and the central square for performance, clue finding and editing of the film captured by the gamers during play. Passersby joined in and were able to be made up by a team of makeup artists. Some came along dressed as zombies on the day to engage with the game and the space, such as the zombie knitter who took over one of the empty shop units encouraging others to join her in knitting (see Figure 6).

Zombie nation, supported by Hub successfully acted as a partnership between the local community and the creative industries to draw unlikely audiences to Salford as a regeneration project. This project used the urban screen in the form of handheld devices and live replay of the event, to create networks, bringing people together who would not otherwise meet. The interdisciplinary nature of this project enabled knowledge transfer between the partners and industry as well as the local community offering digital media training to the youth groups and members of the public who participated. In this way the young local community directly benefited from projects like this and potentially raised their own expectations of their life changes and as one of the participants stated, could potentially work at MediaCityUK as a result one day, ensuring that

Figure 6. Zombie nation, let's go global Eccles festival, Eccles Salford (© 2010 Paul Sermon & Charlotte Gould. Used with permission)

the local community can benefit from the regeneration brought about by the move of the BBC to the North of England and not just a migrating professional workforce. Through their work with youth groups, Lets Go Global aim to offer young people a taste of potential opportunities. Hub developed projects across the city of Salford to encompass the broad range of social strata from the fast developing and slick MediaCityUK to Eccles, a faded symbol of past-misconstrued hopes making up two highly contrasting parts of greater Manchester reflecting the complexities of the contemporary city.

CONCLUSION

Saskia Sassen's keynote at the Urban screens Conference in Sydney in 2008, when talking of the global city, introduced the notion of the "global slum" and she argues that "the slum enables the possibility of complexity" as we experience homogeneousness of space there arise new possibilities of "Placeness" (Sassen, 2009). It is then these complexities that can add to our notion of uniqueness of place. The site specific nature of interactive works such as "Zombie Nation," "Urban Intersections," and "Picnic on the

Screen," and the way that they talk about their environment encourage the audience to reflect on the space though history, politics or playfulness, enriching our understanding of our environment and its unique qualities and the multiple roles that we play within our communities as well as ways of healing old wounds or raising esteem. The location of these projects in a variety of urban environments from wealthy areas to pockets of poverty, from old established spaces to the newly defined ones, mean that the audiences are representative of all walks of life offering a richness to the responses and stories that unravel. Resulting in a diversity of participants, with interactions occurring between people who would not usually make social contact and bringing audiences to an environment to which they would not usually travel. The audiences have not always been deemed 'desirable' by the organisers but the projects remain inclusive because of their location in public urban spaces offering new possibilities for "placeness" as well as making us mindful of our presence and of what it is to be present in our new digital infrastructure. We are able to explore multiple possibilities for identity and reflect on our past relationship to space and community as well as consider new possibilities and new ways of engaging with each other and our urban space in the future.

When Sheenah Delayney, author of *A Taste of Honey,* set in Salford in the 1960s and iconic film, was interviewed for the BBC documentary "Monitor" in 1960 she was critical of the demolition of the red brick terraced housing in Salford, arguing that communities were being dispersed and moved far away "to sterile places" and that the local council "never think of putting anything like a theater there." This underlines the important role that culture plays in creating communities. Hub has now moved from its permanent residence in Salford as the area became very suddenly upwardly mobile and the property owners had plans for development just as our lease ran out. Just over the bridge in Manchester, "Spinning Fields"

emerged complete with aspirational brand's flagship stores. Hub had contributed to a wave of cultural activities in Salford, and contributing to its 'cool' factor. This in turn made the area more desirable and so the property developers moved in and the artists moved out. There is, however, potential for more egalitarian uses of urban screens, as this is not about permanency or ownership but about programming and interactive works offer the public an ongoing framework within which to engage and have a voice.

REFERENCES

Allen, P. (2008). Framing the body in augmented public space. In de Cindio & de Cindio (Eds.), *Augmented Urban Spaces.* Farnham, UK: Ashgate.

Baudrillard, J. (1995). *Simulacra and simulation.* Ann Arbor, MI: University of Michigan Press.

Boellstorff, T. (2008). *Coming of age in Second Life: An anthropologist explores the virtually human.* Princeton, NJ: Princeton University Press.

Broeckmann, A. (2009). Intimate publics: Memory, performance and spectacle in urban environments. In McQuire, S., Martin, M., & Niederer, S. (Eds.), *Urban Screens Reader* (pp. 109–120). Amsterdam, The Netherlands: Institute of Network Cultures.

de Saussure, F. (2011). *Course in general linguistics.* New York, NY: Columbia University Press.

Eco, U. (1986). *Travels In hyperreality.* New York, NY: Pan Books Ltd.

Lacan, J. (2007). *Ecrits: The first complete edition in English.* London, UK: W. W. Norton.

Maguire, S. (2009). Mobility, cosmopolitanism and public space. In McQuire, S., Martin, M., & Niederer, S. (Eds.), *Urban Screens Reader* (pp. 45–64). Amsterdam, The Netherlands: Institute of Network Cultures.

Sassen, S. (2009). Reading the city in a global digital age. In McQuire, S., Martin, M., & Niederer, S. (Eds.), *Urban Screens Reader* (pp. 29–44). Amsterdam, The Netherlands: Institute of Network Cultures. doi:10.1016/j.sbspro.2010.05.057

Sennett, R. (2002). *The fall of public man: On the social psychology of capitalism.* London, UK: Penguin Books.

Stephenson, N. (2000). *Snow crash.* New York, NY: Spectra.

Struppek, M. (2006). Urban screens - The urbane potential of public screens for interaction. *Intelligent Agent, 6*(2).

Virilo, P. (1997). The third interval. In Graham, S. (Ed.), *Cibercities Reader* (pp. 78–81). Oxford, UK: Routledge.

Yue, A. (2009). Urban screens, spatial regeneration and cultural citizenship. In McQuire, S., Martin, M., & Niederer, S. (Eds.), *Urban Screens Reader* (pp. 261–275). Amsterdam, The Netherlands: Institute of Network Cultures.

ENDNOTES

[1] Barbara Kruger, a prominent American artist, coined the phrase "I shop therefore I am" in 1987, as a pun on consumerism and René Descartes' statement "I think therefore I am".

Chapter 5
Living between Worlds:
Imagination, Liminality, and Avatar–Mediated Presence

Denise Doyle
University of Wolverhampton, UK

ABSTRACT

This chapter interrogates the notion of the liminal in relation to the virtual and the imaginary through a consideration of the field of art and technology and current creative practices in virtual worlds and avatar-mediated space. In particular, the art project Meta-Dreamer (2009) is considered through the manifestation of the avatar as digital object. In its attempt to explore the experience of "living between worlds," it reflects the concerns of contemporary arts practice exploration of time and space relationships.

INTRODUCTION

In the field of Art and Technology, the ease in which we experience the liminal through virtual space is even more pronounced when the space is avatar-mediated creating an oscillating state of existence between the virtual and the physical[1]. Yet both consciousness and the imagination depend on this liminality of space. With a focus on the 'threshold,' this continual 'about to become' is almost a necessary condition of being. Some virtual environments (or worlds) deliberately play with this "existential overlay to the physical" (Lichty, 2009, p. 2). Working with a new framework of the emergent imagination consideration is given to the transitional spaces created in artworks in virtual world spaces where aspects of the liminal come to the fore.

The chapter considers to what extent we can examine imaginative or liminal states that are, as Edward Casey notes, "remarkably easy to enter into," yet their "very ephemerality renders

DOI: 10.4018/978-1-4666-2961-5.ch005

[them] resistant to conceptual specification of a precise sort" (Casey, 2000, pp. 6-7). It considers to what extent transitional spaces share similar characteristics to the liminal.

- Does the liminal always find the point of the threshold?
- Does avatar-mediation (re)space the imagination to a place geographically distant from the body?
- Do we experience liminality in a similar way? Or is the liminal more closely bound to the temporal?
- To what extent are both conditioned by the virtual?

The relationship between the transitional and liminal, and the avatar experience, sets out a particular view of the imagination and its elusive, and sometimes liminal, qualities.

A PRELUDE: ON THE VIRTUAL, THE IMAGINARY, AND THE LIMINAL

Casey comments in his book *Imagining: A Phenomenological Study* (Casey, 2000) that, at the time of its first publication in 1976, a "concerted phenomenological study of the imagination had yet to be done" (Casey, 2000, p. xi). Further, there is yet to be a substantial study in which the virtual and the imaginary are considered in relation to each other. There have been some passing associations, such as Massumi's link to the imagination as a "mode of thought" that is most suitable to the virtual (Massumi, 2002, p. 134), or that of Levy, describing the imagination as one of the three vectors of the virtual (Levy, 1998, p. 28). Any dialogue on the virtual and the imaginary might begin by placing them in direct relation to each other (with the two terms on an equal footing). This pairing throws up some initial thoughts on what pulls or pushes them together, what attracts them, and conversely what pulls them apart. When

paired together, as relatives, or at least as an associated grouping, three shared characteristics or impulses are revealed. Firstly, both terms are often associated with an 'elsewhere' or to a place or space not immediately associated with the real. Secondly, each appears to be multi-faceted, whose meaning changes quite dramatically when seen as an act or as a description, when a verb (imagine), a noun (virtuality, imaginary), or equally as an adjective (virtual, imaginary). Finally, each term can be as elusive and fleeting as the other.

When identifying what would differentiate them, one can make the distinction in what may be the very impulse that stirs or moves them. In fact, other than the imagination being more closely aligned with creativity, or a creative impulse, (which does not necessarily incorporate or include notions of virtuality), one may quickly flounder in attempts to keep them separated, rather falling back on the transitional or liminal qualities that they both share. Yet each term cannot necessarily be exchanged as freely as an initial analysis may suggest. Two aspects of what we understand to be the meaning of the liminal are of relevance here; firstly that it denotes "a position at, or on both sides of, a boundary or threshold" (Oxford Dictionary, 2012), and secondly it relates to a transitional or initial stage of a process" (Oxford Dictionary, 2012). Spaces such as *Second Life*, with their combination of immersive qualities, avatar mediation, and user-generated content, are presenting new circumstances and conditions under which to undertake a study of the imagination and in particular to study its own liminal states.

BACKGROUND

Art and the Virtual

Some would agree that there has been a relationship between art and the virtual at least since the Renaissance, with the invention of linear perspective. More recently, in the field of Art and

Technology, the relationship between art and the virtual appears implicit in its scope and engagement (Ettlinger, 2009; Lindstrand, 2007; Grau, 2003). However, Or Ettlinger describes the 'fog of multiple meanings around the term the virtual' (Ettlinger, 2009, p. 6), and he suggests that, in fact, contemporary and digital art has lost its interest in the art of illusion, and is only now marginally concerned with the pictorial. There is a history to the relationship between art and the virtual which spans a number of decades from the early 1990s, from early experiments in virtual environments (Sermon, 1992; Laurel & Strickland, 1993; Gromala & Sharir, 1994; Davies, 1995, 1998) to the networked environments of the early 21st century (Zapp, 2002, 2005) and finally to the networked virtual spaces found in online virtual worlds such as *There.com* and *Second Life*. There is an argument that as soon as linear perspective was invented painting became another kind of virtual space, and in fact, Lindstrand suggests that:

...before the invention of linear perspective, spatial experience was detached from imagery. Once the tools to depict three-dimensional space on a two-dimensional surface were developed, architecture and the understanding of space leaped into a new era. (Lindstrand, 2007, p. 354)

For Lindstrand, the possibility for the viewer to imagine herself walking around inside a painting opened up a whole new chapter in art as well as causing a fundamental shift in the experience of space. Ettlinger would most certainly agree with this perception of space. In developing The Virtual Space Theory, he states that at its heart lies 'the interpretation of virtual space as the overall space which we see through pictorial images, and of 'virtual' as describing any visible object which is located inside of that space' (Ettlinger, 2009, p. 6).

The notion that the concept of space can be seen as Cartesian, definable, and contained, is at odds with the concept of space as lived, as experienced such as the Thirdspace that Edward W. Soja describes, and discussed further below

(Soja, 1996). In *The Production of Space*, Henri Lefebvre (1991) attempts to define the experience of space from both a metaphysical and an ideological perspective. Initially he outlines two terms in relation to space, that of the *illusion of transparency* and the *illusion of opacity* (or the realistic illusion). Of the illusion of transparency, he writes that the emphasis of the written word is to the detriment of, what he terms, social practice. In what he describes as the grasping of the object by the act of writing, he suggests that this is supposed to bring:

[The] non-communicated into the realm of the communicated [...] such are the assumptions of an ideology which, in positing the transparency of space, identifies knowledge, information and communication [...] the illusion of transparency turns out [...] to be a transcendental illusion: a trap, operating on the basis of its own quasi-magical power (Lefebvre, 1991, pp. 28-29).

In turn, the illusion of opacity, of substantiality, being philosophically closer to naturalistic materialism, leads Lefebvre to assert that:

[Language], rather than being defined by its form, enjoys a 'substantial reality.' In the course of any reading, the imaginary and symbolic dimensions, the landscape and the horizon which line the reader's path, are all taken as 'real,' because the true characteristics of the text [...] are a blank page to the naïf in this unconsciousness [original emphasis] (Lefebvre, 1991, p. 29).

However, and most interestingly, Lefebvre continues to say the two illusions are not necessarily in opposition to each other and do not 'seek to destroy each other.' Rather, that:

[Each] illusion embodies and nourishes the other. The shifting back and forth between the two, and the flickering or oscillatory effect that it produces, are thus just as important as either of the illusions considered in isolation (Lefebvre, 1991, p. 29).

This flickering, from opaque to transparent to opaque again, these oscillations suggest a complex system of relationships between a space and the objects found in that space. We become uncertain if space is transparent at all. Yet, Lefebvre (1991, p. 29) writes that it is the texture of space that allows us to create space through social practice as sequences of acts that become a signifying practice in itself. Ettlinger's and Lefebvre's understanding of space, appear at odds with each other. More particularly, does Lefebvre's interpretation of the construction of our experience of space suggest a liminal experience that is inherent in its qualities?

An article by Axel Stockburger, *Playing the Third Place* (2007), extends Lefebvre's ideas to the work of Soja and his definition of what he terms the Thirdspace. As Stockburger notes, beyond the dualism of subject and object Lefebvre suggests that spaces can be understood within the triad of the perceived, the conceived, and the lived. According to Stockburger, Soja 'identifies perceived space (Firstspace) with the real, and conceived space (Secondspace) with the imaginary, leading to lived space (Thirdspace), as a field of both, imagined and real' (Stockburger, 2007, p. 232). Stockburger continues with his interpretation in the context of game space and describes the hybrid mix between real and imagined spaces created through digital game universes as resonating strongly with the concept of Thirdspace. He notes that 'this insight is crucial because it defies the idea of computer games as merely 'virtual' or purely imaginary spaces. It is precisely the interaction between real and imagined spatiality that makes this medium so compelling and unique' (Stockburger, 2007, p. 232). A concept of space that suggests a mixed experience of both real and imagined spatiality proves to be useful when considering online and networked spaces, whether they are games-based or not.

Privileging the Body over the Eye

According to Mark Hansen (2004, 2006), there has been a repositioning of the body in relation to technology within new media arts practice. Hansen's claim, along with others (Ihde, 2002; Biocca, 1997; Hillis, 1999; Pallasmaa, 2005), is that the eye no longer dominates, and it is now the body that mediates our experience 'in the ensuing shift from perception to affectivity' (Hansen, 2004, p. 13). He argues that, because of new media technologies, there has been a move away from the image based in 'perception' to that of embodied experience. The question, or rather the inevitability, that new technologies are changing us has been taken up by Jean-Francois Lyotard as he suggests that "technology wasn't invented by us humans. Rather the other way round [...] any material system is technological if it filters information [...] if it memorizes and processes" (Lyotard, 1991, p. 12). In what he terms the "myth of disembodiment," Steve Dixon (2007), in *Digital Performance*, claims that as bodies embody consciousness, "to talk of disembodied consciousness is a contradiction in terms" (Dixon, 2007, p. 212). In the context of digital arts practice, Bolter and Gromala note that it is digital artists in particular:

[That] insist on the materiality of their work. They will never abandon or disparage the ways of knowing that the senses give us. For them, even the experience of seeing is not disembodied; it is visceral. Seeing is feeling. What fascinates digital artists is the ways in which their embodied existence is redefined in cyberspace. So they use digital technology to examine the interaction between the physical and the virtual (Bolter & Gromala; in Dixon, 2007, p. 216).

There are a number of points here that are relevant to the discourse in this chapter, and most notably that of the examination of the interaction between the physical and the virtual, and the liminal experience that the transitional space between the physical and virtual creates.

New Technologies and Liminal Space

From early writings on virtual reality (Rheingold, 1991; Heim, 1993; Damer, 1998; Heudin, 1999; Schroeder, 2002), to Jones suggesting that "virtual reality is the contemporary and future articulation of the philosophical and psychological question of how we define (and create) reality" (Jones, 2006, p. 4), the issues, definitions, and experience of reality find rich and challenging ground in virtual environments. Writing in 2001, Grosz describes virtual realities as:

Computer-generated and [computer]–fed worlds that simulate key elements of "real space" or at least its dominant representations – for example, its dimensionality, its relations of resemblance and contiguity – acting as a partial homology for a "real space" within which it is located (Grosz, 2001, p. 40).

The early use of virtual environments for artistic practice were explored in a series of projects undertaken at the Banff Centre, Canada in the early 1990s and subsequently documented in *Immersed in Technology: Art and Virtual Environments* (Moser, 1996). In the preface to the book, Douglas Macleod, the Project Director, likens this "moment of virtual reality" to a similar moment in time when Vertov's *Man with the Movie Camera* was released in 1929, cataloguing the potential of the film medium (Macleod; in Moser, 1996, preface). Of particular note were works such as Brenda Laurel and Rachel Strickland's (1993) *Placeholder*, the *Archaeology of the Mother*

Tongue byDove and Mackenzie (1993), and the virtual reality performance, *Dancing with the Virtual Dervish: Virtual Bodies*, by Gromala and Sharir (1994). These projects were particularly innovative in their exploration of virtual reality environments in an art context.

Artists such as Char Davies moved from painting to exploring virtual space in virtual environments in the early 1990s, resulting in the works *Osmose* (1995) and *Ephémère* (1998). In *Osmose* (1995), the participant, or 'immersant' must concentrate on their breath as a device to navigate vertically through the spaces represented. Many immersants explain their experience in similar terms to Hansen:

You are floating inside an abstract lattice [...] you have no visible body at all in front of you, but hear a soundscape of human voices swirling around you as you navigate forward and backward by leaning your body accordingly [...] Exhaling deeply causes you to sink down through the soil as you follow a stream of tiny lights illuminating the roots of the oak tree (Hansen, 2006, pp. 107-108).

In *Landscape, Earth, Body, Being, Space, and Time in the Immersive Virtual Environments Osmose and Ephémère* (2003), Davies says that "within this spatiality, there is no split between the observer and the observed" (Davies, 2003, p. 1). She argues that this is not tied to a Cartesian paradigm, but rather allows "another way of sensing to come forward, one in which the body feels the space very much like that of a body immersed in the sea" (Davies, 2003, p. 1). In this private virtual space:

[By] leaving the space of one's usual sensibilities, one enters into communication with a space that is psychically innovating [...] For we do not change place, we change our nature (Bachelard; in Davies, 1997, p. 3).

In the introduction to *Changing Space: Virtual Reality as an Arena of Embodied Being,* Char Davies (1997) suggests that the medium of immersive virtual space offers the potential for "exploring consciousness as it is experienced subjectively, as it is *felt* [original emphasis]" (Davies, 1997, p. 1). She likens much of her work to the experience of meditational practice.

The work that defines the early exploration of telepresence in telematic spaces by artists engaged with technology is that of UK-based artist, Paul Sermon (1992) and his work, *Telematic Dreaming*, which Dixon describes as a "wonderful, exquisitely simple and ground-breaking installation [that] creates a type of magic, a sort of lucid dream" (Dixon, 2007, p. 220). Over the last two decades, Sermon has built upon this very simple concept of two geographically remote spaces being connected in time. In *Telematic Dreaming* (Figure 1) images of two beds, one in Finland, and the other in England, are projected onto each other, and that enabled a real time interaction with the performer in one space, and the visitor in the other (Sermon, 1992).

Susan Kozel (1994) writes an interesting account of her experience of being the performer in this piece in *Spacemaking: Experiences of a Virtual Body*. Other projects developed by Sermon such as *Unheimlich* (2005), a telematic theatre performance claimed to be the world's first interactive play, and more recently in work such as *Picnic on the Screen* in collaboration with Charlotte Gould (2009) presented at the Glastonbury Festival, he explores the concept of telematic presence.

Toni Dove (2005), in writing about her experiences of making *Spectropia*, an interactive performance piece using responsive interface technologies, likens the experience of the user to the experience of swimming: "this is a different form of attention—a kind of sustained tension which creates a space for reception; vertical eruptions in a horizontal field of time" (Dove, 2006, p. 67). She discusses the effects of the embodied

Figure 1. An interaction in Telematic Dreaming © (1992 Paul Sermon. Used with permission)

interface and the use of 'flow' rather than the 'cut' as the architecture for the media experience. For Dove, this charged space is a key characteristic of telepresence: "it is the space through which the body extends itself into the movie or virtual space. It is the invisible experience of the body's agency beyond its apparent physical edge" (Dove, 2002, p. 210). This space, between real space and the virtual space of the screen, is the charged space described by Dove; this is the space where the experience of telepresence is acted out. This is the same charged space that can be experienced when interacting with a virtual character in Luc Courchesne's (1997) interactive film installation, *Landscape One*, being invited to go on a journey in a park in Montreal.[2]

These are the similar imaginary and metaphorical spaces that Andrea Zapp (2004) describes in *Networked Narrative Environments as Imaginary Spaces of Being*. Additionally, the augmented spaces created in *Human Avatars*, an interactive installation also by Zapp (2005), construct a visual dialogue between real and virtual participants on a networked stage, as the visitors in the exhibition space discover a wooden hut that they are invited to enter. A live image of the visitor was projected inside a model version of the hut seen, and the disproportionately large faces were then seen at the windows of the second hut.

Whilst *Human Avatars* (2005) could be defined as a networked augmented space, it is not actually an avatar-mediated space that is created. The virtual embodiment of people as avatars is a term used in many online worlds, with avatar being the Sanskrit word which originally referred to the incarnation of a Hindu god and particularly the god Vishnu (Boellstorff, 2008, p. 128). The first use of the term in the context of technology was around 1986 for the graphical representation of participants in the *Habitat* virtual world (Dixon, 2007, p. 259). However, Tom Boellstorff notes that:

While "avatar" [...] historically referred to incarnation – a movement from virtual to actual – with respect to online worlds it connotes the opposite movement from actual to virtual, a decarnation or invirtualization (Boellstorff, 2008, p. 128).

He suggests that "avatars make virtual worlds real, not actual: they are a position from where the self encounters the virtual" (Boellstorff, 2008, p. 129) whereas Mark Meadows advocates that "an avatar is a social creature, dancing on the border between fact and fiction" (Meadows, 2008, p. 16). In using the term avatar-mediated online space this chapter distinguishes between the term virtual worlds and the experience of presence through an avatar representation in virtual space as discussed above.

METHODOLOGY: EXPLORATIONS OF AVATAR-MEDIATED SPACE

The very construction of matter is at stake when we consider the virtual: matter is permeated with ephemeral and dynamic elements, such as memory and kinaesthetic processes. Once again, we see that the virtual cannot be pinned to one side of the tenuous divide between the material and the immaterial (Kozel, 2006, p. 138).

A Prelude: The Virtual Body

Kozel suggests that "the virtual does not have to be confined to a set of relations external to the body; we can consider the meaning of traces of virtuality within our bodies" (Kozel, 2006, p. 138). James B. Steeves notes that:

Without the virtual aspect of the body schema, the body's original set of abilities could not be developed into more complex modes of behaviour. This realm of possibility exists through the virtual body, which is an embodied mode of the imagination [my emphasis] (Steeves, 2007, p. 23).

In *Performing in (Virtual) Spaces* Morie (2007) notes that when a participant engages in virtual space through a third person avatar, the form of embodied experience they take on has 'an experiential locus that is outside their perceptual self.' She explains that this is, in fact, "in front of the experient's physical and imaginal locus" (Morie, 2007, p. 132). According to Morie the act of emplacing a body into an immersive environment signifies "a shift to a dualistic existence in two simultaneous bodies" (Morie, 2007, p. 127). She claims that, now, the lived body has 'bifurcated and become two' (Morie, 2007, p. 128). In her article, she explores the representation of the body, or presence, in virtual environments in five ways: as no representation/no avatar, as the mirrored self, as a partial or whole graphical personification, as a third-person/observed avatar, and the representation as experience in shared environments. She suggests that virtual environments such as those created by Char Davies become a:

... sacred, encompassing space, where mind transcends body even as it references the body, the felt organism even in visual absence. This body, as felt phenomenon, is how we know the world, true as much within the virtual as in the real (Morie, 2007, p. 133).

Morie returns to Merleau-Ponty's phenomenological standpoint as he views the body as "the common texture of which objects are woven" (Merleau-Ponty; in Morie, 2007, p. 133), but suggests that he did not have to grapple with "new forms of immaterial bodies beyond the phenomenal" (Morie, 2007, p. 133) as we do now in light of new technologies. The chapter now considers a practice-based project that furthers the discussion on the nature and meaning of the avatar representation as a body that lives and moves between worlds.

Living between Worlds

I have the experience of embodiment, although I know my body is virtual. Of course I do. There is little true form here, only a series of associations. I took a friend of mine to a volcano last night. He was in awe of it. In his mind's eye, in his imagination he saw before him a 'real' volcano. Well, real enough to evoke his awe. Is that not 'real' enough for it to contain a form of reality? A form of presence? (Wanderingfictions Story; in Doyle & Kim, 2007, p. 216).

Working within the realm of Art and Technology (and as an artist who engages with narrative as method), my exploration of virtual space over the last decade has often been based on the retelling of narratives in a new context. An early practice-based project was to re-interpret Italo Calvino's (1997) *Invisible Cities* through an interactive artefact. The story was of Marco Polo's adventures to imagined cities with Calvino providing the descriptions of the fantastic, symbolic, and often conceptually based places. In the introduction to the project, I considered:

How do we understand time in virtual space? Real and imaginary, real and virtual. Is this a suitable dialectic offered by the introduction of 'net space'? Is it truly a dialectic, or a 'parallel' world we can draw upon to explore issues of time,

our experiences of the world as, in fact, a type of non-linear time, a time mixed up with past, present, and future. (Doyle, 2000, p. 4).

Of equal note were my closing remarks, where I suggested that the creation of a figure in the virtual space, that of Eleni, was worthy of further study:

To produce Wandering Fictions for the Web remained essential for the concept. The impact on the process, above technical constraints, of constructing a character to exist within this space was continually evident. The net space, if it has borders and boundaries, are not yet visible. A very different potential space could still emerge (Doyle, 2000, p. 24).

In Figure 2, two stills can be seen of Eleni, the protagonist in the interactive arts project. Here, a vectorized film of movements of a figure was created in an attempt to create a figure that could explore the virtual spaces of Calvino's imagined cities. What was of interest was this exploration of online, or cyberspaces, in a human form.

Following my introduction to *Second Life* in 2007, it was a relatively short time before I created *Wanderingfictions Story*. The origin of the maiden name was based on Siegfried Zielinksi's early writings on the Internet, in which he notes that:

Figure 2. Studies of Eleni (© 2000 Denise Doyle. Used with permission)

In the motion of crossing a border, heterology encircles the impossible place, that is unlocatable, that is actually empty, that in practice is created in the motion of crossing the border [...] this is what taking action at the border, that which I call subjective, targets in relation to the Net: strong, dynamic, nervous, definitely process-orientated aesthetic constructions, that are introduced into the Net as Wandering Fictions (Zielinski, 1996, p. 285).

Having already developed a number of artist projects utilizing and investigating *Second Life* as a space for artistic experimentation, in 2009, my interest in the notion of *Wanderingfictions Story* as a manifestation of, and from, virtual space became the basis of a new project, *Meta-Dreamer* (2009). After reflecting on the work of the performance artist Joseph DeLappe's *MGandhi* series[3], I began working with digital materialization expert Turlif Vilbrandt[4] to create a series of digitally materialized objects of *Wanderingfictions Story*. By experimenting with digital processes that extracted data from *Second Life* and investigating different types of materials, attempts were made to represent jade, and clouded glass, amongst other textures. The end result can be seen in Figure 3, the qualities of the figure are cloud-like and ethereal as though *Wanderingfictions Story*, the meta-dreamer, is 'almost there.' The digital object was presented in the Golden Thread Gallery space (as part of the ISEA2009[5] exhibition) alongside DeLappe's figure of *MGandhi 1* (2008). The visitor could also experience the virtual installation on Kriti Island that included the presentation of *Wanderingfictions Story*, the meta-dreamer, through captured images and her meta-dream writing.

This process of extracting data from virtual space, to be manifested in some way in physical space, forms an aspect of what Lichty terms an Evergent modality of art in virtual worlds. In his article, *The Translation of Art in Virtual Worlds*, Lichty (2009) outlines a number of interesting questions with respect to artists working between

Figure 3. Wanderingfictions Story as part of the meta-dreamer project at the golden thread gallery, Belfast (© 2009 Denise Doyle. Used with permission)

the virtual, and what he terms the *tangible*. He presents four modalities of art in which each modality "refers to the location and vector direction of the work's relation between worlds" (Lichty, 2009, p. 2). He notes that in terms of artistic praxis (beyond the associated problems of audience and questions of form) it is "the representational modality and the permeability of the boundary between worlds" that is of particular interest in the creation of meaning in artworks produced in virtual world spaces (Lichty, 2009, p. 1). He explains that:

...the nature of communication of the work is dependent upon its location and vector. What I mean by vector is a gesture of direction, simultaneity, concurrence, or stasis in regards to its movements between worlds (Lichty, 2009, p. 2).

In suggesting that there are four modalites of art being produced in virtual worlds, the Transmediated, the Evergent, the Cybrid and the Client/Browser work, he explains:

This epistemological "movement" within and between worlds has four basic structures; work that is essentially traditional physical art translated to the virtual, "evergent" work that is physically realized from virtual origins, the virtual itself, designed entirely for the client/browser experience, and "cybrids" that exist concurrently between various modalities (Lichty, 2009, p. 2).

According to Lichty, the semiotics of two modalities, the transmediated and the client/browser, are "a straightforward affair" (Lichty, 2009, p. 2). However, the Cybrids, "are less concerned with continuity, but are interested in the differences and distinctions between worlds and scales" (Lichty, 2009, p. 5). Both the Cybrid and the Evergent works demonstrate a "movement from virtual to tangible, which includes the consideration of works existing in simultaneous physical and virtual components, [and] present more complex models" (Lichty, 2009, p. 2). Manifesting from the virtual to the physical (or tangible) certainly has its parallels with manifesting from fictional worlds. Whatever the movement, this is a complex play and suggests in particular that it is those "enigmatic liminal works that live between worlds" (Lichty, 2009, p. 11) that create spaces that are the most potent for the imagination, demonstrating an array of creative potential for artists engaging in the *Second Life* space itself.

In an analysis of the emergence of *transitional spaces,* the four modalities of art as described by Lichty can be used to note the directions and creations of meaning between the physical or tangible world, and the virtual world, and movements within and between virtual and liminal spaces themselves. My intention within the *Meta-Dreamer* project and specifically in the production of Wanderingfictions Story as a digital object was

to explore, and represent, the almost becoming condition of the avatar-mediated experience. As an artist creating in what is a third-person and multiple perspective I was not alone in finding a complex and liminal state formed during the creative activities within *Second Life* (Doyle, 2010, see Appendix).[6]

Imagining Bodies

Computer artist Myron Krueger's (1974) early experiments resulted in what is considered to be the first virtual world, *Videoplace*. In this, he demonstrated that we can feel and sense other bodies in virtual space through this purely visual experience (Krueger; in Boellstorff, 2008, p. 44). In addressing issues of location in virtual space fellow artist Taey Kim (Iohe) and myself worked on a project *Map to Grid* (2008), employing methods of psycho-geography to determine where our non-human bodies were positioned on the grid[7]. Through this research it was noted, "understanding our geographical position in this digital era is absolutely essential as we are able to live in, and embody, multiple realities. Our 'I's travel through multiple spaces and times" (Doyle & Kim; in Doyle, 2008, p. 24).

Robert Bosnak, in writing of the dreaming brain, agrees with a current set of 'stories' of neuro-science as expounded by both Mark Solms and J. Allan Hobson, that dreaming is related to an experience of space (Bosnak, 2007, p. 36). In fact, a key element of what Bosnak terms the "embodied imagination" is that there is "an *inversion* of the notions of inside and outside [that] *changes the very nature of the space* [original emphasis]" in which we find ourselves (Bosnak, 2007, p. 20). Giving an explanation of how to visualize the experience of multiple embodied emotions, Bosnak explains that if dreaming was considered to be a narrative of simultaneous embodied states that unfold along a timeline, then equally, if the timeline "tilts […] into a vertical *axis* [original emphasis], a cross-section of multiple embodied stories […] making its many story times visible at a glance" (Bosnak, 2007, p. 39). In suggesting that emotions are "fully embodied states existing throughout the physical body" he further explains that dreaming could be considered to be "a simultaneous spatial experience of multiple embodied emotions" (Bosnak, 2007, p. 38). He uses the term "image-presence" to explain the environment, or space, we might find ourselves in when experiencing the embodied imagination. For Bosnak the process of embodiment precedes any mental or emotional knowing. For him "embodiment is the fundamental archaic way of knowing" (Bosnak, 2007, p. 71). It is clear that this approach to, or view of, embodiment through Bosnak's embodied imagination can be related to the avatar-mediated experience and the experience of the liminal in virtual world space.

Time-Spaces of the Liminal

In this section a Groszian reading of time and space in light of the virtual is closely examined to further explore the notion and experience of the liminal. Of the concept of the in-between Grosz writes that "one could say that the in-between is the locus of futurity, movement, speed; it is thoroughly spatial and temporal, the very essence of space and time and their intrication" (Grosz, 2001, p. 94). Grosz claims that space itself actually requires two kinds of time: the first being "the time of the emergence of space as such, a time before time and space" (Grosz, 2001, p. 110); the other being "the time of history, of historicity, the time of reflection, the time of knowledge – a time to which we are accustomed" (Grosz, 2001, p. 111). In her examination of the time and space of architecture, she explains that she is interested in the relevance of the first sense of time:

… a concept that requires not only a time before time but also a time after time […] the times before and after time are the loci of emergence, of unfolding, of eruption, the space-times of the

new, the unthought, the virtuality of a past that has not exhausted itself in activity and a future that cannot be exhausted or anticipated by the present (Grosz, 2001, pp. 111-112).

The digital object realised in *Meta-Dreamer* (2009) implies a state of in-between, of a "time *before* time" and the "loci of emergence" itself. Perhaps it could even be a representation of a "time *after* time," of a passing through, of leaving rather than entering. Equally, a sense of a frozen-ness is suggested in the material chosen to represent the figure in physical form. Dew Harrison suggests, in *Crossing Over: Oscillations between the Virtual and the Real* that this renders the *Wanderingfictions Story* avatar "inanimate," "being frozen from the life she had in SL" (Harrison, 2011, p. 238). Rather it is an attempt to represent the "position at, or on both sides of, a boundary or threshold" (Oxford Dictionary, 2012) that of the liminal state itself. Grosz proposes a re-enervation of space through duration in the "restoration of becoming to both space and time," and equally that when in "virtual time becoming virtual space" (Grosz, 2001, p. 120) a new kind of time-space relationship is established.

Doreen Massey, in an essay responding to the work of artist Olafur Eliasson, attempts to illustrate a set of relationships between time and space by using a narrative account of a journey between Manchester and Liverpool. In the process of travelling she suggests, "if movement is reality itself then what we think of as space is a cut through all those trajectories; a simultaneity of unfinished stories. Space has time/times within it" (Massey, 2003, p. 111). Further:

Space has its times. To open up space to this kind of imagination means thinking about time and space together. You can't hold places and things still. What you can do is meet up with them […] 'Here,' in that sense is not a place on a map. It is that intersection of trajectories [original emphasis] (Massey, 2003, p. 111).

Harrison takes up Nicholas Bourriaud's notion of "journey-forms" to explain the art concerns of a number of artists who developed art works for the *Second Life* platform (Harrison, 2011, p. 237). In fact, the use of "journey-forms, which is a combination of, a way to exchange, time and space values" (Bourriaud; in Harrison, 2011, p. 238). If each space has a particular time, as Massey implies, then the transitional and liminal spaces identified in avatar-mediated space may also have a particular time attached to them. Not only, then, are there heterogeneities of space but also different sets of time-spaces that can also be located in the avatar-mediated experience. Casey writes of "edges in time" (Casey, 2008, p. 12), where these edges are forms of boundaries of what he calls "further wrinkles in the face of the temporal field" (Casey, 2008, p. 12). All of these expressions suggest a plasticity to time as a lived experience, but also to the specificities of time-space relationships.

RECOMMENDATIONS

In the field of Art and Technology, the positioning of each successive 'innovation' is acknowledged as each rupture enables new associations and links to be made. This chapter points towards virtual worlds and avatar-mediated online space as another rupture and an opportunity to articulate both the experience of the liminal and the experience of living between worlds created through the avatar experience. However, the specificity of the platform of *Second Life* or any other may have to be taken into account as each 'time,' or as *Wanderingfictions Story* suggests, 'each decade has its own curiosity' (Doyle & Kim, 2007, p. 217).

Space can be understood and described as metaphoric, visual, Cartesian, and imaginary. However, in this chapter, space, and more particularly avatar-mediated online space, is considered to be more heterogeneous and complex in its nature and construction of the lived experience. The very experience of telepresence, as noted in

a number of the artworks presented, means that there has to be at least a third space, which is based on Soja's mix of the real and the imagined. The new modalities of art being developed in virtual worlds as suggested by Lichty are still somewhat undeveloped, yet are useful as a starting point to begin to explore the vectors of meaning created between the tangible (or physical) and the virtual. To return to the questions outlined at the beginning of the chapter, does the liminal always find the point of the threshold? Most certainly there is a sense that when living between worlds there must be a threshold between them, yet even as outlined by Zielinski's original writings in 1996 that inspired the naming of my avatar, new places are often created "in the *motion* of crossing the border [my emphasis]" (Zielinski, 1996, p. 285). Liminality is bound to the temporal—to passing, to the passage—of time itself. In that sense, *Meta-Dreamer is* a representation of that 'feeling' of time, of what Grosz considers to be the times before and after time, that place and loci of "unfolding" (Grosz, 2001, p. 112). If *Wanderingfictions Story* as a transluscent digital object is a representation of that "time" or if she indeed as Harrison suggests "an inanimate being frozen from the life she had in SL" (Harrison, 2011, p. 238) there is no doubt her new existence is a reminder that living between worlds is a new condition of what must now be termed a developing the contemporary cosmology of real and virtual space.

REFERENCES

Bachelard, G. (1994). *The poetics of space*. Boston, MA: Beacon Press.

Bergson, H. (1991). *Matter and memory*. New York, NY: Zone Books.

Biocca, F. (1997). The cyborg's dilemma: Progressive embodiment in virtual environments. *Journal of Computer-Mediated Communication*, *3*(2). Retrieved from http://jcmc.indiana.edu/vol3/issue2/biocca2.html

Boellstorff, T. (2008). *Coming of age in Second Life: An anthropologist explores the virtually human*. Princeton, NJ: Princeton University Press.

Bosnak, R. (2007). *Embodiment: Creative imagination in medicine, art and travel*. Hove, UK: Routledge.

Calvino, I. (1997). *Invisible cities*. London, UK: Vintage.

Casey, E. (2000). *Imagining: A phenomenological study*. Bloomington, IN: Indiana University Press.

Courschesne, L. (1997). *Landscape one: Interactive film installation*. Retrieved from http://courchel.net/

Damer, B. (1998). *Avatars! Exploring and building virtual worlds on the internet*. Berkeley, CA: Peachpit Press.

Davies, C. (1995). *Osmose: Virtual reality environment*. Retrieved from http://www.immersence.com/osmose/index.php

Davies, C. (1998). Changing space: Virtual reality as an arena of embodied being. In Beckman, J. (Ed.), *The Virtual Dimension: Architecture, Representation, and Crash Culture* (pp. 144–155). New York, NY: Princeton Architectural Press.

Davies, C. (1998). *Ephémère: Virtual reality environment*. Retrieved from http://www.immersence.com/

Davies, C. (2003). Landscape, earth, body, being, space, and time in the immersive virtual environments osmose and ephemere. In J. Malloy (Ed.), *Women, Art, and Technology*. Cambridge, MA: MIT Press. Retrieved from http:///www.immersence.com

Dixon, S. (2007). *Digital performance: A history of new media in theater, dance, performance art, and installation*. Cambridge, MA: MIT Press.

Dove, T. (2002). The space between: Telepresence, re-animation and the re-casting of the invisible. In Rieser, M., & Zapp, A. (Eds.), *New Screen Media: Cinema/Art/Narrative*. London, UK: BFI.

Dove, T. (2005). *Spectropia: Interactive feature film*. Retrieved from http://tonidove.com/

Dove, T. (2006). Swimming in time: Performing programmes, mutable movies - Notes on a process in progress. In Hill, L., & Paris, H. (Eds.), *Performance and Place*. Basingstoke, UK: Palgrave Macmillan.

Dove, T., & Mackenzie, M. (1993). *Archaeology of the mother tongue: Virtual reality installation*. Alberta, Canada: Banff Centre for the Arts. Retrieved from http://www.banffcentre.ca/bnmi/coproduction/archives/a.asp

Doyle, D. (2000). *Wandering fictions 2.0: Eleni's journey*. (MA Thesis). Coventry University. Coventry, UK.

Doyle, D. (2008). *Kritical works in SL*. Morrisville, NC: Lulu Publishing.

Doyle, D., & Kim, T. (2007). Embodied narrative: The virtual nomad and the meta dreamer. *The International Journal of Performance Arts and Digital Media*, *3*(2&3), 209–222. doi:10.1386/padm.3.2-3.209_1

Ettlinger, O. (2009). *The architecture of virtual space*. Ljubljana, Slovenia: University of Ljubljana.

Grau, O. (2003). *Virtual art: From illusion to immersion*. Cambridge, MA: MIT Press.

Gromala, D., & Sharir, Y. (1994). *Dancing with the virtual dervish: Virtual bodies, virtual reality installation*. Alberta, Canada: Banff Centre for the Arts. Retrieved from http://www.banffcentre.ca/bnmi/coproduction/archives/d.asp#dancing

Grosz, E. (2001). *Architecture from the outside: Essays on virtual and real space.* Cambridge, MA: MIT Press.

Hansen, M. (2004). *New philosophy for new media.* Cambridge, MA: MIT Press.

Hansen, M. (2006). *Bodies in code: Interfaces with digital media.* New York, NY: Routledge.

Harrison, D. (2011). Crossing over: Oscillations between the virtual and the real. In *Proceedings of the Cyberworlds 2011 Conference.* Cyberworlds.

Heim, M. (1993). *The metaphysics of virtual reality.* Oxford, UK: Oxford University Press.

Heudin, J. C. (Ed.). (1999). *Virtual worlds: Synthetic universes, digital life and complexity.* Reading, MA: Perseus Books.

Hillis, K. (1999). *Digital sensations: Space, identity, and embodiment in virtual reality.* Minneapolis, MN: University of Minnesota Press.

Ihde, D. (2002). *Bodies in technology.* Minneapolis, MN: University of Minnesota Press.

Jones, D. E. (2006). I, avatar: Constructions of self and place in second life and the technological imagination. *Gnovis, Journal of Communication, Culture and Technology.* Retrieved from http://gnovis.georgetown.edu

Kozel, S. (1994). *Spacemaking: Experiences of a virtual body.* Retrieved from http://art.net/~dtz/kozel.html

Kozel, S. (2006). Virtual/virtuality. *Performance Research, 11*(3), 136–139.

Laurel, B., & Strickland, R. (1993). *Placeholder: Virtual reality installation.* Alberta, Canada: Banff Centre for the Arts. Retrieved from http://www.banffcentre.ca/bnmi/coproduction/archives/p.asp#placeholder

Lefebvre, H. (1991). *The production of space.* Oxford, UK: Blackwell Publishing.

Levy, P. (1998). *Becoming virtual: Reality in the digital age.* New York, NY: Plenum Trade.

Lichty, P. (2009). The translation of art in virtual worlds. *Leonardo Electronic Almanac, 18*(12). Retrieved from http://www.leonardo.info/LEA/DispersiveAnatomies/DA_lichty.pdf

Lindstrand, T. (2007). Viva pinata: Architecture of the everyday. In Borries, V. F., Bottger, M., & Walz, S. P. (Eds.), *Space Time Play: Computer Games, Architecture and Urbanism - The Next Level.* Basel, Switzerland: Birkhauser Verlag AG.

Lyotard, J. (1991). *The inhuman: Reflections on time.* Palo Alto, CA: Stanford University Press.

Massey, D. (2003). Some times of space. In May, S. (Ed.), *Olafur Eliasson: The Weather Report.* London, UK: Tate Publishing.

Massumi, B. (2002). *Parables for the virtual: Movement, affect, sensation.* Durham, NC: Duke University Press.

Meadows, M. S. (2008). *I, avatar: The culture and consequences of having a second life.* Berkeley, CA: New Riders.

Morie, J. (2007). Performing in (virtual) spaces: Embodiment and being in virtual environments. *International Journal of Performance Arts and Digital Media, 3*(2&3), 123–138. doi:10.1386/padm.3.2-3.123_1

Moser, M. A. (Ed.). (1996). *Immersed in technology: Art and virtual environments.* Cambridge, MA: MIT Press. doi:10.2307/1576254

Packer, R., & Jordan, K. (Eds.). *Multimedia: From Wagner to virtual reality.* New York, NY: W.W. Norton & Company. Retrieved from http:///www.immersence.com

Pallasmaa, J. (2005). *The eyes of the skin: Architecture and the senses.* Chichester, UK: John Wiley & Sons.

Rheingold, H. (1991). *Virtual reality*. New York, NY: Summit Books.

Schroeder, R. (Ed.). (2002). *The social life of avatars: Presence and interaction in shared virtual environments*. London, UK: Springer.

Sermon, P. (1992). *Telematic dreaming: Performance installation*. Retrieved from http://creativetechnology.salford.ac.uk/paulsermon/dream/

Sermon, P. (2005). *Unheimlich: Multi-user performance installation*. Retrieved from http://creativetechnology.salford.ac.uk/unheimlich/

Sermon, P., & Gould, C. (2009). *Picnic on the screen: Interactive public video installation*. Retrieved from http://creativetechnology.salford.ac.uk/paulsermon/picnic/

Soja, E. W. (1996). *Thirdspace: Journeys to Los Angeles and other real-and-imagined places*. Malden, MA: Blackwell Publishers. doi:10.1177/030981689806400112

Steeves, J. B. (2007). *Imagining bodies: Merleau-Ponty's philosophy of imagination*. Pittsburgh, PA: Duquesne University Press.

Stockburger, A. (2007). Playing the third place: Spatial modalities in contemporary game environments. *International Journal of Performance Arts and Digital Media, 3*(2&3), 223–236. doi:10.1386/padm.3.2-3.223_1

Zapp, A. (2002). *The imaginary hotel: Networked installation*. Retrieved from http://www.azapp.de/ha_01.html

Zapp, A. (2005). *Human avatars: Interactive installation*. Retrieved from http://www.story-rooms.net

Zielinski, S. (1996). Thinking the border and the boundary. In Druckrey, T. (Ed.), *Electronic Culture: Technology and Visual Representation*. New York, NY: Aperture Foundation.

KEY TERMS AND DEFINITIONS

Embodied Imagination: A term used by the Dutch psychoanalyst Robert Bosnak that he closely associates with the dreaming brain, in which multiple spatial embodied states are experienced simultaneously. The term is also used here to denote the experience of sensing a spatial presence in virtual space through a *sense imaginary* and the association of the body of the avatar.

Emergent Imagination: A term used to denote the most active state of the emerging imagination when interacting with avatar-mediated online spaces and particularly those that reflect the laws and logic of the physical world.

Imagination: The Latin (and English) origin for the imagination is the verb *imaginari*, whereas the Greek term is *phantasia*. The etymological implications of this term are discussed in the thesis. Edward Casey defines the imagination as the complete phenomenon composed of two phases; the act phase and the object phase. The term is used here to imply a state of creation and *act of becoming*: a bringing into being rather than as the inverse of the physical or tangible.

Liminal Space: A term used to denote a space that creates the condition of being at, or on both sides of a threshold or boundary, and relates closely to the state of being in-between.

Transitional Space: A term used to denote the movements of the imagination in which vectors of meaning are created out of the relationships between physical and virtual world spaces.

ENDNOTES

[1]   The use of the terms virtual and physical (also tangible later in the chapter) are used here rather than the virtual and the real given the experience of virtual space can often considered to be as 'real' as the experience of the physical or tangible world.

2   My experience of the installation *Landscape One* was like being invited *into* the screens that surrounded me by the characters, yet still experiencing all the physical sensations of remaining static in front of the screen. This is possibly the first experience of telepresence I had, and it was something that I was curious about for a number of years afterwards.

3   During an artist residency at the Eyebeam Gallery, New York, in 2008, Joseph DeLappe experimented with a range of data materialisation processes to produce *MGandhi 1* (8" rapid prototyped 3D print), *MGandhi 2* (15" rapid prototyped 3D print finished in genuine gold leaf), and *MGandhi 3* (17' tall monumental sculpture constructed from cardboard and hot glue).

4   Turlif Vilbrandt is an expert in the field of Digital Materialisation. He is currently completing his PhD research at the SMARTlab Digital Media Research Institute, University College Dublin.

5   The Inter Society for Electronic Arts organises an annual Symposium and related exhibitions. In 2009, it was held in Belfast on the Island of Ireland.

6   Joseph DeLappe and Annabeth Robinson note their experience and relationship with their avatars in interviews conducted with both artists in 2010.

7   Using a real doll called *Dongdong,* Taey Kim exchanges narratives and stories with the author's avatar *Wanderingfictions Story* in the project.

Chapter 6
LPDT2: La Plissure du Texte 2

Elif Ayiter[1]
Sabancı University, Istanbul

Stefan Glasauer[2]
Ludwig-Maximilian University, Munich

Max Moswitzer[3]
University of Fine Arts, Zürich

ABSTRACT

This chapter will discuss the artistic processes involved in the creation of the three dimensional, virtual art installation La Plissure du Texte 2, which is the sequel to Roy Ascott's ground breaking telematically networked art work La Plissure du Texte, created in 1983 and shown in Paris at the Musée de l'Art Moderne de la Ville de Paris during that same year. While the underlying concepts of the original art work, as well as its capability of regenerating itself as an entirely novel manifestation based upon the concepts of distributed authorship, textual mobility, emergent semiosis, multiple identity, and participatory poesis will be underlined, the main focus of the text will be upon the creative strategies as well as the technological means through which the architecture was brought about in the contemporary creative environment of the metaverse. A further topic that will be covered is the challenge of exhibiting what is after all an art work that requires full virtual immersion to bring about a deep level experience and understanding of it, in the physical world, i.e. 'Real Life'[4]—in a gallery or museum space in which such a virtual immersion cannot be readily obtained.

INTRODUCTION

La Plissure du Texte 1983

The title of the project, *La Plissure du Texte: A Planetary Fairy Tale*, alludes to Roland Barthes's book *Le Plaisir du Texte* (1973), a famous discourse on authorship, semantic layering, and the creative role of the reader as the writer of the text. As was also the case in its first incarnation "distributed authorship," a term coined by Ascott (2003, pp. 191-208) has been the primary subject of investigation of LPDT2. Since La Plissure du Texte 1983 is the inspiration as well as the precedent of our own endeavors; we believe that, before we present our ongoing work in the three

DOI: 10.4018/978-1-4666-2961-5.ch006

dimensionally embodied metaverse, it will be well placed to delve into a brief description of Roy Ascott's original work, which was shown during the exhibition 'Electra: Electricity and Electronics in the Art of the XXth Century' at the Musèe Art Moderne de la Ville de Paris in the fall of 1983. The invitation had been extended by Frank Popper, the curator of the show, to Ascott in 1982; and the artist felt that this presented him with a perfect opportunity to create a large scale telematic event that would incorporate ideas which he had formed over the previous twenty or more years. La Plissure du Texte sought to set in motion a process by which an open ended, nonlinear narrative might be constructed from an authoring 'mind' whose distributed nodes were interacting on a planetary scale (Ascott, 2005).

One of the pathways to La Plissure were the psychic systems that Ascott had been studying since the early 1960s, such as telepathy across oceans, communication with the disincarnate in distant worlds; as was evidenced in some of his writings such as his text entitled 'The Psibernetic Arch' from 1970. These convictions led him, a decade later, to formulate ideas of distributed mind and the concept of distributed authorship which were embedded in LPDT. However, coupled with his interest in the world of the psychic was also Ascott's strong preoccupations with cybernetics, which drew him to, what was for him at that point, the equally mysterious world of computer mediated telecommunications. Further inspirations were also in signs, in semiotics, and in myths which was also fed by Vladimir Propp's study of narrative structure and the morphology of the fairy tale.

Ascott (2005) conceived of LPDT as "a project involving multiple associative pathways for a narrative that would unroll asynchronically according to the centers of action that determined its development. The outcome would be multilayered, nonlinear in all its bifurcations." This also had a precedent in a project which Ascott had previously set up as part of Robert Adrian X's 'The World in 24 Hours,' an electronic networking event held at

Ars Electronica in 1982 which involved participants at their computer terminals around the world tossing coins for the first planetary throw of the I Ching. Just as was the case with this earlier work, La Plissure du Texte also utilized ARTEX, an early email system that was initiated under the name of ARTBOX in 1980 by Adrian X, Bill Bartlett, and Gottfried Bach to offer artists a cheap and simple alternative to business oriented communication programs which were beginning to increasingly be available in the early 1980s.

When Ascott posted a description of the project on the ARTEX network in July 1983, artists and art groups in 11 cities in Europe, North America, and Australia came into the project. In November of that year each participating node was allocated the role of a traditional fairy tale character, such as princess, witch, fairy godmother etc. Beyond this simple concept of the fairy tale however, Ascott was careful not suggest to a story line or a plot; instead the participants were asked to improvise. The notion behind this was that Ascott also wanted to bring in the element of surprise which would be generated by the differences between time zones which would cause the narrative to often overlap and be fragmented, thus inevitably leading into a multiplicity of directions.

La Plissure du Texte was active on line twenty-four hours a day for twelve days: from December 11 to 23, 1983. With terminals in eleven cities, the network grew to include local networks of artists, friends, and random members of the general public who would happen to be visiting the museum of art space where the terminals were located. Over the three week period of the project hundreds of "users" became involved in a massive intertext, the weaving of a textual tissue that could not be classified, even though ostensibly the project was to generate a 'planetary fairytale' (Ascott, 2005).

La Plissure du Texte 1983 turned out to be a fulcrum point in Ascott's work, showing him the importance of text as an agent of not merely theory but also of practice, demonstrating the potency of distributed authorship in the creative process. However, not only has the concept of distributed authorship been important to the artist himself, it has also strongly resonated with many others between then and now, and has managed to retain its freshness and its inspirational power—as indeed we hope our interpretation of LPDT will attest to as well.

LPDT2

LPDT2 consists of a geography/architecture constructed entirely out of dynamic input text, which is built in a three-dimensional, online, participatory virtual world, i.e., a metaverse. While an earlier version of the work was created in the proprietary metaverse of Second Life ®, the current location is an independent artist's grid called the New Genres Grid, which is a part of the newly emerging independent online hypergrid system.

In both versions of the build, the architecture stretches itself over an entire metaverse simulator and reaches thousands of virtual meters into the sky, materializing on several platforms, which show differences both in terms of visual appearance as well as content (see Figure 1).

Beyond this, the second incarnation of the project does not copy or mimic what was created in the first version but strikes out into different visual investigations, searching for novel means of utilizing the generated text in a significantly more restrictive environment: While at a cursory glance the open metaverse operates in a similar fashion to the enclosed world of Second Life, nonetheless there are considerable differences when it comes to scripted objects and especially those involving virtual physics. This inevitably necessitated omissions of architectural components upon which the success of the Second Life structure had much relied. However, as is all too often the case, necessity gave rise to invention and the second version of LPDT2 shows marked

Figure 1. LPDT2 avatars cavorting in a virtual landscape of text: Second Life (© Elif Ayiter 2010. Used with permission)

differences as well as improvements. As an example, the ground level of the second build puts us into a space of letter columns, which form sentences from the harvested text. These columns surround a space filled with one hundred tables. Tablets of a single sentence each have then been placed upon these tables and through them the entire 'table hall' bears testimony to the anonymously distributed authorship of the authors coming to us via Project Gutenberg, whilst at the same time reflecting upon the symbolic attributes of the 'tabletop,' a recurring conceptual element of Ascott's throughout his artistic career.

Whereas in 1983 the text was pleated by a number of human storytellers positioned around the globe; in the three dimensionally embodied metaverse the storytellers show novel and unexpected attributes: An emergent textual architecture/geography, as well as a population of autonomous 'robot' avatars which dwell inside this bizarre, literary landscape are pleating the text by acting as communication nodes between the narrators of this new version of the tale: The primary persistent distributed authorship is now accomplished by many writers throughout the ages.

A text generator telling a non-linear, multifaceted, often times poetic, story harvested from the online Project Gutenberg is now distributing its output amongst an architecture and its inhabitants, generating dialogues and iterations taking their trajectories from masterworks of classical literature. The pleating resembles musical sampling, the connection between the sentences fades, text becomes noise, from which the audience generates meaning.

While the virtual structure on the simulator provides the primary layer of pleating by visually mixing the different sources of text, yet another layer of textual input has been provided through which Real Life visitors can contact LPDT2 by sending SMS messages as well as re-pleating the text via Twitter. All pleated text—the generated, the contributed, and the stored—is simultaneously visible as a massive, ever evolving literary conglomeration. Consequently, the participatory pleating involves not only a meeting of individuals from the same timeframe but extends into a meeting between the past and the present, the bringing together of voices of many ages, then and now.

Although LPDT2 has been planned as a virtual installation which will nonetheless be predominantly visited in a physical gallery space, the interaction with LPDT2 is by no means limited to the physical realm alone: Since the project unfolds in a freely accessible, participatory online virtual world visitors throughout the globe can visit the installation with their avatars at any time of their choosing. Thus, an added layer of participation is provided through the three dimensionally embodied interactions of geographically dispersed individuals amongst each other, with the 'resident' robotic avatars, as well as the avatars of the artists themselves.

Creating a System: Generating the Text

Various means of gathering the input text which would get the entire system operational were discussed during the early phases of the project; however even from the onset a wish to create a system whereby the text would be generated rather than be contributed by discrete individuals was seen as an exciting option. That this was a distinct

possibly was evident from the existence of various online text generators and particularly the Dada Engine (Bulhak, 2000).

Although text can be harvested from many different sources such as search engines and even text determined upon by the artists themselves, Project Gutenberg (Hart, 1992) proved to be an inspired choice since not only does the vast repository provide a huge resource but also the text thus harvested reinterprets Roy Ascott's key phrase of "distributed authorship" by adding to it a dimension of temporality, if not indeed a transcendence of the here and now: The repository holds over 30000 texts which have been authored by countless individuals throughout history. However, beyond this aspect of temporality, the startlingly poetic nature of the harvested text has proven itself to be an additional blessing which came out of utilizing Project Gutenberg as a means for achieving "participatory poesis."

The central idea of the text generator's algorithm is that any meaningful flow of text is based on the semantic connection of subsequent sentences. This is a linkage, which is usually imposed by the author, however at the same time the reader expects such a connection. The present algorithm exploits both the intentions of the numerous authors and the expectations of the reader/spectator, but instead of relying upon an understanding of the text in order to choose appropriate sentences, it uses the statistical properties of written text in a similar fashion to what has been proposed by Claude Shannon more than half a century ago for generating messages (Shannon, 1948). In Shannon's terminology, such an algorithm would be best called a simplified second-order sentence approximation to language. The simplification consists in reducing a sentence to the word that has the highest amount of information (in Shannon's sense), ergo usually the longest word of a sentence. The algorithm can thus be described through the following recipe: 1) choose a random text from Project Gutenberg and then randomly select a sentence as the starting point, 2) take the longest word in this sentence and search for this word in another text, again randomly chosen from Project Gutenberg, 3) once the word is found in the new text, take the sentence immediately succeeding the sentence containing the word, 4) take this succeeding sentence as a new sentence to be added to the generated text, 5) continue ad infinitum. Evidently, the two newly connected sentences share a statistical relation via the conditional probability of the succeeding sentence sharing information with the first. These consecutive sentences are then sent to an HTML server from where they are mapped onto the architecture. However, the same text generator also sends aggregated text via email directly into the metaverse where it is used as the conversational material for the robotic avatars who are the indigenous residents of the architecture (see Figure 2).

Although the text generator does provide the bulk of the text, additional input is provided through an AI system contributed by i-DAT from Plymouth University through which visitors to the physical gallery space can send SMS messages which are then displayed as an additional text layer by means of a screen based heads-up-display. Finally, visitors to the virtual installation can send Twitter messages by clicking on a message board which displays a short sentence obtained from the text generator.

The Aesthetics of LPDT2: Typographic Deconstruction

What remains consistent throughout both the first as well as the second formation of LPDT2 is an adherence to the basic key phrases formulated by Ascott: Textual mobility, distributed authorship, emergent semiosis, multiple identity, and participatory poesis.

This brings about the installation in which the generated text is mapped onto architectural components such as floors, walls, as well as spaces, which are more difficult to make sense of, such

Figure 2. LPDT2, the lettercube: Second Life (© Elif Ayiter 2010. Used with permission)

as a strangely configured cube upon which an ever changing text flow is mapped, or an ever changing labyrinth of sentences and letters of the alphabet. While the text can be read as full stand-alone sentences on the individual planes onto which it has been mapped, oftentimes the layering of the planes as well as the juxtaposition of typographic elements results in typographic deconstruction. This dissection is mirrored by interspersed streams of floating characters forming sentences, which vanish into the sky or crash into the virtual ground, dissolving into flocks of slowly tumbling letters. Thus, just like the ASCII letter which were used in the original La Plissure du Texte from 1983 became a pictorial element forming images, which nowadays are called ASCII art (Ascott, 2003, Figure 17), in LPDT2 the letter as carrier of information becomes a sculptural element.

In the early 1990s, the potential unleashed by desktop publishing and graphics software, allied with the methodological potential offered by deconstructionist philosophy, produced a style of graphic design and typography known sometimes as deconstructionist graphic design, and sometimes as 'The New Typography.' Although the later influx of deconstructionist philosophy cannot be denied, nonetheless deconstructivist typography has its origins in the early 20th Century. Thus, Marinetti writes in 1913:

My revolution is aimed at the so-called typographical harmony of the page, which is contrary to the flux and reflux, the leaps and bursts of style that run through the page... With this typographical revolution and this multicolored variety in the letters I mean to redouble the expressive force of words (Marinetti, 1913).

Modernist typography had engaged in such structural games, even before Marinetti. The printed word was liberated from printing's traditional constraints by Stéphane Mallarmé with 'Un Coup de dés' in 1987, pioneering an expressive form of visual presentation for poetic language. One might have expected Marinetti to enthuse over 'Un Coup de dés,' however he had other views:

Moreover, I combat Mallarmé's static ideal with this typographical revolution that allows me to impress on the words (already free, dynamic, and torpedo-like) every velocity of the stars, the clouds, aeroplanes, trains, waves, explosives, globules of sea foam, molecules, and atoms (Marinetti, 1913).

One of Marinetti's basic Futuristic tenets, the relegation of human experience to a continuum of sensations, underlay the techniques he proposed to use in achieving a Futurist literary expression. Marinetti described these procedures by declaring that *"nouns will be scattered at random, infinitives with their greater elasticity will replace the pedantic indicative"* (Cundy, 1981, pp. 34-352).

Marinetti's attack on typographic convention, taking Mallarmé's work several stages further, had considerable prescience. His directness, vigor and visual augmentation of the power of words, the entire Futurist ethos of treating words as ammunition, helped formulate the solutions which the new needs of the 20th century demanded (Bartram, 2006, p. 9).

Although separated in time though a period of 80 years, Ellen Lupton seems to pick up on certain aspects of Marinetti's outcry when she sees deconstruction in graphic design as a process—an act of questioning typographic practice. In Derrida's original theory deconstruction asks several questions which are crucial to typographic design as well: How does representation inhabit reality? How does the external appearance of a thing get inside its internal essence? How does the surface get under the skin?

A crucial opposition in Derrida's theory of deconstruction, and one, which is also highly pertinent in terms of typographic design, is speech versus writing. The Western philosophical tradition has denigrated writing as an inferior, dead copy of the living, spoken word. When we speak, we draw on our inner consciousness, but when we write, our words are inert and abstract. The written word loses its connection to our inner selves. Language is set adrift.

Parallel questions for graphic design which preoccupy Lupton are how visual form may get inside the 'content' of writing and through what means has typography refused to be a passive, transparent vessel for written texts, instead developing as a system with its own structures and devices throughout the ages? A typographic work can be called 'deconstruction' when it exposes and transforms the established rules of writing, interrupting the sacred 'inside' of content with the profane 'outside' of form (Lupton, 1994, pp. 45-47).

Added should also be that, more often than not, deconstructionist typography exhibits a fascination with contemporary technology, in both its utopian and dystopian possibilities, as well as its glamour, adopting tropes and strategies of appropriation, juxtaposition, détournement, montage, collage, repetition, facilitated by, or reflecting upon the extraordinary capabilities of digital technologies. It is thus of no surprise that the outcome oftentimes resonates upon a world of diffused and distributed communication mediated through networks of powerful information technologies. Even when the artifact itself is presented as a static printed page the reference to a cyberspace driven by hypertext is very often implicit, underscoring that *"communication for the deconstructivist is no longer linear, but involves instead the provision of many entry and exit points for the increasingly over-stimulated reader"* (Cahalan, 1994, p. 1). Thus the page is no longer to be just 'read' but also to be 'perceived,' beyond the pure textual content, into all of its associative conjunctions: We are also meant to 'feel' rather than just to 'read' a page.

In LPDT2 typographic deconstruction is mostly achieved through space; that is the Z axis of virtual three dimensionality. The typeface used throughout the installation was deliberately reduced to two fonts, the standard monospaced typewriter font Courier for the two-dimensional panels (Figure 4) and a classic 5x7 pixel font for the three dimensional letters (Figure 7) and the avatar attachments (Figure 3). Both these choices serve as homage to the history of the work, given that the original printouts of La Plissure du Texte required monospace fonts to be displayed correctly: The 1983 press release was typed in Courier, and the only available font types for screens at that time were simple pixel fonts. As one wanders through the conglomeration the text planes containing their individually coherent sentences will inevitably fall upon one another, creating overlapping layers and presenting the visitor with configurations which will juxtapose as well as superimpose different sizes and angles comprised of many

Figure 3. LPDT2, robotic avatar: Second Life (© Elif Ayiter 2010. Used with permission)

different sentences, enabling readings which may present many entry and exit points. However, since the input text not only manifests upon two dimensional planes but also materializes as three dimensional objects, another juxtaposition which deconstructs the typography is the perception of two dimensional and three dimensional text simultaneously, often one blending into the other, falling upon each other, creating waterfalls and cascades of words, which are indeed meant to be 'felt,' as well as 'read.' The 'conversations' held by the robotic avatars, as well as the SMS text sent from the physical realm add further layers to this deconstructive process. Furthermore, the entire typographic system is in an ever changing state of flux depending upon the motion and view point of the avatar who traverses it.

This visual deconstruction would appear to enhance the transmission of Ascott's fundamental key phrases: Textual mobility, distributed authorship, emergent semiosis, multiple identity, and participatory poesis are augmented not only through the contributions of the countless historic authors whose words reside inside Project Gutenberg, but additionally through the layers of deconstruction which brings these words and sentences together in ever changing novel visual expositions.

EXHIBITING METAVERSE ART

When looking at artistic activity in virtual worlds it very soon becomes apparent that a considerable amount of creative output is created very much along the lines of its physical counterpart; with the objective of being viewed within a gallery/museum setting—albeit virtually. This accounts for the proliferation of virtual galleries and museums inside Second Life to which visitors are meant to come to with their avatars, very much as one would do so in Real Life with one's physical body; complete with openings and purchases of the displayed work—more often as limited edi-

Figure 4. LPDT2, 'the syncretic cathedral': Second Life (© Elif Ayiter 2010. Used with permission)

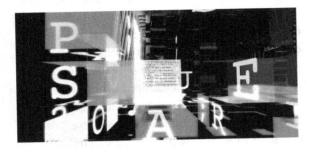

tions but sometimes also as a unique original (in which case the buyer would inevitably have to rely upon the word of the creator that there is no further copy of the bought item).

During such events, the exhibited artworks consist of standalone virtual artifacts, such as sculptures that are created in-world or virtual photographs which are presented as framed paintings and more recently also video art which is played back on virtual screens inside the virtual gallery. These exhibitions usually have fixed time-spans—again very much in the way that a physical art gallery would allot a specific period for a show. Since the experience of the visitor seems to be one which is based upon an objectively externalized viewing, rather than a subjectively internalized or experientially immersive meeting with the virtual nature of the artwork, it is conceivable that exporting such an exhibit into Real Life would be eminently doable simply by exporting the virtual output (which in the case of the 'paintings' would have to have been imported into the virtual world as bitmap textures to begin with), printing it on 2D or 3D printers, and then displaying the outcome in a physical gallery to which visitors can go to with their biological bodies as opposed to their virtual representations.

Yet another approach, mostly used by artists who appear to visit the metaverse for this sole purpose, is the utilization of the metaverse viewer and its native building devices as the software through which artwork which is intended to be shown primarily in Real Life is rendered. This type of work may also involve a merger of Real Life and virtual life, and may very often also incorporate performances in which virtual avatars are expected to interact with a Real Life audience. However, regardless of whether there is a performative aspect or not, since the work in question has been conceived of as one which is meant to come into effect through the participation of a physical audience, it is to be assumed that bringing such artworks into the physical world would pose no major conceptual challenges: Given that bringing the virtual artifact into Real Life is the primary objective of the undertaking, the strategies for doing so would already be built into the creative system from the onset.

Exhibiting LPDT2 in the Metaverse

There is however a further type of creative undertaking to be found in the metaverse which is extremely difficult to replicate in Real Life, and LPDT2 falls very much under this category: These are creations that are all-inclusive environments which come into being through a custom created geography and climate, usually stretching themselves out over an entire metaverse simulator which is used to create a continuously engaging experience, comprised of many interrelated artifacts that cannot be easily separated from one another and which provide a complex visual/sonic system that calls to be perceived in its entirety, growing out of its own artificial ecology, meant to be visited and experienced therein. Indeed these types of experiences can also be seen as the virtual counterparts to exhibitions such as Robert Morris' 'Bodyspacemotionthings'[6], which explicitly form an environment in which the visitor becomes part of the artwork rather than remaining a spectator. Thus, at the very least these spaces require a walkthrough in order to be seen with full impact; however, at their best they will evoke remarkably heightened states of engagement in their visitors.

Such spaces may be thematic, indeed sometimes follow tangible concepts and storylines which may even be potentially defined as artistic Role Play environments in which visitors are meant to experience the artwork by following up on the presented concepts/storylines by taking on the roles which are made available to them within the environment itself. However, in many cases, these ecologies may also be based upon concepts and abstractions from which visitors are expected to derive their own meanings and experiences. To achieve such heightened levels of engagement in many of these all-inclusive virtual ecologies the creators also often provide avatar costumes, which are deemed to be very effective devices in bringing about enhanced states of identification—a strategy which we also put to good use in LPDT2.

As a general rule such virtual art ecologies do not have a specific duration or a statically defined appearance; more often than not they will be around for many months if not indeed for years, whilst undergoing continuous changes during their lifespan. As is already implicit from this lack of predetermined timeframe, with this type of output the objective can be defined as an invitation for others to come and live inside the created space—to make it their own, and ultimately to become creatively active in it. The desire is that the piece slowly unfolds through many lengthy visits, some lasting for days or even weeks, and that the incomers proceed to utilize the landscape for their own ends—to play in, and by extension to become creatively active in on a personal level.

It is our observation that one of the most noteworthy things about metaverse creativity is that it breeds creativity in others; that one of the most vital forms of artistic interaction manifests in the form of a 'cadavre exquis' in which artwork gets built through progressive layers in which an artist will use an existent artwork to further construct upon. Such second order output is usually evidenced as virtual photography and machinima which has become a major creative outlet for many virtual world residents, and through which they will derive their own imaginative interpretations which are often evidenced as remarkably sophisticated documentations of their experiences and playful activity within such ecosystem artworks. Other forms of output may involve storytelling which takes its trajectory from the art environment, either as in-world performative sessions which are acted out inside the artwork itself or as creative writing displayed on the many blogs which metaverse story-tellers are known to keep.

Although we were aware from the onset that LPDT2 was to be exhibited in Real Life, nonetheless we could not help but think of the work as such a metaverse environment first and foremost. We believe that what makes metaverse creative output uniquely valuable as an art form are its immersive characteristics, especially in regards to how this brings about a wish, which very often culminates into an ability to generate further creativity in others. All three of us had taken this noteworthy attribute of the metaverse into consideration in our prior output; we had mostly created full geographies into which other avatars had come to play and to create. After discussing our standpoint with Roy Ascott and obtaining his approval, which given his own life-long emphasis regarding the behavioral nature of contemporary art was of course very easily attained (Ascott, 2003, pp. 109-126), we proceeded to build LPDT2 as an immersive, participatory, all-inclusive environment/ecosystem of no fixed temporality, put at the disposal of all avatars for investigation, creativity and play - in accord with the emergently creative nature of the metaverse.

Exhibiting LPDT2 in Real Life

Following from the above, exhibiting LPDT2 in Real Life is a challenge, which we have always been much aware of, and continue to be so. Although the work has been exhibited three times over the past two years it has to be acknowledged that our preparations in the summer of 2010, when we were actively building the system, actually only took into account the affordances of the first of these displays and that subsequent showings were adaptations and/or documentations of the initial output. This first showing was projected into Real Life in Korea during the INDAF new media art festival, which also hosted a major retrospective of Ascott's work, held at Tomorrow City, Songdo Incheon, throughout September 2010.

In this first exposition we were extraordinarily lucky since the organizers of the festival provided the means whereby a live event effectuated by a number of 'tour guide' avatars, which we custom created for the occasion (and who were dressed in the proper LPDT2 attire), could be realized: Even in a culture as technologically advanced as Korea it still cannot be expected that all visitors will be savvy enough to operate a virtual world avatar by themselves; therefore a docent who can assist visitors in this task and who is available throughout the viewing hours of the work is of the essence. It was the provision of such assistance that enabled us to project LPDT2 as a work into which visitors could become interactively immersed and play—both with the environment/architecture that surrounded them as well as with the robotic avatars that resided within it. Since the environment was open to virtual visitors in Second Life, and since the simulator was very well visited by avatars from all over the globe, an added layer of interaction was also achieved between the visitors that accessed the environment from the physical gallery space in Korea and those that came from elsewhere through virtual means (see Figure 5).

The availability of a docent through whom an immersive virtual visit could be actuated for the gallery audience was indeed a blessing, which greatly encouraged us to proceed with our plans for realizing the work as an immersive environment, as discussed above. However, as preparations in Korea progressed it became apparent that our luck actually extended even further than this;

that LPDT2 was to be projected into Real Life in a very special way: For this we have to thank Roy Ascott's already mentioned preoccupation with the metaphor of the table-top as a viewing system, which through its many associations almost automatically brings with it a heightened sense of engagement, and through which the long held western tradition based upon a single view point can be broken most effectively. Further thanks go to the curator of the show, Byoung Hak Ryu (2010, pp. 29-31), who realized Ascott's wish by projecting the display onto a horizontal flat surface which was surrounded by an elevated viewing platform from where visitors could gaze down upon the display. Thus, LPDT2 could be experienced from many viewpoints depending upon where one stood in relation to the projection upon the ground.

While the table-top viewpoint is a noteworthy concept in and of itself, in the case of LPDT2 for which the textual deconstruction described earlier in this chapter is the predominant visual element, a viewing system which enabled multiple viewpoints to a textual conglomeration that is meant to be 'felt' rather than 'read,' in which the coming together of the words of many authors from the past provides the context for a non-sequential, non-linear narrative with many simultaneous entry and exist points, provided an additional, unforeseen and yet highly desirable stratum of complexity.

The second and third showings of LPDT2 in Real Life occurred as a part of Ascott's retrospec-

Figure 5. LPDT2, conversing robotic avatars: Second Life (© Elif Ayiter 2010. Used with permission)

tive exhibit 'The Syncretic Sense' at the (SPACE) gallery in London in May/June 2011[7]; and as one of the works shown in the 'Uncontainable: Hyperstrata' exhibit[8] which was a part of the ISEA2011 art gallery during the early autumn of 2011 in Istanbul. In both cases, the organizers were in no position to provide a docent who could assist gallery audiences and therefore the display had to be adapted from direct, real-time immersion through an avatar to viewing a documentation of the work.

Since we had foreseen such an eventuality, we had documented the work extensively both as videos and photographs. Thus, we did in fact have ample material to work with. What we had also taken care to do whilst shooting the footage was to work in such a way that the documentational output would be of artistic merit in its own right, with proper lighting and sky settings, sound capture, diverse camera angles comprising many alternative shots of the same locations which would enable us to conduct extensive video editing. Consequently, what we obtained as an end result was not a raw documentation, but a 20 minute long, HD narrative walkthrough video of the environment which also showed the behaviors of its indigenous residents, the robotic avatars—in short, something which could be enjoyed almost as standalone artifact, that we hoped could stand in lieu of the genuine item[9]. That there was no way in which we could replicate the experiential qualities of the immersive virtual environment no matter how expertly we put together its documentation was a foregone conclusion, however we worked very diligently to minimize such loss as much as we possibly could (see Figure 6).

While at (SPACE) gallery in London we only presented the video, which was projected in a very large size onto a wall located in a darkened part of the gallery, for the 'Uncontainable: Hyperstrata' exhibit we were given an entire room at Kasa Gallery, a well regarded venue for conceptual/new media art in Istanbul. The curator of ISEA2011, Lanfranco Aceti, urged us to utilize all four walls for a documentation of the work which would also incorporate sketches, drawings, plans, diagrams and screenshots of the work that went beyond a mere showing of the video itself. This led us to the idea of creating a documentation of the entire history of La Plissure du Texte; that is not only LPDT2, the virtual incarnation of Ascott's earlier work in 2010, but also what came before it in 1983.

To achieve this we created a frieze of text, set against a dark narrow background, which went along the walls of the room. Upon this, we placed a second layer of semi-transparent screenshots of the virtual environment, as well as samples of text from 1983 and 2010. The LCD screen which showed the video was also mounted against this dark band. Thus, when walked along from left to right the informational content allowed the visitor to trace the history of Ascott's seminal work and observe its extraordinary capability for transformation, adaptation, and regeneration, as invigorative today as it was three decades ago when first conceived.

WORK IN PROGRESS

La Plissure du Texte 2 continues its residency in the open metaverse, at the independent New Genres Grid[10], started by Max Moswitzer in 2011. The decision to move out of Second Life into the open metaverse was brought about due to a pricing policy change of Linden Labs whereby the vastly reduced tier cost for non-profit land was effectively done away with. This has caused a mass exodus of many universities and non-profit organizations, as well as individuals who were renting land for their own creative endeavors, from Second Life. While it seems to us that the majority of institutions and individuals that left Second Life may have left virtual worlds as a creative/learning platform altogether, some like us, have set up in the open metaverse.

Figure 6. ISEA2011: panorama stitch showing LPDT2 at Kasa Gallery, Istanbul (© Elif Ayiter 2011. Used with permission)

While the open metaverse appears to be the future of virtual worlds, it has to be acknowledged that in its current state the technical system does not yet match Second Life when it comes to properties such as virtual physics, the workings of certain scripted objects such as sound prims[11] and the like; although the gap with regards to these is closing almost on a daily basis. While performance and stability are vastly improved to what they were even only a few years ago (indeed the improvement of these being the main factors that have made the current move feasible), again it has to be acknowledged that, although here again the gap is speedily closing, at this date Second Life is still far more stable in these regards as well. That said, it would not appear to be overly optimistic to state that when it comes to technological issues the open metaverse is likely to resolve all current shortcomings within a foreseeable future. As a point in case: Virtual Physics, the lack of which

has been a major hindrance to creative activity, is now being tested and implemented in many standalone grids and is likely to become endemic to the entire system within the next few months.

However, the main shortcoming resides neither in scripting or performance, but rather in the lack of a socio-economic system, which has brought about the proliferation of virtual goods and artifacts that is on staggering display in Second Life. For this to come about there would seem to be a need for a critical mass of player-consumers for which the, as of yet, sparse population of the open metaverse cannot account for at this moment in time. In addition, it has to be acknowledged that much of the creative activity that goes on in the metaverse needs this type of economic sustenance to come about: The goods provide the toys with which residents play, and then by extension proceed to become creatively active. In addition, it is these player-creators who come into ecologies such as LPDT2—bringing about the participation, and the level of engagement that goes towards the 'cadavre exquis' described earlier on in this chapter, that our work ultimately calls for (see Figure 8).

Consequently, in terms of the near future, a crucial portion of what needs to be accomplished is out of our own immediate control, depending upon an improvement of the overall social conditions of the open metaverse; only through which our work, which at the end of the day intrinsically relies on virtual participation, can realize its full potential.

Figure 7. LPDT2 at NGrid, 2011: the table hall and the letter columns (© Elif Ayiter 2011. Used with permission)

While we are aware of and note upon these current deficiencies, we are nonetheless optimistic for the future: Virtual worlds and the metaverse are in their infancy, and furthermore incorporate the vastly novel experience of an existence enacted through a three dimensionally materialized, and yet elusive and intangible, 'body in code'[12] that it will take some time for humankind to adjust to. While a proprietary world such as Second Life, with its rules, assistance and safeguards that are administered through a centralized authority, has made these initial steps relatively easy accomplishments for its members; the unstructured, open ended nature of the open metaverse remains as a daunting experience in which one is meant to forge one's own way in the most fundamental sense of the word.

However, with all of the shortcomings—and maybe even because of them—there also comes an exhilarating sense of creative freedom, and it is this license to do precisely as one wants that is making our current sojourn in the open metaverse so very worthwhile. Although we have stressed the importance of a virtual participation for art ecosystems in the metaverse to truly come into their own, nonetheless their absence brings about a mindset in which experimentation as well as extended contemplation and reflection upon one's own output can take place in an unhindered manner, spread over lengthy periods of time. Indeed, in the open metaverse the simulator transforms itself into something that is akin to a Real Life studio in which an artist can work in seclusion, away from prying eyes, and away from the pressure to perform that the immediate presence of art consumer avatars which the crowded milieu of Second Life tends to bring with it. We have therefore become far more experimental while we are working on the second incarnation of LPDT2.

As previously mentioned, the New Genres Grid version of LPDT2 is not a replication of what we built in Second Life. Again, some of this does have to do with technical restrictions, especially

Figure 8. LPDT2 at NGrid, 2011: selavy's spirals (© Elif Ayiter 2011. Used with permission)

those concerning physics through which we managed to obtain the deconstructed text waterfalls in Second Life.

One of the visual elements of which we have been making far greater usage of is color. Whereas the Second Life build was largely monochromatic with only judicious splashes of color here and there, in the New Genres Grid version color is used far more boldly, also painted over great expanses of space and onto large, imposing visual elements, such as 'Selavy's spirals' in the image above. While the Second Life build was highly abstracted, at New Genres Grid recognizable elements such as the tables in the entry level table hall have been integrated into the visual language. Semitransparent 'doors' textured with ASCII images and sentences from Ascott's original work are another element of this language that anchors the new installation within the historical context: The doors serve as a means of transport, as teleportation portals which take the virtual visitor from one location to another within the environment, and thus, to other portions of the text, again alluding to the textural mobility, by pleating the virtual space and allowing connections between previously distant elements. Robotic avatars have not yet been placed; however, we are planning for them to be a much greater part of the work. Unlike the Second Life build in which very few of them placed onto separate floors, in this version we plan on using much greater number, maybe even crowds of them in action—in short, as many as we can depending upon system capabilities. Yet another addition to the avatar population are clone avatars which can be manipulated to behave as intricate animated systems that operate within the architecture. Finally, the appearance of all these inhabitants is expected to be far more colorful, in accord with the ecosystem, which they are a part of.

Future Technologies

We are well aware that as online, three dimensional technologies which bring together the physical realm and virtual worlds continue to develop many new interventions to the existent structure of LPDT2, as well as entirely new structures which may or may not emerge from the already existent one can be contemplated: As an example, a potential increase in the availability of kinesthetic and somatic interfaces which can be expected to vastly augment avatar agency into states of online hyperpresence were already forecast by Frank Biocca in 1999 when he said that:

Robotic…it may be possible to develop a medium in which one feels greater "access to the intelligence, intentions, and sensory impressions of another" than is possible in the most intimate face-to-face communication. One aspect of what might be called hyperpresence" (Biocca, 1997) may be possible in the social presence domain as well. Of course, it is hard for us now to imagine a medium that can create greater intimacy than face-to-face communication. But this misses the point of social presence and the very artifice of the body itself. … But, for example, inner states might be communicated more vividly through the use of sensors that can amplify subtle physiological or nonverbal cues. These can augment the intentional and unintentional cues used in interpersonal communication to assess the emotional states and intentions of others (Biocca, 1999, pp. 113-144).

In terms of kinesthetic interfaces for avatar interactions headway is already being made by adapting devices such as Microsoft's Kinect or the Nintendo Wii controller to provide 3D gesture-based input to 3D gaming worlds and the metaverse (Sreedharan, et al., 2007, pp. 227-230).

When it comes to robotic avatars, which are a component of LPDT2 that we are paying much attention to, there is much promise for their future in a study currently conducted at the Rensselaer Polytechnic Institute, where 'Eddie' a virtual agent in Second Life has his own set of beliefs, as well as the ability to reason about these beliefs and to draw conclusions in a manner that matches the reasoning patterns of human children whose biological age corresponds to his virtual age. This includes a partially developed 'Theory of Mind,' which allows him to understand, predict and manipulate the behavior of other agents and human players (Bringsjord, et al., 2008, pp. 87-98).

In terms of display systems, much improvement is also likely to be in the offering in the immediate future. While sophisticated display systems which combined the visual/sonic experience with other sensory data have been around for quite some, recent developments lead to the hope that such systems may soon become widely available to the general public: An innovation such as the amBX[13] lighting system, originally developed by Phillips, is already impactful enough for hardware, peripheral and device manufacturers to have embarked upon the process of creating amBX enabled products for all types of users, from large businesses to home consumers. One such device which can be effectively used at home is the Sensory Effect Media Player (SEMP)[14] by means of which a team of researchers from Klagenfurt University are working upon transmitting physical effects such as lighting, wind and tremor through fans, a wrist rumbler, an enhanced sound system, and a lighting system which are most efficiently rigged up around a personal computer; presenting the effects within the real world by utilizing the amBX equipment (Wlatl, et al., 2010, pp. 124-129).

Through such novel technologies it is to be expected that interactions between humans (and as importantly those between human and non-human agents) inside virtual worlds will be taken to altogether new levels of communication over the next few years. The manner in which artistic output generated within these worlds is projected into the physical realm is also likely to undergo vast changes in the near future. In terms of our own work, we are delighted to foresee that the input of display systems such as amBX, which extend the impact of visual/sonic virtual material to encompass sensory effects as well, will vastly increase the effect of our undertakings during future Real Life showings of our work.

REFERENCES

Ascott, R. (2005). Distance makes the art grow further: Distributed authorship and telematic textuality in la plissure du texte. In Chandler & N. Neumark (Eds.), *At a Distance: Precursors to Art and Activism on the Internet,* (pp. 282-297). Cambridge, MA: MIT Press.

Ascott, R., & Shanken, E. (Eds.). (2003). *Telematic embrace: Visionary theories of art, technology, and consciousness* (pp. 109–126, 191–208). Berkeley, CA: University of California Press.

Bartram, A. (2006). *Futurist typography and the liberated text*. New Haven, CT: Yale University Press.

Biocca, F. (1999). The cyborg's dilemma: Progressive embodiment in virtual environments. *Human Factors in Information Technology, 13*, 113–144. doi:10.1016/S0923-8433(99)80011-2

Bringsjord, S., & Shilliday, A. Taylor. J., Werner, D., Clark, M., Charpentier, E., … Bringsjord, A. (2008). Toward logic-based cognitively robust synthetic characters in digital environments. In *Proceedings of the 2008 Conference on Artificial General Intelligence Conference,* (pp. 87-98). Amsterdam, The Netherlands: IOS Press.

Bulhak, A. C. (2000). *On the simulation of post-modernism and mental debility using recursive transition networks. Dept Computer Science Technical Reports*. Melbourne, Australia: Monash University.

Cahalan, J. M. (1994). The guilty forgiving the innocent: Stanislaus, Shaun, and Shem in Finnegans Wake. *Notes on Modern Irish Literature, 6*, 5–11.

Cundy, D. (1981). Marinetti and Italian futurist typography. *Art Journal, 41*(4), 349–352. doi:10.2307/776445

Hansen, M. (2006). *Bodies in code: Interfaces with digital media*. New York, NY: Routledge.

Hart, M. (1992). *The history and philosophy of Project Gutenberg*. Retrieved from http://www.gutenberg.org/wiki/Gutenberg:The_History_and_Philosophy_of_Project_Gutenberg_by_Michael_Hart

Lupton, E. (1994). A post-mortem on deconstruction? *AIGA Journal of Graphic Design, 12*(2), 45–47.

Marinetti, F. T. (1913). *Destruction of syntax—Imagination without strings—Words-in-freedom*. Retrieved from http://www.unknown.nu/futurism/destruction.html

Ryu, B. H. (2010). Your mobile is tomorrow museum. In *Exhibition Catalog of Incheon International Digital Art Festival 2010* (pp. 29, 31, 38–39). Korea: Nabi Press.

Shannon, C. (1948). A mathematical theory of communication. *The Bell System Technical Journal, 27,* 379–423.

Sreedharan, S., Zurita, E. S., & Plimmer, B. (2007). 3D input for 3D worlds. In *Proceedings of the 19th Australasian Conference on Computer-Human Interaction: Entertaining User Interfaces*, (pp. 227 – 230). New York, NY: ACM Press.

Wlatl, M., Timmerer, C., & Hellwagner, H. (2010). Increasing the user experience of multimedia presentations with sensory effects. In *Proceedings of the Quality of Multimedia Experience (QoMEX), Second International Workshop*, (pp. 124-129). IEEE Press.

KEY TERMS AND DEFINITIONS

Avatar: Originally a Sanskrit word which denotes a computer user's representation of himself/herself or alter ego, whether in the form of a three-dimensional model used in computer games, a two-dimensional icon (picture) or a one-dimensional user-name used on Internet forums and other communities. The term 'avatar' can also refer to the personality connected with the screen name or handle, of an Internet user. This sense of the word was coined by Neal Stephenson in his 1992 novel *Snow Crash*, who co-opted it from the Sanskrit word 'avatara,' which is a concept similar to that of incarnation.

Metaverse: A fictional virtual world, first described in Neal Stephenson's 1992 science fiction novel *Snow Crash*, where humans, as avatars, interact with each other and software agents, in a three-dimensional space that uses the metaphor of the real world. The word metaverse is a portmanteau of the prefix 'meta' (meaning 'beyond) and 'universe'.

ENDNOTES

[1] Avatar name: Alpha Auer.

[2] Avatar name: Selavy Oh.

[3] Avatar name: MosMax Hax.

[4] Given that 'Real Life' is the term with which virtual world residents refer to the real world which we all inhabit with our biological bodies we too shall be using these words to refer to physical realm throughout this text.

[5] Given that 'Real Life' is the term with which virtual world residents refer to the real world which we all inhabit with our biological bodies we too shall be using these words to refer to physical realm throughout this text.

[6] http://www.tate.org.uk/modern/exhibitions/bodyspacemotionthings/default.shtm

[7] http://www.spacestudios.org.uk/whats-on/exhibitions/roy-ascott-the-syncretic-sense

[8] http://isea2011.sabanciuniv.edu/other-event/uncontainable-hyperstrata

[9] http://lpdt2.blogspot.com/2011/04/documentational-video-of-second-life.html

[10] http://newgenresgrid.blogspot.com/

[11] Prim: the universal three dimensional building block of online virtual worlds, a cube of 0.5 meters in its default state.

[12] See Hansen (2006).

[13] http://www.ambx.com/

[14] http://www.youtube.com/watch?v=xWpDCABp6zg

Chapter 7
Can Duchampian and Darwinian Virtual Objects Ever Behave Themselves?

Dew Harrison
University of Wolverhampton, UK

Eugene Ch'ng
University of Birmingham, UK

ABSTRACT

The chapter presents the trajectory of a collaborative art practice towards intuitive interaction for visitors accessing virtual spaces to achieve a shared holistic understanding of a complex system. From initial explorations into the efficacy of associative media for constructing conceptual-based artworks, in that hypermedia developed from the intent of augmenting human intellect, behaviours were applied to hypermedia data items. The rationale for this is explained through developments in the ongoing 'Deconstructing Duchamp' project, where 'flocking' behaviours have been applied to Duchampian digitised items to observe the familial relations within, and key to his work, at play. Following this project, a second work 'Shift-Life' has proceeded to further develop the idea of allotting animal-like behaviours to electronic data items giving them the appearance of possessing a basic intelligence. By then, observing their response to our physical interactions, we can glean a clearer understanding from their inter-relationships of a complex conceptual framework.

INTRODUCTION

While Marcel Duchamp offered the art world one of the most complex and formative pieces of art ever, initiating the shift of values from aesthetics to idea, Charles Darwin developed the theory of evolution, the 'big' idea of survivability through adaptation. Shift-Life was created as part of the national Darwin 200 project for the international bicentenary in 2009. It is a complex system of virtual life forms struggling to survive in an environment made volatile through human interaction. Central to this installation work is the artificial life ecosystem as a self-sustaining, self-reproducing

DOI: 10.4018/978-1-4666-2961-5.ch007

equilibrium of creatures and plants living in it. The general behaviour of each organism was more sophisticated than those allotted to the 'creatures' taken from Duchamp's work, mainly his 'Large Glass,' in that they were equipped for survival strategies and the reproduction of progenies, while the Duchampian items merely adapted to familial relations. An exposition of the Shift-Life program is therefore presented followed by reflection on both projects and future directions for this collaborative research where potential emergent behaviours are concerned.

As an artist, the principal author continue to explore the extent to which hypermedia is privileged in the creation and interpretation of concept-based art. Dew Harrison's work is based on the understanding that a way forward for contemporary art practice is through this partnership of conceptual art and hypermedia technology. A view which may be seconded by current Internet artists such as Jodi, Heath Bunting, and Vuk Ćosić in that hypermedia is the structuring mechanism underlying the World Wide Web. In keeping with hypermedial concerns, the principal author creates multimedia non-linear art systems in various forms as computer technologies advance. Hypermedia art enables the viewer to connect short strands of information in ways, which make sense and give meaning to the whole work. These works have no beginning, middle, or end in the formal linear narrative sense instead they have an interface, means of navigating the system itself and offer the option to 'quit' whenever.

Neo-conceptualist art practise and hypermedia technology are both concerned with the linkage of multimedia items by their semantic associations. Hypermedia is an evolving conception of the possible applications of the computer leading to the smooth synthesis of Human-Computer Interaction (HCI). Many people have contributed to the idea but the original vision is attributed to Vannevar Bush, President Roosevelt's Science Advisor, who first approaches a description of hypertext in his article "As We May Think" published in *Atlantic Monthly* (Bush, 1945), describing a hypothetical

'Memex' analogue machine, a memory extension system which was to mimic human memory by letting the user 'browse' and make associative links between any two points in a library of scientific literature, sketches, photographs and personal notes. Bush termed this procedure "selection by association" based on an understanding of human thinking where

The human mind...operates by association. With one item in its grasp, it snaps instantly to the next that is suggested by the association of thoughts, in accordance with some intricate web of trails carried by the cells of the brain. It has other characteristics, of course; trails that are not frequently followed are prone to fade, items are not fully permanent, memory is transitory. Yet the speed of action, the intricacy of trails, the detail of mental pictures, is awe-inspiring beyond all else in nature. Man cannot hope to fully duplicate this mental process artificially, but he certainly ought to be able to learn from it...Selection by association, rather than indexing, may yet be mechanised (Bush, 1945).

This was before computer technology was sophisticated enough to fulfill the vision, he did not anticipate the power of the digital computer and so his *Memex* used microfilm and photocells to do its magic.

Almost 20 years later, Bush's work influenced Douglas Engelbart at the Stanford Research Institute (the inventor of the 'mouse') who then published "Augmenting Human Intellect: A Conceptual Framework" (Engelbart, 1962). Engelbart envisioned that computers would usher in a new stage of human evolution, characterised by "automated external symbol manipulation" and his proposed system included the human user as an essential element. The system considered the user and the computer to be dynamically changing components in a symbiosis, which had the effect of 'amplifying' the native intelligence of the user (an 'interactive' system).

He then constructed the *Augment* system, or *NLS* (oN Line System) at the Augmented Human Intellect Research Centre at the SRI in 1968 to augment human intellect. This system had a database of non-linear text, 'view filters' which selected items from this database and 'views' which structured the presentation of this information for the terminal. The availability of workstations with high-resolution displays shifted the emphasis to more graphical depictions of nodes, links and networks, such as using one window for each node.

Meanwhile another hypertext visionary was developing his own ideas about augmentation. Ted Nelson, the originator of the term "Hypertext" defined as "non-sequential writing," was creating *Xanadu* a unified literary environment on a global scale. His intention was to place the entire world's literary corpus online "Under guiding ideas which are not technical but literary, we are implementing a system for storage and retrieval of linked and windowing text." Nelson (1987) states that the value of hypertext is that "it more closely models the way we think," allowing us to explore a subject area from many different perspectives. The mental model underlying a hypermedia system is non-linear, mimicking the brain's ability to store and retrieve information by referential links for quick and intuitive access. Randall Trigg (1983) wrote the first PhD thesis on hypertext in 1983 describing non-linear text as "primitive pieces of text connected with typed links to form a network similar in many ways to a semantic net."

Semantic networks are an Artificial Intelligence (AI) concept for knowledge representation consisting of a directed graph in which concepts are represented as nodes, and the relationships between concepts are represented as the links between them. These networks are 'semantic' in that the concepts in the representation are indexed by their semantic content rather than by some arbitrary (e.g. alphabetical) ordering. Semantic networks are natural to use as related concepts tend to cluster together and an inconsistent or ill-defined concept is easily identified by its neighbouring linked concepts, which provide it

with a meaningful context. Trigg's analogy with hypertext holds where the nodes are hypertext nodes representing single ideas with links between them representing the semantic interdependencies among these ideas. Hypertext can then capture an interwoven collection of ideas without regard to their machine interpretability, which is the way semantic nets are employed by AI knowledge engineers. Hypertext, and now hypermedia, can enable the building of ideas in multimedia form into overarching concepts.

DECONSTRUCTING DUCHAMP

Hypertext has developed in parallel to Conceptual art from the 1960s, they are both concerned with the linkage of associated ideas into concepts, with the structuring of text items into meaningful associations. Where hypertext has developed into hypermedia and the connectivity of multi-media items by association, Conceptual art has moved beyond discourse to incorporate materials other than language. Contemporary art with a conceptual base now incorporates cultural imagery and social narrative resulting in works of great complexity for example Christopher Williams's (1991) *Bouquet, for Bas Jan Ader and Christopher D'Arcangelo*, a continuation of a previous piece *Angola to Vietnam* 1989. For William's work, the viewer needs to become, in part, a researcher with some knowledge of art history and social politics. Hypermedia is designed to manage complex systems in a web-like structure of interrelated items. Perhaps the most complex piece of artwork from the last century has been that of proto-Conceptualist Marcel Duchamp's 'Large Glass' entitled *La Mariée mise à nu par ses célibataires, même* or *The Bride stripped bare by her bachelors, even.* This piece, together with its accompanying 'Green Box' (Duchamp, 1934) and white box of notes *L'infinitif* (Duchamp, 1966), is generally regarded to be both the culmination and the summation of his work, occupying his thoughts between 1912-1923 when he abandoned it as finally unfinished leaving us with a seemingly unfathomable puzzle to interpret. For Duchamp, all artwork is only ever completed by the viewer's interpretation "a work of art is dependent on the explosion made by the onlooker" (Duchamp, 1957).

The *Large Glass* has been explored through re-presentation by other artists, the most well-known replicas are those of Richard Hamilton in 1966, and Ulf Linde 1961. However, the *Large Glass* together with the boxes completes a corpus of non-linear, semantically associated ideas ripe for transposing into hypermedia. Although there are many Duchamp websites available online for example the Dada Companion, the Marcel Duchamp World Community, none are artist re-presentations using the hypermedia format of the Web. While Andrew Stafford's *Making Sense of Duchamp* is an excellent timeline of Duchamp's work and ideas it is in a linear, un-linked form which does not exploit the Web's hypermedial affordances. The sites of P.22, Tony Smith and Fresh Widow 3000 are specific to the inter-linkage of ideas within the *Large Glass*, but then they were all part of the initial *Deconstructing Duchamp* project set up to transpose the work into a hypermedia system.

Duchamp's body of work is riddled with cross-references and complex meanings generating many different interpretations through its apparent ambiguity. The *Large Glass*, was originally constructed as a 9' x 5' sheet of glass with abstract forms over 88 years ago, this display of connected ideas was the nearest Duchamp could get to his goal. It is only recently that technology has made possible that which was impossible in Duchamp's time. Duchamp was exploring ways of portraying his 'Bride' in the 4th dimension he began with painterly abstractions of the figure culminating in the flatness of glass as a material nearing 'no thickness' or 'inframince' and therefore acting as signifier to the fourth dimension. He replaced traditional (thick) paint and canvas as tools for picture making and renounced painting, declaring his *Large Glass* to be "a three-dimensional physical medium in a fourth-dimensional perspective"

(Duchamp, 1966). From Duchamp's notes, mostly in the 'White Box,' it would seem that his interest in the 4th dimension was not aligned to the, then contemporary, 'relativity theory' proposed by Einstein but to the ideas of Poincaré, that the 4th dimension could be understood through geometry progressing from the n-dimension.

A single point has zero dimensions, two points define a line and have one dimension, two lines create a plane and have two dimensions, two planes create a volume or a three dimensional space or object so what do two volumes create? Duchamp suggested that they should create a fourth dimensional space/object. Western art has been traditionally concerned with 2D representations of 3D spaces. Duchamp considered that if 2D images could stand for a world of 3D images it would follow that 3D objects could represent things in a 4D world. He conceived the 'Bride' as a 3D representation of a 4D being, as a "two-dimensional representation of a three-dimensional bride who herself would be the projection of a four-dimensional bride in the three-dimensional world" (Duchamp, 1966). Painters are 2D artists working on a flat plane, sculptors are 3D artists working with objects/space and now we have digital artists working in the 4D of cyberspace concerned with the space/object incorporating time.

In order to project Duchamp's Bride into the fourth dimension of cyberspace for a closer understanding, the Internet was the perfect vehicle for my first hypermedia version of his *Large Glass* and *4D Duchamp* was constructed, within the on-going project *Deconstructing Duchamp*. *4D Duchamp* was a collaborative venture involving 25 participants to lateralise the *Large Glass* by reconfiguring the work from a material 2D field into 25 interlinked elements across the electronic Network field. Each element of the *Large Glass*, e.g. 9 Malic moulds, the Chocolate Grinder, the Bride etc., had its own Web page for an artist's response, gathering the ideas, theories, quotes, diagrams, illustrations, sounds, images...surrounding that particular element. The *Large Glass* was then structured in the fourth dimensional space of the Internet by the inter-linkage of its element websites. Linkage was arranged through the semantic associations within the *Large Glass* elements according to Duchamp's notes. The discrete elements were thus connected across the world into the overarching concept of the *Large Glass*, finally presenting the Bride in her fourth dimensional world (Harrison, 1997).

Other pieces in the *Deconstructing Duchamp* project followed suite, being hypermedia based they were all interactive and relied on the point and click, and rollover of mouse, keypad and screen projection. Online and offline works were created and developed towards a closer engagement between viewer and work. As technologies have advanced towards invisible and pervasive computing, so have methods of interaction moved towards smoother immersion for the viewer. More recent pieces are exploring the semantic inter-linkage within Duchamp's ideas using animation and 'flocking' to reveal their relationships and coherence within the *Large Glass* conceptual framework. The Bride and her bachelors are being allotted behaviours to allow them to return to their familial co-items from the *Large Glass* and boxes of notes. Scanned images of Duchampian objects and writings reduced in scale are each being given animal flocking behaviours such as 'follow the one in front,' to allow them to swarm and herd into male/female positions on the screen. When an item is mouse-held, it expands to a larger image, and when released it shrinks back and moves around to find its family. The small images are slightly blurred giving them the appearance of micro-organic life forms swimming around the screen (see Figure 1).

SHIFT-LIFE

The strange Duchampian life-forms led to the next work *Shift-Life* commissioned for the International Darwin bicentenary where the idea of allotting animal behaviours to data objects has been em-

ployed to elicit an understanding of adaptation and survival. *Shift-Life* was created for exhibition at 'Shift-Time—a festival of ideas' in Shrewsbury, UK—Darwin's birthplace. A number of artists have worked with AI life-forms and intuitive interfaces, for example Jane Prophet's screened virtual world of artificial creatures *Technosphere*, 1995, although this afforded no hands-on interaction, and Squid Soup's *Pest Control 2*, 2010, which is similar to *Shift-Life* in that the virtual bug-like creatures are projected into a physical box, however this interactive installation allows visitors to play with their 'glow bugs' only, there is no ecosystem involved. The *Shift-Life* interactive installation focused on the 'hands-on' potential for witnessing a Darwinian process, the survival of the fittest, in alternate biology as they struggled to adapt to a volatile environment.

Figure 1. Flocked Duchampian objects (©2008, Dew Harrison. Used with permission)

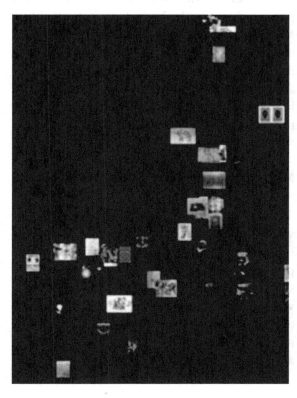

AI behaviours were embodied within a virtual world of fantasy animated objects designed by animator Sam Moore and featured as 2D 'jelly sweet' creatures and 'pick and mix sweet' plants. Their self-sustainable world was projected into a wooden sand-pit box equipped with hidden sensors, where visitors could then cause physical upheavals in their virtual environment by directly pouring in liquids, hammering on the box to simulate earthquakes, and adjusting a physical light source and temperature to increase the virtual sunlight and temperature, to which the bug-like creatures would respond instantly in an attempt to survive. The anthropological 'virtual climate change' via physical interfaces has both positive and negative consequences. The reward or penalty is simple, creatures adaptable to change survive and those unable to adapt die, creatures at the fringe of survival are weakened and produce less progeny.

In response to Darwin's 'big idea,' the aim of this work was to create an 'alternate' biological life as a set of artificial or virtual organisms that possessed similar biological processes to their 'real' counterparts, such as growth, reproduction, and adaptation. The virtual life forms existed in a nutritional (trophic) relationship of predator/prey, and included both rooted (sessile) and free roaming (vagile) organisms. Animal-intelligence was programmed into the virtual organisms to allow them survival strategies.

Mixed Reality Sand-Pit Box Interface

The interface between the physical and the virtual world is the construction of a pervasive computing sand-pit box (Figure 2). The virtual world is projected onto a piece of semi-transparent muslin sheet covering a 1.2m^2 wooden box half-filled with polystyrene beads representing the physical terrain of the virtual environment. The interface to the virtual world is via electronic sensors that are connected to 'tools' of climate change.

Figure 2. The shift-life installation. A mixed-reality sand-pit box showing the projected virtual world on the muslin sheet covering the polystyrene bead terrain. Climate change physical to virtual interfaces can be seen around the borders of the table. (©2009, Dew Harrison. Used with permission)

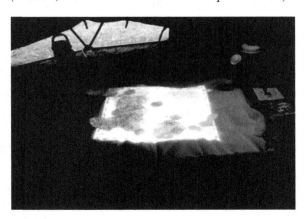

The set of manipulative tools which, when activated, could affect in real-time the projected virtual world of creatures causing them to adapt to survive in their rapidly changing ecosystem. The tools were for hammering earthquakes that affects the stability of the landscape, watering (directly into the box, into the virtual watering holes of the projected virtual world) to alter the humidity and *pH* count of the planet environment and altering light sources to affect temperature and depth of shade. The sensor network was centralised and reported back in a best-effort fashion. A number of optimisations were made to enable the application to appear to be responding immediately.

These physical interfaces allowed visitors to change the condition of the virtual environment supporting the creatures. These interfaces encouraged interactivity for visitors who could use the watering cans, lights, and hammers to radically alter the living conditions of the virtual creatures in their ecosystem. From their activities around and inside the box, visitors could see immediate responses from the animated ecosystem as the projected bug-like 'sweets' creatures adapted to survive. Interaction with the real world landscape and observing its instant affect on the creatures, proffered an understanding of how causing change in environmental conditions enforces the Darwinian concept on resident life forms (see Figure 3).

Sweet Bugs as Actors in the Virtual World

In attempting to both respond to the idea of a young Darwin and to elucidate his adult thinking in a holistic hands-on way, the bug-like creatures in the box reflected his childhood interest in natural life forms by taking the form of jelly sweets and allsorts. Darwin was born and spent his childhood in Shrewsbury, where he began his vast collection of beetles leading to his great insights later in life. The virtual fantasy creature aesthetic was developed as a 'sweet' bug form to make them as approachable as possible to a cross-generational audience diverse in multimedia and games experience. The images moved away from the hyper-reality aesthetic of computer-games towards a deliberate mixed-reality-neither digital nor real. The creatures were bright and cartoon-like; they are essentially flat 2D graphics. They were overtly rather than covertly 'made', and referenced a clear fantasy world avoiding any photo-realism. The bugs were based on 'pick-and-mix' sweets; the carnivore was a 'liquorice allsort,' the herbivore was a jelly sweet and the varied foliage (for shade, sustenance, etc.) were based around a selection of penny sweets. The creatures were two-dimensional in that they were to be observed from above and were given a set of biological preferences and behaviour embodied within them. The herbivores were much larger than their predators and had good eyesight while the carnivores, though small and short sighted, had a fast scuttling gait compared to the lumbering movement of their prey, this balanced the relationship.

The trophic network ecosystem comprises of a hierarchical level of individual, meta-population, community, and environment. There are two species of creatures and three types of vegetation. These are herbivores, carnivores, and plants, which are edible, poisonous, and a large tree that acts as a canopy. The organisms were short-lived (60 seconds minimum and 150 seconds maximum). The general behaviour of each organism concerned its survivability and the reproduction of progenies. The survival of the entire ecosystem depended on the balance of the organisms that inhabited the landscape. If the predator out-grew the prey, an imbalance would occur and the system would perish. If the prey out-grew the edible plants, the food would be scarce leaving the system in a dilemma. If the canopies (large trees) over-reproduced, the predator had little space left to hunt. If the red poison plants outgrew the vegetation, more herbivores would eat them and become toxic; consequently, their newly acquired toxicity would kill the carnivores. When the environment particularly suited them, a plant species would thrive (the poison plants loved high pH levels). The difficulty of such development was the maintenance of equilibrium within the complex system.

The herbivore and carnivore individuals are characterised by:

- **Dynamics:** Speed (hunting, fleeing), eyesight, Field-of-View (FOV).
- **Physique:** Age, deterioration (affects the maximum age), energy, hunger threshold, flesh index.
- **Behaviour:** Impulse, safe distance (security boundary), feeding distance.
- **Reproduction:** Number of progenies, and sexual maturity.
- **Ecology:** Adaptability to sunlight, temperature, seismic vibrations, and humidity.

Figure 3. An illustration depicting the mixed-reality interface: a physical sandpit with electronic sensors that interface the virtual world (©2009, Eugene Ch'ng. Used with permission)

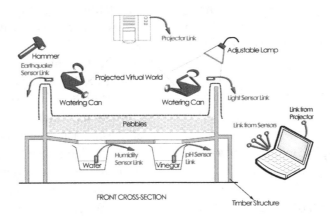

Vegetation are characterised by: energy, resource index, seed count, reproduction age, dispersal distance, and the ecology of the virtual environment—adaptability to sunlight, temperature, soil *pH*, availability of space and humidity. Populations are characterised by size (the number of individuals in a given species) and the community interacts within their trophic network. Populations can be controlled (culled) when a threshold is reached. The simulation environment is discrete, i.e., the smallest unit of movement is one pixel, and time is discrete. Carnivores, herbivores, and vegetation have different behaviours. The sections below describe their rules.

Sweets Plant Behaviour

The plant behaviour is a simplified version of an Individual-Based Model (Ch'ng, 2009) presented in another paper (Ch'ng, 2011). The simplified model has minor changes to suit the difference in the creatures' sensing of environmental factors generated by the electronics sensor networks. The process and scheduling of a single plant in each time step is described in the pseudo code below. Within each time step processes (simple rules) occur—state changes, growth, interaction, adaptation, reproduction, and senescense:

```
For Vegetation
  Sense the environment (Temperature,
Sunlight, Humidity, pH level, Space)
  Grow (aging) and die of senescence
(Maximum age)
  Compete with nearby plants for
space
  Reproduce when sexual maturity is
reached
  Die when the fitness is depleted
```

The environmental factors that the agents take into account are temperature, sunlight, humidity and soil *pH*. Competition for space and the risk of being consumed by Herbivores are threats in the environment. Each environmental factor is measured by the Adaptability Measure (*AM*) (Ch'ng, 2007) and contributes to the fitness measure,

$$f_i^t = \varphi_i \left(CTS\eta \right)_i^t \tag{1}$$

where the output of *AM* for each fitness related to biotic or abiotic interactions are computed: φ_i is the interaction fitness of the *pH* level of the soil for plant *i*, C_i^t is the only biotic local interaction fitness of the current condition C_i^t (Equation 3) at time t, T_i^t is the interaction fitness of the plant related to the temperature, S_i^t is the fitness affected by the sunlight and η_i^t is the fitness of the plant in the current humidity. The interaction of the factors is a logical way for deciding the fitness of the plant. The variable Resource Index ρ, defined as the storage of energy is decremented $K=1$ unit in the condition in Equation 2. Death occurs when

$$\rho_i^{t+\Delta t} \leq 0.0. \qquad (2)$$

Plant competes for land resources. The collective occupation of the space used by the competing plants contributes to the accumulated space C_i^t at time t for the plant i in Equation 3. Competition for space is defined as an interaction. A plant interacts with its neighbour in the condition shown in Box 1, where n is the number of competing plants, and P_i is the effective space used by a single plant. $P_i = 0.05$ if the undergrowth species (vegetable or poison) competes against its own species, $P_i = 0.12$ if the undergrowth compete against a canopy, and $P_i = 0.2$ among canopy competition. The differences in P_i adjusts the space so that the canopies are not too crowded together. $O_{x,y}^t$ is the position of the competitor and $u_{x,y}^t$ is the position of the source plant at time t. O_{size}^t and u_{size}^t, , O_{age}^t and u_{age}^t are respectively the diameter and the age of the two competing plants.

Growth and reproduction depended on the simulation time. Plants aged by the milliseconds and die when the maximum age is reached. Reproduction for Canopy and Vegetable depends on the parameter Reproduction Age and the number of seeds s. Poison plant reproduces quicker on the high pH level of the soil. Reproduction simply disperses the seeds in every direction of the parent plant. The pseudo code below describes the process:

```
For Canopy and Vegetable
  nextReproductionAge = lastReproduc-
tionAge + reproductionAge
  IF age ≥ nextReproductionAge
Reproduce n seeds
lastReproductionAge = age
For Poison
  nextReproductionAge = lastReproduc-
tionAge + reproductionAge
  IF age ≥ nextReproductionAge -
acidity (φ)
Reproduce s seeds
lastReproductionAge = age
The variable acidity is conditional:
φ=10 IF pH ≥ 0.9, φ=5 IF 0.6 ≤ pH <
0.9, ELSE φ=0
```

Sweets Carnivore and Herbivore Behaviour

Similar to plants, carnivores and herbivores senses the environment, but via their eyesight within the field of view (90°). Creatures roam the landscape when not feeding. When they are hungry, they target the lower food chain and chases after them. Predator behaviour and prey fleeing behaviour uses energy reserves, when energy is low, the creatures rest. The process and scheduling of the creatures in each time step is described in the pseudo code below. Within each time step processes (simple rules) occur-state changes (see Figure 1 and Figure 2), growth, interaction, adaptation, feeding/fleeing, reproduction, and inheritance, and senescense:

```
For Carnivore
  Sense the environmental (Tempera-
ture, Sunlight, Humidity, Earthquake)
  Change States
  Grow (aging) and die of senescence
  Avoid Canopy and Poison
  Reproduce when sexual maturity is
reached
  Die when the fitness is depleted
```

Box 1.

$$c_i^t = \sum_{i=1}^{n} P_i \left[\sqrt{\left(O_x^t - u_x^t \right)^2 + \left(O_y^t - u_y^t \right)^2} - \left(O_{size}^t + u_{size}^t \right) < 0 \right] \left[O_{size}^t \geq u_{size}^t \right] \left[O_{age}^t \geq u_{age}^t \right],$$

$$\text{for } 0 \leq c_i^t \leq 1$$

(3)

For Herbivore
  Sense the environmental (Temperature, Sunlight, Humidity, Earthquake)
  Change States
  Grow (aging) and die of senescence
  Avoid Carnivore
  Change colour when toxic plant eaten
  Reproduce when sexual maturity is reached
  Die when the fitness is depleted

The adaptability measure (Ch'ng, 2007) is used for measuring the fitness of the environment. The environmental factors are temperature, sunlight, and humidity:

$$f_j^t = \left(TS\eta \right)_j^t$$

(4)

where the output of *AM* for each fitness related to environmental interactions is computed: T_j^t is the interaction fitness of creature j at time t in the current temperature, S_j^t refers to the interaction fitness with sunlight, and η_j^t is the fitness in the current humidity. When $f_j \leq 0.0$ the agent dies.

Carnivores and herbivores aged in milliseconds, when the maximum age is reached, they die. Reproduction depends on the parameter *Maturity Age Ratio*, *Reproduction Age* and the number of *Progenies n*. The pseudo code below describes the process:

For Carnivore and Herbivore
  IF age ≥ age*MaturityAgeRatio
    nextReproductionAge=lastReproductionAge+reproductionAge
  IF age ≥ nextReproductionAge
    Reproduce n number of progenies
    lastReproductionAge = age

The *Maturity Age Ratio* formula below describes the number of progenies,

$$\varsigma_j^{t+\Delta t} = \varsigma_j^0 + \frac{1}{1 + e^{\left(1 - A_j^{-1} 4t \right)}}$$

(5)

where g is a constant ($g=5.0$) is the *Rate of Growth* to reach full size, it is the growth spurt, A_j is the *Maximum Age* of the agent, and ς_j^0 is the *Initial Size* of creature at birth (see Figure 4).

EXPERIMENTS ON LOCATION

The wooden virtual bug box was large enough to allow for small groups of people, families, and individuals to interact with it and with each other, it was accessible to both children and adults. The box was equipped with sensors to respond to the visitors' actions and relate their physical activities directly to the virtual ecosystem projected into it. As they poured water, for instance, the humidity would alter and some species of plants that are intolerable of the condition may die, this would mean less food for the herbivore (green jelly sweet bugs), and consequently less bugs to eat for the carnivores (pink predators). Switching the lamp on would dry out the atmosphere and enable plants to grow again, however too much 'sun' might be detrimental to the point of wiping out the carnivores entirely. They could, in fact, become extinct due to their reproduction method of cloning, unlike the egg laying herbivores. When this occurred, we had to re-start the programme to reassure the smaller children that they were not responsible for a complete genocide! Pouring vinegar (poison) from a watering can would 'feed' the red poison plants, toxic to all the creatures except for the herbivores. This condition could be remedied by pouring baking soda liquid (plant food) for restoring the *pH* balance of the soil. As herbivores consume the toxic plants, poison saturates their bloodstreams until biological processes flush it away tens of seconds later. Carnivores which happen to eat these herbivores would die of poison. Hammering on the box sends the carnivores into panic mode and they would spin around and run for cover under the trees—in the alternate biology, the carnivores are the only creatures that are afraid of earthquakes.

The low-tech approach to a hi-tech installation encouraged active participation but also a state of contemplation and reflection in passively observing other people's actions and watching the subsequent life form changes taking place. The jelly bug world was set at a self-sustainable and stable level without the intervention from human meddling and as such was visually mesmerising, it was essentially a sugar-coated version of 'nature red in tooth and claw.' Through listening to the participants' conversations, it was evident that there was room for deep thought, where the virtual world could be understood as an analogy for human activity and its effect on global climate change within our own real world.

DISCUSSIONS

From both these projects, *Deconstructing Duchamp* and *Shift-Life*, we have employed basic artificial life behaviours by applying them to data objects, these objects have been grouped into families or types of virtual creatures and exist in a sustainable but simplistic social order. However, according to Reynolds (1987), 'Flocking' can give rise to emergent behaviours in that allocating the same set of behaviours to each entity within one family, and then situating that family in an environment shared with others, each with their own familial traits, may lead to unpredictable shifts in the behavioural patterns. This leads the project to conjecture that if more sophisticated behaviours were allotted to our digital creatures, could they organise themselves into more complex social systems?

Would the Shift-Life animals evolve their social orderings with or without human intervention, as a means of survival? We could certainly extend the behavioural perimeters to include features such as procreation, multiplication, fighting and cannibalism, hiding and carrying, within the Shift-Life world. We could also allow for extra environmental changes in their physical environment (the sandbox) for them to adapt to, such as chasms appearing from the earthquakes (hammer action), or strong winds (from blowing instruments) damaging plants and burying creatures. To what extent could they work together to survive, as a positive analogy for coping with environmental change?

Would the Duchampian objects begin to arrange themselves into new forms of thoughts and ideas from Duchamp's oeuvre? The data items exist as text, image, sounds, and short animations and tend to signify Duchamp's larger ideas, which have had, and continue to have, a significant impact on the art world. His art pieces have been determinedly left in an incomplete state as 'open works,' waiting for closure by the viewer via interpretation and re-readings as each new generation

Figure 4. Shift-life life forms. The projected virtual world showing different periods of the simulation. Top left: the carnivores emerge from the canopies after an earthquake, top right: newly hatched herbivores heading towards the clusters of edible plants, bottom left: carnivorous feeding frenzy. Two herbivores have died (multi-shaded blobs) due to being attacked by a carnivore. Bottom right: herbivores clustering around the group of plants. Some carnivores have died due to senescence and the poison from a herbivore that has just eaten from a poisonous plant. (©2009 Dew Harrison. Used with permission)

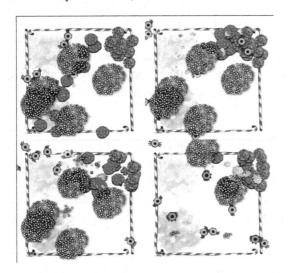

meets them. We now live in a hi-tech culture surrounded by computers in our everyday environs, we use laptops, digital tablets, and smart phones to communicate and exchange information, and play interactive electronic games for entertainment. We have the capability of bestowing Duchamp's writings and imagery with behaviours to allow them to have familial traits. If we were to give more precise behaviours beyond basic flocking, would the texts and images begin to make another sense than that achieved from linear readings of his work and ideas—and would these be more in keeping with our computer literate culture? Such a cut-and-paste approach, re-combining his texts

and images into shifting positions of semantically associated new meanings would be absolutely within the Duchampian methodology of wit, play and chance, particularly if the re-positioning were achieved from the emergent behaviour of the objects themselves.

CONCLUSION

From a review of earlier work exploring a positive alliance between the developing hypermedia technology and concept-based art where both were concerned with the semantic association of ideas into overarching concepts, a place was made for bestowing animal-like behaviours to multimedia data objects. The subject for this alliance was initially the *Large Glass* of Marcel Duchamp, which was transposed into the fourth dimension of cyberspace where Duchamp intended his original idea to live. The first transposition within the *Deconstructing Duchamp* project produced the piece *4D Duchamp*, which consisted of 25 inter-linked websites directly related to the *Large Glass*. Subsequent pieces ensued with each moving towards more intuitive and participatory interactions and finally bringing the notion of allotting flocking behaviours to Duchampian graphic and text objects. These small, blurred graphic forms resembled micro-biotic life forms and informed a new work commissioned by Shrewsbury Museum Service and funded by Arts Council England to create a work in response to Darwin's theory of evolution, adapt to survive.

The hands-on installation *Shift-Life* is a virtual ecosystem of sweet-like herbivores and carnivores, they have been given sets of behaviours according to the needs of their type, and are shaped and coloured to give visual indications of their groupings. The creatures exist in a stable environment until visitors arrive to disrupt their world with hammers, light source, watering cans, etc. This is a mixed-reality work where the virtual world is projected onto the real world—the sandbox pit surrounded with sensors and implements which, when activated, directly alters the ecosystem of the virtual life forms. Interaction is relational and participatory, intuitive and with immediate responses, the installation also allows for quiet contemplation and deeper considerations of creature behaviour and survivability in volatile environments. The installation with its virtual creatures is a complex adaptive system where simple rules and biological determinants generate collective behaviour.

These two projects now require new considerations. One concerning the intuitive nature of the interface, which needs developing towards a sustainable system that still allows a smooth and more natural access to the ecosystem for *Shift-Life* visitors. Squid Soup's *Pest Control 2* had a different agenda to *Shift-Life* but presents an excellent example of an intuitive interface where the projected light-stencils of insect-like creatures appear to respond directly to visitor actions, for example, running away from being touched. *Shift-Life* can accommodate this closer relationship between visitor and creature while addressing environmental changes in the ecosystem for the creatures to respond to. A second consideration is for expanding sets of behaviours, currently 3 links per set, and the number of creatures to enable self-organisation. The potentials for emergent behaviour and self-organisation (De Wolf Holvoet, 2005) in the mixed-reality interactive installation could be fully realised when opportunities for coordination-based simple rules and behaviours are bestowed on both the Darwinian and Duchampian virtual creatures. It is only when we experiment with larger installations with a wider range of sensors, thousands of bugs and a 10 link set of behaviours for each one, can we truly begin to observe emergent dynamics in Darwinian and Duchampian virtual creature adaptability and survival, and display new ideas and understandings for art within the Duchampian oeuvre.

REFERENCES

Bush, V. (1945). As we may think. *Atlantic Magazine, 176*, 641–649.

Ch'ng, E. (2007). Modelling the adaptability of biological systems. *The Open Cybernetics and Systemics Journal, 1*, 13–20.

Ch'ng, E. (2009). An artificial life-based vegetation modelling approach for biodiversity research. In Chiong, R. (Ed.), *Nature-Inspired Informatics for Intelligent Applications and Knowledge Discovery: Implications in Business, Science and Engineering*. Hershey, PA: IGI Global. doi:10.4018/978-1-60566-705-8.ch004

Ch'ng, E. (2011). Spatially realistic positioning of plants for virtual environments: Simple biotic and abiotic interaction for populating terrains. *IEEE Computer Graphics and Applications, 99*.

De Wolf, T., & Holvoet, T. (2005). Emergence versus self-organisation: Different concepts but promising when combined. *Lecture Notes in Computer Science, 3464*, 1–15. doi:10.1007/11494676_1

Duchamp, M. (1934). *Green box*. Paris, France: Rrose Sélavy.

Duchamp, M. (1957). The creative act. *ARTnews, 56*, 28–29.

Duchamp, M. (1966). *L'infinitif*. New York, NY: Cordier & Ekstrom.

Engelbart, D. (1962). *Augmenting human intellect: A conceptual framework*. Palo Alto, CA: Stanford Research Institute.

Harrison, D. (1997). Hypermedia as art system. *Art Journal, 56*(3), 55–59. doi:10.2307/777837

Nelson, T. (1987). *Computer lib/dream machines* (revised ed.). Redmond, WA: Tempus Books.

Reynolds, C. (1987). Flocks, herds, and schools: A distributed behavioral model. In *Proceedings of the Computer Graphics, SIGGRAPH 1987 Conference*. ACM Press.

Trigg, R. (1983). *A network-based approach to text handling for the online scientific community*. College Park, MD: University of Maryland.

KEY TERMS AND DEFINITIONS

Associative Media: Computer applications that enable the linkage of data items through semantic association, for example Hypermedia, which uses associative relationships amongst information contained within multiple media data. 'Associative relations' is a term used by Ferdinand de Saussure for what later came to be called technologies or a broad understanding of media.

Behaviours: Refers to AI behaviours, the coding of digital objects with animal/human-like behaviours, for example 'flocking' first introduced into an arcade game, 'Rip-Off,' in 1980, and first simulated on a computer as 'Boids,' in 1986.

Bio-Life System: A digital ecosystem of virtual life-forms mimicking real-life. An alife modeling approach will generally seek to decipher the most simple and general principles underlying life and implement them in a simulation.

Darwinian: Relating to the ideas of English Scientist Charles Darwin, 1809-1882. The first of the evolutionary biologists, and originator of the concept of natural selection.

Duchampian: Relating to the ideas of the French born artist Marcel Duchamp, 1887-1968. Considered by many as the forefather of Conceptual Art.

Mixed-Reality: Refers to the merging of real and virtual worlds, where both reality and virtuality are augmented to interface with and produce new environments.

Chapter 8
The Virtual and Interdisciplinarity

Alistair Payne
Glasgow School of Art, UK

ABSTRACT

This chapter explores the philosophical notion of The Virtual in response to the writings of Gilles Deleuze and unfolds this thinking through its interdisciplinary and transformative affects upon contemporary fine art. The Virtual will be discussed in relation to forms of contemporary painting, yet provides a model for thinking through interdisciplinarity within, and from, other media. The Virtual acts as an instigator for change, which effectively destabilises the pre-formity[1] attached to medium-specific practices. It is for this reason that The Virtual forces external relationships and connections to come to the fore in order to radically alter and transform the physical and conceptual constructs of different disciplines. This chapter will highlight these important ideas and present new ways to consider The Virtual in relation to contemporary fine art practice, with a particular focus upon current issues in Painting.

INTRODUCTION

I was invited to write this chapter in response to a video discussion on the virtual created for a panel at the ISEA conference in 2011. It was evident that the ideas that were being proposed from my perspective were very different from thinking around the virtual in relation to digital media and technologies.

Therefore, it is important to emphasise that the writing in this chapter has directly evolved from my practice as a painter. Having trained in painting, concerns relating to its contemporary condition led directly to my doctoral and post-doctoral research. This chapter examines the notion of the virtual from a philosophical perspective and so proposes an understanding of the virtual that is different from common parlance relating the virtual directly to, or embedded within, the digital.

This chapter outlines the relevance of the virtual as a philosophical idea that leads towards interdisciplinarity and will be articulated through the practice of painting, using contemporary architectural theory as an exemplar for the practi-

DOI: 10.4018/978-1-4666-2961-5.ch008

cal application of the idea. Examples of my own practice will also be discussed in order to present how the notion of the virtual can potentially be actualised in form.

Questions surrounding the condition of contemporary painting particularly its formal concerns, have led towards new thinking in relation to painting, specifically as an 'expanded practice'[3] (Krauss, 2002). Formal methods effectively lead towards a 'grounding'[4] within the questioning of the specific materiality of painting, in terms of how this affects its closure or completeness and the creation of its identity as a (specific) object—painting.

The contemporary condition of painting constitutes it as a vastly expanded form, which leads towards potential methods for rethinking the characteristics or traits of a, or the, medium employed within the work. The many questions regarding the limits and/or boundaries of painting drive the physical and structural problematics of its condition. These physical (or structural) questions have necessitated the examination, or testing, of the perceived boundaries of painting. The most prominent form, or type of painting practice, which typifies this method, is an internally structured critique of the medium. Where this may change the physical material dynamic of the work, it does not question that materiality, but rather examines the physical limitations of the materials thought to constitute painting. This consequently leads towards a structural or formal shift in the materiality of painting, yet, can be said to relate and conform to its particular identity as painting through the materials themselves. This form of rigorous internal questioning obviously leads towards difference in terms of the physical structure of 'painting' however, this difference is still determined through the constraints the medium itself presents. This chapter highlights alternative possibilities in order to challenge, transform, and rethink the potential of painting as a contemporary practice.

In this context, the notion of change needs to be considered and defined in terms of its importance and how it can be forced into action. Change is not simply the reordering or internal deconstruction of prior arrangements in order to instigate difference within. It is also *not* the shift within a process that instigates a subtle altering of specific identity. In fact, the idea that identity should have this internal focus is alien to the proposition that will be promoted. That is to say that the specifics of particular identity (in terms of painting – or other alternative media), needs to be re-established, for, this is not a search for truth or the essence of 'being' of a thing but rather a very different way of thinking. This involves investigating an opening of 'systems' across boundaries or alternatively where territorial or boundaried 'schematics' are not perceived as (or to be) static and internally specific. This opening of systems also presents a position and the potential for painting to be less reliant upon internal combinations (oppositions or contradictions) for change and the creation of the new.

In contrast to the acceptance of the physical constraints of the medium, this chapter presents an alternative approach to the idea of painting (establishing a method for rethinking other media or disciplines) and constructs new and different ways for painting to be thought. In effect, the investigation of Gilles Deleuze's discussion of the notion of 'the Virtual' instigates an interdisciplinary approach towards painting where *external* connections and relationships are introduced and developed. This equates to the opposite position of the internal critique of medium particularity or specificity connected to the Hegelian (dialectical) dependence of Clement Greenberg's formalist critique, and will radically alter the way in which painting can be created and consequently thought.

Research into the notion of the 'Virtual,' which advances the potential for an interdisciplinary practice driven from painting, effectively constitutes a new methodological model for thinking through the space of painting, as well as the material structural qualities of painting. In contrast to prior methodological models used, primarily within the critique (or theorisation) of painting, an investigation into Deleuze's methodological processes creates a more open position within, or from which to challenge and redefine the limits or constraints of painting.

Interdisciplinarity is an often-used term through which connections between things, and in particular reference to fine art practice, different media can be discussed. In this specific context the ideas of interdisciplinarity stem from a particular position, that of painting, a discipline well known for its internally focused critique and rejection to all that is exterior to, or different from it (Greenberg, 1995). By exploring the potential of the outside, external forces, or those things that do not normally pertain to the specific characteristics or traits of the medium, a greater series of connections and relationships can be established. In turn, this radically alters the potential construction and structural dynamics of the work. For example (as will be discussed), the space of painting can shift, changing the conventional static and two-dimensional constraints within painting, towards the inclusion of movement, fluidity and three-dimensionality. The form of the work alters through these connections (for which the virtual is the instigator) whilst at the same time retaining, or allowing painting to persist. These ideas (aims) challenge the theoretical and practical identity of the work as painting, whilst serving to explore new and under-considered possibilities for the work, essentially this proposes a form of 'becoming,' or 'becoming-other' through externality, a liminal space for the construction of painting as a contemporary practice.

The key literature surrounding the philosophical notion of the virtual; is proposed through Henri Bergson and later taken up by Deleuze in *Difference and Repetition*. Brian Massumi in *Parables for the Virtual*, John Rajchman in *Constructions*

and *The Deleuze Connections* and Elizabeth Grosz in *Becomings and the Time of the Future* as well as *Time Travels* also propose the potential of the virtual. Often this can be seen in very abstract terms; however, there is a practical application of the virtual, which will be discussed through the practice of painting and its interdisciplinary potential later within this chapter.

THE VIRTUAL

The Virtual acts as a method for actualising change, and this chapter will focus upon the notion, or concept, of the virtual and actual according to Bergson and Deleuze. It explores how these ideas can radically alter the way in which contemporary (painting) practice can be made and considered. Initially, an outline of the virtual in this context needs to be discussed, thus presenting the potential of the virtual from a position within painting, forcing or moving towards painting as an interdisciplinary practice.

The virtual is bound into the process of becoming, but not a becoming through a systematic (or concrete) dialectical method; this is an open-ended becoming, where the virtual can be seen as a series of potentials. Rajchman discusses the notion of the virtual in 'Constructions' (2000) and states that,

The idea of the Virtual is quite old. The word comes from virtus, meaning potential or force, and often comes coupled with the actual, that through which the potential or force becomes at once visible and effective (p. 115).

Deleuzian philosophy is based within the virtual; it is the virtual that constructs the actual and the actual that is defined by its virtual intensities. These virtual intensities are the becoming actual of the virtual and this is not used as a way of defining the actual in the sense that it will subsequently have its own identity but rather it is a method for opening the actual to continual and further virtualities. The term 'becoming' here relates to that which is to come, and is directly linked to the virtual, as the virtual itself is tied to the process of becoming as the action of that becoming. As Massumi suggests in 'Parables for the Virtual,' "… the virtual does not exist. It comes into being, as becoming. Its nature is to come to be: to make ingress" (Massumi, 2002. p. 237).

It is in this way that the virtual through this process of becoming opens a different series of potential through which ideas and structural form can develop. The virtual creates, through becoming, a more open future. It is based within this 'open' future or 'to-come' that dramatic change, a shift in the internal dynamics of form (or the interdisciplinary potential evident in external connections), can take place.

The virtual, and therefore the notion that it is becoming or embedded in the process of (continual) becoming[s], focuses upon it being an instigator, or trigger, for change, highlighting difference and a way to upset or disorientate stability and control, through newness, creativity and innovation (Grosz, 1999, p. 16). The virtual's coexistence with and relationship to the actual are both linked to the possibility of openness and the new, in terms of the future incarnation (or genesis) of objects, forms, and spaces.

Importantly, in presenting the particularity of the notion of the virtual (and the actualisation of the virtual) Deleuze (2001b, pp. 212-214) discusses the fact that there is a very different emphasis placed behind the different concepts of the possible and the real and the virtual and the actual. The contrast between the two (the possible/real and the virtual/actual) is embedded in difference. There is effectively no difference between the possible and the real whereas the virtual and the actual (or its actualisation) are constructed through difference itself. To further this, the possible is real in that it is what it becomes. It is a reflection of that which it will be, embedded in sameness

(the resemblance of) the possible does not allow for the radical levels of difference evident within the potential of the virtual and the actualisation of the virtual. The possible contains identity within the form of the real, whereas the actualisation of the virtual does not (or cannot). Actualisation moves towards difference and diverges through the process of its becoming, it is multiple in that it can generate a more complex and varied series of potential within the virtualities from which it comes, or which it is to-come.

In relation to this distinction, between the possible and the virtual Deleuze states:

The possible and the virtual are further distinguished by the fact that one refers to the form of identity in the concept, whereas the other designates a pure multiplicity in the Idea which radically excludes the identical as a prior condition (Deleuze, 2001b, p. 211).

This evidences the action of the virtual and the force of change (or difference) embedded within the process of its actualisation that moves away from the identical, opening out from what was, to what can be.

The virtual is real yet not actual; the actualisation of the virtual is a process linked to, both, being and becoming, an 'open-endedness' where the virtual acts as a 'plane' of differentiation, not for the pre-forming of identity but instead an open, bifurcated, mutated or folded actuality. The virtual is an 'open' multiplicity which differentiates and becomes 'other' through actualisation. In 'Difference and Repetition' Deleuze suggests,

Such is the defect of the possible: a defect which serves to condemn it as produced after the fact, as retroactively fabricated in the image of what resembles it. The actualisation of the virtual, on the contrary, always takes place by difference, divergence, or differenciation (Deleuze, 2001b, p. 212).

It is this difference generated through the virtual, which defies pre-formed 'identity.' As Deleuze states, "Actualisation breaks with resemblance as a process no less than it does with identity as a principle" (Deleuze & Guattari, 2003, p. 212). It is the operation of the virtual, and the vital difference this injects within systems, that challenges the fixed notions of identity and structures a challenge against previous thinking concerning identity (in particular *Hegelian* dialectical thinking).

Deleuze differs from Hegel in many ways, but perhaps the most important distinction between the two rests on the notion of contradiction, and Deleuze refers to Bergson to emphasise the point, "The originality of the Bergsonian conception is in showing that internal difference does not go and must not go to the point of contradiction" (Deleuze, 1999, p. 49) and he goes on to discuss the importance of the virtual,

In Bergson and thanks to the notion of the virtual, the thing differs from itself in the first place, immediately. According to Hegel, the thing differs from itself in the first place from all that it is not, such that difference goes to the point of contradiction (Deleuze, 1999, p. 53).

In this way, the main point of contention in Hegel (for Deleuze) rests on the notion of difference itself as well as the importance of the concept of the virtual. In contrast to internal difference seeking contradiction Deleuze, through or via Bergson, maximises the potential of the virtual, through external, and interdisciplinary series of potentials.

Rajchman provides an interesting suggestion for establishing a particular way of understanding the virtual and how it relates to both space and the construction of form within space, when he states:

A virtual construction is one that frees forms, figures and activities from a prior determination or grounding, of the sort they have, for example, *in classical Albertian perspective, allowing them to function or operate in unanticipated ways; the virtuality of a space is what gives such freedom in form or movement (Rajchman, 2000, p. 119).*

In essence, the virtual allows form to be loosened (freed) from the static preconceived notion of grounding, or fixity in terms of prior identity. This freedom allows different variables to be considered and activated and permits alternative potential options to be evident within the final form.

The openness mentioned in relation to the notion of the virtual hinges upon this question of identity and the idea that the actualisation of the virtual inflects, bifurcates, or 'morphs' with the actual in other words, creating a dynamic change in terms of something's identity and an open-ended becoming. In many ways, this is a shift from the linear concept of resemblance (and identity) embedded within the transition from the possible to the real, towards an 'interactive' combination of the virtual and the actual where the final identity is tied into (or located within) memory and potential. It is in this way that the virtual is linked to the concept of 'becoming,' creating, through becoming, a more open future. It is based within this 'open' future or 'to-come' that dramatic change, a shift in the internal dynamics of matter/material (and the space in which it rests) can take place.

It is important to state that Deleuze's notion of the Virtual is structured through Bergson's discussions surrounding time, space, memory, and duration. Bergson's complex interweaving of materiality (or matter) and space as well as time, which inflects, or disrupts, our perception presents the potential for a new understanding of the potential for, or the structure of the new, the "insertion of duration into matter that produces movement" (Grosz, 2000, p. 230). This 'movement,' or 'sudden, unpredictable' change is structured through difference, a series of divergent potentialities that lead towards new and challenging arrangements or organisations. The important aspect to this is the actualised *material* thing, which at once differs from what it was (at least the implication that it is, or could be, tied to a specific unifying identity), whilst reorganising the potential of itself through its own becoming.

What Bergson's understanding of duration provides is an understanding of how the future, as much as the present and the past, is bound up with the movement and impetus of life, struggle and politics. While duration entails the coexistence of the present with the past, it also entails the continual elaboration of the new; the openness of things (including life) to what befalls them. This is what time is if it is anything at all: not simply mechanical repetition, the causal effects of objects on objects, but the indeterminate, the unfolding and emergence of the new (Grosz, 2000, p. 230).

In essence, as Grosz mentions, both Bergson and Deleuze support the notion of becoming as a rupture of emergence, a change instigated through difference.

Realisation is the concretisation of a pre-existent plan or programme; by contrast, actualisation is the opening up of the virtual to what befalls it. Indeed, this is what life, élan vital, is of necessity: a movement of differentiation in the light of the contingencies that befall it (Grosz, 2000, p. 228).

This returns to the possible/real and virtual/actual again, the first static, or at least it deals with the formulation of itself, whilst the other is open, dynamic and instrumental in the production of change, or enabling the becoming of more than itself (or other). The first formulation relates to the 'materialisation' of the possible within the real (direct resemblance), the second through differentiation allowing for a new divergent actuality. The virtual does not act as a plan or 'blueprint' for the actual; rather it generates or produces interconnections, differences, networks, and morphological, hybridisable actualities within both the actual and also the actualisation of the virtual. It is in this

way, through external connections, that the opening of the work creates the potential for change (change embedded in difference), that *a* becoming is generated. Deleuze suggests that a 'becoming' is not a reduction or a leading back, it is a movement forwards, the openness and potential of the future. Grosz also states, in reference to Bergson and Deleuze, that "each conceptualises time as becoming, as an opening up which is at the same time a form of bifurcation and divergence" (Grosz, 1999, pp. 3-4) and the virtual is vital to the notion of becoming. The virtual allows consistent movement away from identity, or the idea of an (en)closed entity, and effectuates the becoming, the move into the future instigated through change and difference.

The space opened by the virtual, and its actualisation, brings external potentialities to the fore. As mentioned, the virtual as a multiplicity explores connections that lie outside of fixed identity effectively, this forces a certain break with the idea that different media are 'closed,' and contain fixed boundaries that delineate their particular or specific essence (or traits), that which makes them something and instantly recognisable as that thing and that thing alone. This break, or rupturing of these boundaries allows interconnectivity, it presents the challenge of interdisciplinarity, but from a point where the multiplicitous potentialities of its future force the becoming of what will be. In effect, this could be considered a 'liminal space', a state between one thing and another. The idea of liminality needs to be seen as a position that rests between things, as a movement from one state to another, in effect a process of becoming in its own right, and the virtual can be seen to relate at this juncture as the multiplicitous potentialities of breaking with resemblance (possible/real) as the principle of change. This in-between state, or space, is subversive in that it brings often inharmonious or conjectural principles together in order to explore potential correlations between them. It is for this reason that interdisciplinarity, at least interdisciplinarity effectuated through the virtual can be seen as a subversive process, a subversion that leads away from the pre-formity of media, discipline and form, and our understanding of them.

INTERDISCIPLINARITY

Transformative qualities are often overlooked within painting practices, outside of the constraints of its perceived boundaries. The virtual affects painting directly in this way. Connections external to the physical, structural constraints of the medium can actually force a change in the form of the work, whilst allowing the persistence of itself within the final arrangement. This happens even though its appearance may have radically altered, at times to the point of unrecognisability. The virtual opens a multiplicitous space through which many differential options can be considered with the work becoming other than that which it was. In effect the form can morphologically change, adapting to include external potentialities, which include architectural possibilities, movement, and three-dimensionality, as well as questioning the materiality, time and duration within it.

In terms of painting the notion of the virtual becomes complex, and in effect the way of thinking of the virtual does not come from painting itself (although it can be considered a virtual element), rather it has to be constructed through spatial and temporal connections opening it out into different spatial and temporal opportunities and a series of potential. In this way, the virtual operates as a trigger for interdisciplinarity and this happens in the way it acts, in order that it question the specific 'internal' nature of the, or a, medium. The virtual can be used as a way of re-thinking or re-negotiating the space of theory within which the practice can be actualised. It necessarily incorporates interdisciplinarity by forcing connections and proposing ways of re-structuring new, transformative and different dynamic forms of practice. It is in this way that the virtual has to be thought in terms of painting, acknowledging

relationships with other disciplines, challenging its theoretical ground, and subsequently integrating or folding itself upon different media creating new forms of 're-territorialised' practice. The virtual proposes the external, in contrast to the internal (in terms of disciplinarity), and it is this integration through the notion of multiplicity that orientates the interdisciplinary affects upon painting and creates the potential for painting to redefine itself in terms of its form and its spatial and temporal context.

Miwon Kwon states that; "the fluidity of subjectivity, identity, and spatiality as described by Deleuze and Felix Guattari in their rhizomatic nomadism, for example, is a powerful theoretical tool for the dismantling of traditional orthodoxies that would suppress differences, sometimes violently" (Kwon, 1997, p. 109). This method of disruption within the methodological process challenges the boundaries of the medium from within. The 'conventions' of the medium are used to subvert themselves, not through a particular material dependency but rather through a method enabling the act of painting to spread into the world a different relationship to objects around us, a challenge to our confirmation of an object as something and only that thing, a quasi-hybrid form referencing painting whilst seeping out - spreading out and incorporating other possibilities. This formless condition depends upon Deleuze's notion of the virtual and allows a 'spacing,' a slippage or the 'bringing forth'[5] of potential within painting. The development of this methodology situates painting as a virtual element, an element which itself contains the potential for change within the work through integration and transformation.

Alternatively, in terms of a multiplicity—being the form of the work—painting could be seen as the virtual component, driving the dynamic and orchestrating the manner in which connections and combinations can be made. From the theoretical ground orientating its particularity, the virtual proposes different methods for creating practice by amalgamating the theoretical and physical potentials within other mediums. It is important to state that the notion of the virtual changes our understanding of painting as a practice. It redefines the way in which painting can be created and necessarily shifts from an internal disciplinary approach to an external interdisciplinary one.

Thus, the notion of the virtual allows painting to be considered in a very different way from before from a boundaried, rule-dependent specific material form, the notion of the virtual permits a fluctuating space for painting where the virtual inflects, informs and deforms the actual (through its actualisation). It is therefore a position in which painting can exist without being painting.

However, painting is still embedded within the larger form and considered as a virtual element. This enables it to 'persist'; that is to say, the notion of persistence is central to the place of painting, as the virtual extends the potential of the medium. This 'persistence' is not defined by the medium, but rather found through the integration of painting within larger systems. Persistence is not to be considered in the same manner as repetition. Repetition implies the reformulation of the 'same'; persistence is continuity in a similar way to repetition but enables a greater degree of difference. This can be seen as painting 'becoming-other' whilst retaining different or certain/particular 'qualities.'

The transformative affects of the virtual as a concept, thought-through painting as a practice, force change in terms of the form of the work and they also subversively work towards inclusion rather than exclusion of external potential for the work. These transformative qualities work towards full morphological shifts rather than purely hybridised adjustments. This means that the virtual can affect a full change within the form of the work, rather than a doubling of one thing with another, and this allows for complete difference from the original identity (painting) and a break with resemblance as a principle. This form of transformation acts through interdisciplinarity, structured by the virtual, which takes firmly into consideration external elements. For instance, the static nature of painting can be radically altered through time-based media like film, where movement and time conjecture the constraints of conventional painting processes that is, they enhance the facticity of the process in the final form the work takes. Projection and light also construct different approaches for considering the potential of painting.

In terms of the connections that can be approached through this form of thinking, the frame, particularly in reference to painting can be reconsidered alongside the frame of the architectural, discussed at length by Bernard Cache in 'Earth Moves: The furnishing of territories.' "Like Deleuze, Cache defines his domain in terms of operative function rather than an essence or property: architecture is the 'art of the frame'" (Harris, 2005, p. 39). The framic reference of these ideas relating to architecture can be thought through the virtual link with the framic potential of painting. Yet, these series of potential can only be activated through a loosening of the ties to specific boundaries allocated to, from and within medium specific disciplines.

The virtual as a multiplicitous space allows connections to be made; it presents bifurcating and divergent paths for thinking through the work, structuring difference from the outset and forcing new arrangements, combinations and configurations. This can be considered in or through external disciplines like architecture (and architectural theory) where a piece of work like *'Leviathan's Slumber'* (Figure 1) stretches across and away from painting (seeps or spreads out) into the surrounding space, incorporating elements of the architectural surroundings, like the water fittings normally internal to and covered by the walls. These elements allow for colour to be present, to move and flow through the space. The architectural, both considerations of the internal architecture and the actual space within which the work is placed, become integral to the work. As a form, the work consists of multiple elements, where the considerations of painting, being the

Figure 1. Leviathan's slumber: water, food colouring, Grundfos pumps, 120m transparent tubing, wooden platform, and fixings (© 2012, Alistair Payne. Used with permission)

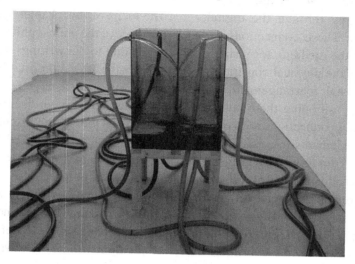

initial driver behind the work, are inflected and become morphed into a larger whole. The transformative qualities of the work hinge around the widening (or opening) out and interdisciplinary approach alongside the potential evident within the virtual, which allows the concerns evident within painting to be retained whilst being transformed through the divergent and mutational potential when combined, blended or folded into a complex multiplicity. In terms of painting, the frame (the conventional frame of painting) becomes deformed through the architectural. This happens alongside the deframing of the architectural as well as the deframing of the architectural in reference to its location and the deframing of painting in relation to its architectural site. These combinations allow for a 'fluid' mixing, where the different elements come together, or are actualised in a new form.

In this way, the elements of the compositional parts become loosened so that they can be remapped. This loosening creates the openness for the external relationships with alternative media, disciplines, methods, functional possibilities, and materials to interweave and blend towards the construction of new forms evidencing difference, divergent from their original identities,

yet, persistent in their concerns. As painting becomes *loosened,* that is to say positioned so that it can flex or distort, it moves into a space where its potential becomes far greater, greater than the mere provision and articulation of its own constraints. This can be articulated through a split between the 'frame,' or armature/support, linked across and with the skin, the canvas or paint, as initially discussed by Jeremy Gilbert Rolfe (1999). In loosening the way in which these elements can be considered, importantly not from a deconstructive (internalised position), and the inter-connective potential of other fields of practice, new alignments and configurations can be mapped. This effectively leads to a direct affect upon the way in which painting can be considered through the virtual. Once the armature or framic support is freed, as can be considered in the early work of Fabian Marcaccio for instance, its alignment to the wall and the architectural surrounds can and need to be rethought. Therefore, the framic potential of the architectural space can consequently be driven as the framic potential of painting, blended, or mixed together in new arrangements to reconfigure previous alignments.

Another option, one of many potential connections, relates to time and movement, the displacement of painting through the digital, even becoming digital. These connections can be considered through the medium, for instance from deconstruction of the physical constraints, not as a way of internal rearrangement, but through methods of repositioning them outside of themselves, following connections with other potentially rearranged elements in a multiplicitous system. The short film loop 'Lost Angel's' (Figure 2), constructs a fluid interplay of coloured liquids, which at rest remain separate, yet, once forced, create an aggressive and at times violent interaction—produced through the repellant (non-mixing) characteristics of the two liquids. The digital projection is instantly derived from painting yet is structured through film and the movement inherent within the work, destabilising the static fixity of a painted surface.

The two projects outlined above present the potential within practice for the reformulation of painting as a practice, thought through the virtual and the interdisciplinary potential embedded within it.

CONCLUSION

The focus of this chapter was to outline the importance of the philosophical notion of the virtual in relation to the writings of Gilles Deleuze and explore the affects this may have on current practice, particularly in reference to painting outlining the potential for interdisciplinarity. It is for this reason that the chapter discusses the virtual in the context of the writing of Deleuze, John Rajchman, Brian Massumi, and Elizabeth Grosz amongst others, then proposes the more practical possibilities evident within this way of thinking. The strategies of the virtual promote interdisciplinarity through openness, the loosening of the framework of medium-specificity towards inclusion of the external. In many ways, this includes a folding of all the elements, so that the potential for change (the construction of new form/work) is not forced from purely one direction. The composition of the final multiple creates a new form that relates all the individual elements but does not reductively identify them. In this way, the inclusion of multiple elements creates a space for interaction; this is the basis for interdisciplinary thinking and practices.

Figure 2. Lost angels (film stills), looped DVD, 9 mins 28 sec (© 2012, Alistair Payne. Used with permission)

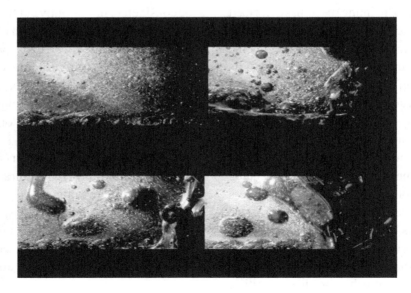

Therefore, the affects of the virtual can be seen to dramatically alter the way in which painting can be considered. The identity of the final form will have effectively been changed or altered, with the new form structured through connections and difference.

The virtual constructs methods for disrupting the specific 'structural' elements of painting through connections that can be brought through other media. This enables new strategies for painting, where considerations outside of the specific medium, across the perceived boundaries of its condition, enhance a new series of potential for the construction of form.

REFERENCES

Ansell Pearson, K. (2002). *Philosophy and the adventure of the virtual: Bergson and the time of life*. London, UK: Routledge.

Benjamin, A. (2004). *Disclosing spaces: On painting*. Manchester, UK: Clinamen Press.

Bergson, H. (1920). *Creative evolution*. London, UK: Macmillan and Co. Ltd.

Bergson, H. (2002). *Matter and memory*. New York, NY: Zone Books.

Cache, B. (2001). *Earth moves: The furnishing of territories*. Cambridge, MA: The MIT Press.

De Landa, M. (1999). Deleuze, diagrams, and the open-ended becoming. In Grosz, E. (Ed.), *Becomings; Explorations in Time, Memory and Future*. Ithaca, NY: Cornell University Press.

Deleuze, G. (1999). *Foucault*. New York, NY: The Athlone Press.

Deleuze, G. (2001a). *Bergsonism*. New York, NY: Zone Books.

Deleuze, G. (2001b). *Difference and repetition*. London, UK: Continuum Books.

Deleuze, G. (2002). *Cinema I*. New York, NY: The Athlone Press.

Deleuze, G., & Guattari, F. (2002). *A thousand plateaus*. London, UK: Continuum.

Gilbert-Rolfe, J. (1999). *Beauty and the contemporary sublime*. New York, NY: Allworth Press.

Greenberg, C. (1995). *The collected essays and criticism: Modernism with a vengeance, 1957-69 (Vol. 4)*. Chicago, IL: University of Chicago Press.

Grosz, E. (1999). *Becomings: Explorations in time, memory and futures*. Ithaca, NY: Cornell University Press.

Grosz, E. (2000). Deleuze's bergson: Duration, the virtual and a politics of the future. In Buchanan, I., & Colebrook, C. (Eds.), *Deleuze and Feminist Theory*. Edinburgh, UK: Edinburgh University Press.

Grosz, E. (2002). *Architecture from the outside: Essays on virtual and real space*. Cambridge, MA: The MIT Press.

Harris, P. (2005). Deleuze, folding architecture. In Buchanan, I., & Lambert, G. (Eds.), *Deleuze and Space*. Edinburgh, UK: Edinburgh University Press.

Krauss, R. (2002). *The originality of the avant-garde and other modernist myths*. Cambridge, MA: MIT Press.

Kwon, M. (1997). Notes on site specificity. *October, 80*.

Lynn, G. (1998). *Folds, bodies and blobs*. New York, NY: Books-by-Architects.

Massumi, B. (2002). *Parables for the virtual*. Durham, NC: Duke University Press.

Melville, S. (2001). *As painting: Division and displacement*. Cambridge, MA: MIT Press.

Meyer, J., & Bochner, M. (2001). How can you defend making paintings now? In *As Painting: Division and Displacement*. Cambridge, MA: MIT Press.

Moos, D. (1996). Architecture of the mind: Machine intelligence and abstract painting. In Moos, D. (Ed.), *Painting in the Age of Artificial Intelligence*. London, UK: Academy Editions.

Patton, P. (1997). *Deleuze: A critical reader*. Oxford, UK: Blackwell Publishers Ltd.

Rajchman, J. (2000). *Constructions*. Cambridge, MA: Massachusetts Institute of Technology.

Rajchman, J. (2001). *The Deleuze connections*. Cambridge, MA: Massachusetts Institute of Technology.

Walker Bynum, C. (2001). *Metamorphosis and identity*. New York, NY: Zone Books.

ENDNOTES

[1] The term 'pre-formity' is used here in reference to Gilles Deleuze's distinction between the possible/real and the virtual/actual, where he states that the real is already preformed in the actual, as a given, whereas the virtual is not fixed, structured through a greater level of movement and difference through actualisation (Deleuze, 2001b, pp. 210-214). As Elizabeth Grosz suggests: "The field of the possible is wider than that of the real. Deleuze suggests that implicit in this pairing is a preformism: the real is already preformed in the possible. The possible passes into the real through limitation, the culling of other possibilities. Through resemblance and limitation, the real comes to be seen as given" (2000, p. 226).

[2] The term 'pre-formity' is used here in reference to Gilles Deleuze's distinction between the possible/real and the virtual/actual, where he states that the real is already preformed in the actual, as a given, whereas the virtual is not fixed, structured through a greater level of movement and difference through actualisation (Deleuze, 2001b, pp. 210-214). As Elizabeth Grosz suggests: "The field of the possible is wider than that of the real. Deleuze suggests that implicit in this pairing is a preformism: the real is already preformed in the possible. The possible passes into the real through limitation, the culling of other possibilities. Through resemblance and limitation, the real comes to be seen as given" (2000, p. 226).

[3] The term 'expanded practice' is used in this context in relation to painting but is derived from the ideas proposed by Rosalind Krauss in her essay 'Sculpture in the expanded Field' (Krauss 2002).

[4] The term 'grounding' in this context relates to a form of leading-back, a cyclical return to the conventional constraints of the, or a, medium.

[5] The term 'bringing forth' in this context relates directly to Martin Heidegger's use of the term. Heidegger describes *poēsis* as a 'bringing-forth' this is the bringing-forth of the work (the 'irruption'). Heidegger states that, "bringing-forth brings out of concealment into unconcealment" (Heidegger, 2002, pp. 311-341); this is revealing—*alētheia*—the revealing of truth (the technical aspect of the work and the subject being taught).

Chapter 9
Behind the Sonic Veil:
Considering Sound as the Mediator of Illusory Life in Variable and Screen-Based Media

Ross Winning
University of Wolverhampton, UK

ABSTRACT

Drawing firstly on animation, this chapter will consider how applications of sound may demand new conceptual frameworks for animated work to develop. Making reference to audio-visual sound theory, the acousmatic and cinematic histories, the discussion surveys aspects of animation sound, and suggests the potential for exposing the sonic elements of the form to evaluation using means beyond current film-sound concepts. The application of recorded sound and the role it performs in the re-creation of synthetic life in new animated situations brings unconsidered possibilities for sound-image concepts. How sound functions and how it combines with an image on screen, in order to create a listening involvement in animation, is central to this consideration. Nevertheless, as the form transgresses, it is evolving from the structured sound space of the traditional screen; new spaces may present different challenges that motivate different sound to picture equations.

INTRODUCTION

Animation has a relationship with drawing that is almost fundamental to its definition. The system of mark making directly on film or photographing artworks somehow seems to define the genus of an art form that, whilst having many visual antecedents, is not generally thought of as a medium rooted in sound. The development of the contemporary animated form, now mediated by computer, suggests that there are new ways to develop animated work. This process is not a new one as a culmina-

DOI: 10.4018/978-1-4666-2961-5.ch009

tion of technology led practices now means that animation and the cinematic product engage less with the lens-based and chemical process and more with mediation via digital machines. The move to treat cinema as a text, once considered itself as a radical move, has gained ground at a time when the audio-visual product is now mostly written to machines rather than photographed (Altman, 1992). This suggests revitalized production sets for traditional animation as well as a common grounding in machine-based production shared by proliferating entertainments. Mutations of any primary definition that might be based on the indexical nature of film may also need to be considered. The mediation of many film processes even if they currently originate on film stock, are also often digitally post manipulated. The implication for this sound and image relationship therefore is for it to evolve from its former specified indexed limitation. In addition, sound can then be considered with equanimity in the creative process both practically and theoretically with a greater symbiosis between them.

This chapter examines current and developing definitions of the relationship of sound to vision in the animated form. It also has inter-related aims. Firstly, one aim is to build part of a narrative derived from a scope of personal practice and research about sound and image whilst seeking to question the audio-visual marriage with a particular respect to animation on the understanding that evolutions of the form are now transgressing boundaries. The discussion reviews aspects of the animated form's theoretical relationship with sound whilst acknowledging the facilitating role of digital production in the sound image partnership. Secondly, there is a consideration of the developments that are bringing new manifestations of animated work to be made such as the expansion of sound into other digitally facilitated areas that have animated content, such as games and virtual worlds. A consideration whether part of these differently structured sound spaces present challenges for the conceptual landscape of the sound-image contract based is also undertaken.

The chapter therefore forms a case for the pivotal function of sound in this process of recreation and that the Pythagorean principle of the acousmatic[1] may be fundamental to engaging spectators for animated forms. The extension of this veiled sonicity in the moving image to animation and other animated and variable experiences, such as Virtual Worlds and Games is considered for its new potential where that off-screen principle might evolve. That is, sound, is the unseen mediator in the recreation of convincing animated encounters. In addition, the sonic is central to immersion for the spectator and is therefore traceable across related digital art forms as the desire to communicate and transport audiences is a key aim.

Acousmatic Sound

The notion of the acousmatic was researched by Pierre Schaeffer to describe a sound heard independently from its source and without knowledge of its origin. Extracted from its semantic Greek origins for the contextual discourse of musique concrete, it has connotations for the on screen/off screen use of all sound as well as the voice to which it originally referred. (Murray Schafer, 1977; Chion, 1983). Its origins describe the Akousmatikoi, a sect of Pythagorean disciples who would listen to the master speaking from behind a curtain so that the message would not suffer from visual distraction. This emphasis on listening not only had resonance for the development of concrete music and the modernist aspirations of the composers of the twentieth century but also suggests an implication for the original sonification of cinema and the animated form. From that point on from the possibilities of sound's insertion into the animated film, experiments with synchronous and asynchronous sounds for their own sake, punctuating the visual, making time elastic and without an identifiable source became a source of regeneration for the cartoon film. "Both immersing and altering the graphic narrative along the way" (Klein, 1993, pp. 8-18).

Film theoretical models and sonic theories provide a departure point to consider what new theoretical frameworks might evolve in future. The ubiquity of sonic phenomena, its effect in everyday life and its increasing pervasiveness into our noisy urban environment will underpin a case for the potency of recreated sound in media forms. The cultural relevance of the voice will provide further context for this chapter about sound and potential for immersing the audience.

BACKGROUND

Engaging with the Senses

"The sense of hearing cannot be closed off at will. There are no ear lids" (Schafer, 1977, p. 11), suggests that the act of listening continues after we have averted our eyes, it is reasonable then to ask, why is the world so primed to vision? Sound is the sensual phenomenon that reaches us first in the assailment of the senses. In terms of its implementation in cinema, sound is deployed, with vision, as a cross modal tool to rediscover acoustic effects from the "formless mass of din" of our everyday lives (Balazs in; Weiss & Belton, 1985, pp. 117–125). Sonic experiences, when added to the speed in which we see things are a major part of the human sensorium. Humans perceive movement through vision in the real world, closely after perceiving sound suggesting that the "ear analyses, processes and synthesizes faster than the eye" (Chion, 1990, pp. 10-11) suggesting that sound is not only of primary importance to the awareness of the immediate environment but also in cinema spaces. Additionally, sound, hearing and listening is necessary to human survival in primates and humans, is a corroboration of this embodied sense to sound and its role in awareness of the wider environment. It is suggested that this as an evolution of the senses in order to meet the challenges of pre-historic life as hunter-gatherer (Morris, 1973).

The terms of hearing and listening are sometimes inter-related and inter-changeable, but as Rost (2001) states, "Although both hearing and listening involve sound perception, the difference in terms reflect a *degree of* intention" (p. 11). These two senses combine with such expediency, that they present important eventualities for our real world spatial orientation. A sense of security is negotiated in the world and mediated by this symbiosis (Classen, 1993). This is also a discussion that is relevant to the sensual experience in screen media and virtual spaces.

Extending this to other senses; touch, taste, smell, sight, and sound are the five senses first classified by Aristotle[2]. Our knowledge of the exterior world is mostly defined by these traits. They are links to how we might locate and position ourselves in the world as physical beings. We create much of our human experience from these senses. Kant, in 1700s, posited that modes of perception are dependent this sense awareness. Of these sensations, sight is usually accepted as primary in the human scheme. Sound is accepted as secondary in our human design and the other physical senses are subsidiaries in making up human sensorium.

Additionally humans also have a sense of balance temperature pain and motion. The co-ordination of the primary senses affects perceptions and actualities of the secondary senses. For example, kinesthesis, a knowledge of muscle and joint movement, is affected by the primary senses awareness of how we move and where we are in the world. Synaethesia highlights a phenomenon that is present in some people where the senses are confused and stimulation in one sense promotes a sensation in another.

It is accepted that the means and efficacy by which the organs and their cellular structures receive and transmit the specific sense stimuli to the nervous system can vary between individuals. However, to compensate adjusting one sense over another's impairment appears to be a strong trait in the human being. The ability of the sensorium to compensate for hearing or sight loss has been the subject of recent studies[3]. The musician who is deaf or the artist who is blind illustrate this ability of the sense organs to adjust and compensate for the other diminished faculties.

What of the other embodied feelings of taste, touch and smell that may have a role to play in sensing the world? Apart from a few attempts, either real or imaginary, to incorporate these other senses into cinema, the sight, and sound duopoly continues. Aldous Huxley, in *Brave New World,* wrote of a cinema-like mass entertainment that used smell and touch in attempts to engage marginalized social groups. This prescient description of a future cinema albeit of an insidious utopian future, predated actual attempts to introduce other sensory stimuli to the cinema audience. Competing systems[4] made attempts to engage other senses to effect the audience's emotional responses other than sight and sound[5].

These attempts to engage all the senses in entertainment forms have antecedents from before the outset of the first wave of mass communication. Technologically derived entertainments such as cinema re- revitalized by the science of optics and photography and subsequent evolutions through digital means continue to animate the senses. From village fair and Music Hall to Cinema, Animation, Games, Virtual Reality through to contemporary location based entertainment, all have sought to motivate the totality of the senses.

Sight, Sound, and Film

Whilst there may be wider cultural reasons as to the domination of the visual, in our mediated forms of entertainment such as film, animation, and Computer Games, the role of the visual remains a primary consideration. The screen is the pre-dominant method of mediation. This reliance on the frame suggests an origin from previously established forms of entertainment that are framed by a proscenium arch. Theatre, Music Hall, Lectures, and the travelling show are all forms that have used this convention suggesting

a proto-cinematic reliance on the frame preceding early cinema. Wider access to television screens permitted wider coverage, as does the computer screen where invocationally mediated forms of media proliferate. The image is therefore primary to what an audience or spectator detects.

An extension of those principles that make the eye look outward and the ear inwards in the assailment of the senses is fundamental to a spectator coding the animated sound film, (as in all film). When considering the conventional application of sound and image, one might question why the image in cinema is thought to be primarily spatial and the sound temporal thereby diminishing the role of vision in temporality and sound in spatiality? Assertions by acousticians would be that the conflict between visual and acoustic space in the environment emphasizes the visual but that a sound has spatial properties. The measured space in which a sound can be heard is one example. Ultimately, a space affects a sound's properties. Sound is modified by reflection from soft and hard materials in that space, the interior sound, and the outdoor sound have different characteristics that affect both production and reception of that sound (Murray Schaffer, 1977, pp. 214-217).

Contemporary moving images now use digital media devices for production. The proliferation of this means of production co-incides with recent narrowing of distinctions and definitions in a range of media forms. Terms that divide animated forms and live action have become blurred and remain undefined. This oscillation, brought about by the currency of digital media that can assist traditional modes of production can also aid the generation of new and revitalized industrial methods in these cinematic forms. The computer game, LA Noire (Rockstar Games, 2010) is a significant milestone in the cross flow between game play and cinematics. The period atmosphere and genre that the LA Noire aspires to takes on the terms and conditions of a film. This is apparent in both in the cut scenes that trace the narrative arc and in the use of music appropriate to the period during interactive game play. From a sonic perspective, these manifestations of similar art forms that are present in one product bring in to question the terms and conditions of sound's function as they cross modal boundaries between forms. The implication for the structuring of sound with picture in the range of moving image media production further suggests possible cross-fertilization of approaches in both the craft and theoretical assimilation of sound.

Established concepts of film sound are therefore borrowed for other forms whereas new aspects of sound are being challenged by game play and interactive modes. A recorded soundtrack that structures the sound-space complements the visual image in cinema. Significantly, this implies passivity by the spectator. Soundtracks and indeed films and animation are also characterized by a designed linear progress. In contrast, the basis in sound for interactive works is further qualified by that user interaction in direct response to different scenarios being encountered in a game world, virtual world or artwork. The specification for sound, music, and vocalization is not linear in this case. Even so, the audience, spectator, or user's experience remains partly defined in terms of this overall space made for sound. Altman (1992) further qualifies this "sound space" in describing the film "industry's desire for a match between sound scale and image scale (p. 46).

Sound and Added Value

The definition for this sound space in cinema has a conceptual basis set out by screen sound theorists. This "added value" for sound is the basis of a concept of what has been termed an "audio-visual contract" (Chion, 1990, pp. 3-123). According to Chion, this is where the sound and image combine to produce effects that help to immerse the spectator. Whilst there may be similarities in the deployment of sound between these screen based works and games for example, the building of a sound space in interactive worlds spring more from invoking pre-programmed routines or devised scenarios of artificial intelligence.

This suggests that sound could, at least, be a significant agent through which we can signify and build meaning in audio-visual media of all kinds. With this expansion of sound application in combination with the visual image in those traditional media forms of animation and cinema, for example, a conceptual re-evaluation of the function of screen sound seems inevitable. The structuring of sound in contemporary works may demand new conceptual observations and specific practical applications to be developed as the added value of sound is stretched in these new media.

Additionally, sound's function and relationship in other mediated forms that are invoked by digital means such as computer games and virtual worlds is central to the concept of immersion. The level of involvement born of deep immersion is considered desirable for convincing game play, for example. The suggestion is that sensory immersion and challenges in games promotes engagement. That "imaginative immersion" and aspiration to recreation of reality is a challenge that this can be met and augmented by audio (Collins, 2010, p. 134). Conversely, this chimes with Manovich's (2001) assertion that interactivity denies the function of any imaginative and interactive engagement in all pre-digital works is a contemporary digital myth. A condition that he suggests is brought about by a danger that lurks within the term interactivity. Further stating that it is not a new phenomena and is "a structural feature of the history of modern media" (Manovich, 2001, p. 57).

Bela Balazs wrote in the 1930s that the timbre of a sound changes according to its placement next to an image:

A sound changes in accordance with the physiognomy or gesture of the visible source of the sound seen together with the sound itself in a sound film in which acoustic and optical impressions are equivalently linked together into a single picture (Balazs; in Weis & Belton, 1985, p. 117).

Sonic functions in new and evolving contemporary interactive arenas therefore pose new questions for the deployment of sound. In considering the function that sound has in a range of media artifacts, an attempt to draw distinctions and similarities between those various media forms, from the perspective of its theoretical function, could be made. Contrasts and similarities between cinema, for example, with its predominant forms of live action movies, animation and games and virtual worlds and audio visual artworks in distributed spaces could be drawn by appropriating the use and function of sound. The role that sound has to play in immersing a spectator or audience is therefore considered fundamental in this respect. The audio-visual contract, and the unseen voice, both concepts that are forwarded as central in film sound, could prove to be appropriate to all audio-visual forms.

LOOKING AT SOUND BEHIND THE VEIL

Evolution in Film Sound-Animation Sound-Interactive Sound

"More than any other medium of human communication, the moving picture makes itself sensuously and sensibly manifest as the experience of experience by experience" (Sobchack, 1992, p. 3). Vivian Sobchack in discussing phenomenology and film suggests that this experience of the heard and the seen is a reflexive and objective experience. That it is a "more discrete, systematic and less wild form of communication" (Sobchack, 1992, p. 4). This echoing of Maurice Merleau-Ponty, who states that cinema is reversible in terms of the aural and visible world that it creates, both perceptively and expressively and that the embodied modes of existence that cinema appropriates, are in addition to the frameworks and "stuff" that life itself is constructed from. A further qualification of that it is "not necessary to reassemble them into a synthesis" might also suggest that this life

expressing life syndrome, especially as it refers to live action cinema, indicates animation could be considered as a different form playing to different set of rules and governances. In considering that these are phenomenological references to the photographed and filmed image, the suggestion arises that a different task may surface when considering the signifying possibilities of the aural and visual conjunction of a synthesized animation in a post-photographic age. However, the reciprocating possibilities of that cinema is considered to be two aspects of a "reversibility that is an ultimate truth" (Merleau Ponty, 1968, p. 155), With changing means of production, there is the suggestion that these observations, are now complicated by the continuing primacy of the visual, the expanding fluidity of the animated (synthesized) form and the new digital production processes of sound and image that questions origination and doubts the veracity of the real, bringing the cinematic closer to the animatic arrangement. Furthermore the extents that sound phenomena inhabit the picture in imbuing these arranged images with the anima is an area for a discussion that could occur around its debatable, dialectical role in the complete construction of an animation.

In this process of recreation that cinema and animated forms strive for, the sound operates behind the veil of the image. In the recreation of games and virtual spaces that aim to engage a spectator within the bounds of illusory space, the sound elements that are present, create a bifurcation of the real and imaginary presence that the player might sonically be influenced by. Sounds that are part illusory and part a re-creation of the senses. Sounds that sometimes follow cinematic or animatic principles, and those that circumscribe the soundscape of environment, even if that environment is virtual or illusory.

Some games demonstrate that they intermittently share cinematic principles but in open play the notion of a sonic contract may be supplanted by an evolving concept of sound that responds to motion in the game. This kinaesthetic relationship is addressed in those products that seek immersion from the spectator. Games can have cut scenes or FMV that will display the sound characteristics of the motion picture film. Conversely, the engagement of the spectator or user begins to locate the viewer "as if they are there!" Experiencing sound aspires to the real occurrence of sound in these instances. Terms such as adaptive audio are relevant here and serve to illustrate the contrasting function of sound in cinematics and games. Adaptive sound functions helps to create immersion in games helping to provide convincing play. Immersion is further described in terms of classification or degrees noted as curiosity, identification, empathy, and transportation (Glassner, 2004).

Whilst indications for the use of sound and image in early cinema abounded with explorative novelty, immersion was also seen as an important element. The masking of projector noise for example is a function of this desire to promote disappearance of the frame (Gorbman, 1987). Ironically, the first uses of sound limited the progress of the image, enthralled, as it was the visual language of photographing live action and documentary pictures. The later coming of synchronized sound to cinema and by implication, language, was a complicating addition to the purity of this visual form. Despite testimony to the proliferation and addition the sonic with film before synchronization, the perception remains, therefore, of the visual primacy of early cinema. The period following the inception of asynchronous sound and vision, marks the beginning a re-vitalization in Animation that was energetic and inventive, embracing the new abstract possibilities and aesthetic aspirations that synchronous sound brought to animation, notably the cartoon (Russet & Starr, 1976; Goldmark, 2005; Abel & Altman, 2002).

The Problem of Sound Description

This progress of sound in animation towards a full symphonic approach epitomised by Walt Disney and the subsequent reaction of the seemingly

discordant (Warner Brothers) has provided a neat distinction for the description of animated sound in a historical context. (Brophy, 1991, pp. 67-102). Whilst a basis for a comparative model, the curiously unwieldy terminology that sound exposes will often find form through the substitution of musical concepts into the attempt for classification of tempo pitch and beat and so on. Somehow, the terms "don't quite fit the phenomena" (Brophy; in Altman, 1992, p. 192). In acknowledging this state and accepting that language is the only semiotic system capable of interpreting another semiotic system, then, the path towards a tentative semiology for sound and a further exploration of the function of sound in various mediated forms presents a challenge of classification.

Although language, itself a system of sound organized for communication, it is making a poor attempt at interpreting sound. On the range of sound possible, language occupies a very small part. Music and its performance are often described in the most facile terms and translated into "the poorest of Linguistic categories" (Barthes, 1977, p. 179). This refers to an inevitable use of the adjective in such description. Barthes explains this tendency in the use of the epithet in descriptions of music as providing a bulwark against which the subject's threat (perceived) against the imaginary is protected. This is also claiming that music is possessed of access to joy or loss (in some cases). It is therefore an extension of the Platonic idea. Extending this to Cage's notion that music and noise qualities are interchangeable and therefore also open to re-contextualization further demonstrates that the attempt to qualify and create firm classifications for sound presents linguistic challenges. The expansion of the diegetic and non-diegetic concept to cope with the challenge to sound in animation is a case in point.

Commentary in animation study has signaled directions in this endeavour so that new categorizations could be evolved from animation's interrogation of the diegetic and non-diegetic use of sound. When Tom, or Jerry collide with walls and obstacles accompanied by a sound, it is both part of the musical orchestrations and a description of the speed or trajectory or hardness of that impact. It is non-diegetic in terms of its musical origin, as there is no orchestra visible, yet, at a certain point of emphasis in the narrative flow, it becomes diegetic as a sound effect. The music also functions in the moment and can also emphasise direction and motion with the characters movements that is often accompanied by short musical figures. Daniel Goldmark affirms this when discussing Carl Stalling and his contribution to cartoon music stating, "Stalling's music informs the audience about the action at hand, providing a functional replacement for the dialogue" (Goldmark, 2005, p. 36). The continuation of this application, switching between modes of music operating as sound additions and its other role in qualifying the ambience, tempo, and punctuation, is a main sonic characteristic of the animations in this particular corpus. The synchrony between image and musical effects interspersed by dazzling passages of musicianship are played out both beyond and within the virtual construct of the screen space so that definitions of the diegetic are stretched in sympathy with the cartoon depictions of Tom and Jerry.

Scott Curtis argues for a different terminology to be employed in the pursuit and classification of animated sound. It is, as suggested a presupposition to assume a sound image hierarchy. In addition, the vague description that separates dialogue from effects and music is a strange point of departure when thinking about the animated cartoon where these classifications are immediately dissolved upon meeting extreme cartoon physics. Sound relationships, such as iconic and isomorphic, although not exclusive to animation, are described by Curtis as analogous to the pictorial depictions of cartoon characters on the screen. When applied to sound, they help describe the fluidity between sound and image that is often present in animation. These evolutions suggest that new terms are possible as the form evolves.

Harrison Birtwhistle puts forward a composer's view in his statement from 'Insects, Urine, and Flatulance: On the Radical Potential of Mickey Mousing' (Birtwistle, 2002).

Not only does Mickey Mousing destroy the notion of an isolated Specificity, of an abstraction from all else, but it also introduces ideas of other kinds of structuration, other ways of considering structure, other ways of thinking music, and other ways of thinking about music (Birtwistle, 2002, p. 26).

Birtwhistle takes the view that an audio-visual relationship weakens the structure of both prioritizing the isolation of audio and vision as disciplines. This is counter to the expanding notion of contemporary media, which maintains its trajectory towards the proliferation of sound and image combinations across many cultural divides. In addition, it accepts the value of audience. It also seems to favour abstraction as a pinnacle. The denial of the cartoon as a modernist exemplar of abstract sound and vision is completed by:

Sound described as being within the diegesis or extra to the diegesis seems to find a more complex and fluid state when the beats of an animated sound film unfold.

This suggests that the diegetic audio-visual concept appears to become untenable and beyond description when applied to the animated film. The expansion and compression of space and time, possible in even the most conventionally represented cartoon or animation, seemingly makes extra demands on this non-diegetic, diegetic framework.

Experiences of Sound in Variable Forms

Schismogenesis refers to the creation of a division in anthropology to describe a range of social behaviours[6]. In reworking this original concept,

R Murray Schaffer supplants this idea of dislocation, into his concern for the acoustic ecology. Murray Schafer's invention of "Schizophonia" derived from Bateson, suggests sonic events that are effectively divorced from their origins. These observations begin to provide a conceptual framework not only for an understanding of the acoustic ecology and the reality of the sonic world but significantly, begin to create a context for recorded sounds, those sounds that are more familiar as the soundtracks to a range contemporary entertainment works. The consideration of this kind of sound is more conceptually linked with the audio-visual in film and TV as well as the further possibilities for sound in virtual media.

We have split the sound from the maker of the sound. Sounds have been torn from their natural sockets and given an amplified and independent existence. Vocal sound, for instance, is no longer tied to a hole in the head but is free to issue from anywhere in the landscape (Mathieu, 1994. p. 223)[7].

This re-contextualisation of sound that pertains to recorded sound and may also suggest ways in which audio-visual concepts might be constructed for virtual reality world encountered in Computer Games for example, which are presently expanding a use of image with sound[8] through evolutionary technological means. It also conveniently describes the conceptual dislocation encountered with experiencing recorded electro-acoustic sounds as opposed to the sonic realties encountered in our day-to-day lives. R Murray's Schafer's conception of the soundscape appears have resonance for virtual world creation, where the aim is a convincing recreation of life itself. In addition, what might be construed to be the more traditional synthesis of sound and image, such as those approaches found in animation and film production can also be derived from these sonic realities. The sonic concern of the illusory in animation deals mostly with recorded soundtracks, however. It is also linear in conception but nonetheless, has a relationship with space and time in accordance with sound. The interactive requirements of virtual worlds demands the implementation of sound in other ways that may be closer to and reminiscent of the real world. This suggests that these approaches to sound might be a world apart or, as is implied schizophonic. However, the role that sound has in audio-visual construction for these technologically related forms, is increasingly valued for its potential in constructing viable experiences. The illusion and ultimate goal of immersion is due to the successful implementation of sound, in relation to what is being seen.

With the means of production increasingly mediated by digital tools, the conceptual implications for the sonic worlds of the film soundtrack and the synthesis of virtual reality through CGI would appear to be more and more closely interrelated but very much in a state of flux. Concepts of audio-vision synchresis, audiovisual contracts, and spatial magnetisation may be more or less effective for interactive environments. The diametric opposition of the diegesis and iconic and isomorphic descriptions, the concepts of synchresis, and spatial magnetization (Chion, 1990) as suggested, already draws a distinction between film and animation in its sonic attributions.

Sonic Histories

Walter Murch in stating that we "gestate in sound and are born into sight" (Chion, 1990, p. vii) reinforces a case for the sonic in cinema. This foremost sound designer, refers to a "mechanistic reversal of this biological sequence" (Chion, 1990) in cinema after "cinema spent its youth (1892-1927) wandering in a mirrored hall of voiceless mirrors" (Chion, 1990) This is further posited as a "mechanistic reversal of the natural order" which suggests the analysis of sound in cinema has always presented a challenge that is both intangible and contentious. The challenge for filmmakers, animators, and new media artists is to find a way to structure the sound space.

Sonic elements in audio-visual entertainments are often under-considered both conceptually and practically. Although subservient to a dominance of the visual, which has been to the foreground in our understanding of cinematic functions, attempts to immerse audiences from early developments of the so called silent cinema does not ignore sonicity. The live musical accompaniment, the illustrated Magic lantern show, vaudeville, "the itinerant exhibition model" (Altman, 2004, p. 133) and pre cinematic forms of entertainment engaged the full possibilities of interactivity with an audience through sound as well as vision. Visual metaphors as well as devices for sound were deployed to engage the aural sense. With the subsequent application of synchronized sound in cinema, the animated cartoon considered how abstractions through sound might evolve. This synchronization of sound and image lent new potential for revitalizing the landscape of the cartoon. These initial responses to combining sound and vision separated animation from the complication that sound brought to a naturalistic and live action cinema predicated on vision. Live action also made a sonic preoccupation of the language and a vocalization of the human presence in films whereas animation experimented with the abstract potential of the sound effect.

Animated cinema before sound synchronization existed for the short period in a politically universal dimension. The hope for cinema was that it could function as a form of trans-national communication that would highlight different cultures but emphasise the similarities between people. A tool in the service of world peace after the initial wave of globalisation had caused mechanized division. A panacea. It is documented that soldiers across the divide in the 1914-1918 war would have the same star picture on show in their respective trenches. During the so-called

silent era, this seemed attainable. The early period between the world wars marked social upheaval and economic fluctuation but the escapist cinema flourished across the world uncomplicated by the addition of synchronized sound and therefore spoken language (Gomery, 2005).

The short-lived hope for the propagation of a universal cinema that bound societies together went into demise as national and cultural separations were again to the fore. These were propagated through a medium that was being complicated by the addition of sound and therefore, the highlighting of language differences. The promise of a sound cinema and its related technological optimism also implied cultural and economic upheaval. There were many countries with film industry aspirations, seeing the commercial and social potential that were unhindered by the necessity to create films in obscure languages up until the addition of synchronized sound. The visually dominated film without the division created by language meant that film products could easily transport to other countries. Coinciding with depressed world economies the fledgling film industries in certain European countries went into sharp decline (Gomery, 2005).

It is a misconception to describe film as not possessing any language during these nascent years. The addition of intertitles, to support the story structure became a manifestation of sonically connecting to audiences through graphic means, for example. The exportation of a range of films was easily accomplishable through re-configured titles allowing the products to transport across national boundaries. The oncoming synchronization of sound in the image marked the addition of the human voice and therefore further obscuring the potential for the medium of film to be accepted universally. (Murch; in Chion, pp. iv-viii). As such, the role and function of this coming vocalization opened up new areas to be sonically exploited, voice of cinema mutated from the noisy audience along with the piano accompaniment and orchestra pit to the screen.

Central Voices

The use of sound within the wider situation of animated cinema that has, in the mainstream feature at least, evolved the voice's position towards the centre of the sound continuum. Therefore, by placing it at the summit of a sound hierarchy in animated movies, it curiously echoes, the centrality that language had in live action movies soon after the inception of synchronized sound. For Michel Chion, the debate about this aspect of sound infers that it is a "vococentric" and therefore "verbocentric" part of the cinematic form (Chion, 1990, p. 6). This elevated position for the voice has historical and cultural resonance and suggests a further political implication that can be invoked in cinema whether this design is intended or serendipitous. There are also implications for a pre-dominance of the vocal implementation in animation, where it now an increasing element in the commercially orientated animated feature. Furthermore, the complication of this celebrity voice invokes further discussion in terms of its political implication. The role of the vocal is also situated and considered for its provocation in immersive and imaginative processes and how voice neighbourhoods can define the register of a range of animated films.

This discussion is further compounded and informed from both a technical and historical perspective that has privileged the spoken voice since the inception of a synchronized performance of sound to picture (within the expanding superfield of sound). Chion, writing on the application of voice and image claims the cinema to be "verbocentric." "The presence of the human voice structures the sonic space that contains it" (Chion, 1999, p. 5). Chion paraphrases this as sonic space whereas the original statement by Christiane Sacco refers to the human body as the structuring agent. This is further clarified by if the cinema is vococentric, as Chion claims, it is probably because "we as humans, are as well" (Chion, 1990, p. 6). It suggests that we are habitually so and are now attuned to those voices structuring both our interior and exterior worlds. We are attuned to and prioritize human voices in the sound space.

Mainstream animated cinema is also at a stage where the voice is becoming more centrally placed within the traditional definition of dieges and this is increasingly apparent in the most commercially dominant forms. These cultural objects that continue the conventions of cinematic sound also happen to feature the added complication of the celebrity voice, a practice now prevalent in the field. This throws modern, commercial entertainment agendas into sharp relief. It should also be noted that this not a new phenomena. Specialist voice actors working in the profession, and those that do not have public personae have faced stiff competition from the demand for celebrity voices in animation for some time. Now that productions in animation are publicity hungry, the extra potential that the celebrity voice brings is undoubtedly beneficial to any commercial success.

Therefore, it cannot be a surprise this verbosity of the form also continues to inhabit those new and contemporary advances in animation that have been re-vitalised by the digital and that these cultural products are both technologically and commercially driven. The added complications of the theatrical voice and the simultaneity of the dubbed celebrity voice, whilst challenging the animators to new heights of characterisation, poses problems for audio-visual poetics.

Functioning of the Cartoon Voice

The successful technological marriage of sound to picture in the late 1920s gave permission for the people's desire to see the stars of the silent era speak. This synchronization of the voice to the body continues to be exploited in contemporary commercial animation. Of course, cartoon stars were destined to gain voices when the sound additions were seen not to be a passing phase. They would also burst into song adding extra vitality to the early musical invasion of animation, but a lasting irony is that Steamboat Willie (USA

1928) was made as a vehicle for the testing and demonstration of successful synchronization and subsumed the musical sensibilities in favour of the previous vision of concrete effects that showcased rhythmic congruity between sound and image. These original concrete and iconic uses of sound in animated form are woven into the consciousness of the cartoon form, abounding and underscoring the soundtrack (Goldmark, 2002).

Whilst the complication of the voice and in particular the addition of language and speech proposed deeper and possibly more politically charged layers, the form of animation utilised the notion of natural effects in a more empathetic/ sympathetic relationship with their kinetic origins than the cinema of the real exploits. This is the domain of the animated film in terms of sound visualisation. Capitalisation upon this sound/kinetic link found an early reference in Mickey-Mousing. This is also acknowledged at the early inception and use of sound in animation where the action of characters and objects is closely followed with sonic equivalents of the spatial trajectories.

However, children will vocalise as they play with toy cars and so on and it is not the mimetic sonification of the object that is being vocalised but the kinetic qualities of the real object as understood by the child. Slowing down, speeding up and changes of direction are expressed as sounds to qualify the movement and not the actual sound of the object in question. These relationships between sound and object are the codes of an emerging musical system that also give direction to the tangential motion being spontaneously voiced in the soundtrack. They therefore have potential to describe both direction and magnitude, and as Chion would say, supply a "vector" accompanying the shape, as depicted. Although not exclusively related to animation, these aspects of sound are most closely most affined with the cartoon form.

In asking "why do cartoon characters have funny voices?" (Altman, 1992, p. 202), Scott Curtis exposes the function of the cartoon voice and illustrates that synchronous speech, functions as index where as the cartoon world lacks this property although "the voice matches the body." The analogy is to their "distorted bodies" as no index or "match between sound and image is required" as Curtis further explains. If this is correct, then the accepted relationship between the diegetic and non/diegetic and the acousmatic applications of sound in animation may be open to further investigation and scrutiny. Curtis also forwards arguments for the isomorphic and iconic notions of sound in animation and considers these as distinction to the form. These arguments go some way to enervating the perceived hierarchical structure between sound and vision (Curtis; in Altman, 2002, pp. 191-203).

In addition, one might consider what this aspect of sound says about the status of the animated film. If one observes that the sound in the cartoon, is often voiced as a child would whilst playing, therefore underscoring its acceptance as a child's medium! Conversely, the persistence of the form suggests because, like a child, the form refreshes continually in the moment and in the case of sound to image is more able to extend the audiovisual contract in its own powerful small world terms. So, with the animated form so often complemented and enhanced by music and sound it is clear to see how much of the image relies on sound to determine the mise-en-scene and actions. With the diegesis of an animated film often confused by the suspending of disbelief, as it does within a world prey only to its own physics, the markers for the definition of the diegesis are once again challenged. Music and sound can be both diegetic and non-diegetic in the animated film, as in all film. The cartoon form creates sound that begins to oscillate between the two.

These "mutual" (Wells, 1998) sound and image relationships in animation help to stretch the limits of the diegetic and non/diegetic definition. Wells further explains this symbiosis as: "Voice, music, song, and sound effect may all be evaluated separately for the particular contribution each makes to the collective aural vocabulary that simultaneously illustrates, interrogates, comments upon and narrates the visual image" (p. 99).

CONCLUSION

Sound Crosses Boundaries

It should be noted that the main focus for this discussion has been animation and the form has been observed through the prism of sound. This has been from a historical and theoretical perspective. The debate has attempted to frame technological change through examining the challenge that sound has for its theoretical basis in the animated form. The definition of animation has seen new waves of development that challenge its basis. Indeed this has prompted debates as to the nature of the medium migrating between live action and animation and as to the end of film; it is also precipitating commentaries such as "at the end of animation history" (Langer, 2002, p. 4; cited in Coyle, 2010).

The marginalisation of similar art forms is an argument that could well be challenged and framed by examining sound as it currently emerges in cinema, games animation virtual worlds, etc. The ontological potential from this brings into sharper focus the possibilities for a re-assessed standard of sound design and new theoretical basis as the digital supplants analogue processes. This has a historical resonance. Previously, and referring to the animated art form in particular, mediated as it was through the film material, Cholodenko (1991) suggests that animation should not be accepted as a subset of film and that "animation is traced in film" (p. 213). Animation is reframed as coming from a historical position of: "the manual construction of images loop actions, the discrete nature of space and movement—was delegated to cinema's bastard relative, its supplement, and shadow—animation" and was a "repository for nineteenth century moving image technology left behind by cinema" (Manovich, 2001, p. 298). Therefore suggesting that moving image born of animation has itself become "one particular case of animation" (Manovich, 2001, p. 302). Extending this notion, it is possible to see Games traced in animation and Virtual Worlds traced in games.

Evolving Technology

The revolution in digital sound recording and its wide availability preceded the corresponding development in visual media. A parallel debate as to the definition of sound and its primary origins exists in trying to articulate the difference between recorded sounds and actual sound. This is asserted by Altman (1992) when he states that, "current approaches to film systematically borrow a musical model" (p. 15).

A new question arises from this kind of technologically driven development where the democratic means of both production and dissemination of the product offer a wide diversity of scale. How much has the debate regarding the off screen and onscreen notions of recorded voice and sound in applications of audio-vision been affected by those developments? Conceptual frameworks that make up the audiovisual scene and those that constitute the contract are also open to evolving agents such as technology and are founded on moving ground (Chion, 1997). Statements, such as these, from instigators of such concepts are an admission of a developing theoretical terrain for sound. Modifications of the cinema product that use sound in increasingly larger superfields of sonic material also cause these classifications to fragment. In the face of developing sound technology, the experience of the audience is further mediated by multi speaker systems.

The diegetic definition of "hearing and voicing of animation" in distributed spaces is therefore a further case for examination of this analogue and digital development. There are suggestions regarding new terminology for this aspect regarding vocalization and sound. In attempting to advance the terminology, in computer games, for example, the terms "teledigetic" and "ideodigetic" serve better the function of an interactive diegesis (Grimshaw & Schott, 2007a, 2007b). Chion also suggests that the importance instilled in some concepts of sound theory for screen are breaking down, suggesting a technological determinism that is in a state of flux. Additionally, more immersive qualities are being achieved for the feature film engaged in a sound space through the use of technology and analogue speakers. The blurring of the computer Cartesian spaces with the cinematic bring the virtual and film product closer. The position of the spectator in this extended space might be better served by game sound terms and conditions.

The use of multi speaker set ups, in theatrical presentations adds deeper spatial awareness of sound and higher levels of immersion that can be very subjective to individual audience positioning. Zonal phenomena for sound tracks in such spaces could then become part of the strategy for soundtrack design. Add to this; a diversity of arenas and scales of consumption of animation and audio-visual products that are inspired through digital mediation, then audio-visual concepts should also be revised to meet this.

Whilst most processes of moving imagery production can be completely synthesized, sound provides a basis in the analogue. An attempt to illustrate this has been made in this chapter through aligning the use of sound in games and virtual worlds with a definition of the soundscape. How it might inform future debates as to the address of audio-vision in new form is posited for future deliberation. This will be especially pertinent where forms are thought to be transgressing boundaries. Demands are such that for the designers of these new genre-defying entertainments, engagement with interdisciplinary ideas and topics is necessary. The abstraction of sound is one such arena where a conceptual cement can be found. The terms and conditions of soundscapes therefore could provide energy to a new conceptual model in the quest for greater immersivity. However, not all conceptual sound theories may automatically apply across forms.

Appropriating Sonic Theories

A model of sound design borrowed from animation and live action cinema presents a readymade scheme for sonic additions to the visually dynamic and interactive environments that computer games inhabit. The audio-visual design in both disciplines, aims to work with narrative, movement, space and time. This condition would therefore seem to encourage opportunities for similarities in the sonic design to naturally migrate between forms. This seemingly natural migration may not be so straightforward.

This loose relationship has grown as games have become more allied to visual spectacle and narrative. Increasingly, sonic forms in games are also continuing to be borrowed from cinema origins. In those gaming environments that inherit the visual language of a specific film genre, the design of the sonic terrain can also be introduced for mood and atmosphere. This wholesale importation of sound design from existing film genre would further seem to be the natural cornerstone upon which to build sound design in all kinds of genres and virtual game-play.

Whilst this annexing of one cultural form with the conceptual frameworks of another would appear tempting, this kind of colonialisation needs to be further examined for suitability. Whilst there are similarities in the appropriating of sound theories for a range of audio-visual products that seek to engage the senses, the pace of developing technology in digital audio and visual production might help loosen the determinist argument that tends to inhabit media from time to time.

Therefore, "games are not films" (Collins, 2008, p. 5) but the immersion and levels of psychological engagement that characterise certain kinds of role playing games are transgressing across permeable boundaries, sharing ideas on sound as well as vision for cinematics and game audio. In the game LA Noire, the motion capture enhances the animated content increasing involvement for the spectator. The audio transports users through cinematic means set in synthesized and illusory 3D space, often both in game play and in the linear full motion video sections or cut scenes. Importantly, the aspects of sound in game play are proposing new ideas to construct around the use of audio. Concepts such as adaptive and responsive sound, applicable to the positioning of players, are deployed. The dynamic positioning of sound is now both a challenge for the audio designers and an aid to the construction of immersive and convincing gaming experiences that are superseding the traditional diegetic and non-diegetic relationship (Collins, 2008, p. 125).

Such examples from contemporary animated cinema, games and virtual world creation, demonstrate and suggest different and emerging relationships between sound and image and are new arenas for comparing how sound is catalyzing the development of new conceptual frameworks for these related animated works. The application of sound and re-imagining of life in these animated situations suggest unconsidered possibilities that might be due partly to the nature of how sound functions in real life rather than how a recorded sound combines with the image.

Voices in the Stratosphere

Carefully structured economics that respond to the need for popular idioms are driving the centre of entertainment industry's output. In the range of media that seek to portray and represent spaces and the human body with increasing realism, additions of sound and music need not just support the actuality of game play but also encourage sonic ambiguities to enhance the imagination and form a counterpoint to the highly specified visual sensations. There are many other genres of games that are not so allied to the film form but are also animated and therefore simulated, and reference live action. They include Action Shooters, Action Adventure Role-Playing and Simulation of Life, Vehicle/Racing Simulation, and Management and Construction. This simple categorization process, however, immediately draw observations. For example, games development is fast moving and that individual games may belong to more than one category. It is also crucially the result of changing and innovative marriage of technological and creative ideas. It is therefore, not a

surprise that artists and educators are migrating to virtual spaces for dialogue and opportunities for new expression.

The Pythagorean principle of the acousmatic has been described as pivotal to creating powerful illusions in cinema and animation in this chapter. The extension of these veiled sonicities to animation in variable situations can also be considered as a new potential area for transporting concepts. However, when the locations of the body or its tele-present form in virtual worlds alter and are in an unspecified flux, the relationship between spectator/user and immersed character are subject to an oscillation that could have a bearing on the acousmatic principle in such artistic virtual spaces

Second Life (Linden Lab, 2003) is debatable across genre and its sonic potential supports this. Neither a game nor an Animation or movie, in its original designation, it takes on the traces of both. It is however, increasingly becoming regarded as a creative, social, and artistic space. The objectives are not defined, as in a conventional game. It is interactive and user controlled whereas screen Animation is defined through its passive audiences. It shares, with Animation and Games, themes of motion, dynamics, and kineticism. Second Life builds its environment from Cartesian coordinates and Computer Graphic processes as does Games and more recently, so do popular forms of feature animation. All are modern spectacles widely consumed by different cultural groups.

Whilst it is difficult to define what Second Life is, its sound attributes conditions a response, just as in these other forms. It can be seen in the sonic potential of Second Life that the unseen voice for example, even if it is expressed as written language on a command line, vocalization, and language are still rendered powerfully through the anonymity of the acousmatic. The take up by education establishments to use this artistic virtual space with its open architecture and user driven content has been progressively rapid since its inception. Nearly 4000 educators were listed in 2007 seeing the potential for learning spaces where geographical boundaries and social and cultural boundaries are diminished. Whilst this number might have ebbed and flowed recently, the value of a self-constructed artistic space for persuasive interactions in virtual worlds is an interesting testament to the desire for humans re-imagining of the self in alternative ways. These environments provide a place to fail safely, in a wide range of artistic and learning situations, that is, for the most part, without repercussion. The Pythagorean example of the Akousmatikoi, where the teacher is veiled and unseen and relying only on the remote voice to enhance listening, is alive and full of potential in Second Life, as it is in other MMOs.

REFERENCES

Abel, R., & Altman, R. (2002). *The sounds of early cinema*. Bloomington, IN: Indiana University Press.

Altman, R. (Ed.). (1992). *Sound theory sound practice*. New York, NY: Routledge.

Altman, R. (2004). *Silent film sound*. New York, NY: Columbia University Press.

Barthes, R. (1977). *Musica practica, in image, music, text*. London, UK: Flamingo.

Chion, M. (1990). *Audio-vision: Sound on screen* (Gorman, C., Trans.). New York, NY: Columbia University Press.

Chion, M. (1999). *The voice in cinema* (Gorbman, C., Trans.). New York, NY: Columbia University Press.

Cholodenko, A. (Ed.). (1991). *The illusion of life*. Sydney, Australia: Power Publications.

Collins, K. (2008). *Game sound: An introduction to the history, theory and practice of video game music and sound design*. Cambridge, MA: The MIT Press.

Coyle, R. (Ed.). (2010). *Drawn to sound: Animation, film music and sonicity*. London, UK: Equinox Publishing.

Curtiss, S. (1992). The sound of early Warner Bros. cartoons. In Altman, R. (Ed.), *Sound Theory Sound Practice* (pp. 191–203). New York, NY: Routledge.

Goldmark, D. (2002). *The cartoon music book*. Chicago, IL: Chicago Review Press.

Goldmark, D. (2005). *Tunes for toons: Music and the Hollywood cartoon*. Berkeley, CA: UCP. doi:10.1525/california/9780520236172.001.0001

Grimshaw, M., & Schott, G. (2007b). *Situating gaming as a sonic experience: The acoustic ecology of first-person shooters*. Paper presented at Situated Play. Tokyo, Japan.

Klein, N. M. (1996). *Seven minutes: The life and death of the American animated cartoon*. London, UK: Verso.

Manovich, L. (2001). *The language of new media*. Cambridge, MA: The MIT Press.

Merleau Ponty, M. (1969). *The visible and the invisible*. Evanston, IL: North Western University Press.

Rost, M. (2001). *Teaching and researching listening*. London, UK: Pearson Education.

Russett, R., & Starr, C. (1976). *Experimental animation: An illustrated anthology*. New York, NY: Van Nostrand.

Schafer, R. M. (1994). *The soundscape: Our sonic environment and the tuning of the world.* Rochester, VT: Destiny Books.

Sobchack, V. (1992). *The address of the eye: A phenomenology of film experience.* Princeton, NJ: Princeton University Press.

Weiss, E., & Belton, J. (1985). *Film sound theory and practice.* New York, NY: Columbia University Press.

Wells, P. (1998). *Understanding animation.* London, UK: Routledge.

ADDITIONAL READING

Barthes, R. (1977). *The grain of the voice, in image, music, text.* London, UK: Flamingo.

Bordwell, D. (1989). *Making meaning: Inference and rhetoric in the interpretation of cinema.* Retrieved from http://en.wikipedia.org/wiki/Harvard_University_Press

Chion, M. (2009). *Film a sound art* (Gorbman, C., Trans.). New York, NY: Columbia University Press.

Clair, R. (1929). *The art of sound.* Retrieved, January 16, 2012 from http://lavender.fortunecity.com/hawkslane/575/art-of-sound.htm

Crafton, D. (1993). *Before mickey: The animated film 1898-1928.* Chicago, IL: University of Chicago Press.

Deleuze, G. (1992). *Cinema 1: The movement image.* London, UK: The Athlone Press.

Doane, M. A. (1980). *Ideology and the practice of sound editing and mixing.* Academic Press.

Feld, S. (1994). From schizophonia to schismogenesis. In Keil, C., & Feld, S. (Eds.), *Music Grooves* (pp. 257–289). Chicago, IL: The University of Chicago Press.

Furniss, M. (1998). *Art in motion: Animation aesthetics.* London, UK: John Libbey.

Glassner, A. (2004). *Interactive storytelling: Techniques for 21st century fiction.* Wellesley, MA: AK Peters.

Halas, J. (1976). *Visual scripting.* London, UK: Focal Press.

Halas, J. (1987). *Masters of animation.* London, UK: BBC Books.

Lauretis & Heath. S. (Eds.). (1985). *The cinematic apparatus.* London, UK: Macmillan.

Manovich, L. (2000). *What is digital cinema? The digital dialectic new essays in new media.* Cambridge, MA: MIT Press.

Mathieu, W. A. (1994). The musical life. Boston, MA: Shambhala.

Merleau Ponty, M. (1962). *Phenomenology of perception.* London, UK: Routledge.

Moholy-Nagy, L. (1947). *Vision in motion.* Chicago, IL: Paul Theobald.

Stokes, M., & Maltby, R. (Eds.). (1999). *American movie audiences.* London, UK: BFI.

Westercamp, H. (2002). *Linking soundscape composition and acoustic ecology. Organised Sound: An International Journal of Music and Technology, 7(1).*

KEY TERMS AND DEFINITIONS

Acousmatic: Off screen and unspecified sound source.

Interactivity: Active engagement by the spectator either physically or mentally.

Listening: A function of hearing.

MMO: Massively Multiplayer Online Games.

Sense: Means through which a range external stimuli are received.

Sonicity: That which relates to sound and vibration.

Sound Space: Dimension of sonic material in a space either real or recorded.

Voice: The specific vocal part of a soundtrack. Can also refer to the context of an artifact.

ENDNOTES

[1] Pierre Schaffer attributed with the researching a definition of the term "acousmatique" which signifies a sound with an unspecified source.

[2] Aristotle 384 BC-322 BC.

[3] Recent studies have revealed that the brain has a capability to compensate for losing one sense such as sight or hearing. but that the best results are with people who were blind or hearing impaired from birth. The indication is that there is plasticity in the brain that can acquire and compensate for such losses. An interesting brief primer on this topic can be found at http://health.msn.com/health-topics/blind-people-hear-better-truth-or-myth-1 or http://www.livestrong.com/article/268986-how-does-becoming-blind-affect-other-senses/. A recent study by Dr Robert Zatorre at the Dept of Neurology and Neurosurgery provides a more in depth view of this phenomenon.

[4] In 1959, A travel film: *Behind the Great Wall* director Crlo Lizzani was released with a system called "AromaRama" a method to accompany films with scent injected into the air conditioning of theatres.

[5] Smell-O-Vision was another competing system that emitted smell during the projection of a film so that the viewer could "smell" what was happening in the movie. Working in time to a soundtrack, various odours would be released at appropriate times. It was only used once in a film directed by Mike Todd Jr., *Scent of Mystery*.

[6] Borrowed from the Greek word skhisma meaning cleft. Attributed to Gregory Bateson, English anthropologist, social scientist, linguist, visual anthropologist, semiotician and cyberneticist.

[7] See Mathieu (1994).

[8] See Feld (1994).

Chapter 10
Para–Formalistic Discourse and Virtual Space in Film

Ian P. Stone
Independent, UK

ABSTRACT

Cinema remains current and saleable by constantly revolutionising the mode of its distribution. Film Auteurs are affected by these changes, using the contemporary "tools of their trade" to their advantage. This chapter focuses on two Auteurs' use of digital technologies. Jean Luc Godard, one of the most innovative filmmakers of the last fifty years is a recent convert to digital film, having denounced the medium previously. Mike Figgis has been an advocate of digital filmmaking until recently, when he has been more circumspect. These filmmakers employ techniques indebted to Sergei Eisenstein and Bertholt Brecht. The "active" variant of third text understandings applied represent a "para-formalistic discourse" where the audience is made aware of the film's artifice, projecting the audience into an ontological virtual space where they are compelled to confront conditions around them. A tentative advocacy of the digital as an aid to enhancing this experience is here advanced.

INTRODUCTION

This chapter addresses issues concerning the production and reception of digital films; the ability of the auteur to shape such films, and the impact of the films on their audience. A broad definition of new media exemplifies the spirit of such specific explorations into digital filmmaking, noting; 'formal and technological experiments' and 'a complex set of interactions between new technologies and established media forms' (Lister, et al., 2003, p. 10). Such a conceptualisation recognises the potential for innovation present in the digital medium but also continuity with the older analogue form. An effect of the proliferation of digital film technologies such as CGI and

DOI: 10.4018/978-1-4666-2961-5.ch010

state of the art 3D has been to create the illusion of virtual worlds. The virtual here is characterised as a simultaneous depiction of 'real' conditions (virtual as *nearly*), and a liminal bridging to alternate or meta-realities. This chapter argues that para-formalistic discourse, being aware of its own artifice, is a necessary corollary of the film industry; namely an antithetic, countercultural approach that must strive to superimpose itself over and above the existing status quo. In repeated usage, it conjures forth a multiplicity of possible 'virtual worlds.' Para-formalistic discourse is third text narrative that responds to ontological givens and attempts to subvert them; that summons commentary from non-film based mediums (e.g. theatre) in order to form a meta-critique; and is an expressly political manoeuvre, grounded in theory indebted to Marxism and existentialism.

BACKGROUND

The creation of virtual worlds in film has been a facet of cinema since its inception. As an enclosed virtual space, cinema necessarily removed the spectator-consumer from the external physical reality of the outside world. Filmmakers continue to exploit new technologies to maintain the mystique of this virtual space. Digital film is the latest of these innovations. This chapter focuses on two progressive directors who have had different initial responses to the digital, Jean Luc Godard (France, 1959-present) and Mike Figgis (UK, 1980-present). Their similarity in outlook and approach has eventually caused a convergence of sorts in their attitude to the digital via a circuitous route that takes in issues of cultural context, aesthetic preference, and political positioning. As exemplars, their work embodies continuity in film that has always grasped as presciently at the future as it has drawn selectively from the past.

A cursory analysis of Godard and Figgis' approach to the digital suggests divergent paths. Godard expresses apparently negative comments about the digital in an interview of 2001, where

he references a cautious approach to the potential manipulation of new technologies. Godard's contention is this: "The so-called 'digital' medium is not a mere technical medium but a medium of thought. And when modern democracies turn technical thought into a separate domain, these modern democracies incline towards totalitarianism" (*The Guardian*, 10/10/2001). Nine years after this statement, *Film Socialisme* (2010) is Godard's first fully digital work. As one of digital cinemas innovators, Figgis was one of its foremost advocates. Yet more recently he has stated, as evinced by icewaterpictures (2008): "Digital technology has just indicated the acceleration of the problem of cultural saturation...."

When Godard made *Film Socialisme*, it seemed to parallel the work of cultural theorist Lev Manovich (2003), whose book *The Language of New Media* was as a new advocate of the digital and appeared a few short years after Manovich's (1998) own technophobic communique *On Totalitarian Interactivity*. As with Godard, the adjustment was not as stark as it first appears. Manovich's realignment was based around the political and social potentiality of the new medium; this facet has become more apparent as innovations such as digital streaming have developed. Digital streaming can now be used not just to relay cultural events at geographic distance but also create the possibility of multiple political meetings from one, by streaming the speaker to other locations. It is difficult to chart Godard's own change in judgement since there is scant evidence to suggest it was purely political. Perhaps more importantly to Godard the digital represented a total *realisation* of his own aesthetic.

The denial or delay of this realisation has its origin in allegiances in French Cinema dating back to the 1940s. Godard had belonged to a social set that had frequented the Cine'-Club du Quartier Latin (CQQL) founded in 1947 by one of Eric Rohmer's students (Brody, 2008, p. 15). Amongst this social set was a disavowal of the orthodoxy in French film at the time, which favoured weighty literary adaptions. The response to such fare was to advance a youthful internationalism that valorised directors who took control of their films and exacted an authorial stamp on their works. This approach was concretised in an article by Francois Truffaut in *Cahiers du Cinema* in 1954, which advanced a *politique des auteurs*. The article drew opposition from editor-in chief Andre Bazin, whose advocacy of non-intervention in filmic terms cast the director as facilitator rather than master (Cook, 2007, p. 390).

Importantly, there was openness towards American cinema that was not a facet of the contemporary French filmmaking status quo. The emerging outlook had important consequences for Godard as he made the transition from established film critic to filmmaker. Though Truffaut would be the first French filmmaker to release a Hollywood tribute with *400 blows* (1959) it was Godard's *Breathless* (1960), that spearheaded the *Nouvelle vague* movement as an aesthetic and commercial concern, successfully alchemising a pastiche that stood askance of US 'reality,' whilst being a fond enough portrayal of Hollywood production values to guarantee the film a successful reception in the U.S. Stylised editing was back on the agenda, a tribute to Hollywood film noir. Godard was able to deploy techniques such as the 'jump-cut,' which were viewed as not just artistic innovations, but proved to be money saving devices too.

ISSUES, CONTROVERSIES, PROBLEMS

Jean Luc Godard and Brechtian Form

The unique aspect of the editorial interventions of Godard was that he was, if not the first to pastiche Hollywood film, the first to enact pastiche that simultaneously cannibalised recognisable Hollywood tropes while questioning their right to exist. He might have appreciated some Hollywood films, notably those of Hitchcock (See Milne,

1972, pp. 37, 51), but he also resented having to work to a formula even as he stood askance from it. *Breathless* was dependent on the existence of the Hollywood machine it critiqued, and he was relieved when it was commercially successful. He now had free rein to make more overtly experimental films, and kept pace with developments in popular culture as he sought to fulfil an aesthetic vision that drew on a neo-classicism indebted to a Bourgeois upbringing. Godard's father was a doctor and his maternal grandfather a Banker who was also a close friend of Paul Valery and Andre Gide. (Mac Cabe, 2003, p. 7) *Cahiers du Cinema* hinted at this when an interviewer from the time of *Une Femme est Une Femme* (1961) posited: "Only a fraction of the Nouvelle Vague have this [i.e. Godard's] cultural equipment" (Milne, 1972, p. 172).

Godard's' background provided him with a broader pallet to construct his films than his contemporaries and also an insightful affinity with the films of the old guard such as Roberto Rossellini (Milne, 1972, pp. 140-142). It also allowed for a unique positioning; he was fully integrated into the Nouvelle Vague. Developments in film generally at this stage are predicated largely on an understanding of cultural developments of the previous generation, a juncture where traditional art: "...starts to foreground its own processes and practices...this moment of foregrounding takes place in a specific context-the advent of universal education in democratic societies of the west" (Mac Cabe, 2003, p. 158). Moreover, in this paradigm Bourgeois invocations of 'understood art' are insufficient. So too are Romantic ideals of the 'artist as genius.' Reactions include 'the aesthetic, where the audience is projected into a virtual future' (Mac Cabe, 2003, p. 158), or a retreat into a regressive version of Modernism that denigrates the role of art. Two other options remain, to produce art that follows a political agenda, or to produce art that articulates a political situation (Mac Cabe, 2003, pp. 158-159).

The first and fourth reactions reference the reflexive political theatre of Bertholt Brecht. Brecht seeks to project his audience into a virtual future. He also produces theatre art that articulates a political situation. He does this by reference to Ancient Greek epic theatre forms, for example Godard himself admitted that the twelve "formal tableaux" (Barthes, 1977, p. 70) that segmented *Vivre sa Vie* (1962) were used to showcase his "Brechtian side" (Godard, 1998, p. 221). More explicitly, "Epigrammatic, compressed gestures (*gestus*), sophisticated arrangements of movement; stylization, cool elegance, and a relaxed enjoyment of the technicalities of art replace a correct imitation which is 'true to life'" (Demetz, intro pp. 7). The influence of Brecht in Godard's work is important because it allowed for a transfiguration of form that produced effects that would have been difficult to capture ordinarily through use of analogue methods. This transfiguration of form is indebted to para formalistic discourse, narrative that is self-aware of its own artifice. This is an 'active' third text narrative (Barthes, 1977, pp. 51-68) of which Brechtian form is a variant.

As early as the second of Godard's articles for the short lived *La Gazette du Cinema* 'Towards a political cinema' (1951) Godard is theorising film in an expressly political way (Milne, 1972, p. 16). Godard began to foreground political issues in his films as his fame grew. As Godard's films grew more political, so the technique of separating the spectator from the fiction became essential in order to achieve the effect he desired (Morrey, 2005, p. 39). This foregrounding was expressly Brechtian. It was fascinating to Godard that a form external to cinema could be so useful within the cinema, and if anything confirmed his modernist tendencies.

It is in Godard's excellent portrayal of a student Maoist group in *La Chinoise* that his Brechtian concerns reach their apotheosis. Jean Pierre Leauds' character may rub Brecht's' name from a blackboard (La Chinoise: 45:30) but he nevertheless haunts the film. A group of revolutionaries have taken over one of their parents out-of-town apartments for the summer, to plan revolutionary activity and conduct a theoretical 'summer school.' Here the mundanely day-to-day life of the Marxist cell, expressed through rituals such as exercise and the recitation of Marxist tracts (*La Chinoise*, 1967, 14:37) lulls us into acceptance of its veracity as a wider concern, before reality asserts itself as surprise in the shape of Veronique's botched assassination attempt (*La Chinoise*, 1967, 1:22:18), Serge's anomic suicide (*La Chinoise*, 1:21:33) or even cries of "revisionist!" (*La Chinoise*, 52:30) designed to disrupt the flow of an unapproved speech.

Brechtian *motifs* are also used to notable effect in Godard's 1972 film *Tout Va Bien*. There is an extensive prologue where we are informed that the film is fictional, that Yves Montand and Jane Fonda will play the lead characters (*Tout Va Bien*, 1972, 2:47), and that they live in the country which is "in the city" (*Tout Va Bien*, 4:08). Prologue is an intrinsic aspect of Brechtian form. As Walter Benjamin mused: "Like no one else, Brecht started at the beginning again and again. And this, incidentally, is the distinguishing mark of the dialectician" (Benjamin, 1934, 1973, pp. 37). Prologue is used in *Tout Va Bien* as irruption, to challenge repeatedly the viewer's precepts as to what a film should contain. In particular, a film does not typically contain commentary on itself; less often still does it question its own assumptions. This stop-start 'choppiness' is not just a philosophical manoeuvre but has narrative implications; 'stockpiling' Para-formalistic discourse, and allowing for longer, meditative scenes at the end of the film. In particular, the dreamlike tracking shot across the breadth of the supermarket ten minutes from the end of the film (*Tout Va Bien*, 1:19:02) revisits the romantic preoccupations of *Le Weekend* (1967). There it seemed to have been a fin de siècle expression of inward collapse, where the viewer was invited to examine the artefact of the destruction of civilisation. Indeed, the spectre evoked had theoretical parallels with the Paris of the late 19th Century, as depicted in Benjamin's *Arcades Project* (1999). In *Tout Va Bien* that civilisation re-emerges, coated in consumerist sheen.

Tout Va Bien ends up having the sense of a neo-realist film in respect of being a contextual piece. It illustrates a dialogue with everyday life that has become essential to deal with mass production and mediation. The bulk of the characters appear to be typologies, as is the case with *La Chinoise*. Two pointed differences to *La Chinoise* emerge. *Tout Va Bien* draws on the beginnings of notions of poststructuralism and postmodernism in its articulation of a personification of the political. For instance, the scheming factory boss espouses an ideology (*Tout Va Bien*, 13:30) is simultaneously an enunciation of the situation as much as one of class location. Nevertheless, he still comes across as somewhat of a manqué. He represents in this sense, incomplete, virtual Capitalism. Susan de Witt, meanwhile, emerges as the only character to truly break out of her typology, as evidenced by the extraordinary level of self-awareness she exhibits in the argument with Jacques (*Tout Va Bien*, 1:06:45). Her assertions, underlined by *Gestus* render both Jacques and the viewer stunned with sudden recognition. It is a masterful Brechtian manoeuvre.

Para-Formalistic Discourse in Film Theory

Crucial to Godard's aesthetic is that his favourite filmmakers were steeped in theory and articulated para-formalistic methods. One of these theorists was the filmmaker who would provide the inspiration for the name of the collective that Godard and Jean Pierre Gorin formed when Godard 'retired' from mainstream filmmaking in 1968, Dziga Vertov (see Brody, 2008, pp. 319-320). Vertov employed a primarily documentary-based filmmaking style in films such as *Man With a Movie Camera* (1929). However, his innovative camerawork created the sense of being slightly

'beside oneself' (Eisenstein, 1938, 1987, p. 27) as a viewer. Vertovs' *The Essence of Kino-Eye* (Vertov, 1927, 1984) essay could be understood as a valorisation of naturalism, but there is a counter-tension in his writing. He writes of "the decoding of life as it is" and "using facts to influence the workers consciousness" (Vertov, 1927, 1984, p.49). The first statement is indicative of a passive chronicler of 'found' life, who may ruminate about what is real but not act on it. This aspect informs the aesthetic position of Andre Bazin, who favoured minimal camera 'trickery' in order to convey reality (Neupert in Cook, 2008, pp. 532-533). By contrast the second statement is almost an atavistic automatism. Both impulses are at work in Godard-Gorins Dziga Vertov films, indeed usually within a single film.

British Sounds (1969) is the most apposite example of this tension. The film opens with an eight minute naturalistic factory scene, simultaneously sound tracked by ear-splitting atonal music and an undercurrent of speedily read Marxist theory. As the end of the scene approaches, the atonal music smothers the sound of the theory and reaches a crescendo (*British Sounds*, 8:27). The next scene features three competing voices, a man, woman, and later a child, intoning over the image of a naked woman walking between upstairs rooms, then descending the stairs (*British Sounds*, 9:00). A later scene features a politician making a racist speech (*British Sounds*, 15:30); it is clearly staged, but shot in a documentary style. This is juxtaposed with a scene of 'found life,' unadorned by music or speeches, of workers talking between themselves at their workplace, on a cigarette break (*British Sounds*, 21:00). It contrasts strikingly with the artifice, which has gone before.

Sergei Eisenstein is the second of the two filmmakers that most influence Godard's conception of reality. Eisenstein's aesthetic is one of "organic unity and pathos" (Eisenstein, 1938, 1987, p. 11). This encapsulates "wholeness and an inner law" where the work is "governed by a law of structuring, all its separate parts are subordinated to this law." The second element is that the canon of natural phenomena is present in the work and replicates itself in the structure (Eisenstein, 1938, 1987, pp. 11-12). A synthesis of the two elements represents the embodiment of an "organic unity of a particular or exceptional order" (Eisenstein, 1938, 1987, p.27). The pathos in the Meta element generated by this synthesis takes the work past a mere internal dialogue and into a relationship with external meta-reality. The auteur generates an effect that allows the receiving subject, the viewer to double in objectivity, to "be beside oneself" (Eisenstein, 1938, 1987, p. 27). Eisenstein articulates a version of para-formalistic discourse here. Another version is *Mise-en-Scene*, a "graphic projection of the character of the action" (Eisenstein, 1938, 1987, p. 15).

Eisenstein suggested that in *Mise-en-scene* the framing of shots are sometimes necessary to illustrate a more universal point. To this end, they lose their metaphorical positing and return to the non-metaphorical, performing re-integration with the 'naturalistic' world (Eisenstein, 1937, 1991, p. 21). It is another favoured manoeuvre in Brecht's theatre. However, Eisenstein considered *Mise-en-Scene* in filmic terms to be the more primitive forerunner to montage (Eisenstein, 1938, 1987, p. 15). Eisenstein preferred montage in the sense that it allowed him to produce a realist piece that he could exert enough authorial control over to direct it to the soviet authority's specifications. Though this was not imperative when he started filmmaking, Eisenstein quickly fell out of favour when Stalin came to power and *Bezhin Meadow*, a notable departure from his normal aesthetic, was forcibly taken out of production (Kleiman in Eisenstein, 1991, p. 17).

Godard distanced himself from the Hollywood machine seemingly with every film up until 1967. If *Le Weekend* was his critique of European civilisation and *La Chinoise* a critique of both US imperialism and the media, the next logical step was to step outside the industry entirely, a move

befitting of someone who was keen to continue to maintain his independence as an auteur. Godard saw the establishment of the *Dziga Vertov* group as the answer to his problems, though he did then use the New York film festival to promote his film *Le Gai Savior* (Wheeler Dixon, 1997, p. 101). This period of Godard's career was experimental in the extreme.

The grand staging of the *Le Gai Savior* (1968) premiere is evidence of this. The audience walked out *en masse* thirty minutes in Wheeler Dixon (1997, p. 101) due perhaps to the efficacy of Godard's inversion of Brechtian method. An edifice of theory is built up in the early scenes, centred on two characters talking to each other against a black background, the only prop in evidence a multi-coloured umbrella. Crucially, the two characters are named Emile Rousseau and Patricia Lumumba and are thus representatives of Bourgeois romanticism and postcolonial revolution respectively (Brody, 2008, pp. 316-317). The characters are 'students' of images and sounds, which they are to collect, criticise, and then make their own models of. Two unenlightening interviews follow, one with an elderly man, the other with a young boy (*Le Gai Savior*, 27:40). The typical Brechtian method is to alienate the audience first, then invite them back in with a surprise that chimed with their lives, the idea of *Gestus* (Jameson, 1999, p. 126) where a gesture can have both particular and universal significance. Instead, an intimate setting of supposed import had been constructed, with plenty of interest contained for both fan and critic, and then seemingly wasted with a dreary interlude that gave no indication of letting up. More patient moviegoers were rewarded with the knowledge that it was an aberrant ten minutes of an otherwise interesting film, though Godard attempts to alienate his audience later through the deployment of intrusive atonal music.

One Plus One is One (1968), meanwhile, suffers from not knowing if it wants to be a commercial film or an art film. The Rolling Stones had asked Godard to chronicle the making of their most menacing song, 'Sympathy for the Devil' (1968). The naturalistic camerawork is appropriate but for once the band are bland in all aspects apart from their bright clothing. The accompanying vignettes are underdeveloped, and provide insufficiently interesting counterpoint to what seems like routine and uneventful recording sessions. Godard himself vehemently disagreed with the producers edit (Brody, 2008, pp. 340-341). In later films, the experience was to prove instructional, in the sense that Godard began to visibly obsess over getting every aspect of his films right. We see this in *Numero Deux* (1975), his first film to be part-shot on video, and our first encounter with Godard as actor: "We're back in the editing room with Godard, who seems to have collapsed over his desk…his effort to control the world, to reduce human nature to strips and tape have apparently failed. The manipulator is being manipulated" (Kehr, 2011, p. 147).

Godard's aesthetic from the mid-sixties on seems to be this desire to get to 'reality,' to control the agenda, the mark of the auteur. Despite his love of elements of expressionist cinema, evidenced by the appearance of Fritz Lang in *Le Mepris* (1963) and in his *Cahiers* writings, there is not the sense of leaving anything to chance. Godard could not be the passive recorder of life that one reading of Andre Bazin would suggest (Thompson & Cook, 2007, p. 525), and at times resisted the auteur impulse too. For instance, an aspect of his films that was truly naturalistic was that the scripts were open ended, with only rough guidelines as to where the story was going to go (Andrew, 2002, p. 29), allowing for a lot of improvisation. For Godard, the debate between and Expressionism, on-going since the thirties (e.g. Adorno, et al., 2007) was something of a straw man. Modernism and its striving for objectivity through technical means was not as much about the inhuman as social realism could ever be said to be a completely human rendering of a supposedly accurate portrayal of reality.

Figgis: Para-Formalism and the Digital

Occupying a place between these two extremes are the films of Mike Figgis, already an accomplished director when in 1999 he shot *Timecode*, his first major digital feature. *Timecode* had proved Figgis to be an innovator not only in terms of his use of multiple location set-ups, and his holistic translation of this to a quadruple split screen format, but also by way of the use of a continuous live take. Four apparently separate stories bleed into each other, working towards a *denouement* where several of the central protagonists meet to catastrophic consequence (*Timecode*, 1:23:10). This is preceded by a speech from the female filmmaker character, who references both Sergei Eisenstein and Dziga Vertov (*Timecode*, 1:12:45), highlighting them as being the vanguard of a former era. She talks of a new age of filmmaking, one conditioned by digital technology and mediation, the response to which she believes should be a return to Leibniz's "monadology" (*Timecode*, 1:13:30). Figgis is a Godard fan and intimately familiar with Godard's indebtedness to Eisenstein and Brecht (see Figgis interview extra on Criterion Collection DVD).

Timecode was a fulfilment of a trajectory Figgis had been on since his earliest productions. *Redheugh* (1980) combined film, live music, and theatre. Figgis called it a 'performance-art theatre piece' (Figgis, 2006, p. 20). Similar productions followed over the next few years. Even when Figgis tried his hand at making mainstream movies, jazz prominently underscored the images. Unusual too was the extent of Figgis' input into the films; writing the scores, and often playing on the soundtrack. Even Godard as auteur did not have this level of control over his films. In the months immediately prior to *Timecode*, Figgis shot a version of Strindberg's *Miss Julie*; 'which makes use of fluid, hand-held camerawork, and split-screens. The film was shot within one set using digital cameras in a series of long takes which add to the intensity and claustrophobia of the piece' (Stail, 2007, p. 62). One of Figgis' many striking similarities with Godard is his vacillation between 'high' and 'mass culture,' often within the same film. We get a sense of this with *Leaving Las Vegas*, essentially a story about decay and degradation set to a soundtrack of refined music. The Nicolas Cage character has a drinking problem that is both a general comment on the destructive potentialities of modern capitalism and also has a rarefied uniqueness about it in its very extremity.

Robert Stail (2007, pp. 61-62) in his sketch of Figgis's work is frustrated by a lack of consistency, seeing it as a weakness. A particular complaint is the fact of Figgis's Hollywood excursions followed by a return to the UK. As with Godard, the twin Europe/America obsession has played out over time, and conversely seems to have a unity of purpose in its blurring of the boundaries between those cultures, each new film suggestive of a different combination of European/US influences, both old and new. In many ways, this parallels Godard's experimentation. For instance, when Godard realised his documentary based location films were not making him money, he employed Jane Fonda and Yves Montand as stars of *Tout Va Bien* and shot in France, on an independent label. He then kept on Jane Fonda to shoot the resolutely uncommercial *Letter to Jane*, filmed in Vietnam.

SOLUTIONS AND RECOMMENDATIONS

If Godard's most effective films might properly be called 'an anticipation of the immersive' then Mike Figgis uses digital video to enable him to develop this aesthetic. In Godard, music is used usually to illustrate key narrative moments, as with the ironizing faux-classical Stockhausen *motif* used pointedly to underline pretension in *La Chinoise* (e.g. *La Chinoise*, 6:50), though this is less true in his Dziga Vertov period films, where music

is used more randomly and abstractly. Music in Figgis' films is used not so much as surprise, but as a constant. While Godard's use of music seems to permit us entry into an immersive world, there is the sense that with post-*Timecode* Figgis we are already in that immersive world. Timecode's script was written on music paper, broken into four *movements* around the plot device of four earthquake tremors (Figgis, European Graduate Lecture, 2008). In fact, the tremors might properly be called a positioning device, in the manner of Brecht, as they were indicators to the actors of where they were in their allotted ninety minutes in a largely improvised film. The shocks are rendered banal as the viewer comes to realise what they represent.

Figgis has been quoted as saying that Filmmaking had become 'boring and perhaps needed to become worse before anything better could emerge' (Figgis, 2005). The suggestion of boredom here as a liminal gateway to revelation is Brechtian. It also neatly juxtaposes the tension at work in digital cinema; for one, Francis Ford Coppola's idea that "any eight year old girl from Ohio" (Figgis, 2005) could now make a digital film is either potentially very liberating or allows for the possibility of a lot of dross to flood the market. There is also the sense of the high budget CGI films of the day conversely appearing as a 'glass ceiling' to upcoming filmmakers. These films are often made by established filmmakers with major film companies.

Berys Gaut uses *King Kong* (2005) as an example of a neo-realist film in the sense of being a film prepossessing of *photorealism*. This means that while the total scenario depicted in *King Kong* is unrealistic, the king Kong ape is assembled by reference to how a photograph of Kong *would* look, "if he existed with the properties that the animation image ascribes to him"(Gaut, 2010, p. 66). Moreover, it is a film with *content realism* in that we give *Kong* credulity due to the fact that he fits in with the 'reality-fantasy' world around him

(Gaut, 2010, p. 62). For these reasons, the high-end of the CGI market, i.e. the GCI blockbuster tends not to be dross as it does not treat it's audience disdainfully by trying to do something it cannot do. Rather, in operating within the realm of *the spectacular* it creates a world that is true to itself.

However, this does not recommend the *spectacular* as film art. If we apply a truly Brechtian, Para formalistic reading of the digital Hollywood blockbuster, as Slavoj Zizek does, an interesting juxtaposition emerges. Zizek states that we tend to accept the introduction of digital characters into the 'real' worlds of the *Star Wars* and *Lord of the Rings* films (Zizek, 2004a). Yet what is truly surprising to the viewer is when 'real characters' are incorporated into a digital world, as in the film *300*: "It is only with *300* that the combination of real actors and objects and digital environment come close to create a truly new, autonomous aesthetic space" (Zizek, 2004a). So, for Zizek, it is only this radical incongruity between the characters, made more real by being taken out of their ordinary context, and the virtual world they are forced to inhabit that creates antagonism as a precondition for truth.

Zizek's interpretation of the virtual is of it as a kind of 'Deleuzian excess' (Zizek, 2004b, p. 3). Apropos of Eisenstein, he cites the scene in *Ivan the Terrible* where Ivan's friends pour golden coins from large plates onto his newly anointed head: 'This veritable rain of gold cannot but surprise the spectator by its magically excessive character…' (Zizek, 2004, p. 3). The coins continue to flow even as the evidence suggests that there are far too few coins on the plates to produce such an excess. This is a typification of "the reality of the virtual as such…its real effects and consequences"(Zizek, 2004, p. 3). Such effects are produced firstly by a disparity between what human perception is able to visually interpret and the range of colour and visual information that science has hinted at but we have been unable to experience, and I would add, still less to nominalise. The second

aspect is that the human eye expands perception to interpolate and incorporate narrative into our visual experiences. The incongruity between these two modes forms a "Deleuzian transcendental" (Zizek, 2004b, p. 4).

Mike Figgis' *Timecode* and *Hotel* represent the generation of worlds within worlds. Each of the four simultaneous stories in motion in either of these films can be seen as external to any of the other three. Moreover, in both there is a meta-story at work, omniscient to all four: in *Timecode* concerning the making of a film, in *Hotel* the making of a production of Webster's' *The Duchess of Malfi* (1915). The fact that the meta-stories each involve the creation of a story is a tip of the hat to Godard's *Tout Va Bien* and about as kaleidoscopic as is possible to get within a film.

Hotel is a film Figgis had problems getting shown in its digital mode; it was typically re-formatted and projected in 35mm form, often at great cost (Figgis, 2006, p. 8). This is very curious in light of the clamour for digital films just a few years later. Though Figgis was an advocate of digital filmmaking when he released his book of the same name, in the years since he has been cautious in his application of the praise of the medium, perhaps coloured by his initial difficulty in getting his films shown, and now somewhat bewildered by the suffusion of variable examples of the form. He chose to make digital films as he saw its potential for the distortion of received narratives, and construction of new narratives, not to fetishize the medium but to use it as a tool. Theodore Adorno reflected that:

Underlying the element of truth in aesthetic hedonism is the fact that the means and the ends are not identical. In their dialectic, the former constantly asserts certain, and indeed, mediated independence…[As Alban Berg said], it is a prosaic matter to make sure that the work shows no nails sticking out and the glue does not stink (Adorno, 1997, p. 17).

While Figgis's work may sometimes look threadbare in contrast to a CGI blockbuster, that seems to be the point. The aim is to show the 'join' in the work since that is the moment of process that philosophy can then interrogate. This is not to confuse an interrogation of process as deconstruction for its own sake. Though they are both sometimes implicated in such readings of film, the predominance of postmodern theory from the 1980s onwards (See Callinicos, 1989) did as little for Mike Figgis as it did for Giles Deleuze, the major Cinema theoretician of the period.

Certainly theoretical rethinking in both cases was never merely about the object, or about adopting an ideology. Therefore, while some of the situations in *Timecode* are ridiculous, they are staged in such a way to stand out from the rest of the narrative; they are atypical. For example the '*Trotsky in the house*' rap/opera crossover is made more cringe worthy than it should be, as it immediately follows an earthquake tremor (*Timecode*, 1:10:30). This is also homage to Godard's "*It's the little red book, that makes it all* move" Mao song from *La Chinoise* (42:55), which also commented on the radical incongruity between politics and enacted situation.

Deleuze expressly references new technology, but again the emphasis is on using it to illustrate process: He writes of a closed system, much like Eisenstein's idea of everything being contained in one shot, that enables a 'becoming' (Deleuze, 1983, 1986, p. 145). The closed system is also "the detailing of how a film takes shape." Moreover, 'In this technical process, regulated by what Deleuze and Guattari called the "*machinic processes*" of social formations, a self-affective transformative "metacinema" arises from the cinematographic shot, cuts, and framed composition' (Colman, 2011, p. 43). The next stage of Deleuze's taxonomy is that: "...the virtual worlds created by screen forms intervene in all aspects of things in the world on screen and the bodies in the worlds external to that screen" (Colman, 2011, p. 1). The former aspect is certainly achieved by both Godard and Figgis, and it seems that instances of the use of Para Formalistic discourse have achieved the latter effect to a significant degree, though it is difficult to quantify such an experience.

FUTURE RESEARCH DIRECTIONS

Figgis's own characterisation of his productions have emphasized "a limited multi-media approach." In his version of the opera *Lucretia Borgia* (2011) this included 'a new overture' written for purpose "which is entirely cinematic" (English National Opera, 2011). Opera shares with epic theatre an exaggerated, projected style of reality that is para-formalistic. In the case of 'Lucretia Borgia,' 3D technologies are also used. Of whom might be called the 'modern auteur' directors Peter Greenaway has also used a multimedia approach in recent years. Greenaway cites Godard as an influence, though some have seen this as a Hegelian end-of-art/cinema influence (Willoquet-Maricondi & Alemony-Galway, 2008, p. 13). His recent films and art installations have used digital technology as a precept for experimentation.

Lars Von Trier's practice has parallels too. He was a founder of the experimental Dogme label (www.filmbug.com). He has since become an advocate of digital cinema and in his *Dogville* film, he references both Brecht in his use of stage positioning and the Godard of *Le Gai Savior*. To somewhat square the circle, it is notable that Dogme films, whilst being very structured in terms of the rules they obeyed, were not so much the films of the auteur but of the cast (www. Filmbug.com). This does not counterpose them to Godard's films, less still to Figgis's, as both directors incorporated elements of cast input; certainly more than many Hollywood films would. In their rigorous pursuit of naturalism, the Dogme films recall Andre Bazin's aesthetic.

The new versions of virtuality are not so different from the old. Zizek's version of virtuality is one that adheres to a model pursued by Eisenstein some seventy years ago: "a new sense: the ability to reduce visual and sound perceptions to a common denominator" (Eisenstein, 1988, p. 119). Here Eisenstein's invocation of gestural sound as an echo is illustrated by an example from Kabuki theatre where sobbing off stage "graphically corresponds" to the movement of the knife that enacts *hari-kari*' (Eisenstein, 1988, p. 119). Eisenstein attempted to provide a total cinema, yet did so in the silent era, where soundtracks could illustrate the action. There was no characterisation necessary: everything had to be apparent enough for the viewer to see. Though the quadruple screen format of *Timecode* might seem fussy presentation, it is perhaps easier on modern cognition than might at first be expected. As consumers, we are conditioned to process a multiplicity of images. Computer images are pixelated, a result of digital processing. Each pixel contains information, a part of the story of an image. In Figgis' *Timecode* or *Hotel,* the parts that make up the whole are held up to the light and examined. In such a way we are allowed into the world of the filmmaker. We are entreated to an exposition on process in the most direct of ways: "Digital media do not refer. They communicate" (Cubbitt, 2005, p. 250).

In pursuing Brechtian methods with digital technology, Mike Figgis has answered some of the questions Andre Bazin posed in the middle of the last century. He pondered why there had been no adaptions of theatre: "It has always been a temptation to the filmmaker to film theatre since it is already a spectacle-we know what comes of it" (Bazin, 1967, 2005, p. 54). In fact, Bazin shows his unfamiliarity with Brecht, by not thinking through how that form might be subverted. From *Redheugh* (1980) on, Figgis has been attempting to film theatre in a number of ways, each of them surprising. Digital technology has been the mode by which Mike Figgis has chosen to create an aesthetic space that articulates a political situation. When, in *Hotel,* for example we are confronted with a series of distressing scenes being played out we are somewhat comforted by the fact that

they could be staged, as the film is a film of an adaption of *The Duchess of Malfi* (1915). We are provided with the essential knowingness that Hollywood film can provide, but are on the precipitous border between that and a state where we confront conditions around us.

CONCLUSION

Thus, digital cinema provides the potential, if executed with care, to short circuit mediation. Slavoj Zizek showed how juxtaposition of real and unreal elements in the digital spectacular *300* could subvert the genre of the spectacular for the good, requiring us to question our ontology in a Brechtian way. Such questioning necessarily causes us to also question our position in the world. More prosaically, the amateur filmmaker is also advantaged in the practicalities of creating exposes or critiques of the system:

While digital production tools certainly had a strong impact on narrative feature filmmaking, they also affected documentary production in a positive way, offering filmmakers a viable method for producing low-budget films (Willis, 2005, p. 33).

This directness is something that would have appealed to Jean Luc Godard when making *Film Socialisme* at age eighty. Digital was a technique that he had not yet pursued and his long-term collaborator Ruth Walderburger as co-producer had a significant role in the cinematography of the piece. As with his collaboration with Gorin in *Tout Va Bien,* the subtext seems to be that in each case a pivotal moment in Godard's career sees his vision fulfilled only through the intervention of another. *Film Socialisme* is an extraordinary experiment that references the expansiveness of films such as *Russian Ark* (2000) in its cinematography, while conjoining the neo-classicist bourgeois realism of the films of his youth with an apposite counterweight of anti-colonial narratives referencing Palestine and Iraq. It does not try to compete with the films that a younger digital auteur might try to produce. Rather the film affects a stately pace that is suggestive of Godard as an omniscient elder. Godard eternalises his place in film whilst at the same time restating his claim to be current.

Adopting an antithetical approach has always been part of Godard's aesthetic. And yet it has never been more pertinent to reflect that what has made Godard a truly revolutionary director has been a rigorous application of theory to back up the impressive look of his work. It is imperative that such rigour must be consistently applied in the digital age, since the tools at the disposal of the modern filmmaker can just as easily be used in a slapdash way rather than for innovation. Mike Figgis amongst others has shown how the philosophical precepts at work in Godard's films can be effectively applied to the digital medium. He has simultaneously shown that Brechtian form is a pedagogical tool, but is not rigid in its effects. Indeed, the multiplicity of outcomes that can be generated through a philosophical application of para-formalistic discourse using tools such as the continuous live take provides a virtual space far more revolutionary and imaginative than the countervailing technism of CGI. What has set Godard, Figgis, and the like apart is not the determinisms of the prescribed fantasies that Hollywood has routinely produced. They both favour the use of active third text, or para-formalistic discourse to project their audience into a virtual future, where a situation articulated presents itself as incongruous as to be necessarily political.

REFERENCES

Adorno, T. W. (2007). *Aesthetic theory*. London, UK: Continuum.

Adorno, T. W., Benjamin, W., Bloch, E., Brecht, B., Lukacs, G., & Jameson, F. (Eds.). (2007). *Aesthetics and politics*. London, UK: Verso.

Andrew, D. (2002). *Concepts in film theory: An introduction*. Oxford, UK: Oxford University Press.

Barthes, R., & Heath, S. (Eds.). (1977). *Music, image, text*. London, UK: Harper Collins.

Bazin, A. (1995). *What is cinema? Volume one*. Berkeley, CA: University of California Press.

Benjamin, W., Eiland, H., & Mc Laughlin, K. (1999). *The arcades project*. Cambridge, MA: Harvard University Press.

Benjamin, W., & Mitchell, S. (1973). *Understanding Brecht*. London, UK: NLB.

Brody, R. (2008). *Everything is cinema: The working life of Jean Luc Godard*. New York, NY: Metropolitan Books.

Callinicos, A. (1989). *Against postmodernism*. Oxford, UK: Polity Press.

Canton, M., & Barnett, S. (Producers), & Synder, Z. (Director). (2009). *300* [Motion picture]. United States: Warner Brothers Pictures.

Colman, F. (2011). *Deleuze and cinema: The film concepts*. Oxford, UK: Berg.

Cook, P. (Ed.). (2007). *The cinema book*. London, UK: BFI Publishing.

Cubitt, S. (2005). *The cinema effect*. Cambridge, MA: MIT Press.

Deleuze, G., & Tomlinson, H. (1989). *Cinema 2: The time-image*. London, UK: Athlone Press.

Deleuze, G., Tomlinson, H., & Haberjam, B. (1986). *Cinema 1: The movement-image*. London, UK: Athlone Press.

Eisenstein, S. (Producer and Director). (1947). *Ivan the terrible part one* [Motion picture]. Soviet Union: Mosfilm.

Eisenstein, S., & Marshall, H. (1987). *Nonindifferent nature*. Cambridge, UK: Cambridge University Press.

Eisenstein, S., & Taylor, R. (Eds.). (1996). *Selected works volume one: Writings 1922-1934*. London, UK: BFI Publishing.

Eisenstein, S., Taylor, R., & Glenny, M. (Eds.). (1991). *Selected works volume two: Written circa 1937-1938: Towards a theory of montage*. London, UK: BFI Publishing.

English National Opera. (2011). *Mike Figgis on Lucretia Borgia*. Retrieved 28/5/2012 from http://www.englishnationalopera.com

Figgis, M. (Producer and Director). (1980). *Redheugh* [Motion picture]. United Kingdom: Artsadmin.

Figgis, M. (Producer and Director). (1988). *Miss Julie* [Motion picture]. United Kingdom: Metro-Goldwyn Mayer.

Figgis, M. (Producer and Director). (1996). *Leaving Las Vegas* [Motion picture]. France: Lumiere Pictures.

Figgis, M. (Producer and Director). (2000). *Timecode* [Motion picture]. United Kingdom: Screen Gems.

Figgis, M. (Producer and Director). (2002). *Hotel* [Motion picture]. United Kingdom: Moonstone Entertainment.

Figgis, M. (2007). *Digital filmmaking*. London, UK: Macmillan.

Figgis, M. (Producer and Director). (2011). *Lucretia borgia* [Motion picture]. United Kingdom: Sosho Productions.

Figgis. (2005). *Wikipaedia*. Retrieved 23/5/2012 from http://Wikipaedia.comMikeFiggis

Filmbug. (2012). *Website*. Retrieved 2/6/2012 from http://filmbug.com/dictionary/dogme95.php

Gaut, B. (2007). *A philosophy of cinematic art*. Cambridge, UK: Cambridge University Press.

Gibbs, J., & Pye, D. (2005). *Style and meaning: Studies in the detailed analysis of film*. Manchester, UK: Manchester University Press.

Godard, J. L. (Producer and Director). (1960). *A bout de Soufflé* [Motion picture]. France: Les Productions Georges des Bureaugardes.

Godard, J. L. (Producer and Director). (1961). *Une femme est une femme* [Motion picture]. France: Euro International Films.

Godard, J. L. (Producer and Director). (1962). *Vivre sa vie* [Motion picture]. France: Les Films de la Pleiade.

Godard, J. L. (Producer and Director). (1963). *Le Mepris* [Motion picture]. France: Les Films Concordia.

Godard, J. L. (Producer and Director). (1967). *Deux or trois choses que je Sais d'elle* [Motion picture]. France: Argus Films/Nouveaux Pictures.

Godard, J. L. (Producer and Director). (1967). *La Chinoise* [Motion picture]. France: Anouchka films.

Godard, J. L. (Producer and Director). (1967). *Le weekend* [Motion picture]. France: Ascot Cineraid.

Godard, J. L. (Producer and Director). (1969). *British sounds* [Motion picture]. Unreleased.

Godard, J. L. (Producer and Director). (1975). *Numero deux* [Motion picture]. France: Bela Productions.

Godard, J. L., & Gorin, J. P. (Producer and Director). (1972). *Letter to Jane: An investigation of a film still* [Motion picture]. France: Son Image.

Godard, J. L., & Gorin, J. P. (Producers and Directors). (1972). *Tout va bien* [Motion picture]. Italy: Anouchka Films.

Godard, J. L., & Milne, T. (Eds.). (1972). *Godard on Godard*. New York, NY: Da Capo Press.

Icewaterpictures. (2008). *Mike Figgis*. Retrieved 1/6/2012 from http://www.youtube.com

Jackson, P. (Producer and Director). (2001). *The fellowship of the* ring [Motion picture]. New Zealand: Entertainment Film Distribution.

Jackson, P. (Producer and Director). (2002). *The two towers* [Motion picture]. New Zealand: Entertainment Film Distribution.

Jackson, P. (Producer and Director). (2003). *The return of the king* [Motion picture]. New Zealand: Entertainment Film Distribution.

Jackson, P. (Producer and Director). (2005). *King kong* [Motion picture]. New Zealand: Universal Pictures.

Jameson, F. (1999). *Brecht and method*. New York, NY: Verso.

Kehr, D. (2011). *When movies mattered: Reviews from a transformative decade*. Chicago, IL: University of Chicago Press.

Lister, M. (2003). *New media: A critical introduction*. London, UK: Routledge.

Mac Cabe, C. (1980). *Godard: Images, sounds, politics*. London, UK: BFI Publishing.

Mac Cabe, C. (2003). *Godard: A portrait of the artist at seventy*. London, UK: Bloomsbury Press.

Manovich, L. (2001). *The language of new media*. Cambridge, MA: MIT Press.

Manovich, L. (2012). *On totalitarian interactivity*. Retrieved 2/6/2012 from manovich.net/TEXT/totalitarian.html

Morrey, D. (2010). *Jean Luc Godard*. Manchester, UK: Manchester University Press.

Quarrier, I. (Producer), & Godard, J. L. (Director). (1968). *One plus one is one* [Motion picture]. United Kingdom: Pro Cupid Productions.

Sider, L., Sider, J., & Freeman, D. (2003). *Soundscape: The school of sound lectures 1998-2001*. New York, NY: Wallflower Press.

Stail, R. (2007). *British film directors: A critical guide*. Carbondale, IL: Southern Illinois University Press.

Truffaut, F. (Producer and Director). (1959). *The 400 blows aka les quatre cent coups* [Motion picture]. France: Les Films du Carrosse.

Vertov, D. (Producer and Director). (1929). *Man with a movie camera* [Motion picture]. Soviet Union: VKUFU.

Vertov, D., Michelson, A., & O'Brien, K. (Eds.). (1984). *The writings of Dziga Vertov*. London, UK: Pluto Press.

Von Trier, L. (Producer and Director). (2003). *Dogville* [Motion picture]. Denmark: Lions Gate Films.

Waldburger, R. (Producer), & Godard, J. L. (Director). (2010). *Film socialism* [Motion picture]. United States: Vega Films.

Webster, J., & Gibbons, B. (Eds.). (2001). *The duchess of malfi*. London, UK: AC&Black.

Wheeler-Dixon, W. (1997). *The films of Jean Luc Godard*. Albany, NY: State University of New York Press.

Willis, H. (2005). *New digital cinema: Reinventing the moving image*. New York, NY: Wallflower Press.

Willocquet-Maricondi, P., & Alemony-Galway, M. (2008). *Peter Greenaway's postmodern/poststructuralist cinema*. Blue Ridge Mountain, PA: Scarecrow Press.

Zizek, S. (2004a). *The true Hollywood left*. Retrieved 25/5/12 from http://www.lacan.com/zizhollywood.htm

Zizek, S. (2004b). *Organs without bodies: Deleuze and consequences*. London, UK: Routledge.

KEY TERMS AND DEFINITIONS

Gestus: A 'fateful historical act' illustrated by a gesture that articulates both the general and particular.

Jump Cut: An editorial device in film used to signify dynamism.

Kabuki: Gestural Japanese theatre.

Liminal: A threshold/bridge between states: here, reality and the virtual.

Mediation: An ideological intervention between the reality of an image/situation and the way in which it is received.

Para-Formalistic: Discourse that, in adopting an exaggerated or ironical stance demonstrates the ideological dimension of conventional form.

Third Text: A reading of an image that is not constrained to either an analysis of it's contents or an assessment of its symbolism, but a mixture of the two, creating a third meaning.

Virtual: Nearness to reality/access to meta-reality.

Chapter 11
Database Narrative, Spatial Montage, and the Cultural Transmission of Memory:
An Anthropological Perspective

Judith Aston
University of the West of England, UK

ABSTRACT

This chapter discusses ways in which the database narrative techniques of virtual media can be used to explore the relationship between real-world oral storytelling and embodied performance in the cultural transmission of memory. It is based on an ongoing collaboration between the author and the historical anthropologist, Wendy James, to develop a multilayered associative narrative, which considers relationships between experience, event, and memory among a displaced community. The work is based on a substantial living archive of photographs, audio, cine, and video recordings collected by Wendy James in the Sudan/Ethiopian borderlands from the mid-1960s to the present day. Its critical context relates to the 'sensory turn' in anthropology and to 'beyond text' debates within the arts and humanities regarding ways in which we can capture and represent the sensory experiences of the past.

INTRODUCTION

The chapter relates to an ongoing collaboration between the author as a visual anthropologist and lecturer in creative media production, and the Oxford-based historical anthropologist, Wendy James. This work, which has been proceeding on an intermittent basis over the past ten years, explores new possibilities for the use of interactive digital media in the communication of anthropological ideas and arguments. The work sits alongside James' writings on her long-term fieldwork in the

DOI: 10.4018/978-1-4666-2961-5.ch011

Sudan/Ethiopian borderlands, and is intended for distribution within museum gallery settings and networked environments, and as DVD publication. It is articulated within the context of the 'sensory turn' in anthropology (Howes, 2003) and 'beyond text' debates within the arts, humanities, and social sciences, which seek to bring non-textual forms of communication into the heart of scholarly discourse. In terms of technique, it builds on Manovich's aesthetically orientated work on spatial montage (Manovich, 2001), to consider new possibilities through which to create narrative meaning. The focus of the work is on using multiple windows on a computer screen to juxtapose sound, still, and moving image recordings and create authored routes through a multimedia archive. The audience for this is mixed, to include academic experts, members of the public with a more general interest in the work, and the people themselves who are represented in the archive.

LONG-TERM FIELDWORK

Wendy James has been conducting intermittent fieldwork with the Uduk-speaking people from the Blue Nile area of the Sudan/Ethiopian borderlands since the mid-1960s. When she began her fieldwork, the Uduk were living as subsistence farmers in small hamlet communities but, with the outbreak of civil war in the late 1980s, they were forced to leave these hamlets and became subjected to a series of displacements across Ethiopia and the Sudan. Most of the survivors ended up living in a semi-permanent refugee camp just inside Ethiopia, where they remained until 2006, when an official repatriation scheme was initiated following the Sudan Peace Agreement. In 2011, when South Sudan became an independent state, the Uduk found themselves living just north of yet another border under the ongoing jurisdiction of the Republic of the Sudan. Recent fighting in the area has subsequently led to them to once again becoming displaced. Although James' last trip to the Sudan/Ethiopian borderlands was in 2000,

she has continued to work with the Uduk, both as a humanitarian advocate and through ongoing fieldwork with diaspora communities in the United States.

From the outset, James used audio-visual recording techniques as an integral part of her fieldwork, initially working with Super-8 film, reel-to-reel audio and photographic slides, moving on to Hi-8 video, audio cassettes and photographic prints, and more recently helping the Uduk themselves to buy their own digital cameras. In spanning more than a forty-year period, from the mid 1960s to the early 2000s, these recordings reflect the changing nature of her fieldwork through time, as she has moved from being a PhD student and participant observer, through becoming a historical witness of war and displacement, to writing advisory reports for various agencies working in the region. They also reflect the materiality of the range of recording technologies employed, which adds to the sense of a changing context of engagement through time (as described in depth in Aston & James, 2012). However, on another level there is a strong sense of consistency in James' recording style, which combines observational footage with informal interviews often using long takes. This enables comparisons to be made across time and place, to highlight aspects of both continuity and change among the Uduk people and their neighbouring communities, and to link this to James' own reflections and analysis on her experiences.

Many of the recordings are highly emotive in nature, as they combine observational material of everyday life and events, such as dance, music making, work rhythms, and children at play, with footage of traumatic events and spoken memories of these events. The observational material can be used to embody a sense of village life as well as to show continuities and changes that the people have undergone in their journey from the Sudan to the Ethiopian refugee camp. The transformation of tradition becomes evident, as formerly separated neighbours are thrown together in the refugee camp and children learn to combine older and newer forms of expression. The spoken memories range from serious reflection on traumatic events to humorous accounts of past traumas, conveying a strong sense of resilience in the face of extreme adversity. What becomes evident as one spends time with the materials is the extent to which James has become embedded in the community, and that her recordings are based very much on the subjective eye/ear of someone who has gained a good deal of trust among the people she has been studying.

SPATIAL MONTAGE

Through the collaboration with James, techniques of how 'spatial montage' can be applied to these materials are examined. The art historian Lev Manovich coined this term in relation to his ideas about interactive cinema and emergent cultural interfaces for the 21st century. In his work on *The Language of New Media*, he describes spatial montage as representing "an alternative to traditional cinematic temporal montage, replacing its traditional sequential mode with a spatial one" (Manovich, 2001, p. 322). He states, that "whilst twentieth century film practice has elaborated complex techniques of montage with different images replacing each other in time, the possibility of what can be called a 'spatial montage' of simultaneously co-existing images has not been explored as systematically" (Manovich, 2001, p. 323). He goes on to say that the advent of an aesthetics appropriate to the user experience of multitasking and the multiple windows of graphical user interfaces offers an opportunity to move away from "a logic of replacement' towards 'a logic of addition and co-existence" (Manovich, 2001, p. 325) and it is this idea that forms the basis of this collaborative work.

Manovich (2005) has applied these ideas through his *Soft Cinema* project to create new possibilities for digital filmmaking, focusing on the generative aspects of computation to randomly

juxtapose multiple images within a linear form of cinematic delivery. In this sense, his interest lies in the aesthetic qualities of juxtaposition as a form of collage from which viewers can create their own sense of narrative meaning as they watch the films that are generated by the software. This work, on the other hand, is more concerned with the creation of meaning through more carefully choreographed juxtapositions. The materials are juxtaposed, and are pre-selected to communicate discrete points and create documentary meaning within the context of an ongoing narrative based on the temporality of James' long-term fieldwork. This approach to juxtaposition is not without its antecedents, as it builds upon the work of experimental film-makers, such as Abel Gance (*Napoleon,* 1927) Jean Luc Godard (*Tout Va Bien,* 1972), and Mike Figgis (*Timecode,* 2000), whose work employed split screen techniques to convey multiple perspectives and multiple points of view through non-conventional approaches to narrative structure. However, the argument here is that digital interfaces can extend these possibilities by offering new forms of human computer interaction through non-linear delivery systems. A good example of a commercially produced digital work which uses spatial montage to good effect is the interactive documentary *Gaza/Sderot* (Arte, 2009), which draws comparisons between everyday life over a period of forty days across two cities in Palestine and Israel.

Building on these ideas, the project works towards the creation of authored routes through an organised archive of James' materials. This archive is currently under development as a parallel but interlinked endeavour to the work described here. For a technical exposition of how this work links to the current discussion, see Matthews and Aston (2012). The authored routes are designed to illustrate the personal stories of the handful of people that James knew well, and who helped her in her original research in the 1960s. The stories "weave in and out of the whole tragedy of the Sudanese civil war and the deadly choreography of its entanglements with the struggles in Ethiopia" (James, 1999, p. xii). She has always tried to include these stories in her work and has expressed frustration that "the discussion of emotion, culture, and language is greatly hampered by the format of written ethnography alone, and even by the written version of the recorded and translated vernacular" (James, 1997, p. 124). Through our collaboration, techniques of spatial montage are used to combine carefully chosen clips in such a way as to tell the 'story' of the events and changes that have occurred as far as possible 'through the words and experiences of the people themselves' (James, 2007, p. ix). In this sense, the point of view of the anthropologist as narrator does not take final authority, with contradictory ideas and different styles of speech being able to co-exist in a more dialogic form.

Application of Technique

In terms of technique, this is to be achieved by using multiple windows to juxtapose meaningful combinations of sound, moving and still image recordings within a single screen. Primarily based on juxtaposing two, and occasionally three, moving image clips alongside each other in discrete windows, some of these juxtapositions employ techniques of parallelism to compare similar activities or points of view across time and place, whilst others focus on antithesis to show opposing activities or different points of view. Parallels are drawn between circular forms of dance recorded in the 1960s and the recreation of these dances in the refugee camp. Differences of opinion in the refugee camp are shown, such as one man expressing his desire to return to the Sudan whilst another expresses his desire to emigrate to a better life in the USA. Soundscapes that are resonant of life in the village hamlets of the 1960s are presented and simultaneous activities are shown from different perspectives to illustrate ways in which work rhythms operate at different levels within the refugee camp. Juxtaposition has also

been used to look at the non-verbal transmission of culture across generations, such as placing video footage of children performing a 'frog dance' in the refugee camps in the 1990s alongside video footage of children in a resettlement in Rochester, New York watching this dance on a video and then attempting to perform it themselves.

The juxtapositions are presented on screen in such a way as to enable fluid and tactile engagement with them. This is achieved by the creation of an interface through which the user can discover resonances between the materials and choreograph relationships between them. In so doing, it opens up opportunities for in-depth engagement with archival materials in ways that are only possible within interactive digital environments, using playful interfaces to facilitate exploration and discovery. This tactile engagement with the materials is designed to be experiential rather than functional and sensory as opposed to informational, giving users privileged access to primary data that usually remains in the hands of the anthropologist who recorded it. The interface is very simple, currently designed for one to one interaction whilst sitting at a computer with a keyboard and a mouse but open to further exploration on tablets or in an installation context. It employs the keyboard to enable users to turn clips on and off and call up supplementary narration if required. Although pre-selected to make discrete points, the user can choreograph their own interaction between the two (or three) clips on a frame-by-frame basis. This degree of fine-grained interaction is designed to increase the user's sense of tactile engagement with the content. It is particularly effective when comparing observational footage of activities across time, such as dancing or grinding grain, and when presenting multiple points of view and different modes of remembering past events.

If users want to focus more closely on one clip or call up text-based subtitles, they can enlarge it and consequently go back to the two or three screen juxtaposition at will. The fluidity comes from the fact that the clips will continue to play in forward motion as the user interacts with them. In order to provide additional context to the materials, various techniques were tried, whilst always endeavouring to let the materials speak for themselves wherever possible, using appropriate combinations of text and voiceover where needed. The contextual material is secondary to the presentation of the archival materials themselves, giving primacy to the experiential nature of the juxtapositions. The aim is to evoke a sense of place and embodied experience, building on the corporeal power of sound and image to create synesthetic responses that require more of the viewer than the mental facility afforded by language (MacDougall, 2006, p. 242). Much of this work is still in a prototype stage, as it needs to be re-versioned for delivery across the Web. However, some examples can be found in an online article (Aston, 2010). These give a good sense of the range and scope of the materials from which the comparisons are being drawn.

Whilst each set of on-screen juxtapositions communicates a discrete idea, ways to combine these screens to construct a series of multilayered arguments are explored. This builds on Eisenstein's idea that montage is a unifying cognitive principle in which 'the spectator not only sees the represented elements of the finished work, but also experiences the dynamic process of the emergence and assembly of the image' (Eisenstein, 1986, p. 34). Whilst this recognises James as being the authorial voice behind the materials, I also want to enable users to actively engage with the materials and find their own resonances within them as a means of becoming implicated in the production of meaning. It also draws on Levi Strauss' ideas around deep and surface structures (Levi-Strauss, 1968) by looking at the particularities of everyday life in the refugee camp, whilst also considering universal themes such as relationships between adults and children, the rhythms of work, and the transmission of memory through embodied experience.

In connecting a series of juxtapositions together in linear sequences, the relationship between spatial and temporal montage is being explored, as a form of associational space and chronological sequencing. The aim is to establish a series of different routes through a database of archival materials, in which materials can be combined, recombined, and juxtaposed to make different points. For example, there are clips of Uduk people playing music, singing and performing circular dances in the 1960s, which can be juxtaposed with clips of the recreation of these dances in the refugee camp to show aspects both of continuity and change through time. The same clips from the refugee camp can also be juxtaposed alongside clips of church services in the camp, in which the Uduk are sitting in organised straight lines. This makes a point about how different cultural influences affect their activities. Another example is to place a clip of someone reflecting on an event alongside footage of the event itself, or to place the clip alongside other people talking about the same event to convey multiple points of view. In this sense, a series of authored trajectories is built through the materials to create a database narrative in which the structure exemplifies "the dual processes of selection and combination that lie at the heart of all stories" (Kinder, 2002, p. 6).

ACCESS, AUTHORSHIP, AND ETHICS

Fundamental to this project is the recognition of the subjective nature of the archive and ideas and arguments that are being communicated through it. At one level, this is James' 'story,' with the materials gathered clearly reflecting her ongoing relationships with the Uduk people. The response to this is to make the point explicit in the work by including audio and moving image recordings of her talking about her experiences. In this sense, she becomes both the narrator and a character in the work, opening up the possibility for heteroglossia (Bakhtin, 1981), in which James' enters into a dialogic relationship with the other characters. By placing James within the work in this way, also avoids the danger of the "objectifying gaze of social scientists" in their tendency to present scholarship "as a transparent window of explanation that somehow magically and, apparently effortlessly, hid(es) the conditions of knowledge production" (Ebron, 2006, p. 205).

It is also important to recognize the fact that, had James not made these recordings, there would be no tangible record of this part of the Uduk's recent past, beyond a few materials recorded by the missionaries and any passing travelers. The Pitt Rivers Museum in Oxford has recently created an on-line archive of photographic collections and museum objects from the Sudan (Coote & Edwards, 2006), which has been accessed widely by the Sudanese diaspora. This indicates a strong interest in their recorded 'history,' which is likely to strengthen as and when the people themselves gain greater access to their own means of documentation. Whilst this archive presents the materials as searchable files, unlike this project, it does not attempt to incorporate narrative to draw the user into a world of experiences to engage the subjectivities of informants, their own reflections on the past-including past photographs and films-along with the individuality of their memories and hopes, their musical enthusiasms, their interactions, and silences in conversation with each other and with the ethnographer at different historical periods. This does, however, come at a price because it requires high-end computers and a broadband connection, to which the refugee communities in the Blue Nile borderlands, currently have very little, if any access.

It is also important to acknowledge that there are ethical concerns in relation to making some of James' recordings available on-line, as the political situation in the Sudan/Ethiopian borderlands has created divisions within the Uduk community and between their neighbours that are not always

appropriate to highlight. This is why, to date, the materials that we have put on-line focus more on a celebration of resilience and the transmission of memory through music, song and dance than on the tensions within the community. The project website (Aston & James, 2007) was designed to complement James' most recent book (James, 2007), which looks more closely at the wider political issues. James has also recently received five DVDs recorded by an Uduk elder living in the USA during a recent trip to the site of repatriation in the Sudan. The aim is to add such materials to the archive, creating new possibilities for juxtaposition alongside an on-line forum through which the people themselves can add their comments.

FUTURE CHALLENGES

The challenge here lies in using the Internet and disc-based media to create authored pieces of work, which enable users to engage with the materials in new and interesting ways, whilst at the same time opening this work up to allow the incorporation of user-generated content and user-responses. This work is intentionally expressive and aims to explore new ways of using archival materials to embody sensory knowledge within scholarly discourse for the sensory communication of ideas. Whilst, on the one hand, there are grand plans to create an all singing and dancing multimedia archive with a series of pre-authored routes through it that users would also be able to explore in a more open-ended way, there are also the benefits of creating a series of smaller works designed to complement each other and focus on specific aspects of James' fieldwork. This, in the short term, is a more realistic approach to the delivery of tangible outcomes, as it enables each work to focus on creating an optimum interface and structure through which to deliver its core idea. Given that the materials were originally recorded primarily for research purposes, they have not been planned or structured with these new forms of digital delivery in mind. It is a credit to James' consistent and poetic touch that so many interesting juxtapositions have been created thus far. No doubt, more will be discovered as the project continues to digitize, add metadata, and record James' commentary to the materials.

REFERENCES

Arte. (2009). *Gaza-sderot: Life in spite of everything*. Retrieved June 24th from http://gaza-sderot.arte.tv/

Aston, J. (2010). Spatial montage and multimedia ethnography: Using computers to visualise aspects of migration and social division among a displaced community. *Forum: Qualitative Social Research, 11*(2). Retrieved June 24, 2012, from http://www.qualitativeresearch.net/index.php/fqs/article/view/1479

Aston, J., & James, W. (2007). *Voices from the blue nile: A portait of a refugee community*. Retrieved June 24, 2012, from http://voicesfromthebluenile.org

Aston, J., & James, W. (2012). Memories of a blue nile home: The photographic moment and multimedia linkage. In Vokes, R. (Ed.), *Photography in Africa: Ethnographic Perspectives* (pp. 104–126). Woodbridge, NY: James Currey.

Bakhtin, M. (1981). *The dialogic imagination*. Austin, TX: University of Texas Press.

Coote, J., & Edwards, E. (2006). *Recovering the material and visual cultures of the southern Sudan: A museological resource*. Retrieved June 24, 2012, from http://southernsudan.prm.ox.ac.uk/index.php

Ebron, P. (2006). Contingent stories of anthropology race and feminism. In Lewin, E. (Ed.), *Feminist Anthropology: A Reader*. Oxford, UK: Blackwell Publishing.

Eisensten, S. (1986). *The film sense*. London, UK: Faber and Faber.

Figgis, M. (Producer and Director). (2000). *Timecode* [Motion picture]. United Kingdom: Screen Gems.

Gance, A. (Producer and Director). (1927). *Napoleon* [Motion picture]. United States. MGM. de Beauregard, G., Rassam, J.-P. (Producers), & Godard, J. L. (Director). (1975). *Numero deux* [Motion picture]. France: Motion Picture.

Howes, D. (2003). *Sensual relations: Engaging the senses in culture and social theory*. Ann Arbor, MI: University of Michigan Press.

James, W. (1997). The names of fear: Memory, history, and the ethnography of feeling among Uduk refugees. *The Journal of the Royal Anthropological Institute, 3*, 115–131. doi:10.2307/3034368

James, W. (1999). *The listening ebony: Moral knowledge, religion and power among the Uduk of Sudan*. Oxford, UK: Oxford University Press.

James, W. (2007). *War and survival in Sudan's frontierlands: Voices from the Blue Nile*. Oxford, UK: Oxford University Press.

Kinder, M. (2002). Hot spots, avatars, and narrative fields forever: Buñuel's legacy for new digital media and interactive database narrative. *Film Quarterly, 55*(4). doi:10.1525/fq.2002.55.4.2

Levi-Strauss, C. (1968). The structural study of myth. In Levi-Strauss, C. (Ed.), *Structural Anthropology*. London, UK: Penguin Press.

MacDougall, D. (2008). *The corporeai image: Film, ethnography and the senses.* Princeton, NJ: Princeton University Press.

Manovich, L. (2001). *The language of new media.* Cambridge, MA: MIT Press.

Manovich, L., & Kratky, A. (2005). *Soft cinema: Navigating the database.* Cambridge, MA: The MIT Press.

Matthews, P., & Aston, J. (forthcoming). Interactive multimedia ethnography: Archiving, workflow, interface aesthetics and metadata. [forthcoming]. *ACM Journal for Computing and Cultural Heritage.*

ADDITIONAL READING

Aston, J. (2003). *Interactive multimedia: An investigation into its potential for communicating ideas and arguments.* (Unpublished Doctoral Dissertation). Royal College of Art. London, UK.

Aston, J., Dovey, J., & Gaudenzi, S. (Eds.). (2012). Special issue on interactive documentary. *Journal of Documentary Studies, 3*(2).

Coover, R. (2011). Interactive media representation. In Margolis, E., & Pauwels, L. (Eds.), *Sage Handbook of Visual Research Methods.* Thousand Oaks, CA: Sage.

Deleuze, G. (1986a). *Cinema I: The movement image.* Minneapolis, MN: University of Minnesota Press.

Deleuze, G. (1986b). *Cinema II: The time image.* Minneapolis, MN: University of Minnesota Press.

Dixon, W. Winston, et al. (Eds.). (2002). *Experimental cinema: The film reader.* London, UK: Routledge.

Eisenstein, S. (1942). *The film sense.* New York, NY: Hartcourt.

Eisenstein, S. (1949). *Film form: Essays in film theory.* New York, NY: Hartcourt.

Howes, D. (Ed.). (2005). *Empire of the senses: The sensual culture reader.* Oxford, UK: Berg Publishers.

Iampolski, M. (1998). *The memory of tiresias: Intertextuality and film.* Berkeley, LA: University of California Press.

Laurel, B. (1993). *Computers as theatre.* Reading, MA: Addison-Wesley.

Le Grice, M. (2001). *Experimental cinema in the digital age.* London, UK: BFI.

Marchessault, J., & Lord, S. (Eds.). (2007). *Fluid sceens, expanded cinema.* Toronto, Canada: University of Toronto Press.

Murray, J. (1997). *Hamlet on the holodeck: The future of narrative in cyberspace.* New York, NY: The Free Press.

Murray, J. (2012). *Inventing the medium: Principles of interaction design as a cultural practice.* Cambridge, MA: MIT Press.

Petric, V. (1987). *Constructivism in film: A cinematic analysis.* Cambridge, UK: University of Cambridge Press.

Pink, S. (2009). *Doing sensory ethnography.* Thousand Oaks, CA: Sage Publications.

Rieser, M., & Zapp, A. (Eds.). (2002). *New screen media: Cinema/art/narrative.* London, UK: BFI.

Shaw, J., & Weibel, P. (Eds.). (2003). *Future cinema: The cinematic imaginary after film.* Cambridge, MA: MIT Press.

Tufte, E. R. (1997). *Visual explanations: Images and quantities, evidence and narrative*. Chesire, CT: Graphics Press. doi:10.1063/1.168637

Vertov, D. (1985). *Kino eye: The writings of Dziga Vertov*. Berkeley, CA: University of California Press.

Vesna, V. (Ed.). (2007). *Database aesthetics: Art in the age of information overflow*. Minneapolis, MN: University of Minneapolis Press.

Youngblood, G. (1970). *Expanded cinema*. New York, NY: EP. Dutton and Co.

KEY TERMS AND DEFINITIONS

Beyond Text: Modes of scholarly discourse which employ a variety of media as part of the transmission of meaning.

Cultural Transmission: The process of passing on values, attitudes, beliefs, and modes of expression across time and place, to help create a common sense of cultural identity.

Database Narrative: The use of authored pathways through sets of data to create narratives from the materials contained therein, thus breaking down the usual hierarchies that are inherent in databases.

Fluid Interfaces: Human computer interfaces which facilitate intuitive and Tactile engagement with audiovisual and textual materials, to create expressive as opposed to informational forms of representation.

Sensory Turn: A movement within the arts, social sciences and humanities which looks beyond the visual to consider how the senses inform and affect our ways of knowing.

Spatial Montage: The showing of two or more moving image clips or still images on the same screen in order to make meaningful juxtapositions, the moving image clips being accessible to user interaction.

Visual Anthropology: A sub-field of social and cultural anthropology that is concerned, in part, with the communication of anthropological ideas and arguments through visual as opposed to text-based means.

Chapter 12
Exploring Liminality from an Anthropological Perspective

Rina Arya
University of Wolverhampton, UK

ABSTRACT

The transition from the real to the digital requires a shift of consciousness that can be theorised with recourse to the concept of liminality, which has multidisciplinary currency in psychology and other disciplines in the social sciences, cultural, and literary theory. In anthropology the notion of liminality was introduced by the ethnographer Arnold van Gennep in the context of the development of the rite of passage. Since van Gennep's discussion of the concept, the term has been used in a variety of contexts and disciplines that range from psychology, religion, sociology, and latterly in new media, where it has a renewed emphasis because of the transition from the real to the virtual space of the digital interface.

INTRODUCTION

This chapter unpacks the term the 'liminal' or 'liminality' and examines its applicability in a wider context beyond its original formulation in anthropology. Of particular interest are the behaviours and practices that occur in the liminal state which are distinct from regulations adhered to in the pre- and post-liminal states. This is problematized in digital culture where the transitions between the states are more spatially impercep-

tible. Given that the liminal state is central to the rite and therefore to the relationship between 'self' and 'the world' the confusion of the boundary in digital culture has psychological ramifications for the participant of the video game, for example, as s/he is less able to regulate their behaviour in the absence of clearly delineated boundaries.

One of the first questions that need to be asked is: what does 'liminality' refer to? When something is described as liminal what does this mean; has it undergone a transformation in properties, or

DOI: 10.4018/978-1-4666-2961-5.ch012

merely in the way that it is perceived? The terms 'liminal' and 'liminality' are derived from the Latin '*limen*,' which means *threshold* and refers to the bottom part of a doorway, which must be crossed when entering a room. Ritual passages can be described by the following spatial metaphors: crossings, thresholds, boundaries, and crossroads. In anthropology the notion of liminality was introduced by the ethnographer Arnold van Gennep in the context of the development of the rite of passage, which was a specific ritual that marked what he described as "life crises" (the accompanying stages that mark the transition from one stage of life to another, such as in birth, marriage, death) or seasonal changes (such as the harvest, or the New Year). Rituals in general involve repeated, symbolic activities, but they do not always involve the liminal stage, which marks the crossing of thresholds. It is only a certain subset of rituals, namely the one concerning the rite of passage, which involves the liminal. In *The Rites of Passage* (1909/English translation, 1960) van Gennep analysed different rites of passage performed by ancient tribes, which facilitated the life-changing passage in life, such as the transition from childhood to adulthood. Van Gennep envisioned life in society as a house with many rooms where the individual has to be led from one room to another. The passage from room to room represents abrupt and ritualised transitions, which mark out the different stages in life.

He claimed that they each, irrespective of type and cultural context, shared three common stages of 'separation,' 'transition' (which is the liminal stage), and 'aggregation.' These are: the stage before where the individual has a defined role in the community, the stage during, where the individual is stripped of their role within the community, and the stage after, where the individual is bestowed with a new identity or status and integrated back into the community. The reconfiguring of the new identity in the third stage is usually the cause of great celebration for the community. The three stages can be mapped around liminality as the central concept, where 'separation' involves pre-liminal rites, and where the individual is forced to break with previous practices and extricate him/herself from the community. This is followed by the liminal stage where the rites and rituals are carried out to move the individual across a threshold. In the crossing of this threshold the individual is often spatially segregated from their normal environs. They also become stripped of any determinate identity and are set apart and rendered sacred (untouchable). After the rites have been carried out, which confer the new status on the individual, aggregation occurs and the individual becomes reincorporated into the community. The individual has surpassed the liminal stage (and so is in the post-liminal stage) where they can begin their life as a new being.

This tripartite structure can be mapped onto rites in specific terms. In the traditional formulation of the marriage rite, the individual moves from the status of being single to being betrothed to being married. Moving from one stage to another involves a crossing of the threshold. In initiation rites an adolescent who has undergone an initiation ceremony, such as a Bar Mitzvah ritual (in Judaism), returns to the community not as a boy but as a man. Whilst van Gennep argued for the presence of all stages in a rite of passage, the significance given to each stage was not always uniform. Some rites might develop one of the stages more than other stages in the ritual act. Therefore, whilst the stage of separation may be more central in funeral ceremonies, incorporation is often more significant in marriages. However, all rites involve some degree of experiencing each of the stages before the individuals are fully accepted into society or culture. In the case of death, the three stages aid the community in coming to terms with the deceased. These are complex stages that are clearly demarcated by separation, transition, and aggregation.

The anthropologist Victor Turner isolated the middle liminal stage from van Gennep's analysis and examined its significance further in his works,

"Betwixt and Between: The Liminal Period in *Rites de Passage*" from *The Forest of Symbols: Aspects of Ndembu* Ritual (1967) and The *Ritual Process: Structure and Anti-Structure* (1969). He expanded the reference of the liminal from beyond tribal communities to its resonance in the contemporary world. In this threshold phase, the individual is "betwixt and between" positions or states (Turner, 1969, p. 177). In other words s/he is in-between, is neither one thing nor the other. In this liminal phase of transition, an individual is stripped of their former identity and awaits their future identity. Turner states how "liminal individuals *have* nothing"; there is "no status, insignia … nothing to demarcate them structurally from their followers" (Turner, 1967, p. 98). It is an intermediary phase where the status of the individual is ambiguous.

The undefined nature of the individual can be viewed with suspicion and ambivalence because they do not fit into the social order and may be viewed as threatening the status quo. In rare cases, the liminal state does not resolve itself or progress to the final stage of reincorporation into the community and instead becomes hypostatised. The theorist Michel Foucault's extensive studies on insanity and homosexuality articulate the importance of social boundaries separating the conventional from the transgressive. Individuals that transgressed social boundaries of propriety were rehabilitated through the hegemony of institutions, such as the mental asylum or the prison. In his genealogical studies, Foucault showed that, beneath the veneer of paternalism, lay a fear-laden society that would not accept social deviance. On a more benign level there are certain other groups of society that are regarded as marginalized mainly because they have deliberately placed themselves in that position. For instance, the hippie countercultural movement of the 1960s entailed a fierce resistance against mainstream values and posited instead free-living and opting out of the structural patterns of society.

The anthropologist Mary Douglas explores liminality (although she does not use the term) from the perspective of hygiene and boundaries. She argued that the idea of danger is associated with anything that cannot be placed within social classification. In *Purity and Danger: An Analysis of Concepts of Pollution and Taboo* (1966) and *Natural Symbols: Explorations in Cosmology* (1970). Douglas asserts the importance of the boundary as a way of classifying orderliness, thus separating order (and purity) from the threat of contamination (danger or disorder). What cannot be classified according to traditional classification schemes are regarded as ritually unclean. These rules surrounding boundaries are important in social, religious, and anthropological discourse where the rite of passage operates to mark one boundary from another. Being non-placed or unclassifiable within the normative schemas of social classification, individuals in the liminal stage are regarded as anomalous and polluting. This explains why they are kept apart and segregated from mainstream society. Although essential to the transition from the old to the new in anthropology, the liminal was viewed as ambivalent. What follows is a more detailed analysis of the levels of estrangement experience in liminality.

SPATIAL ESTRANGEMENT

The liminal state in the rite of passage disconnects the moment from the flow of time. Turner notes that "the subject of passage ritual is, in the liminal period, structurally, if not physically, invisible" (Turner, 1967, p. 95). In other words, the status of individuals in the liminal stage is both socially and structurally ambiguous. They have been declassified and await classification. Being in the liminal stage involves two types of separation: the physical or spatial and the psychological. These two ideas are related—the physical act of separation creates a distance from the former state and this may cause psychological feelings of separation. Topographically those in the liminal state are removed from the centre of activity and are placed on the edges or margins of society, in a liminal zone. During a rite of passage, the individual undergoing the transition from one state to another may be temporally removed from the community and taken elsewhere. In such a case, the process of reintegration, which follows, involves the individual being reintroduced to the group, albeit with a different identity.

The concept of the liminal lends itself to the digital because of the dislocation of 'space' from 'place' (Waskul, 2000, p. 54) that occurs in digitally mediated environments. We may be given a sense of place but the real experience of space is withdrawn. This makes users feel displaced in a liminal zone. In the digital context, the physical barrier between the real and the digital interface, however thin, represents an impermeable membrane separating polar realities – the corporeal person from the artificial avatar and the analogue from the digital. What is indisputable is the schism between the two realities and the potential this holds.

PSYCHOLOGICAL DERANGEMENT

As well as being spatially estranged in the liminal state, the individual is also psychologically isolated because its ties with the community are temporarily suspended. This results in the stripping down of their identity where the individual is removed from their existing social ties and where their status is unqualified. The liminal zone bears similarities with Mikhail Bahktin's notion of the carnivalesque as introduced in *The Rabelasian Body* (1965).

The carnivalesque is traced to the folk culture of the medieval carnival. In Bahktin's theory, the carnival represented an ideal way of life where rules and order was flouted and we saw instead a subversion of social conventions. This was seen in

the body during carnival that was typically open and fluid. During carnival, there was an emphasis on bodily processes, such as eating and copulating, and social norms and values were inverted. Carnival was the archetypal liminal event, which was arranged annually in medieval culture in order to celebrate bodily and sensory excess. It brought about a sense of catharsis, or the release of tension. The function of carnival and notion of the carnivalesque has resonance in the post-industrial world. The carnival has an important sociological function, which operated in contradiction to the daily grind. In the realm of the everyday or profane, the focus was on labour and production. Gradually, through the development of Western industrialisation, the individual became to be seen in terms of his/her use value. The carnival as symbolic of an expression of exuberance gave the individual a momentary release from the humdrum nature of reality and an opportunity for self-expression and excess. The carnival was archetypically liminal—it lay beyond normal temporal and spatial boundaries and gave rise to a feeling of the sacred. In *The Elementary Forms of Religious Life,* Émile Durkheim described the sacred in social terms. The irrational behaviour exhibited during rituals was of a qualitatively different kind to the behaviour exhibited outside the event of the ritual.

In his characterisation of the liminal state, Turner contrasts the social conventions of profane activity and the irrationalism of the sacred, where the sacred defines the liminal stage (see Czarniawska & Mazza, 2003, p. 271). In *The Ritual Process: Structure and Anti-structure* Turner posited two notions: 'structure' and 'anti-structure.' 'Structure' refers to society as "a structure of jural, political, and economic positions, offices, statuses, and roles, in which the individual is only ambiguously grasped behind the social persona" (Turner, 1969, p. 177). Everyone has their designated place in this social hierarchy and the functioning of community depends on everyone conforming to social expectations of their individual roles within a larger structure. 'Structure' refers to the states before and after the liminal stage; 'separation' and 'aggregation' respectively. In the liminal stage, the individual has had its former roles and ties suspended and s/he now lies in an uncertain realm where the future is uncertain. In the liminal stage, we see the opposite of structural stratification and have instead 'communitas,' which refers to the anti-structural spirit. 'Communitas' to refer to the true community spirit where nearly everyone is equal (the ritual elders still hold sway) and there is solidarity between group members. Erstwhile social distinctions between individuals, such as social class, are eroded and the social structure is based on the inclusivity of common humanity. People are not viewed in instrumental terms but integrally and holistically.

Turner's two models of human interrelatedness share similarities with other theories of the social, including Durkheim's study of the different forms of solidarity, cohesion and interdependence in *The Division of Labour in Society* (1893), what he termed as 'mechanical' and 'organic' solidarity which approximates to tribal and post-industrial societies. Ferdinand Tönnies developed Durkheim's ideas in his own distinction (in *Community and Society* [1957]) between two types of social groups: *Gemeinschaft* and *Gesellschaft*, where the former is based on community and feelings of mutuality whilst the latter is based on social stratification. The models can be characterised by their expressions of the profane and the sacred, where the profane refers to the principles of organisation that are based around work, instrumentality and efficiency whilst the sacred refers to the values of communality.

In the liminal stage, the individuals cohere through experiences of empathy and the bonds of attachment are sacred. The liminal zone has the propensity to exhibit signs of sacred communality where we witness the Dionysian excess of the carnival that the real-life order temporarily evades. This level of absorption is experienced in the digital where we see the blurring of the boundaries between the self and the digital world, whether this is in the form of the game, or virtual domain (Turkle, 1995, p. 19). The simulated world becomes more real than the real itself and it takes a shift of consciousness to adjust back to the real. In cases of low to moderate use the absorption can be regarded as recreational, an escape from the binds of normalcy. However, in more extreme cases readjustment to real life becomes more difficult. Dennis Waskul discusses the ecstatic dimensions of the liminal state and draws on the etymology of the term *ekstasis*, which means to stand outside of oneself. This happens in the liminal state, and corresponds with Turner's notion of anti-structure. Being deprived of status and all the markers of differentiation, the individual merges with the community. This sense of transformation and transcendence of the individual occurs in digital interactivity. Waskul comments on how "the transformative ecstatic potency of the Internet cannot be denied. We are all just a few mouse-clicks away from endless potential for utter transformation: every one [sic] can be any one [sic] every body [sic] can be anybody; every thing [sic] can be anything; everywhere is anywhere" (Waskul, 1995, p. 56).

The disordered state of the liminal has resonance when thinking about the transformation from the real environment to the virtual space in gaming and digital media in general. Turner defines liminality "as a realm of pure possibility whence novel configurations or ideas and relations may arise" (Turner, 1967, p. 97). This may be present in virtual imagined communities or in social networking sites where the individual may take advantage of their liminal status and construct new identities for themselves. The absence of a real and corporeal representation in the virtual space entices people to creatively explore the possibilities of alternative identities that may even be entirely fabricated. The ramifications of this for inter-personal relations and the welfare of the young and vulnerable are immense. However, the autonomy of the liminal, which offers an escape from the real is compulsive and people will continue to exploit the opportunities to be able to reinvent themselves, or to live vicariously through avatars or online screen personas.

In gaming culture, the player suspends convention in order to fulfill the functions of the game, whether this is about driving a high-speed car or destroying a villain. The screen represents an interface that moves the individual from the experience of the real to the virtual. The increasing sophistication of technology not only enhances the experience of the transition but also makes the boundaries between the real and the hyperreal indistinguishable. In van Gennep's spatio-temporal world the transition from the pre-liminal to the liminal, and then the liminal to the post-liminal is more abrupt, and is demarcated by spatial shifts. In the case of a rite of passage, the individual often experiences structural separation in the liminal stage because they are removed from the community. The re-integration that follows involves the individual occupying a different space. This differentiation is more seamless in the case of new and digital media, which makes the rupture from the state of liminality potentially more problematic because of the extent of absorption in the digital realm. This is especially exacerbated in simulated and virtual spaces where the participant is less able to make a distinction between the real and the unreal.

The liminal is a rich concept that has a wide application from its more traditional origins in the study of the structure of society to its more contemporary use in the digital environment. In its simplest sense it means an undefined and indeterminate space that is characteristically transitory. It is both destructive because it involves transgression, which may lead to violence in rites of passage because of its effuse nature. In reference to its use in social networking, it may lead to uncontrolled and unregulated behaviours.

However, it also harbours creativity in enabling people to redefine the roles between their self and society. The liminal is a critical structural part of the rite of passage because it regulates the transition from one identity to the other. This field of study has become increasingly important because many of our experiences and interchanges with others are via the digital. The liminal applies to the digital in that it refers to the crossing of the physical space into the non-space of the digital, which is not constrained by the physical boundaries of space and time and the mechanics of motion. In our interactions with the digital, we are thrust into a liminal space of interactive possibilities.

REFERENCES

Bakhtin, M. (1984). *Rabelais and his world* (Iswolsky, H., Trans.). Bloomington, IN: Indiana University Press.

Czarniawska, B., & Mazza, C. (2003). Consulting as a liminal space. *Human Relations*, 56.

Douglas, M. (2002). *Purity and danger: An analysis of concept [sic] of pollution and taboo*. Oxford, UK: Routledge Classics.

Douglas, M. (2003). *Natural symbols: Explorations in cosmology*. London, UK: Routledge.

Durkheim, É. (1984). *The division of labour in society* (Halls, W. D., Trans.). Basingstoke, UK: Palgrave.

Durkheim, É. (1995). *The elementary forms of religious life* (Fields, K. E., Trans.). New York, NY: The Free Press.

Foucault, M. (2003). *The birth of the clinic: An archaeology of medical perception* (Sheridan, A. M., Trans.). London, UK: Routledge Classics.

Tönnies, F., & Harris, J. (Eds.). (2001). *Community and civil society*Harris, J., & Hollis, M., Trans.). Cambridge, UK: Cambridge University Press. doi:10.1017/CBO9780511816260

Turkle, S. (1995). *Life on the screen: Identity in the age of the internet*. New York, NY: Simon Schuster.

Turner, V. (1967). *The forest of symbols: Aspects of Ndembu ritual*. Ithaca, NY: Cornell University Press.

Turner, V. (1969). *The ritual process: Structure and anti-structure*. Berlin, Germany: Walter De Gruyter Inc.

Van Gennep, A. (1961). *The rites of passage*. Chicago, IL: Chicago University Press.

Waskul, D. (2005). Ekstasis and the internet: Liminality and computer-mediated communication. *New Media & Society*, *7*(1), 48–63. doi:10.1177/1461444805049144

Chapter 13
The Mirror between Two Worlds:
Multitouch–Multiuser Interaction for 3D Digital Objects

Eugene Ch'ng

IBM Visual and Spatial Technology Centre | Do.Collaboration,
University of Birmingham, UK

ABSTRACT

The information society manufactures, manipulates, and commodifies information. Heritage is one such area that is undergoing digital transformation. Heritage is increasingly being transmuted through digitisation devices such as laser and structured light scans into multiple representations of information. The rich information of a heritage object or an environment can be restructured, transmitted, and recomposed into a mediated form both textual and non-textual. Once digitised, it becomes free from its physical predecessor; it enters another world that defies the physical laws of nature where the imagination of the maker is a limit. Such worlds accompanied by their objects are accessible in new yet intuitive ways via multitouch table computers. The horizontal nature of the multitouch-multiuser table then becomes the mirror that links both worlds, allowing access into a virtual space via the touch-table computing paradigm. This chapter explores multitouch interactions, its technology, capabilities, and limits with the development of two multitouch applications incorporating 3D heritage objects and environments, and the observation of the reactions of initial users. It addresses new issues and challenges surrounding the use of multitouch tables and how the access and transmission of heritage information via multitouch-multiuser tables are able to contribute to the accessibility, teaching, and learning of heritage.

DOI: 10.4018/978-1-4666-2961-5.ch013

INTRODUCTION

The issues related to the value of the digital is increasingly provoking questions that need to be answered. This is becoming more urgent as we transition into an increasingly mediated world where the boundary of the real and that of the simulated is diminishing. One of the characteristics of post-industrial, information society is the manufacture, manipulation, and commodification of information via digital infrastructure. Information can be represented in many forms. Particularly in the sphere of heritage, itself already a valuable asset as we shall soon see, its digitisation seems to greatly elevate its position in accessibility. However, before proceeding any further, we must first define and contextualise heritage within this chapter.

Heritage is conceived as something that is worth safeguarding, protecting or conserving (Jokilehto, 2005). Specifically, cultural heritage in which culture can be defined as "that complex whole which includes knowledge, belief, art, morals, law, custom, and any other capabilities and habits acquired by man as a member of society" (Tylor, 1871), and natural heritage which, in the context of this chapter, is the legacy of fossilised organisms rather than present natural objects and environments. Information associated with heritage objects and environments once digitised can be disseminated widely and quickly via the viral nature of social media. Furthermore, the object itself at its present state in time with its surface details and colour information can be digitised into 3D via laser or structured light scanning, both of which project light on the entire surface of an object in order to capture data stored as 3D points, surfaces, and colours in virtual space. When an object is digitised, it remains perpetually in this state, frozen in time, free from the invisible but destructive hands of the second-law of thermodynamics. Whilst the original fall victim to entropy, the simulacrum enjoy the effects of the elixir of life. There in eternity, it wears many forms, at times compressed, at other times reproduced and decimated, accompanied by and embodying historical and factual information. Guided by binary logic, it disintegrates and recomposes, it materialises on organic light-emitting diodes—the spectators are awed by it.

Whilst the simulacrum is being widely exhibited, the original sits in the archives deserted, and perhaps forgotten. The original's fuller version, the simulacrum seems now to have more worth than the physical. It can be represented in many forms, disintegrated and electronically teleported to another location and re-materialised and produced in a 3D printer with the same form, structure, volume, and perhaps even material. Which philosophical path will this new form of image making take, where the 'new' refers to the transformative nature of the digital in all its interactive and representational possibilities? Since advances in real-time 3D computer graphics and Natural User Interfaces (NUI) may soon make the object indistinguishable from the physical? It could probably supercede the original with the accuracy and power of its imitation so much so that we cannot discern the differences in our visual or tactile experiences. Will it take on a negativity in the public's eye, that "the simulacrum is more than just a useless image, it is a deviation and a perversion of imitation itself—a false likeness" (Plato, 360BCE) where the viewer's subjectivity takes priority over that which is viewed and manipulated? Or in Baudrillard's argument (Baudrillard, 1981, 1983), that reality is usurped and superceded by the simulacrum? Or will such simulation establish a positive outcome as in Deleuze's argument (Deleuze, 1983)—that:

The simulacrum is not a degraded copy. It harbors a positive power which denies the original and the copy, the model and the reproduction. At least two divergent series are internalized in the simulacrum—neither can be assigned as the original, neither as the copy. It is not even enough to invoke a model of the Other, for no model can resist the vertigo of the simulacrum. There is no longer any privileged point of view except that of the object common to all points of view. There is no possible hierarchy, no second, no third...

Already, we are living in a world where the boundary between the physical and the virtual disintegrates, where the mediated is superseding the unmediated. These questions make developments that will allow users to access heritage in innovative digital ways worthwhile. Innovation in digital technology allows us to perceive user behaviours, valuation, and their veneration of digital heritage objects and environments in enlightening ways. It allows us to probe questions that we were not able to ask a decade ago—do laser scanned heritage artefacts carry the same value as its material originals, since they both look the same? Are physical heritage seen to be really of more value than its digital representation? How can we compare a physical heritage object with its fuller virtual version, which possesses deep historical and semantic information embedded within the 'file' and weigh their individual value? What about the 'socialness' of the digitised object, for "objects are a cause, a medium, and a consequence of social relationships" (Riggins, 1994), especially when not long from now, when people will interact and converse around digital artefacts using a multitouch table?

Although the chapter will not attempt to answer the questions stated above, it is an important development along this line of thought, i.e., to simulate heritage objects via real-time computer graphics that bears the same characteristics as their originals, so that further research may be established to engage those questions. However, the initial thesis is that these objects are in fact fuller; they can contain deep information embedded within them, and categorically semantic relationships between objects. They are perpetually preserved, and they can be visually represented in many forms, simulated in an environment with the law of physics, and manipulated via natural gestures. Eventually, they can be printed via 3D

printers. The role of the digital development in this chapter will lead to the accessibility, teaching, and learning of heritage objects, the transmission of its value through public access and eventually, the understanding of the questions stated above.

This chapter aims to address new issues and challenges surrounding the use of multitouch table technology in physical and virtual spaces. It presents ideas of how the access and transmission of heritage information via multitouch-multiuser tables are able to contribute to the accessibility, teaching, and learning of heritage objects. The Mirror between Two Worlds narrates the possible avenues in multitouch tables that researchers could explore, it aims to open up ideas and possibilities in research where the boundary between the physical and the virtual becomes hazy.

THE IMPACTS OF DIGITAL TECHNOLOGY ON THE ACCESSIBILITY OF HERITAGE

Traditional museums present a selection of objects from the archives with accompanying captions displaying associated information. Occasionally, special collections are complemented with a few sheets of paper as narratives for the story. Modern museums provided some form of interactive displays of a mechanical nature for more engaging learning. Others provide a mono-directional display for presenting videos and animation associated with the collection. New museums are becoming increasingly digital with the use of interactive digital display on LCD screens of various sizes. In this context, a museum is a place of great learning opportunity. According to Hooper-Greenhill (1999), "A museum is not a book, or an encyclopaedia, although it has been compared with both; a museum is a complex cultural organization, which is made up of a site that is frequently spectacular, a body of people with rare and fascinating expertise, a collection of objects that in its totality is unique, and a range of values that are currently under intense scrutiny from within the institution, from the academy and from government. All of these elements are susceptible to study, and therefore present learning opportunities. The level of learning can range from early childhood education to postgraduate research."

A museum provides a broad range of collections on display. Hidden in the archives are heritage artefacts encompassing layers of deep history that are inaccessible to the public. An old rule of thumb for large museums is that it typically has only 10 to 20 percent of its collection on display at any given time. Following Burcaw's observations (Burcaw, 1997), "The museum objects on exhibit at any time may actually constitute less than half of the total collections," or "the well-known 40-40-20 proportion" where 40 percent are for the collections, 40 for exhibits and 20 percent for everything else (offices, restrooms, etc.). Some museums with larger archives have only 10 percent on display. The limitations of space mean that not all collections are on display at the same time. Collections from the archives worth displaying are rotated through the archive-preservation-display cycle. The information connected with a relic may be deep, and it may be an unsustainable practice to arrange piles of information on paper associated with that object around display cases. This may be one of the reasons that traditional museum spaces tag a very short caption on the plaques attached to the glass or the pedestal of the display case. Museums are finding such practice quite restrictive on visitor learning and are exploring digital display technology to complement their collections. Interactive virtual spaces like online museums are popular. Others like the Musei Capitolini in Rome are more state-of-the-art. The museum in collaboration with Samsung provides accompanying Near Field Communication (NFC) electronic tags on 300 display items that allows NFC enabled devices to read and display information on mobile screens.

The exploration of digital technology to supplement old exhibits may not necessarily add value to both the institution and their visitors. It may also not create opportunities for economic growth in the larger tourism context. In order to add economic and pedagogical value, museums must find ways to empower visitor access to the tangible and intangible heritage from the archives. The ways in which visitors can access the layers of hidden archives and the deep history associated with each object must provide an intuitive interface from which a vast range of audiences can use. The relationships between objects and the visitor exploration of these relationships via an individual or group collaborative activity are also necessary for deeper learning. In this sense, multitouch tables that support natural gestures and multitouch-multiuser interaction are a potentially useful complement.

An unrestricted access to the archives provides two major benefits. The first advantage allows the rediscovery of hidden source of information that may bridge relationship or chronological gaps amongst objects. This helps extend current knowledge for researchers. One example is the discovery of a new species of dinosaur hidden in the archives for almost a century at the Natural History Museum (NHM, 2011). The discovery allows species to be compared and assists with identification between individuals in the classifications of these animals. According to Paul Barrett, the palaeontology researcher at the NHM, "These embellishments are central to determining relationships between the groups of horned dinosaurs and are a sign of evolutionary relatedness." The second advantage brings indirect economic benefits, through regional and international heritage tourism activities. Heritage is a legacy from the past worth preserving and is important for transmission to future generations. The value of heritage in motivating tourism has been studied in various economic analyses. A study commissioned by the Heritage Lottery Fund conducted by Oxford economics (Economics, 2010) on the impacts of heritage tourism in the United Kingdom reveals that annual visitors for both museums and green spaces amounted to 164.7m generating more than £20.6 billion. The contribution to the gross domestic product is more than the car manufacturing industry, advertising, and entertainment. Spillover benefits suggests a link between the visitor economy and other areas of economy such as retail, manufacturing, health and life sciences (Deloitte, 2008). Heritage tourism also employs 270,000 people in the UK excluding green spaces, and 466,000 including green spaces. Estimates suggest that the tourism economy will grow by 2.6% a year from 2009 to 2018 (Deloitte, 2008).

Contemporary societies are keen on the valorisation of heritage. Greffe's (2004) study reveals that: (1) heritage satisfies the artistic, aesthetic, cognitive and recreation needs for individuals and households, (2) owners of public and private monuments gain benefits through the mobilisation of resources for conservation, (3) companies earn profits from spin-offs related to tourism of such sites, (4) local authorities take advantage of the positive image and opportunities for the improvement of the living environment, and (5) countries benefit from the reaffirming of their national identity and for promoting solidarity. Opening up the archives hidden from the eye of the public via digital technology will have great impacts on research, learning and teaching, public awareness, the transmission of the value of heritage, and the economy indirectly. This chapter posits that multitouch-multiuser table has the potential to bridge this important gap in the GLAMs (Galleries, Libraries, Archives, and Museums).

Heritage and its value can be transmitted digitally, as evident by the surge in virtual heritage research since 1998 via the International Society on Virtual Systems and Multimedia, and in 2000 the Virtual Heritage Network, however the intuitiveness of the interface is an important factor in determining the usefulness of such an access to a wider range of users of a non-computing background. It is important therefore, that the next section looks at the impacts of the multitouch Smartphone revolution and how it has changed the way users access and manipulate information.

NATURAL USER INTERFACES AND THE INTUITIVE ACCESS OF INFORMATION

One of the critical ways in which digital heritage objects can be made more accessible to a wider audience is the development of more intuitive human computer interfaces. Natural User Interfaces (Seow, et al., 2009; Wigdor, Fletcher, & Morrison, 2009) are the next generation of human-computer interaction that can be applied to various platforms. Touch and gesture-based devices such as the Apple iOS (iPhone/iPad Operating System) and Google Android supported Smartphones have revolutionised the way in which users access information via wireless communication networks. The usefulness of these NUI devices prompted developments of larger devices such as Tablet computers (e.g., iPads and Android Tablets). The presentation and access of information is now enhanced with larger multitouch displays allowing a wider set of gestures as evident in the iOS updates for the iPad supporting the navigation between Apps of up to 4 fingers using the 'swipe' gesture as opposed to the PC-era 'Alt-TAB' key combinations on the keyboard. These developments are revolutionising both workflow and leisure. A recent survey suggests that people are spending most of their time using the iPad for personal computing (Yarow & Goldman, 2011). Other surveys observed that the general readership is turning to the digital (Whitney, 2010) with space-saving scanning of books into a digital format (Fleishman, 2011). Hundreds of thousands of NUI games are being developed by professional and amateur developers on Apple App Store and the Android Market, and Microsoft's Windows Phone Marketplace. Computers are now intuitive for a broad range of audiences that never knew the PC-era or are cyberphobic. Computers are for the first time, useful and fun, as evident in news channels and magazines that interviewed the elderly of their experiences of the iPad. There are even various 'Best Apps' for the elderly and toddlers. This is a grand progress since thirty years ago when access to computers was through keyboards with lines of textual instructions, and the mouse.

The commercialisation of horizontally oriented tabletop computers such as Microsoft's Surface, PQLab, and Ideum's MultiTouch-MUltiuser (MTMU) tabletop computers for museum spaces are bringing general and research computing into another dimension. Large High Definition (HD) displays of up to 65" supporting up to 32 touches and 'pop-out' 3D Stereographics already exists (the Heritage and Cultural Learning Hub commissioned Mechdyne MTMU tabletop computer at the do. Collaboration Prototyping Hall, the University of Birmingham). The fusion of cutting edge technological advancement on tabletops ushers in functional capabilities that were not present in traditional computing environments. One such feature is the multitouch-multiuser potential. Traditional computing workflows 'coagulate' our coordination behaviour of supposedly collaborative tasks into a sequential nature. Tasks are passed between chains of 'collaborative' workers in sequence via emails before completion. For example, given an instruction with a set of task where two or three employees were to accomplish together in collaboration. If the task is passed between emails, there will be a sequential back and forth transmission of email conversations. If the task is worked on location at a computing terminal, only one user is allowed to interact with the computer due to the limitations of the input methods—a single keyboard and a mouse. The two other employees can only dictate their thoughts to the computer user. Concurrent versioning systems and computer supported cooperative work (Eseryel, Ganesan, & Edmonds, 2002) groupware such as Google Docs (the online documents, spreadsheets,

and presentation suite) are opening up possibilities for simultaneous editing of documents over the network and on different terminals, there are issues (Dekeyser & Watson, 2006) however. Furthermore, where possible, working together on location might resolve issues of psychological ownership and perceived document quality, as evident in a collaborative Google Doc study (Blau & Caspi, 2009).

Multitouch-multiuser computing opens up possibilities where collaboration is transformed from sequential to simultaneous—all workers work on a task together, at the same time. The viewing and commenting on artworks becomes more natural. Researchers are now able to convene around a table for the purpose of accessing and manipulating digital information. Employees can now collaborate on a set of task without having to exchange digital documents sequentially. The demands on the environment may be lessened through less use of printing. Teachers and learners can now access rich information around a table. Learning becomes fun with n-degrees of freedom between teacher and students, and gaming is brought into another dimension with collaborative play.

Every revolutionary technology naturally gives rise to new ideas and uses. One of such useful ideas is to have MTMU tables in the GLAMs. The existence of MTMU tables in the architectural spaces of the GLAM implies that information access, interaction and presentation requires imaginative and innovative user interface and user experience design. This needs new research that goes far beyond the archaic class of multimedia CD-ROMS and Web pages. The following sections explore the surface computing paradigm, its functionalities, and how users might behave around a collaborative virtual table, and how they would manipulate digital objects if the objects were to look and feel the same as their physical counterpart. The sections also look at the possibilities around the application areas where this technology might provide.

THE MULTITOUCH PARADIGM

Multitouch-multiuser s table conjure many promising application areas and can potentially be a pervasive technology with widespread adoption in the near future. The aim of this section is to explore the capabilities of different multitouch technology and initial observations of user behaviour from a practical angle. The objective is to identify potential application areas for digital heritage where multitouch tables could be used.

Multitouch Devices

Market trends in research shows multitouch technology are reaching the maturity stage in North America and Europe. Prices will drop dramatically. The market is expected to grow 18.18% in the next five years to reach USD5.5 billion by 2016 (GMTM, 2011). A smaller survey sample (InnovationNow, 2011) in the Far East between multitouch hardware and software provider, and end users suggests increasing usage of the technology in advertising, education, retail, museums and art galleries, and media. Clients generally felt that the prices are too high but are positive about the multitouch market.

There are three main categories of multitouch devices based on their size – mobile devices (palm and tablet sizes, 3" to 10"), desktop monitors (15" to 30"), and collaborative multitouch devices (above 30"). We will be looking at the third category.

Various technical reports are available for multitouch technology (Dietz & Leigh, 2001; Downs, 2005; Hodges, Izadi, Butler, Rrustemi, & Buxton, 2007; Ocular, 2008; Rekimoto, 2002; Schöning, et al., 2007; Schöning, et al., 2010). There are four alternate technologies (resistive, capacitance, optical, surface acoustic wave) and variations of it used for constructing multitouch surfaces. Other developments (e.g., 3M's Dispersive Signal Technology (3MDST, 2009)) are available but are not in widespread use. Resistive touch screens is the most difficult to use as they require a certain touch pressure to capture the point of touch, they also have low clarity (75% to 85%) and have risk of damage in rugged environments. Capacitive touch screens have high positional accuracy but is the most expensive to produce but affords superior touch efficiency, and is suitable for rugged environments such as public installations but large screen sizes are limited and the cost is high. Capacitive technology requires electrical conductors (e.g., human body, special capacitive stylus) to work; electrically insulating materials will only work on projected capacitance. Optical multitouch technology uses work above the glass substrate and can be activated by extremely light touch or prior to the user touching the surface. One disadvantage of optical screens is that the effectiveness of interaction may be affected by direct sunlight or bright ambient lighting environments. Surface acoustic wave touch screens determines touch points by measuring the attenuation of acoustic waves across the surface of the glass, response is less precise than capacitive touch screens. Both optical and surface acoustic wave technology's touch functions are affected by contaminants on the surface substrate. Microsoft Surface 2's Pixel Sense is going beyond multitouch. Unlike current touch screen technology, Pixel Sense is an optical technology that allows screens to see in full the different shapes of objects placed over and above it. Every pixel senses information. Special 'Byte Tags' are used for object recognition via infrared reflection.

It is possible to integrate active 3D stereo displays in multitouch computers. However, due to the 'pop-out' nature of the 3D objects (3D objects appear to rise above the table) when viewed with active 3D stereo glasses, there is generally a perceptual problem. Users think that they can touch the 'holographic' objects when what is necessary is to touch the surface, the glass, in order to interact with the objects. This is an area of research that requires additional sensors that make possible 'holographic' interaction. The Kinect or Leap's motion sensor might help.

The survey and testing of the advantages and disadvantages of different multitouch technology conducted in the present research indicates that large rugged display and sensitive surfaces are needed, particularly within the indoor museum spaces where visitor range is broad, public use are in large volumes, and ambient lightings can be controlled. At present, optical multitouch screens are a more appropriate technology.

Human Behaviours in Multitouch-Multiuser Computing

It is not immediately clear how the larger population of users will react to a virtual collaborative table. Our observations of a range of visitors' first encounter with a surface computer at the IBM Visual and Spatial Technology Centre's Open Day (Ch'ng, 2011) where heritage related artefacts are displayed, and various other personal viewing events at the do.Collaboration prototyping hall suggests the following category of general behaviours amongst a small range of users.

- Users new to multitouch technology will first observe before touching the display.
- User behaviours are affected by the number of users actually using the MTMU table and whether they are acquaintances or not.
- Adult users are not acquaintances are courteous in their use of the table, i.e., they will 'queue up' (standing a short distance away from the table and watching for a short time) before they actually touch the table. Children participate freely regardless of whether they know each other or not.
- If a user is working on a task on the table, others will not intrude, they will only watch.
- Children will crowd around a table at close proximity whereas adults tend to leave some personal spaces between each other.

This occupation of space reduces the number of users that can stand around a table at a given time.

- Children of equivalent elbow heights to the table have a tendency to lean on the table, this occupies touch points. On devices where touch points are limited, multiple user interaction will not work.
- A facilitator giving encouragement warms up users to use the table.
- Users are finding the virtual keyboard difficult to use.

Usability research needs to be conducted to leverage the behavioural observations above in order to facilitate collaborative play and learning in various combinations of user scenarios.

An earlier study of direct-touch tables in uncontrolled environments (Ryall, Morris, Everitt, Forlines, & Shen, 2006) reveals the following categorical behaviour: Touch Interactions—"at first, some people are hesitant to touch the table at the same time," "accidental input is common, especially when pointing at something on the table," "GUI elements designed for a mouse need modification for finger-based input," "some people preferred to use a stylus (or other input device) to interact with the table rather than their hands." Organisation of Content—"users appreciate their elbowroom," "bare fingers are insufficient for text input," "for some types of documents, orientation is not a problem." Occlusion—"the actions of multiple people often conflict with one another, both intentionally and accidentally." Physical Setup—"concerns about shadowing caused by top-projected displays are not a problem in practice," "the design of the table's edge and its height impacted its use," and "users do view the interactive table as a 'computer'".

Hornecker's qualitative observation of visitor interactions with touch tables at the Berlin Museum of Natural History (Hornecker, 2008) shows that interface designs that does not resemble computer displays evokes a rich repertoire of multi-fingered and bimanual gestures, with organic elements evoking rich multi-finger gestures, and button-like objects mostly pointing and button-pressing. Aesthetic designs, which appeared user friendly revealed noticeable glitches in interaction, requiring visitors to invest effort into learning how to use the interface, this distracts from actual content exploration. CityWall (Peltonen, et al., 2008), a larger study in an uncontrolled environment with 1199 reveals that users at a display attract other users, and a user's actions on the touch wall is learned by observers. An interesting result was "how these people were configured in groups of users and crowds of spectators rather than as individual users. They were able to use the display both in parallel and collectively by adopting different roles"—the use of the display was highly non-individualistic. Learning from other users may be one of the key explanations for this phenomenon.

Recent research on user-defined gestures (Wobbrock, Morris, & Wilson, 2009) suggests that the Windows desktop paradigm has a strong influence on users' mental models; that users rarely care about the number of fingers they employ; that one hand is preferred to two, and that on-screen widgets are needed. Mental models built around the physical world are affecting users of multitouch tables. The study revealed that their use of tables correlates with the physical objects they have interacted with. Users said that they often used more fingers for "larger objects," as if these objects required greater force. Other participants used more fingers in order to have more reliable contact with the objects, and that more fingers are used for commands that executed "a bigger job." The study published in 2009 when multitouch phones (iPhones, Android phones) are only beginning to be in widespread use. Recent rise in multitouch phone markets may prompt different user behaviours. The multitouch phone paradigm will 'educate' users and transform their mental models on multitouch displays.

Another study suggests that multitouch provides a scope for interactions that are closer to physical interactions than classical windowed interfaces (North, et al., 2009), users who start with the physical setup finish the task faster when they move over to using the MTMU displays with a simulated setup than users who start with the mouse.

SDKs, APIs, and General Limitations

Morgan Stanley research on "Tablet Demand and Disruption" (MSR, 2011) shows that the lack of a physical keyboard on many multitouch tablets (e.g., iPads, Android, Windows devices) are not encouraging the widespread adoption of touch devices for content creation. Although some users are using their tablets to create content, the conclusion is that content creation using touch is still not elegant. We can safely extrapolate this study to larger display screens where keyboards are on-screen and flat on the horizontal table. Our experiences with using multitouch displays of different sizes confirm this argument. Whilst content creation is a challenge on multitouch-based computers, content viewing and interaction is more intuitive than conventional means. This intuitiveness with natural gestures and a 'round the table' computing opens up possibilities in multiuser collaborative research and learning. Various Application Programming Interface (API) and SDKs are available to facilitate rapid development of multitouch-multiuser applications. Gestureworks, which builds on ActionScript's core multitouch event Class, and OpenExhibits, the Open Source SDK based on Gestureworks are popular with museum and art gallery applications. Whilst Gestureworks provides a large collection of predefined gestures, they are not necessarily reflective of general user behaviours (Wobbrock, et al., 2009). System designers' gestures can be compared to a new language, they need to be learned. However, it would seem that certain natural gestures learned through modern multitouch phones are transferable to tablet top applications. The pinch-zoom and sliding gestures are but one of the many. Adobe Flash ActionScript 3.0, from which OpenExhibits is based, has native multitouch event management. Microsoft's Surface 2 SDK, running on Windows Presentation Foundation (WPF), XNA 4.0 and Windows 7 is an efficient SDK to create multitouch applications on. It integrates various controls such as menus, stacks, bar, containers, and drag-and-drop that users can combine to create custom user interfaces. Other SDK's are Nuiteq's Snowflake. The highly flexible and programmable Unity3D game engine with highly realistic Shader technology, physics, lights and shadows, and animation system in combination with XTUIO uniTUIO's C# scripts that simulates multitouch events make it possible to create interactive 3D multitouch applications.

Aside from the limitations with onscreen keyboard, which requires extensive usability research in order to discover new ways in which textual input becomes intuitive, the APIs and SDKs mentioned above allows new applications to be developed for multitouch-multiuser tables. The imagination is the only limitation.

NEW OPPORTUNITIES IN MULTITOUCH DISPLAYS

User interfaces in multitouch displays with simultaneous multiple finger inputs adds another dimension to computing. The user interface is almost disappearing, enabling users to manipulate digital objects with intuitive touch and gestures. This naturally opens up opportunities for new types of user interfaces. Initially, basic applications that browse collections of images appeared. These early adopters of multitouch computing for museums use very basic functionality (see examples Ciocca, Olivo, & Schettini, 2012; Correia, Mota, Nóbrega, Silva, & Almeida, 2010). As multitouch-based hardware, APIs and SDKs mature, more creative use is expected.

The multiple simultaneous inputs that surface computing allow in both 2D and 3D have scope for applications in both the Arts & Humanities, and the Sciences.

Applications of Multitouch Technology to 3D Digital Heritage

The digital revolution has given new meanings to digital simulacra described with bits (binary digits) as compared to their physical versions made of atoms. Bits are weightless, inexpensive, reproducible, can be compressed, disintegrated, and electronically transferred via communications network. It is eco-friendly, apart from the fact that it requires electricity for operation, although no electricity is used to maintain the static state (modern storage devices require only electricity when data is transferred but not when it has been stored). Reproducing digital copies uses simple algorithms; different compression codecs code and decode information to reduce file sizes. The transfer of bits takes advantage of the already available network infrastructure. It is in this sense, inexpensive to maintain. Digital representations of physical objects look the same when advanced Computer Graphics Shader materials and texture mappings are 'applied' to its surface, they have all the advantages of the digital. However, they are not viewed as having the same value as physical objects, and why should they not have the same value? 3D laser scanning technicians are obsessively possessive in their scans of heritage objects and monuments, the digitally scanned objects 'belonged to them' and are not to be given away. 3D artists sell at a high price to the entertainment industry very detailed models that they painstakingly spent hours of efforts 'sculpting' and 'painting.' Are they any different from physical artworks, which requires equal amounts of effort, and which cannot 'come to life' on screen with digital animation and artificial intelligence? The valorisation of digital objects is increasingly a curious area of research. The purpose of the two case studies amongst other aims, were meant to provoke the questions surrounding the value associated with digital objects, in this case digital heritage objects.

This section explores two case studies of the author's development and some general user behaviour observations in 3D multitouch virtual environments. The hardware setup is similar for both cases but the software and content was developed separately for different uses. The multitouch-multiuser table (Figure 1) measures in cm 178.75 (length) x 115.57 (breadth) x 74.77 (height). The diagonal screen size is 65", a Samsung made 3D-ready display. The compute is Intel Quadcore XEON 3.06GHz with 8 threads, and 12 GB of memory. The graphics card is NVIDIA Quadro 5000 with 2.5GB GDDR5 SDRAM. The 3D display is driven by NVIDIA's Stereoscopic 3DTV and MonsterVision's Max3D high-speed shutter glasses. Aside from the multitouch inputs, there is a portable keyboard and a Gyration Air mouse. The applications are developed within the Unity3D Integrated Development Environment (IDE) with multitouch simulation from the uniTUIO libraries. The first application *Accessing Realistic 3D Heritage Artefacts Through Touch* has 13 C# scripts attached as behaviours for the objects, their relationships and the user interface, the second application, a simple agent-based model *Bringing Ancient Creatures to Life: The Trilobite Pit* had 13 other C# scripts for defining the agent behaviour, food, and the user interface. Both applications have been viewed by users on uncontrolled environments in public spaces, and smaller guided previews.

Accessing Realistic 3D Heritage Artefacts through Touch

Heritage artefacts, as it appeared to curators are valuable simply because they are old, unique, and rare. If not for the glass encasements and security perimeters surrounding them, and if artefacts were found in the 'wild,' we would handle them with

Figure 1. 65" Mechdyne integrated 3D ready multitouch table at the do. Collaboration Prototyping Hall, University of Birmingham.

bare hands as we would other objects. If finders did not know the real value of discovered artefacts, and no heritage valuers were available, the objects if not made of precious materials, may not have any real value at all. 'Value' then is in the eye of the beholder, as beauty is. The purpose of this application is to allow Museum visitors to manipulate objects via 'touch' as they would any physical objects that were previously inaccessible due to the reasons stated above (e.g., the Staffordshire Hoard, the 52,500 Roman coins, both valued at £3.3m each, etc). For this to happen, we need to leverage the natural user input that multitouch displays offer, the high definition 3D display, real-time computer graphics rendering techniques, and software algorithms that simulate physical behaviour. Integrating these technologies and building new software modules that helps us accomplish that which is not possible in the physical world is the objective for this application.

The multiuser-multitouch application described here allows users to 'touch' and 'manipulate' treasures. The application answers the question set earlier about how we can pull heritage assets from the hidden archives and engage with them. Using natural gestures such 'pinch-zoom,' 'swipe,' 'poke,' 'drag,' 'rotate,' users are able to interact with objects in an intuitive way. Each object is computationally 'tied' to physical laws such as weight and gravity, collision, inertia, and inflatable effects such as bounciness, and pressure. Our hardware is able to handle mesh collision detection that calculates polygon level collisions. Object materials describe it's bending and stretching stiffness, cloth, metal, wood, rubber, etc. Some objects are chain-linked with inverse kinematics when interacted upon. Material surface can be described by textures and Shader effects; materials can take on the appearance and 'feel' of any physical material. Gold would look like gold with glittering effects, silver, wood, fabric, plastic, etc. The objects appear to 'pop-out' of the screen with the stereo 3D glasses, although touching them requires a direct interaction with the surface. 3D Objects can be created with content generation software and from laser and structured light scanning data.

Among the tools provided, the application simulates a lamp for spotlighting objects, and a magnifying glass for inspecting objects. In addition to the physical effects and real-world tools, the environment integrates digital tools that were not possible in the physical world. One of such tools is the 'connector' and 'disconnector' bases. Items dragged onto the bases are connected to a 'parent' connector, which stores information of the child objects. Objects on the same base as the parent all shared the same parent. Parent connectors are created when an unconnected object is placed on the 'connector' base. The 'disconnector' base allows individual objects to be disconnected with its parent; it also allows a disconnect-all solution by placing the parent at the base. Parent connectors can be moved back to the bases to connect with other objects when desired. Each object embeds its own information. At the moment, the embed information includes a unique ID, name, description, and user comments. The software module provides a WWW port to connect to resources in the Web, such as databases and social media where data can be retrieved and stored. The embedding of information and the relationship-building environment for objects aims to provide an environment for users to use natural gestures as they would a physical workspace to sort, categorise, retrieve, and record information.

The realistic environment and its rich affordances aim to allow visitors and researchers to make meanings and relationships with objects on the table, in a natural way (see Figure 2 and Figure 3).

Bringing Ancient Creatures to Life: The Trilobite Pit

Research in palaeontology, the study of the history of life on earth is extending knowledge about how creatures lived and behaved in palaeoenvironments. Their diets, behaviour, and environmental preferences, and hierarchy in the food chain have become knowledge in various scientific publications. Traditionally, studying fossils teaches us about ancient plants and animals; artists' impression based on fossil remains illustrates their morphology, with backgrounds portraying the environment and potential predator-prey scenarios. Geological museums display fossil remains and reconstructed models of large land-creatures that awed visitors; these are accompanied by little textual descriptions of the animals. Animatronics sit boringly within perimeters and bellows roars on occasions, frightening children and some adults, but they are rarely interactive. The entertainment industry recreated animations of Jurassic park with accompanying "shoot 'em up" dinosaur games, entertaining, but not exceptionally educational to say the least. Geological museums and classrooms should educate in new ways, particularly when knowledge of habitats and animal behaviour is becoming comprehensible. Knowledge of creature behaviour and habitat, in combination with real-time interactive computer graphics and artificial intelligence should bring new ways of engaging

Figure 2. a) Users interacting with the objects using multiple touches. b) Users interacting with 3D objects via touch and using stereo 3D glasses.

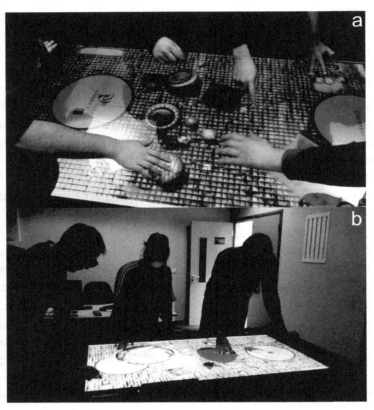

visitors, and contribute to learning, and the heritage tourism economy.

Ancient creatures, especially dinosaurs have been brought to life in movies, but never interactive, and not yet in the museums. The multitouch application covered here is aimed at Geological museums and future classrooms. In the past, there were no endeavours to bring trilobites, these seemingly boring but actually important creatures to life. Their importance was in the fact that they were extraordinarily successful in adapting to various environmental changes; they first appeared in the early Cambrian period, dying out in the mass extinction only at the end of the Permian period—they lived for over 300 million years. Trilobites are Arthropods with the Horseshoe crab as the closest living relative and there were more than 20,000 different trilobites identified to date. They

were predators, scavengers, or filter feeders. The study of trilobites has contributed to many fields in the history of life and geology (see Figure 4).

The multitouch application here prepares an ecological environment for trilobites and a certain type of zooplankton as prey. Users tweak environmental 'sliders' to simulate effects of climate change with temperature, sunlight, and oxygen levels in the ecosystem. Creatures react to the environment in various states of fitness measured by the adaptability measure (Ch'ng, 2007). Different levels of fitness produce different effects in the creatures' speed and survivability; death occurs if the environment surpasses their rate of adaptability. Users interact with the ancient creatures by dropping capsules containing zooplanktons into the pool. The zooplanktons have built in behaviours that swim faster when pursued and

Figure 3. a) Objects with different materials, weights, shapes, and sizes. b) Objects at the 'Disconnect' dish disconnects from the red parent cube. c) Objects that are placed on the 'Connect' dish are connected to the red parent cube. d) The input form for commenting on each object. e) The magnifying glass tool that users 'pulled' out from the side for inspecting objects. At the top right corner is a lamp tool, which users could use for shining a spotlight at objects.

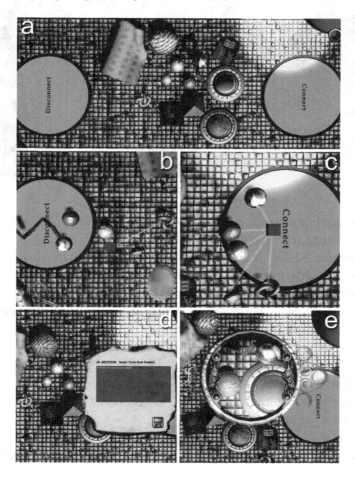

avoids predators via turns and twists. Energy levels decide their ability to survive the trilobite predation. In the agent-based model, each creature has different preferences and capabilities. These are the speed of movement, slope climbing capability, energy levels, turning angles, feeding distance, predation thrust, and adaptability to sunlight, temperature, and oxygen levels. The morphology are created based on fossil records; movements are slightly exaggerated to create a game 'drama' effect—creatures' 'breaths' with inflating and deflating abdomen animation during the idle state, they also wiggles during movements and feeding. These are all controlled via the C# scripts in Unity (see Figure 5 and Figure 6).

Qualitative User Experience on the Multitouch Interactive 3D

The design of interaction styles on multitouch computers are a very new field. The behaviours observed on 2D multitouch-computing applications in the "Human Behaviours in Surface Computing" apply, but mental models differ. From observations

Figure 4. The trilobite pit multitouch table application

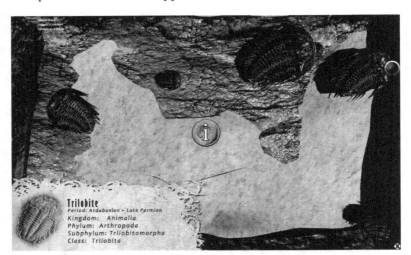

of groups of users using the digital heritage object multitouch application, some user behaviours are learnt. Users generally expected that interactions with the virtual objects are similar to the physical. Their mental models of multitouch interaction follow that of the physical world, but generally any user mistakes done earlier are quickly learned for future developments. List below are a number of user comments and notes, some of which contrasts each other, and suggestions within the quotes with regards to their experience of the multitouch table application with the author's notes at the end:

You can feel the actual weight of the objects, there is resistance.

The objects are set up with different weights, heavier objects are more difficult to 'lift.' When users could not move a heavier object with one finger, they used two to four fingers. When that did not help, the users attempted double tapping on the object, reverting to habits acquired via the Windows paradigm.

The virtual objects are comparable to the real.

The gesture 'pinch zoom' that enlarges objects are very useful for me to get a closer look at them."

The magnifying glass is cool!

Since we've got the pinch zoom, why do we still need the magnifying glass? But having a magnifying x-ray glass that allows you to see inside the object or layers of information might be useful.

Connecting objects requires you to pull objects to the 'Connector' dish, why can't we have gestures that allows objects to be connected when both objects are touched with both fingers?

It is necessary to have the connector dish as multiple people are touching objects at the same time.

Depending on the weight of the objects, moving them with the fingers will leave a gap between the object and where the finger touches the objects due to the resistance of the object. It might be useful to have a line connecting the objects and the position of the fingers, or to have a one to one relationship between finger position and object.

If the interaction is designed so that the objects and fingers are in a one to one positional relationship, the weight of the object might not have been 'felt.'

Figure 5. a) Learning information panel about the trilobites. b) Dropping zooplankton capsules onto the trilobite pit. c) As capsules burst open, zooplanktons are released, resulting in a feeding frenzy by the agent-based trilobites. d) The information panel showing an individual trilobite's bio-profile (fitness, energy, etc). At the top left corner of the application are three slider bars for adjusting the temperature, level of oxygen and sunlight.

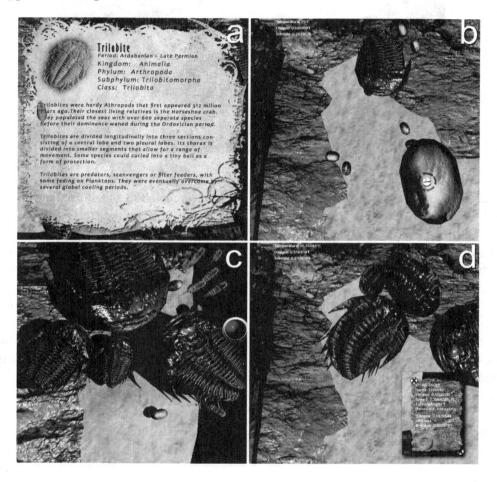

Once I found out that some objects could be enlarged with the 'pinch zoom' gesture, I expected that all objects could be enlarged. There needs to be an indication that only some object can be enlarged.

This could possibly be solved by bringing up a small widget surrounding the touched object indicating its interactivity.

I think that virtual objects can complement real objects but not replace it. But virtual objects have more scope and possibilities than real objects. Examples are the 'pinch zoom' effects.

On stereo 3D table:

I tried to touch the 3D stereo objects but I cannot interact with them unless I actually touch the screen

Figure 6. Users feeding zooplanktons to the trilobites

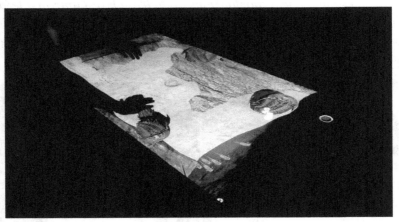

Users have the wrong perception that they can touch 'holographic' 3D active stereo objects popping out of the screen. Users find it difficult to judge the distance between their fingers and the table when 3D is turned on.

The trilobite application has a lesser scope of interaction as it involves only dropping food pellets onto the trilobite pool. The demo however, did create some very exciting responses as users witnessed the 'hatching' of the pellets into zooplanktons that the trilobites attempted to eat.

The qualitative observations here have established areas in which a more formal, quantitative usability research can be conducted.

CONCLUSION

We have explored multitouch computing technology as applied to 3D digital heritage objects and environments in this chapter. The motivation for the chapter was set forth early in the introduction, which is to lay a technical foundation for engaging questions related to the value of the physical as compared to its digital simulacra. Whilst the questions are not answered directly within the text, developments conducted here will pave the way

for research. In order to understand user valuation of digital objects, their accessibility via digital interfaces must first be intuitive—they must not be a barrier that needs a steep learning curve for the majority of users from a non-computing background. In section two, the impacts of digital technology in the access of heritage artefacts was studied. The section concluded that the wider and deeper access to heritage and its value can be transmitted digitally, and that multitouch-multiuser tables have the potential to bridge the gap where digital technology impacts research, learning and teaching, public awareness, and the economy indirectly. Sections three and four explored NUI and the multitouch table paradigm. The sections covered the evolution of NUI interfaces and how it has revolutionised the ways in which users access and manipulate information. The capabilities and limitations, and how previous studies on users' behaviour around multitouch-multiuser displays are surveyed. Finally, two developmental case studies were presented in which hypothesised digital heritage artefacts that allow natural gestural interactions were implemented.

Digital heritage does have a value. The value of the digital is in its transformative nature in both form and structure. The digital simulacrum in the positive sense can take many structures and forms. It can appear to different audiences as different representations, or as the undistorted original itself. It can be reproduced at will, and it can be transmitted from one device into another, from a mobile phone to another or from mulitouch computers to a phone. In the observational studies, users spend a lengthy amount of time interacting with the virtual objects as if they were toddlers being given brand new toys. It was as if that was their very first experience of the world. The vertical computer screen that they once knew had become irrelevant; the table computer is the new world, it is the simulacra, which precedes the original where the distinction between the reality and the representation vanishes. Everything that lies beyond the glass gives a new experience. The glass of the multitouch table has become a bridge from which the physical and the virtual converge. We grew up making sense of our world, forming mental models of physics as we threw objects around the room; we interacted with objects and learned the nature of them. We now have to 'grow up' once more through our interaction with objects beyond the glass of that mirror. Beyond the mirror lies a world where the laws of nature can be ignored, a world where possibilities are bounded only by the imagination of the creator. As natural user interfaces improves, and digital image making matures, we will find ourselves going through iterations of learning how to interact with the real world within the mirror.

ACKNOWLEDGMENT

The author gratefully acknowledges the support of the Hertiage and Cultural Learning Hub. The author would also like to thank Michael Chowen, Mark Glatman, Carol Kennedy, the ERDF, the Garfield Weston Foundation, and the College of Arts and Law (University of Birmingham) whose support made it possible to establish the Hertiage and Cultural Learning Hub and its extensive cross-disciplinary, cross-sector projects.

REFERENCES

Baudrillard, J. (1981). *Simulacra and simulation*. Ann Arbor, MI: University of Michigan Press.

Baudrillard, J. (1983). *Simulations*. New York, NY: Semiotext. [e]

Blau, I., & Caspi, A. (2009). *What type of collaboration helps? Psychological ownership, perceived learning and outcome quality of collaboration*. Paper presented at the Chais Conference on Instructional Technologies Research 2009: Learning in the Technological Era. Raanana, Israel.

Burcaw, G. E. (1997). *Introduction to museum work* (3rd ed.). New York, NY: Altamira Press.

Ch'ng, E. (2007). Modelling the adaptability of biological systems. *The Open Cybernetics and Systemics Journal, 1*, 13–20.

Ch'ng, E. (2011). *IBM visual and spatial technology centre open day*. Retrieved 21 December 2011, from http://www.youtube.com/watch?v=A8yDEMhEkdg

Ciocca, G., Olivo, P., & Schettini, R. (2012). Browsing museum image collections on a multi-touch table. *Information Systems, 37*(2), 169–182. doi:10.1016/j.is.2011.09.009

Correia, N., Mota, T., Nóbrega, R., Silva, L., & Almeida, A. (2010). A multi-touch tabletop for robust multimedia interaction in museums. In *Proceedings of the ACM International Conference on Interactive Tabletops and Surfaces*. ACM Press.

Dekeyser, S., & Watson, R. (2006). *Extending Google docs to collaborate on research papers*. Toowoomba, Australia: The University of Southern Queensland.

Deleuze, G. (1983). Plato and the simulacrum. *October, 27*, 45-56.

Deloitte. (2008). *The economic case for the visitor economy.* New York, NY: Deloitte.

Dietz, P., & Leigh, D. (2001). *DiamondTouch: A multi-user touch technology.* Paper presented at the 14th Annual ACM Symposium on User Interface Software and Technology. Orlando, FL.

Downs, R. (2005). *Using resistive touch screens for human/machine interface.* Dallas, TX: Texas Instruments Incorporated.

Economics, O. (2010). *Economic impact of heritage tourism.* Oxford, UK: Oxford Economics.

Eseryel, D., Ganesan, R., & Edmonds, G. S. (2002). Review of computer-supported collaborative work systems. *Education Technology & Society, 5*(2).

Fleishman, G. (2011). Book transubstantiation. *The Economist.* Retrieved from http://www.economist.com/blogs/babbage/2011/10/media-digitisation

GMTM. (2011). *Global multi touch market, by product (smartphones, tablets, laptops, televisions/LCD, tables, floors), applications (entertainment, infotainment, enterprises, others) & geography, 2011-2016.* Dallas, TX: Markets and Markets. Retrieved from http://www.marketsandmarkets.com

Greffe, X. (2004). Is heritage an asset or a liability? *Journal of Cultural Heritage, 5,* 1–309. doi:10.1016/j.culher.2004.05.001

Hodges, S., Izadi, S., Butler, A., Rrustemi, A., & Buxton, B. (2007). ThinSight: Versatile multi-touch sensing for thin form-factor displays. In *Proceedings of the 20th Annual ACM Symposium on User Interface Software and Technology.* ACM Press.

Hooper-Greenhill, E. (Ed.). (1999). *The educational role of the museum.* London, UK: Routledge.

Hornecker, E. (2008). I don't understand it either, but it is cool: Visitor Interactions with a multi-touch table in a museum. In *Proceedings of IEEE Tabletop.* IEEE Press.

InnovationNow. (2011). *Multitouch market research.* Kuala Lumpur, Malaysia: Innovation Now Sdn Bhd.

Jokilehto, J. (2005). *Definition of cultural heritage: References to documents in history.* ICCROM Working Group 'Heritage and Society'.

3MDST. (2009). *Technology comparison: Surface acoustic wave, optical and bending wave technology.* Methuen, MA: 3M Touch Systems.

MSR. (2011). *Tablet demand and disruption: Mobile users come of age.* New York, NY: Morgan Stanley Research Global.

NHM. (2011). *New horned dinosaur hidden for 90 years in museum.* Retrieved 21 December, 2011, from http://www.nhm.ac.uk/about-us/news/2011/december/new-horneddinosaur-hidden-for-90-years-in-museum106428.html

North, C., Dwyer, T., Lee, B., Fisher, D., Isenberg, P., & Robertson, G. (2009). Understanding multi-touch manipulation for surface computing human-computer interaction – INTERACT 2009. *Lecture Notes in Computer Science, 5727,* 236–249. doi:10.1007/978-3-642-03658-3_31

Ocular. (2008). *Projected capacitive technology enhances clarity, durability and performance of touch screens.* Dallas, TX: Ocular.

Peltonen, P., Kurvinen, E., Salovaara, A., Jacucci, G., Ilmonen, T., Evans, J., et al. (2008). It's mine, don't touch! Interactions at a large multi-touch display in a city centre. In *Proceedings of the Twenty-Sixth Annual SIGCHI Conference on Human Factors in Computing Systems.* ACM Press.

Plato. (360BCE). *The republic: Book X.*

Rekimoto, J. (2002). Smartskin: An infrastructure for freehand manipulation on interactive surfaces. In *Proceedings of the SIGCHI Conference on Human Factors in Computing Systems.* ACM Press.

Riggins, S. H. (Ed.). (1994). *The socialness of things: Essays on the socio-semiotics of objects (approaches to semiotics).* Berlin, Germany: Mouton de Gruyter. doi:10.1515/9783110882469

Ryall, K., Morris, M. R., Everitt, K., Forlines, C., & Shen, C. (2006). Experiences with and observations of direct-touch tabletops. In *Proceedings of the First IEEE International Workshop on Horizontal Interactive Human-Computer Systems, TABLETOP 2006.* IEEE Press.

Schöning, J., Brandl, P., Daiber, F., Echtler, F., Hilliges, O., & Hook, J. (2007). *Multi touch surfaces: A technical guide.* Münster, Germany: University of Münster.

Schöning, J., Hook, J., Bartindale, J., Schmidt, D., Olivier, P., & Echtler, F. (2010). Building interactive multi-touch surfaces. In Muller-Tomfelde, C. (Ed.), *Tabletops - Horizontal interactive displays* (pp. 27–49). Münster, Germany: University of Münster. doi:10.1007/978-1-84996-113-4_2

Seow, S. C., Wixon, D., Mackenzie, S., Jacucci, G., Morrison, A., & Wilson, A. (2009). Multitouch and surface computing. In *Proceedings of the 27th International Conference Extended Abstracts on Human Factors in Computing Systems.* ACM Press.

Tylor, E. B. (1871). *Primitive culture: Researches into the development of mythology, philosophy, religion, art, and custom.* London, UK: John Murray. doi:10.1037/13484-000

Whitney, L. (2010). Nearly 1 in 10 using e-readers, poll says. *TeleRead.com.* Retrieved from http://www.teleread.com/ebooks/survey-shows-nearly-1-in-10-using-e-readers-and-e-readerusers-buy-more-books/

Wigdor, D., Fletcher, J., & Morrison, G. (2009). Designing user interfaces for multi-touch and gesture devices. In *Proceedings of the 27th International Conference Extended Abstracts on Human Factors in Computing Systems.* New York, NY: ACM Press.

Wobbrock, J. O., Morris, M. R., & Wilson, A. D. (2009). User-defined gestures for surface computing. In *Proceedings of the 27th International Conference on Human Factors in Computing Systems.* ACM Press.

Yarow, J., & Goldman, L. (2011). How people really use their iPad: Our exclusive survey results. *Business Insider.* Retrieved from http://www.businessinsider.com/how-peoplereallyuse-the-ipad-our-exclusive-survey-results2011-5

Chapter 14

The Earth Sciences and Creative Practice:
Exploring Boundaries between Digital and Material Culture

Suzette Worden
Curtin University, Australia

ABSTRACT

Artists who engage with the earth sciences have been able to explore all kinds of information about the natural environment, including information about the atmosphere, extremes of physical formations across immense dimensions of time and space, and increasingly 'invisible' realms of materials at the nanoscale. This is a rich area for identifying the relationship between digital and material cultures as many artists working with this subject are crossing boundaries and testing out the liminal spaces between the virtual and the real. After an overview of theoretical links between visualisation and geology, mineralogy and crystallography, this chapter explores four themes: (1) environment and experience, (2) code and pattern, (3) co-creation and participation, and (4) mining heritage.

INTRODUCTION

Within current creative practice, artists engage with the earth sciences for inspiration and as a source of information about the natural environment. This rich and varied source of data, which is increasingly in digital format, includes information on many aspects of our material world: from the conditions of the atmosphere to physical formations; from small scale to gigantic formations; extremes of heat and cold; and the interaction of all these in time and space. Additionally, the

DOI: 10.4018/978-1-4666-2961-5.ch014

models, visualisations, and explanations of these phenomena by scientists can include aesthetic characteristics that are appreciated by a wider audience than immediate scientific peers.

For digital environments, the discussion is most often centred on visualisation, which includes the relationship between an image and objects with a material or physical existence and also between images and mental constructs. These constructs and models can be directly observable or become visible through an instrument or device. Visual characteristics can also be translated from a non-visual state into constructed data, as a 'conceptual' translation.

With digital environments becoming more common in everyday life there is often slippage between the values attributed to the 'natural' or analogue and virtual spaces. This can happen where there is slippage between the virtual and the real, or symbol and matter; or even where there is a reversal of values. As Bruno Latour has noted: "How did we succeed in having the whole of philosophy reduced to a choice between two meaninglessnesses: the real but meaningless matter and the meaningful but unreal symbol?" (Latour, 2008, p. 36).

Instead of accepting, or even creating, binary oppositions this chapter will examine how virtual and material spaces are not oppositional but connected and communicated through creative practice for the earth sciences. Often artists deliberately play with the unfixed boundaries between the virtual and the real. The slippage or reversal, noted by Latour, is intentional and becomes, for the viewer as well as the artist, an intriguing and rewarding aesthetic and emotional experience. Using examples related to the earth sciences, this chapter will discuss the ways in which creative works demonstrate the movement of ideas and concepts to and from the physical to the digital. Many of the works that can be chosen to examine a relationship with, and a response to, the field of earth sciences also demonstrate a strong sense of awareness of the importance of a 'sense of place,'

referring to the values associated with cultural memory and the construction of heritage. These values are aligned with place but facilitated by digital technologies. This makes the resulting slippage culturally rich. In addition, any interpretation of these creative works must also include a study of the construction of 'texts' and within this, whether this is intentionally 'authored' by the artist, or is the result of audience participation. This chapter will therefore investigate distinctions between what is presented in an artifact, and what might be constructed by the audience.

In this chapter, examples of creative practice that takes us from the digital to the physical, or vice versa, will be considered where they make specific reference to mineralogy, crystallography, geology, studies of rock formations and technologies supporting mining activities and resource industries. This includes works that are engaged with related environmental, social, and cultural issues in addition to intrinsic interest in the expression of formal and aesthetic qualities.

In dealing with relationships between the virtual and the real world, it is becoming increasingly difficult to categorise artifacts and environments in one camp or the other. In many cases, digital technologies have replaced traditional analogue production and have provided us with new artifacts, products, and services. These have often included a new kind of feedback loop or allow interactivity between the artifact and the user. Alternatively, a service or product can have hidden differences, in its 'internal' workings, but many of its practical qualities can remain unchanged. It is possible to view television or photography in this way. There may be changes in resolution and delivery, including the ability to choose what to watch at a certain times with digital broadcasting, but programmes are still consumed as time-based linear events. Photographs may be digitally processed, and we may be taking more pictures, but they are still attributed with aesthetic and practical values for recording events and memories that are similar to those found in photographs produced with 'traditional' (wet process) film and a mechanical camera. We can choose to celebrate the new, or continue to amend old practices. This chapter explores the transition points between the digital and the real and particularly how we attribute value and significance to those transitional contexts. This account will mainly deal with examples that are hybrid digital/real but includes the entirely digital or the material artifact to suggest a continuum of possibilities that may still be evolving.

Texts that set the scene for this discussion of boundary crossing between art and the earth sciences include Mark Cheetham on the crystal interface (Cheetham, 2010), George Caffentzis on the theory of crystals, historical materialism and analytic engines (Caffentzis, 2007), James Elkins on the history of crystallography (Elkins, 2001), and Tom Corby on information visualization. These authors highlight themes relevant for artworks connected with the earth sciences, but they also discuss the limitations of interpreting the arts and sciences with reference to a shared methodological point of view. For example, Cheetham offers insights into the metaphorical use of crystals, noting some of the similarities across the arts and sciences but Elkins highlights the difference between scientific and artistic images and the dangers in expecting them to share a united history. This is a useful cautionary note: to make effective readings of artworks, images, and texts it is important to give due recognition to context.

In addition to these current critical reviews, there are historical precedents that point to themes that are relevant for current work. Ideas to be developed for interpreting creative practice dealing with the earth sciences can be found in the writings of John Ruskin (1819-1900), or in the philosophy behind projects such as the Festival Pattern Group's designs for the Festival of Britain exhibitions in 1951.

These texts and historical precedents form the background for an account of examples of creative work that, even though they each have a distinct and individual focus, also allow further discussion of general concepts and socially concerned art

practice. The creative works being considered in detail here are primarily inspired by science or are projects initiated as art-science collaborations. As a sense of scale is relevant to the earth sciences, so are creative works that explore minerals at the nanoscale, either through reference to theoretical modelling or exploring the scientific equipment used to visualise nano particles. With reference to a more familiar bodily scale, other works to be described include *The Sixth Shore*, which combines visualisations of natural phenomena and storytelling being delivered through digital technologies. A further example re-works ideas about materiality to form a collection of creative works that 'translates' crystallography into artifacts made using traditional craft techniques. This encourages us to question our acceptance of digital techniques as a complete replacement for more traditional means of representation. Digital media and technologies have been effectively used for historical depiction and heritage communication. The earth sciences and industrial mineral exploitation, mining activities and its cultural heritage are no exception and form a further area of collaborative creative activity. These works will be described in some detail later in the chapter.

This area of work increasingly situates representations in social media and therefore facilitates new ways of reading of the visual images in the context of expanding ideas about authorship. Such images have the potential to extend cultural references into definitions of space, distance, scale and the relationship of the human body to the natural environment.

The Power of Crystals

When charting the 'crystal interface,' Mark Cheetham has described the ways in which crystals are both part of science and the arts, are chemical and material, have a literal dimension but also a metaphorical presence. For this reason, the crystal is a zone of exchange. Cheetham suggests that "crystals are liminal entities, whether as a substance that marks a crucial position on a continuum from the organic to the inorganic or in their work as metaphor" (Cheetham, 2010, p. 255). Cheetham's examples include the architect Daniel Libeskind's Michael Lee-Chin Crystal facility (2007), at the Royal Ontario Museum, Toronto; the installation 'Seizure' by Roger Hiorns; and the work of Gerard Caris. In 2008, Hiorns filled a room in a house, due for demolition with 90,000 litres of copper sulphate solution, which crystallised to make a blue crystal environment. Gerard Caris explores tiling and the ordering systems of pentagon and dodecahedrons. Cheetham describes theoretical interest in crystals, showing how Arthur Schopenhauer, Wilhelm Worringer, Gilles Deleuze and Félix Guattari, and Donna Haraway have all shown an interest in how crystals straddle the organic/inorganic divide.

Cheetham's examples of artworks are primarily artifacts to be experienced in the physical world. For crystals in theories of visual culture he mentions how, for Deleuze and Guattari, there is no divide between the organic and inorganic, interior and exterior (Cheetham, 2010, p. 253). For Deleuze and Guattari, existence is a continuum. In his discussion of late 20th century cinema, Deleuze has used the concept of crystal-image for cinematographic time to show the relationship between the world and imagery, and as noted by Kozin, the crystal-image "establishes the direction of fit; images to the world (e.g. memory to photographic or cinematographic image)" (Kozin, 2009, p. 109). According to Kozin, the naming of the concept was inspired by the physical properties of minerals:

…the structure of a crystal allows us to see how, with each turn of the crystal, what is opaque and virtual becomes luminous and actual. This reversibility makes all sorts of binaries coalesce…. Our thoughts become matter, while matter becomes an object of our thoughts. The crystal-film is therefore the kind of film that exposes the relations between what is being reflected and the act of reflecting (Kozin, 2009, p. 109).

As Kozin further explains:

The liminal in-between that it explores is not empty; it contains a prime mover, and it is in that pivot that we find one of the most basic conditions for our experience of the world as image: 'what we see in the crystal…is time, in its double movement of making presents pass, replacing one after the next, while going towards the future, but also of preserving all of the past, dropping it into the obscure depth' (Deleuze, 1989:7) (Kozin, 2009, pp. 109-110).

This linking of the structure of the crystal to the liminal provides a 'space' within the movement between matter and symbol, which, as previously mentioned, intrigued Latour.

Interest in the crystal-image is therefore central to ideas of media working with time. However, scientific understanding of crystals has never been absolute. Another view of crystals is found in an account of the theory of machines by George Caffentzis. In a discussion of theories of labour Caffentzis has explained that it is possible to extend Marx's incomplete theory of machines by including another category of machine, the Turing machine. He argues that Marx was working at a time when there was a transition between the substance-theory of the 1840s and the field theory of the 1860s. This meant that there was a transition, at that time, from natural philosophy to physics, although both aspects could be mixed. By the 1860s a mineral's crystalline form was not a given of nature (Caffentzis, 2007, p. 32). Instead, "the crystalline aggregation, which had been studied throughout the early nineteenth century as a way of differentiating chemicals, was seen as part of the great round of the correlation of forces" and:

A new theory of the crystal is made possible. For the crystal simply is a store of energy that in the various mineralogical processes is released and then reabsorbed. Increasingly the internal structure of inorganic bodies were seen by physicists, chemists and mineralogists as a more or less complex pool of 'tensional' or 'potential' energy (Caffentzis, 2007, p. 32).

The process of potential turning to actual and back into potential energy again was a model for Marx in understanding commodity values, with commodities having value locked within them as a consequence of the labour that had gone into them.

To make a claim that services, cultural products and knowledge and communication are 'material goods,' Caffentzis discusses the Turing machine through an account of Charles Babbage's philosophy and related analytic engine and argues against a view of immaterial labour put forward by Michael Hardt and Antonio Negri (Hardt & Negri, 2000) in their discussion of immaterial labour. Babbage's idea had practical 'application' but was not 'practical' until the composition of working groups included an increase in clerical labour and recognition of the Jacquard loom principle as a possible mathematical-industrial space that characterised the labour process in general. This was to be a 20th century phenomenon (Caffentzis, 2007, pp. 39-40). By taking into account a combination of simple machines, heat machines and Turing machines, Caffentzis goes beyond binary semantics and the problematic of conceptualising immaterial and material. He also identifies the historical reasons for the problematic discourse and finding commonalities in measuring value in work. This account, which merges a discussion of scientific theory and philosophy and the economic theory of labour, is useful contextual background for a conceptualisation of the materiality of creative work and is a further example of finding commonalities rather than making binary distinctions. It is also evident that crystallography as part of the earth sciences and science more generally is not to be represented by an absolute viewpoint but is historically constructed. For artists this confirms the relevance of multiple fields of reference.

These theoretical discussions about crystals highlight the in-between space of the liminal. Further possibilities arise in relation to the direction of enquiry, taken within the construction of an argument and descriptive narrative. For example, when examining crystallography, James Elkins starts from science and then moves to art and, as a consequence, is better able to examine process. When comparing the histories of art and histories of crystallography, Elkins starts his discussion by placing the drawings, diagrams and geometric images of crystals, with their 'cold transmission of meaning' in opposition to artworks with 'expressive meaning.' He then provides an experimental reading of crystal drawings to test the limits of art historical interpretation. He usefully tests the boundaries of what is acceptable as 'art,' which he calls the "problem of appropriate explanation" (Elkins, 2001, p. 14). An integral and useful outcome of his discussion is information on the constructed-ness of the crystal drawings and their lack of 'naturalness.' The crystal drawings use a system of notation that has to be learnt. The drawings may have a visual similarity to the use of perspective in paintings but are systems of notation that flatten and distort without seeming to do so (Elkins, 2001, p. 21). In his discussion, Elkins is making us aware of the distinctions between art as expressive and science as the source of objective information. His demarcation of this distinction is based on the belief in a 'canon' for art historical study and a nuanced belief in reading images in context.

Information Visualisation

Although Elkins usefully discusses process, his argument is nevertheless grounded in historical examples and static images. When considering the use of digital formats, information visualisation becomes a process that extends possibilities. In an account of visualisation as a form of image making, Tom Corby identifies that the images produced "are a vehicle capable of enabling comprehension of material realities" (Corby, 2008, p. 461). This is a new type of image "consisting of objective and subjective, informational and aesthetic components, which operates at the limits of what the image is understood to be in the visual arts" (Corby, 2008, p. 467). Corby acknowledges the cultural aspects of reception and interpretation and the use of "intricate formal assemblages of information, space, material, and image" (Corby, 2008, p. 463). He argues that information visualisation can be used to create works that enable a tangible experience of data, or even the physical equivalence of abstract facts. This produces an ambiguous kind of embodied knowledge and has potential for audience participation.

Corby's stress on the subjective and embodied potential of information visualisation means that information visualisation, as integral to a creative artifact, can incorporate the range of referents that are also found in scientific visualisation. Visual representations may refer to objects that exist or to mental and abstract constructs. Material and physical referents may have physical characteristics that are directly observable, or the object or phenomena may only become visible through the use of special techniques and devices, or need to be translated from a non-visible state into visual representations (Pauwels, 2008, pp. 149-150). It is also possible to combine referents.

Phenomenology

Increasingly historians of science have developed a practice-orientated approach to models in science and propose treating models as 'epistemic artifacts.' This means that traces of human agency is present in the model, that models are 'materialised' inhabitants of the inter-subjective field of human activity and are also knowledge objects (Knuuttila & Voutilainen, 2003, p. 1487). Models are mediators and have 'surplus content' which means that "models are open-ended things that have their own history and dwell in our research practices in manifold ways as both tools and ob-

jects of inquiry" (Knuuttila & Voutilainen, 2003, p. 1494). Similarly for scientific image making, there has been a move away from 19th century 'mechanical objectivity' with its separation of self and the world (Anderson, 2009, pp. 119-121). Daston and Galison make a distinction between this 'mechanical objectivity' and new ways of manipulation and making, when they consider scientific imaging for nanotechnology. Here the measuring instrument interacts with nature at the atomic level. In this context, the outcome is a result of aesthetic judgment where images are made and seen at the same time (Daston & Galison, 2007). This is a move to presentation rather than representation. This embodied practice has been the subject of research, where it has been noted by investigators that the exploratory process is enhanced by the use of computer technologies. For X-ray diffraction, crystallographers use the actions of their physical bodies as a resource, and as an interface so that they can interact 'physically' with molecular configurations (Myers, 2008, p. 163). Their visual facts are produced through techniques of manipulation (Myers, 2008, p. 190).

Combining Art and Science

These recent commentaries indicate that examining the crystal image is not only relevant for scientific theory and the natural world but is relevant for a critical understanding of visualisation. Differences between the real and the virtual are varied and often transitional. Over time, there is a shift away from an expectation of objectivity (Daston & Galison, 2007) and this is especially shown through the embodied potential of digitally produced information visualisation (Corby, 2008). It would be too simplistic to see this shift to the embodied potential of visualisation and a greater subjectivity as inevitable or even a constant transition. For this reason, the contribution of John Ruskin, art critic and geologist, provides some themes and preoccupations that are relevant for a critical review of current work that makes reference to the earth sciences. John Ruskin was a formidable art critic, first as a supporter and critic of J.M.W. Turner and then of the Pre-Raphaelites artists. He was also interested in social issues, education, the arts and crafts, and political economy. He travelled extensively, wrote on the natural sciences, especially geology, as well as on architecture and the arts.

The origins of the earth were central to the discussions of religion and evolution in the 19th century. It was against this background that the study of geology and the earth sciences were developed. The critical writings of John Ruskin are a fascinating example of how the earth sciences, especially geology, could be intertwined with art practice in the 19th century. An examination of Ruskin's appreciation of minerals and landscape sets a benchmark for themes relevant for present-day practice. Ruskin included discussions of geology in his writing on art. The second volume of *Modern Painters* is dedicated to description of the Alps and their geology. *Deucalion* (1875-1879) was subtitled *Collected Studies of the Lapse of Waves, and Life of Stones*, and *The Ethics of the Dust: Ten Lectures to Little Housewives on the Elements of Crystallisation* (1866), a discussion of mineralogy with didactic overtones. Ruskin also included over 2000 mineral specimens in the Collection of the Guild of St George, which was put together, from 1875, as a creative and educational tool for the metalworkers of Sheffield, UK (Ruskin at Walkley, 2012). The minerals were part of a collection that also included coins, and drawings and illustrations of architecture art works, and all kinds of natural forms such as landscapes, birds, and flowers. Ruskin's work on geology was frequently published and his view of geology was considered alternative to the mainstream, with much of his work considered "professionally current" (Trowbridge, 2006, p. 18).

Ruskin's contributions are various but for considering mineralogy, as discussed by Feldman (2006), the following themes are important for Ruskin's critical discussions of rocks and crystals. Firstly, crystals brought moral and religious ques-

tions as well as science and art together. Secondly, rocks were important as images of change over time. This means that mutability is a useful theme to consider. Thirdly, the idea of a mineral provides an example of an array or a constellation, which is ordered in itself and can be extended in infinite ways. Lastly, Ruskin's ideas about minerals and rocks point to the significance of order within disorder (Feldman, 2006, pp. 12-15). An interest in changes in scale of physical forms can be added to this list. Ruskin was equally at ease studying the changes in mountain landforms as he was appreciating the beauty of minerals and crystals.

These themes are useful for extending this discussion of current art practice and to the formation of representations and visualisations dependent on digital technologies more generally. Additionally, Ruskin's work had a strong social message. His desire to make art and books available to everyone is relevant to discussions of the ways in which digital media and technologies can provide increased forms of access to artifacts, museums, and art collections. Ruskin's interests in working conditions, aesthetics, morality and ethics are reminders of the importance of cultural and social outcomes. This can be related to 21st century interests in using digital technologies in conjunction with explorations of ecology and sustainable living.

In the 20th century, crystal forms became associated with abstract form and building with glass, as shown by the work of Expressionist architects. Bruno Taut's Glass Pavilion (1914) was based on a crystal form as a symbol of renewal and proposing a utopian vision for the future (Frampton, 1980, p. 116). Crystal forms were used as a metaphor of renewal and for visions of a better future. As was the case with Ruskin, in Taut's work, *Alpine Architektur* (1919) the Alps continue to inspire a sense of sublime awe and wonder.

The flexibility of the crystal metaphor to work at different registers of scale is shown in another 20th century use of crystal imagery by the Festival Pattern Group for the Festival of Britain in 1951. This Group created designs to be used to decorate manufactured objects, based on patterns derived from X-ray crystallography. The initiator of this project was Dr Helen Megaw, a crystallographer at Birkbeck College, London. Although minerals, such as chalk, kaolin, afwillite, mica, and quartz, were the subject of this project, many of the examples were also of proteins, as this was the newest and most challenging area of research for crystallography (Jackson, 2008, p. 11). This exhibition was put together when optimism about science and technology was widespread. In using the crystal patterns as a starting point for patterns on textiles, wallpapers and manufactured objects, there was an expectation of accuracy in the representation of the scientific data. For this, the proper scientific name was used for each crystal pattern and at least one scientist involved expected an explicit description of the extent to which the patterns were interpreted in by design process (Forgan, 2000, p. 229). This interest in crystalline structures and atoms and the aim to make it familiar in everyday objects served to immerse the viewer and "foster a visceral familiarity" (Moffat, 2000, p. 105) where the viewer becomes part of the otherworldly realm.

Increasing Diversity

The creative works, to be discussed here, includes works that are primarily inspired by science or are projects initiated as art-science collaborations. Some of these have a strong social focus or are a commentary on the environment, ecological conditions, historical change, or industrial development by the resources industries. Parallel to this, these industries are responsible for generating further scientific knowledge, for innovation and application of engineering and digital technologies, and for the extract and management of resources for industrial production. These creative works are grouped under four themes: (1) environment and experience, (2) code and pattern, (3) co-creation and participation, and (4) mining heritage.

Environment and Experience

The Sixth Shore, which is part of SymbioticA's long-term project, *Adaptation*, is a soundscape project developed by Perdita Phillips started in 2009 for completion in 2012. It is a creative work that integrates a 3D soundscape, using GPS technologies, with a location renowned for its geological uniqueness. The project is based at Lake Clifton, which is in the Yalgorup National Park, south of Mandurah in Western Australia. The eastern shore of the lake has thrombolites living in the lake. The dome-shaped thrombolites are rock-like formations built by microorganisms. Thrombolites grow as a clotted formation, while the related stromatolites build layers. Thrombolites provide a focus for questions about the boundary between minerals and biological life. They precipitate calcium carbonate and form in shallow water where the microbes have the sunshine they need to photosynthesize (see Figure 1).

The Lake Clifton eco-system is a fragile balance of human and non-human interactions, with decreasing groundwater, as a result of climate change, and Tuart tree dieback due to a fungal infection. Clearing in the locality is in tension with viable bird habitat. The microbial formations of the thrombolites are considered a critically endangered community (Luu, Mitchell, & Blyth,

Figure 1. Thrombolites at Lake Clifton (©2008, Suzette Worden. Used with permission)

2004; South West Catchments Council & Department of Environment and Conservation, 2011). The project builds a picture of the environment in layers, alluding to the immense geological timescale that can be discerned through studying the constituent parts of this landscape. The thrombolites are organisms have a lineage going back 3.5 billion years. For the *Sixth Shore*, multiple stories are woven together from the six themes: Shore 1: thrombolitic time; Shore 2: shifting shores: lake formation and seashore changes; Shore 3: cultivated landscapes: indigenous cultures; Shore 4: a time of clearing; Shore 5: bird migration and hooded plovers; and finally Shore 6: futures.

Inherent in the progression through the six stages is a sense of historical change and, through knowledge and experience the power to see a viable future that is not disconnected from a history that embraces far more than a human timescale. Geological time has its own characteristics but it is also seen as integral to the other narratives of the environment. Equally, the digital technologies used to support the project are integral to other means of collecting data or communicating the project. Digital technologies are used as a means to understand the physical environment rather than overwhelm it and research was undertaken into the design of a system to identify the ground position and orientation of a participant so that the soundscape they hear could be planned. This system had to be comfortable, light and easily wearable and adapted from off-the-shelf technology (see Figure 2).

As well as create an embodied experience supported by digital technologies, the project added to the rich histories of the area through its collection of testimony. As noted by Phillips,

The Sixth Shore aims to push the boundaries of what it means to go on a walk and think like an ecosystem. It addresses the diverse narratives that surround the Lake, directly responding to the area and engaging with the local community

through oral history recordings and interviews. The Lake is a hotbed of diversity surrounded by a rich 'human ecology.' It offers a microcosmic peek into the issues and threats that the world faces, and presents a metaphor for the global ecosystem and a planet in crisis. The project promises both a deeper engagement and dis/re-orientation for the audience (Phillips, 2012).

In this project, Phillips has interpreted the scientific knowledge on thrombolites, along with the changing sea levels and coastal deposits to arrive at metaphorical implications that influence the sound world she is creating. This is a complex story, which enriches the sense of place for the area.

I will be structuring my soundscape to suggest this great distance and depth, and the boundaries of life that the thrombolites represent. I envisage a spiral of tiny sounds like the descent into the geological past and tiny pinprick sounds like the multitudinous field of microbes beneath us with their sharp aragonite grains, oxygen burps, and hydrogen sulphide farts (Phillips, 2009, p. 3).

From the thrombolites, the idea of clotted life is developed as a metaphor and from the fragility of the lake, which becomes dry by the end of summer,

Figure 2. Testing commercial GPS units (©2011, Perdita Phillips. Used with permission)

the idea of a brittle landscape. Phillips uses these metaphors to link her materially driven practice to a theoretical and philosophical positioning of 'artifactual constructivism' in order to reflect the complexity of the work. In this, there is a move towards depth and geological time. For instance, from the position of a single bacterium one might image living within an eco-system of layers and multiple, eroding and advancing, ever-shifting shorelines. The fossil remains have also been ravaged by time. As Phillips explains:

With all fossils what we see are traces, never a complete or full record of the past. It is important to consider the concepts of loss and complexity with the use of scientific data in this project. My development of a sound ecosystem will be the tracing of a place, never a full record, but reflecting the 'sketchy' remnants of multiple pasts found in the evidence of today. Correspondingly the sound installations will be built up of fragments (Phillips, 2009, p. 7).

The metaphor of a clotted structure aims to thicken the narrative and arrive at a more complex structure than a layered or linear narrative (Phillips, 2009, p. 9). This includes forming a balance between incorporating scientific data and "maintaining a connection to the materiality of specificity of a place that science cannot capture" (Phillips, 2009, p. 13). The work therefore deliberately tries to work at the threshold of different value systems. This is not a creative work that is completely dependent on digital media for its execution. It uses digital technologies for collection of data and delivery of soundscapes. The digital resources provide a platform to support the exploration of margins between the inorganic and organic, timescale and the complexity of art and science relationships. For this, the shoreline is an apt metaphor.

Walking is important for the engagement of the audience in the *Sixth Shore* project. Walking is considered central to our perceptions of an environment; it is a multisensory experience where there is emphasis on the performative and the communicative. These are key factors that also make digital environments attractive to users. As ethnographers have noted, it is very difficult to represent the experience of walking with printed words and linear text so new formats of using image and text need to be explored to create a multisensory experience that includes looking, listening and touching (Pink, Hubbard, O'Neill, & Radley, 2010, p. 5). Extended further, the performative role in art has a hybrid space where the visual and textual products can feed into cultural politics and/or social intervention.

This digitally enabled work creates links between the environment and experience through sound narrative and supports a multisensory richness. This includes a slippage between the virtual and the real that is mirrored by links between the social and the geological. More importantly, the work makes the connections and links visible and accessible, and consequently the methodological concerns of art practice also become visible.

Code and Pattern

My next example is of creative work that uses formations from crystallography and re-works the forms using traditional techniques. In doing so, the work reinforces the importance of appreciating the materiality of artifacts. This extends the discussion of metaphor and the 'crystal interface' suggested by Mark A Cheetham, who notes:

Crystals are compelling because they are indexical of existential questions, poised at the crossing point of life and death. While their perfect forms appear lifeless, they suggest life because they "grow" and move. Even as "corpses" they function as physical reminders of life (Cheetham, 2010, p. 251).

Al Munro is an artist who works across textiles, print and drawing-based media. In 2010, her work in the exhibition *Crystallography* was an exploration of mathematical codes and patterns (Craft ACT, 2010). A collection of small pieces form a creative interpretation of scientific representations of crystals. The work is produced in needlepoint, using fabrics, cotton, and sequins, to explore the depiction of 2D and 3D space. We are provided with an opportunity to question our understanding and appreciation of textures, opacity and transparency, reflection and symmetries. The precious, delicate materials used on a flat surface create a tension with the diagrammatic forms of the structures depicted. We have learnt to read these diagrams as 3D forms, which we can also manipulate imaginatively as if revolving in 3D space. These textile depictions freeze any potential movement with the strength of their static and fixed material qualities.

Extending an exploration of crystal structures, Al Munro exhibited prints and constructions at the Brenda May Gallery, Sydney in 2011 (Brenda May Gallery, 2011). These screen prints, with glitter flocking, form a series in which the texture and structure of textiles are uses as a knitted-weave surface decoration in contrast to the lines in crystal diagrammatic structures. A further series of constructions *Patterns that are not* show clusters of repetitive crystal shapes in a variety of sizes, evoking formation and growth. Here there is association with ideal shapes rather than the deformations often found in natural growth. The artificial qualities of scientific depictions are emphasised, but the materials used—constructed coloured glitter and cardboard—signify the creative potential to be found through experimenting with these structural forms in other domains. Munro's work explores the process of defining structure rather than seeing the crystal as a symbol for something else (see Figure 3).

The display of these forms in a gallery can be compared to the display of crystals and mineral specimens in museums. Minerals are most often displayed in cabinets that emphasise classification; we are given an ordered natural environment where visual qualities are emphasised. Munro's textile works are also concerned with texture and reflec-

Figure 3. Al Munro, from the series 'Crystallography Embroideries' (©2011, Al Munro. Used with permission)

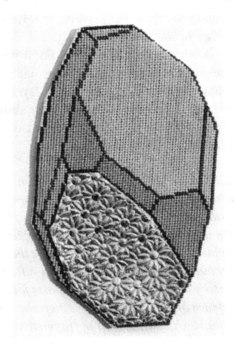

tion. This is imaginatively captured through glitter and sparkle rather than transparency. The prints, in contrast, emphasise the graphic nature of crystallography. This form of notation had its most significant phase of development during the 19th century.

A broad historical survey of crystal imagery includes the neo-platonic and medieval and renaissance symbolism which contrasts crystals as perfect products of nature to mortal decay. After the contribution of Abbé Huäy's *Triaité de Minéralogie* in 1799, the representation of crystals was formalised in science and pure illusionistic devices were no longer used. Huäy established an empirical connection between the external 'secondary' forms of crystals and their internal 'primitive forms' and 'integrant molecules' (Albury & Oldroyd, 1977, p. 195). There was no longer any depiction of textures and shadows. There was a move from naturalistic drawings to geometric notation, based on geometric solids and using various versions of projection, such as the clinographic projection (a version of parallel projection), and gnomonic and stereographic projections, which were both derived from mapping techniques. Crystallography shared an interest in principles of original form and principles of growth abstracted from natural forms with architecture and neoclassical artists (Elkins, 2001, p. 20).

Clinographic projection was invented by Carl Friedrich Naumann in 1829-30 and standardised by Paul Groth by 1876. The projection became a standard representational strategy for crystal drawing after it was chosen by editors of influential German and French crystallography magazines in 1877 and 1899 respectively. The use of the standardised projection was combined with a 19th century interest in realism and descriptive naturalism. Gnomonic projections were used in the analysis of Laue photographs (X-ray diffraction plates) and stereographic projections were important for morphology and symmetry.

A paradigm shift was evident after 1912 when X-ray diffraction was applied to crystallography, based on the work of William Henry Bragg and his son, Lawrence Bragg (Nobel Media, 2012). The earth sciences benefitted from their discovery, which made it possible to study matter at the sub-microscopic level and see the structure of atoms within molecules. As already mentioned, in the 1940s and 1950s, the crystallographer Dr Helen Megaw worked to adapt crystallography patterns for decorative designs, culminating in exhibits shown at the Festival of Britain in 1951.

Munro's embroidery works also bring to mind the applied arts and crafts and makes reference to process. This suits the 19th century version of crystallography, referring to a pre-20th century sensibility before the expanding application of machines and the conception of a modernist vision for science, technology, and aesthetics. In admiring these works, we are encouraged to question the boundaries we hold between pure science and applied technologies.

Co-Creation and Participation

Perdita Phillip's *Sixth Shore* project heightens our awareness of geological time and the capacity of the virtual to appreciate the environment. Al Munro's re-workings of crystallography provide a critique of the artificiality of scientific depictions, also remarked upon by Elkins, and works with metaphor. Taken together these creative works are exploring contrasting possibilities found in the earth sciences. One explores the immenseness of time and endless change in the environment; the other the minuteness of crystal forms and the artificiality of codes and patterns made visible through microscopy.

My next examples are works that explore a more recent development of science that is about manipulating matter, rather than areas covered by a particular earth science sub-discipline, so has implications across all of the earth sciences. This is nanotechnology, which contributes to our understanding of materials in a very general sense. It is a very diverse area that has developed considerably since the 1980s and is not without its controversial aspects related to environmental risks. Moving beyond the power of the microscope, nanotechnology works at a level that is always invisible—phenomena that are smaller than the minimum possible resolution of light (0.2 micrometers or 2,000 angstroms) (Hanson, 2012, p. 59). Exploring the nanoscale is about finding ways to express the invisible. It goes beyond a similar problem that has been relevant for visualising materials through the use of the microscope since the 17th century. Nanotechnology stretches current definitions of the real. According to Cynthia Selin, nanotechnology is an ambiguous technology with its interest in future developments being usurped by a conservative meaning, bound to commercial developments (Selin, 2007, pp. 206-207). It has relevance for the earth sciences where it expands our understanding of material resources, to ideas of scale so inherent in geology, mineralogy, and crystallography and challenges our view of the physical limits of the mining and resources industries that are intimately related to the earth sciences.

Victoria Vesna and Paul Thomas have been inspired by the nanoscale. Since 2001, Victoria Vesna has explored nanotechnology through installations in collaboration with nanoscientist James Gimzewski. This includes *Zero@wavefunction* and *Nanomandala*. She has also created an installation, *Datamining Bodies*, for a defunct mine in the Ruhr, Germany, that explored the social history of mining in conjunction with an interest in relationships between information and human relationships. Paul Thomas has been developing creative works that explore the nanoscale, often in collaboration with Kevin Raxworthy (see Figure 4).

Zero@wavefunction was first shown in 2002. The installation projects moving images of bucky-balls, which are spherical fullerenes, an allotrope of carbon and important for nanotechnology. Participants, through their shadows, are able to interact with these shapes (Vesna, 2012). When interacting with the buckyballs the participant's attention is drawn to changes in scale represented by the changing projection of their shadow in conjunction with visualisations of the buckyballs shown on a large scale. The work draws attention to the possibility of manipulating the mechanics of matter as well as to the body's relationship to scale. The name, *Zero@wavefunction*, refers to quantum mechanics and the energy of atoms and electrons and encourages further comparison between different registers of scale. This work draws attention to the work of the nanoscientist and their manipulation of matter. For example, a scientist using a Scanning Tunnel Microscope (STM) using a tactile sensing instrument is recording shape by feeling and can also use the instrument as tool to manipulate the atomic world by moving atoms and molecules in virtual space (Gimzewski & Vesna, 2003).

The *Nanomandala* installation was also a collaborative project between Victoria Vesna and James Gimzewski. It has been shown in various

Figure 4. Zero@wavefunction, Singapore (©2008, Suzette Worden. Used with permission)

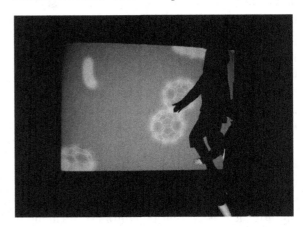

locations since 2003. The installation consists of a video projected onto a disc of sand. The images change from depicting the molecular structure of a grain of sand into an image of a complete mandala and then back again. The images of the grain of sand were created from the visualisations from a scanning electron microscope. The mandala is an image of Chakrasamvara and was created by Tibetan Buddhist monks from the Gaden Lhopa Khangtsen Monastery in India. An accompanying sound track has been devised by Anne Niemetz. These monks had originally created the mandala for an exhibition of Nepalese and Tibetan Buddhist at the Los Angeles County Museum of Art (Vesna) (see Figures 5 and 6).

The images are derived from digital photographs of the full mandala, taken at different stages, using a wide angle and then a maco lens. Next, photographs were taken of the centre of the mandala with an optical microscope and a scanning electron microscope. A final suite of photographs were taken of a grain of sand, taking the images collected to the nano level. The final composition was an animation using the 300,000 images collected from the different stages. When watching this work, the viewer is drawn into a progression of images that explores our sensual response to scale. It also allows us to consider how representations of scale are captured and how

Figure 5. Nanomandala, John Curtin Gallery, Perth (©2008, Suzette Worden. Used with permission)

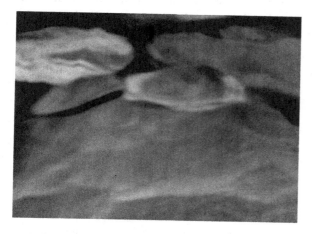

Figure 6. Nanomandala, John Curtin Gallery, Perth (©2008, Suzette Worden. Used with permission)

this stretches our understanding and experience of scale in relation to our own bodily presence. Vesna was also interested in the process of making world views worthy of contemplation and investigation. She noted the following about the installation, saying she was inspired by

Watching the nanoscientist at work, purposefully arranging atoms just as the monk laboriously creates sand images grain by grain, this work brings together the Eastern and Western minds through their shared process centered on patience. Both cultures use these bottom-up building practices to create a complex picture of the world from extremely different perspectives (Vesna, 2012).

In its production, this work uses the computer technologies associated with nanotechnology research and takes on some of the concerns of explaining the nanoscale. The need to read the nanoscale through computer graphics is evident but the work takes us into an enclosed representation of the mandala. This is not in accordance with the depiction of limitless space, which Valerie Hanson has seen as an effective trope for describing the nanoworld. Hanson suggests that images of the limitless space of the nanoworld are not spaces to explore; "they refer to a built world—a world that the viewer may also alter as he or she explores. In other words, the viewer has already entered into the world, as opposed to standing at the threshold" (Hanson, 2012, p. 70) (see Figure 7).

Paul Thomas is an artist interested in the spatial boundaries and in particular the disintegration of territories and boundaries in the nanoworld (Thomas, 2007). Appreciating the potential of exploring the tactile aspects of data gathering within nanotechnology, Thomas uses the metaphor of Midas, to investigate the boundaries between skin and gold and what happens when gold is touched. The experimentation for *Midas* involved using an Atomic Force Microscope (AFM) to "probe topological, conformational changes and interactions of a gold-coated cantilever on a single skin cell as compared with an uncoated cantilever" (Thomas, 2007, 2009). In another experiment, *Nanoessence*, the vibration of atoms with the AFM in force spectroscopy mode was made, where only the vertical movement was recorded. The data was translated to sound files and used in conjunction with 3D stereo images. The resultant work is a combination of this sound data with images of the projection of a single cell where "a genetic algorithm was written for semi-

Figure 7. Midas (©2009, Paul Thomas. Used with permission)

autonomous self-organizing nanobots to affect the digital image of the skin cell translating the data to gold colour" (Thomas, 2007, 2009). The viewer releases the nanobots through using a button, which is physical model of the skin cell and then interacts with the imagery. The resulting experience is visual and haptic. The subject matter of gold relates to the earth sciences as a mineral of great value and therefore a catalyst for mining operations and related applied research.

However, this work deliberately blurs the boundaries between the minerals and the post-biological human existence as it is being articulated through an understanding of the nanoworld. In this context the body has lost its distinct boundaries. Through the work, Thomas asks: if basic atoms and molecules can be manipulated, what does this mean for the human body? Thomas deliberately invites a phenomenological discourse about our understanding of these issues. He focusses on the understanding of a mineral in relation to our own body and combines an investigation of biological and chemical and mineral science. For him, "the concept of reality checking is of greater relevance to us now…Nano art in general allows for a reconfiguring of our conscious understanding of space, which is our lived experience, generating the potential for new spatial understanding" (Thomas, 2009, p. 192).

Both these artists explore the potential of computer technology to create an immersive world where we are literally drawn into another world and requested to ask questions about scale or about our means of accessing that world, especially where the technology can bring into play different senses—of touch as well as the visual—or make us aware of different cultural sensibilities. The artificiality inherent in explorations of the nanoworld also makes a different interplay between the virtual and the real. The 'real' is totally constructed. It is therefore appropriate to use the term simulation and to describe a world that is self-sufficient. As Hanson suggests, "simulations allow for consistent events to happen within their parameters (their worlds) and do not make a transition between the internal world and the external world; these characteristics led to researchers' creation of artificial life" (Hanson, 2012, p. 71).

These works have a dynamic and temporal dimension. The level of involvement is much more embodied and an enactment with a process of change. This is as much the case for scientists engaged in using digital technologies as it is for someone interacting with the creative work. In magnetic resonance imaging, which is based on a combination of reading data from radio frequencies and magnetic fields with the computer, according to Morana Alac (2008, p. 488), "the acts of seeing are managed through the temporal and spatial coordination of gesture, talk, and the manipulation of the digital screen." For Alac, in laboratory practice, "multiple semiotic fields, such as the field of the digital screen and the one inhabited by material bodies, are superimposed and intertwined" …. This provides "an action-orientated, publicly available, and intersubjective character or seeing" (Alac, 2008, p. 493).

The developments in nanotechnology in the 1980s demonstrated a shift to postmodernity. This is a change that has brought forth a new relationship between science and technology. Paul Forman explains in a discussion of science and technology that, in modernity technology is:

The collective noun for all the many ways things are in fact done and made—technology is what it is independently, largely of our conceptions of it. The opposite is the case with science, which is, largely, only what we think it is. That is, the boundary between science and non-science, as well as the bulk of the activities that are science, is not primarily a matter of fact but of a cultural consensus (Forman, 2007, p. 10).

In the 1980s, the distinction between modernity and postmodernity became evident through a reversal in the science-technology relationship. Technology has replaced science as the principal model for knowledge production and has replaced science as the principal model for ordering activities that constitute culture (Forman, 2007, p. 53). There has also been a reversal from modernity's interest in method (and the means) to technology's focus on the end justifying the means (Forman, 2007, p. 71). This shift means that there is no longer an either/or between science and technology, a point also noted by Daston and Galison (2007, p. 395) where they see that nanotechnology departs from ideas of pure science and the activity of working in nanotechnology is a hybrid between science and engineering. Even the name nanotechnology makes this clear.

Mining Heritage

Many of the works, mentioned so far, have the potential to extend cultural references into definitions of space, distance, scale and the relationship of the human body to the natural environment. An early example of this kind of practice was *Geoderma*, from 1996, a collaborative work by David Carson, Brian McClave and George Millward, that was supported by Kalgoorlie Consolidated Gold Mines (KCGM) and the Goldfields Arts Centre Gallery. These artists used 3D imaging techniques, primarily used in mining exploration, to explore digital imaging, exploration of the earth and of the body. They used 3D video images of the mine sites with aerial photographs from the Kalgoorlie

Gold Fields, Western Australia, in conjunction with a stereo soundscape and medical imagery (Carson, McClave, & Millward, 1996).

It is increasingly possible to find representations, using digital technologies, of current mining operations and mining heritage that are using techniques in common usage on the Internet, but on further investigation are capable of extending documentation of mining heritage and offer innovative ways of understanding landscape in the context of industrial exploitation of physical resources. Representations of history or industrial practices are situated in easily accessible interactive and social media formats. These information resources facilitate new ways of reading of the visual images and provide a wealth of opportunities for user participation.

For example, Google Earth can include a provision for making personalised maps for visiting a mining area. Geoscience Australia provides an interactive history of Australia's mineral history. It is possible to view locations for the history of mining from the Goldrush of the 1950s and follow a virtual guided tour of landmarks in mining areas (Geoscience Australia, 2012). This can be used to augment planning for a visit to the area, or just be a virtual experience, and puts a creative process in the hands of the user. A Google Earth 3D map of Sovereign Hill, an outdoor mining museum in Ballarat, Victoria, offers a more immersive experience and is a detailed construction of the museum, itself a re-constructed environment bringing together a collection of buildings to reconstruct the first ten years after the discovery of gold in the area in 1851. The Museum provides an experience that is described as a stepping back in time to bring history to life (Sovereign Hill, 2012). The 3D Google Earth depiction takes this experience into a virtual world. Google Earth has been described as a multidimensional phenomenon by Jakob Jensen, who suggests that "by combining the strengths of maps and globes, libraries, the film media, and the Internet community, it does not only remediate. It is a metamedium" (Jensen, 2010, p. 132). He also states that "it makes no sense to distinguish clearly among virtual and real spaces…Physical, mediated, and imaginary experiences play together" (Jensen, 2010, p. 130). These virtual environments are an extension of other kinds of virtual museum strategies and increasingly have a stronger community and collaborative structure.

CONCLUSION

This chapter has engaged with practice and theory and taken a broad definition of the earth sciences to discuss virtual worlds and art practice. This has included a discussion of technologies that act upon the environment and also the visual technologies that allow us to 'see' that environment and measure the world for scientific disciplines. Artists explore this as their subject and provide a critique of the associated science and technologies. In this context, our understanding of materiality is extended. What becomes more discernible is the means by which the world is understood in scientific terms both to aid technological development and also as a means of understanding our place in the world. Here links between virtuality, as measurement and modelling has become important, as an addition to interest in experiential issues. The works discussed test our understanding of the relationship of real to virtual, particularly for scale, order, moral and ethical issues and between innovation and traditional practices.

A study of these 'translations' to and from the material world to digital spaces has opened up ways of providing a critique of new media works in the context of a broader historical perspective, including ecology and the body in space. Although reference to science and technology is often present, there is also a move to counter some of the trajectories of science. When considering nanotechnology, Robert Frodeman (2006, p. 384) suggests that "Science has ended up, however, describing an invisible mathematical world disassociated from the one we inhabit." For many

this gap between the visible and the invisible makes science an alienating form of knowledge. For Frodeman, the natural sciences "have left the world of experience as a *terra incognito*, uncharted territory whose contours are now explored by poets, artists and other culturally marginal figures" (Frodeman, 2006, p. 385). Making the invisibility visible is a role for everyone-scientists and artists. Frodeman calls for us all to be "embodied perceivers" (Frodeman, 2006, p. 389).

Supporters of new media arts may claim that new media works are different from conventional art forms because of their use of time-based forms, relationship to conceptual art, installation and performance, and exploration of new technologies, and that new media work should therefore be treated as a new paradigm. To some extent, this is helpful but the aim of this chapter has been to take a broader view of what comprises a creative work associated with, celebrating or critiquing the earth sciences in order to break down unnecessary polarities. Returning to Latour's comment on meaninglessness (Latour, 2008, p. 36), I hope I have shown that if we explore relationships between matter and symbol across both the real and the virtual and also include a historical perspective, we arrive at a richer understanding of creative work and the world. Looking at the earth sciences has been a way to test this proposition.

REFERENCES

Alac, M. (2008). Working with brain scans: Digital images and gestural interaction in fMRI laboratory. *Social Studies of Science*, *38*(4), 483–508. doi:10.1177/0306312708089715

Albury, W. R., & Oldroyd, D. R. (1977). From renaissance mineral studies to historical geology, in the light of Michel Foucault's "The Order of Things". *British Journal for the History of Science*, *10*(3), 187–215. doi:10.1017/S000708740001565X

Anderson, N. (2009). Eye and image: Looking at a visual studies of science. *Historical Studies in the Natural Sciences*, *39*(1), 115. doi:10.1525/hsns.2009.39.1.115

Brenda May Gallery. (2011). *Al Munro*. Retrieved 1 February, 2012, from http://www.brendamaygallery.com.au/pages/artists_works.php?artistID=90

Caffentzis, G. (2007). Crystals and analytic engines: Historical and conceptual preliminaries to a new theory of machines. *Ephemera, 7*(1), 24-45. Retrieved from http://www.ephemeraweb.org/journal/7-1/71caffentzis.pdf

Carson, D., McClave, B., & Millward, D. (ProducerS). (1996). *Geoderma 3D video*. Retrieved from http://www.youtube.com/watch?v=M0XPM_CrsAU

Cheetham, M. A. (2010). The crystal interface in contemporary art: Metaphors of the organic and inorganic. *Leonardo*, *43*(3), 250–255. doi:10.1162/leon.2010.43.3.250

Corby, T. (2008). Landscapes of feeling, arenas of action: Information visualization as art practice. *Leonardo*, *41*(5), 460–467. doi:10.1162/leon.2008.41.5.460

Craft, A. C. T. (2010). *Crystallography - Al Munro*. Retrieved 26 October, 2010, from http://craftact.org.au/crystallography

Daston, L., & Galison, P. (2007). *Objectivity*. New York, NY: Zone Books.

Elkins, J. (2001). Art history as the history of crystallography. In *The Domain of Images* (pp. 13–31). Ithaca, NY: Cornell University Press.

Feldman, J. (2006). Ruskin's minerals. *Field Notes, 1*(4).

Forgan, S. (2000). Festivals of science and the two cultures: Science, design and display in the Festival of Britain, 1951. *British Journal for the History of Science*, *31*(2), 217–240. doi:10.1017/S0007087498003264

Forman, P. (2007). The primacy of science in modernity, of technology in postmodernity, and of ideology in the history of technology. *History and Technology*, *23*(1-2), 1–152. doi:10.1080/07341510601092191

Frampton, K. (1980). *Modern architecture: A critical history*. London, UK: Thames and Hudson.

Frodeman, R. (2006). Nanotechnology: The visible and the invisible. *Science as Culture*, *15*(4), 383–389. doi:10.1080/09505430601022700

Geoscience Australia. (2012). *History of Australia's minerals industry*. Retrieved 15 February, 2012, from http://www.australianminesatlas.gov.au/history/index.html

Gimzewski, J., & Vesna, V. (2003). The nanoneme syndrome: Blurring of fact and fiction in the construction of a new science. *Technoetic Arts: A Journal of Speculative Research, 1*(1), 7-24.

Hanson, V. L. (2012). Amidst nanotechnology's molecular landscapes. *Science Communication*, *34*(1), 57–83. doi:10.1177/1075547011401630

Hardt, M., & Negri, A. (2000). *Empire*. Cambridge, MA: Harvard University Press.

Jackson, L. (2008). *From atoms to patterns: Crystal structure designs from the 1951 Festival of Britain*. Shepton Beauchamp, UK: Richard Dennis and Wellcome Collection.

Jensen, J. L. (2010). Augmentation of space: Four dimensions of spatial experiences of Google Earth. *Space and Culture*, *13*(1), 121–133. doi:10.1177/1206331209353693

Knuuttila, T., & Voutilainen, A. (2003). A parser as an epistemic artifact: A material view on models. *Philosophy of Science*, *70*(5), 1484. doi:10.1086/377424

Kozin, A. (2009). The appearing memory: Gilles Deleuze and Andrey Tarkovsky on `crystal-image'. *Memory Studies*, *2*(1), 103–117. doi:10.1177/1750698008097398

Latour, B. (2008). *What is the style of matters of concern? Two lectures in empirical philosophy.* Dordrecht, The Netherlands: Uitgeverij Van Gorcum.

Luu, R., Mitchell, D., & Blyth, J. (2004). *Thrombolites (stromatolite-like microbialite) community of a coastal brackish lake (Lake Clifton).* Wannero, Australia: Western Australian Threatened Species and Communities Unit (WATSCU).

Moffat, I. (2000). A horror of abstract thought: Postwar Britain and Hamilton's 1951 "growth and form" exhibition. *October, 94,* 89-112.

Myers, N. (2008). Molecular embodiments and the body-work of modeling in protein crystallography. *Social Studies of Science, 38*(2), 163–199. doi:10.1177/0306312707082969

Nobel Media. (2012). *The Nobel Prize in Physics 1915.* Retrieved 20 February, 2012, from http://www.nobelprize.org/nobel_prizes/physics/laureates/1915/wh-bragg.html

Pauwels, L. (2008). An integrated model for conceptualising visual competence in scientific research and communication. *Visual Studies, 23*(2), 147–161. doi:10.1080/14725860802276305

Phillips, P. (2009). Clotted life and brittle waters. *Landscapes, 3*(2), 1–20.

Phillips, P. (2012). *The sixth shore details.* Retrieved 28 January 2012, now available at http://www.perditaphillips.com/portfolio/the-sixth-shore-2009-2012/

Pink, S., Hubbard, P., O'Neill, M., & Radley, A. (2010). Walking across disciplines: from ethnography to arts practice. *Visual Studies, 25*(1), 1–7. doi:10.1080/14725861003606670

Ruskin at Walkley. (2012). *Reconstructing the St George's Museum.* Retrieved 4 February, 2012, from http://www.ruskinatwalkley.org/index.php?hotspots=off

Selin, C. (2007). Expectations and the emergence of nanotechnology. *Science, Technology & Human Values, 32*(2), 196–220. doi:10.1177/0162243906296918

South West Catchments Council & Department of Environment and Conservation. (2011). *Glimpses into disappearing landscapes.* Wannero, Australia: South West Catchments Council & Department of Environment and Conservation.

Sovereign Hill. (2012). *Google Earth - 3D model of Sovereign Hill.* Retrieved 18 February, 2012, from http://www.sovereignhill.com.au/sovereign-hill/

Thomas, P. (2007). *Boundaryless nanomorphologies.* Paper presented at the MutaMorphosis: Challenging Art and Sciences. Prague, Czech Republic.

Thomas, P. (2009). Midas: A nanotechnological exploration of touch. *Leonardo, 42*(3), 186–192. doi:10.1162/leon.2009.42.3.186

Trowbridge, C. (2006). Speakers concerning the Earth: Ruskin's geology after 1860. In Clifford, D., Wadge, E., Warwick, A., & Willis, M. (Eds.), *Repositioning Victorian Sciences: Shifting Centres in Nineteenth-Century Thinking* (pp. 17–30). New York, NY: Anthem Press. doi:10.7135/UPO9781843317517.002

Vesna, V. (2012a). *Zero@wavefunction.* Retrieved from http://notime.arts.ucla.edu/zerowave/zerowave.html

Vesna, V. (2012b). *Nanomandala.* Retrieved 20 February, 2012, from http://nano.arts.ucla.edu/mandala/mandala.php

Chapter 15
The Metaplastic Cyber Opencode Art

Gianluca Mura
Politecnico di Milano University, Italy

ABSTRACT

This chapter explores the continuum between old and new media and presents the research area of Metaplastic Art and Design. The description of the Metaplastic Metaspace and its own methodology create interactive virtual spaces for Cyber Art between reality and virtual realities, from living code to software and vice versa through the Metaplastic Opencode Platform.

INTRODUCTION

Technological progress has led to the creation of the interactive media for the Internet by reintroducing and extending Web experiences based on the relationships between digital artwork, audiences, and authors. The computer, in its interactivity, is capable of virtual object reproductions that do not act as "things" any more with forms and immutable properties, but as artificial "beings" more or less sentient, more or less lively, more or less autonomous, more or less intelligent. These achievements were derived from the Artificial Life and Cognitive Sciences research areas. Researchers in the field of artificial intelligence were moving towards non-programmed behaviour by utilizing genetic algorithm properties.

There is a basic principle within these studies: interactivity at its highest level of complexity between basic elements of artificial life (genes or neurons) and their configurations, which correspond to the production of these emergent phenomena. The art of virtual worlds integrates informatic devices and modifies their interac-

DOI: 10.4018/978-1-4666-2961-5.ch015

tion with the audience, too. It cannot be reduced only to technological manipulations. John Cage's artworks have strongly anticipated interactive art experience by introducing spectator participation through objects, combinations and their casual instructions. In the same way, Duchamp stated that artwork becomes physical and objective through its interactivity. Nowadays, research on spectator participation has been used in different areas of media art as performance, kinetic art, conceptual art, body art, and other forms of art. Contemporary interactive media contain dialogues with their spectators that are more than simply observations, they have an active function. Interactive media is created with two actors: the first actor creates or defines programming rules for the user's/spectator's conditions; the second actor-spectator introduces the progress of the artwork with the goal of acting in its potentiality, differently from the traditional spectator/user that has no possibility of interaction. The media-work is therefore composed of two different semiotic objects: the "actor" that is a computer program and the other "object," the spectator/user with the role of co-authoring or co-acting (Mura, 2010). Ted Nelson (1965) and Marshall McLuhan (1967) have previously referred to a new relationship between form and content in the development of new technologies and new media, focusing on social and cultural collaboration across interactive media and software development methodologies. Laurel (1990) explicitly discussed human-computer interaction and interface design research fields, emphasizing the importance of natural experience in our interaction with technological media. She describes a medium in terms of mimesis, imitation, or representation of sensitive world aspects, especially human actions, in literature and art, like the relationships between user and technology from acting in gaming. Engagement, the emotional state of someone using digital media described by Laurel, serves as a critical factor in personal relations.

THE METAPLASTIC ARTS AND DESIGN THEORY

Interactivity has become the main aspect of new media since the fast evolution of digital processes and media convergence on the Web. In brief, the notion of interactivity means the possibility of real time interaction with digital media. The new media along with technological convergence are changing the model of mass communication into new ways for people to interact and communicate with one another. The digital innovations of the Internet have made possible the shifting towards the new media model of communication from the traditional "one-to-many" mass communication to the wide range of possibilities of a "many-to-many" Web communication. The conversational dynamics of mediated communication forms can be considered as a central point in understanding new media.

However, different types of media possess various degrees of interactivity, even some forms of digital and converged media are not interactive at all. For example, digital television uses the most recent technology to increase the number and quality of channels and their services, but it does not transform the user's experience of television into a more fully interactive one. Instead, virtual realities, as an extension of the world we live in, actually appear to be the best possible digital conceptualization in terms of a new interactive media environment. Cybernetic studies transform spectators into actors where the artist invites the spectator to get actively involved, to participate, making a device "alive." In conclusion, last century the interpretation of the machine as a co-operator in human dynamics demonstrated the possibility for the development of actual virtual realities. Virtual realities present new possibilities for society, art, and science.

This disciplinary field is derived from the first developments of cybernetics. New aesthetics of hybrid forms between artwork and spectator has led contemporary art to its concept of physical de-materialization. This phenomenon of de-materialization has allowed dancers to interact with their virtual doubles projected onto screens as digital choreographies in the name of a new form of art. Digital arts can restore their lost technique by introducing a new way to use information automatically. The computer is a hybrid machine and it is the first machine that uses an interpretive language for its functioning. The key to understanding these new levels of mediation environments is through digital plasticity, that is a property of the digital artefact, which is a characteristic defined by the user's activities; within its own interaction process, digital plasticity can create, modify and perform every form and content of the new digital media. It includes the social dimension as another level of possibility for extending human communication and creativity for new virtual communities. The adaptive and pervasive digital plasticity is termed digital metaplasticity, defined also within neuroscience, but in digital terms is intended as an algorithmic plasticity, which provides new media aesthetics and logic for the second media age.

Additionally, Goodman (1988) termed it semantic and syntactic densities for new cultural methods, which is the definition that would be given in the metaplastic discipline.

Metaplastic design is the specific trans-disciplinary research area that includes art, design, architecture, cybernetics, cognitive psychology, artificial intelligence, and computer sciences. From the point of view of technical-scientific studies, it describes plastic qualities of high digital media configurations and their conceptual expressions through the applications of abstract art languages and methodologies to computational symbolic systems (new media). The computer itself could be considered a symbolic cultural system, comprised of computer codes, languages, and informational "object" typologies. It also includes visualization and a screen interface, which

represent so much of media culture that they have become a powerful set of metaphors for human conceptualization.

The metaplastic theoretical model leads to the definition of a fuzzy dynamic modelling system, comprising a visual formal language and implementation of the composition rules of abstract languages to create artworks and design artefacts.

Digital interactivity, a base of every artefacts digital process, is the combination of factors that can create new relationship between users and the digital media. It provides the conceptual basis for metaplastic design (Mura, 2008, p. 176) where "it proposes a different approach to the construction of virtual reality based upon a conceptual poetry of the virtual space" (Mura, 2010).

The main characteristics of metaplastic design are:

- **Interdisciplinarity:** Of existing relations between Art, Design, Science and Technology.
- **Dematerialization:** Of artworks and the processes from their disciplines.
- **Hybridization:** Between Aesthetics and Technology (hybridization type1) becomes a redefinition of the practices of production of sensitive forms. The dynamics of the artwork within the social sphere have different levels of interaction which are: between artwork, author and spectator (hybridization type 3) and between society, science and technology (hybridization type 2).
- **Interactivity:** As a fundamental paradigm of dynamic relations which occurs among author, spectator and artwork.
- **Synaesthetic Immersivity:** Of the spectator through his sensorial and psychological involvement coordinated with the interactive representation.
- **Communication of Wisdom:** As a cultural goal to be obtained through the creation of new metaplastic media.

The term 'Multiplasticity' (Mura, 2011) extends the metaplastic new media qualities to the multi-directional communication properties of the new media. The users within their social networks become informational nodes within their own individual Web structure as a website or a Web-blog.

The perceived immediacy of online and mobile media communications confounds the temporality and the spatiality of the apparent presence, which can occur between one or many people, at varying distances and involve the hybridization of social and cultural mediation in the communicative moment.

To give readers a better idea of the characteristics of the metaplastic framework, in respect to information systems and visual design, we could specify three possible roles: programmer, animator, and viewer. The metaplastic designer is both the programmer and animator and anyone may be a viewer. Regarding its audience, we could define some issues of the metaplastic discipline, as follows:

- **Scope:** The metaplastic framework and its models provide a synthetic, complete event based system customizable by designers/animators to relate autonomous model behaviour.
- **Abstraction:** It is a structural, direct, synthesized model representation expandable by the designer.
- **Animation:** It can be manipulated and playable in any of its own elements.
- **Presentation/Representation:** The designer defines the visual language of the system within the interactive elements of its visual structure.
- **Interface:** Their ring structure makes their visual interface fully customizable through the defined visual language. Other graphical interactive systems could be implemented inside them.

Digital virtual worlds may be related to hyper real representations of the phenomenal world if such a place "exists"; they may be related to the avatar-based engagements of games and hybrid social environments; to geo-spatial systems such as Google Earth 3D; or to abstract spatial constructions, such as the Form Rhythm of the Mura's Meta-Plastic Virtual Worlds (2008). metaplastic virtuality is where the interaction process describes the dimension of presence and should be seen as a performative space-time that produces a kind of synaesthesia through the screen (Mura, 2007). The screen appears to offer the illusion of an entrance to memory, a portal to the past as present, and the present as future past tense, as history in the making. The screen's virtual space-time, according to DeLanda, literally causes space to function as time. Images of events lost to the past are projected into the present, the "irreversible succession of passing presents," which soon disappear into the virtual time of memory (see Rodowick, 2007, pp. 78-79).

The metaplastic metaspace, one of discipline's components, within its own aesthetic and semantic codes define a new culture of representation. Interaction processes defined with metaplastic codes, trace behaviors and plastic multisensorial qualities. The earlier plastic art movements characterized the conceptual basis of the metaplastic media with the spatial and kinetic methodologies activated by the user during the processes of interaction. The conceptualization of Klee's logical-plastic formalism (Thürlemann, 1982) indicates the possibility to define virtual spaces through the conceptualization of the Metaplastic model.

This model is described within three fundamental study fields: the information field for the "Construction of knowledge"; the sensorial field for "Emotional involvement" and the area of "Social Participation." Every field mentioned before, was defined with more subfields. Two external zones were defined, respectively, as the "Private space" and the "Social space," within the use of media and its cultural content. The internal circle's width visually indicated the conditions of being part of the media included or not included in the social spaces. In defining that media property, we defined different reality conditions: virtual reality, extended reality or mixed reality. The level that described the "emotional involvement" area indicated which conditions had improved to create an immersive reality. The resultant models of the metaplastic metaspace, offered useful indications about the shared informations; the definition of the user's activity; the interaction modalities with the information and with other connected users.

According to Domenico Quaranta, when regarding the virtual worlds as cultural constructs, it is important to remember that: "...The philosopher Karl Popper defines three kinds of world experience into the human society: 'First, there is the physical world—the universe of physical objects... this is I will call World 1. Second, there is the world of mental states; this is I will call World 2. But there is also a third such world, the world of the contents of thoughts, and, indeed of the products of the human mind; this I will call World 3.' The human perceptions and cognitions are the links between the real world (World1) and this conceptual world (World3) ...The artists, in brief, with their own artworks create a cultural and conceptual 'world-in mind' realities like many 'World3.'" The conceptual world modelling requires us "to integrate art, science and technology to create integrated culture" (Mura, 2008). Following on from Domenico Quaranta's thought, it is also relevant to underline that in virtual worlds "the subject of artistic projects, including the artist." The cyber art projects of the diffuse virtual world of Second Life's avatar-model generally include a virtual character of the artist and a story is built around the creation of the avatar's personality, as the virtual alter ego of the artist. In his essay, Quaranta gives some interesting examples.

In the "13 Most Beautiful Avatars" virtual world, the avatars confirm their own existence standing in front of the portrait for the photographers. They are a projection of the artist's myth,

turning their virtual body into a mask of the artist itself. Gazira Babeli is probably one of the most famous Second Life artists and one of the most successful cases of virtual identity construction. Gazira deforms her avatar and literally donates the virtual body to other avatars within her performance of creative script manipulation, which cause this event's result. All the case studies demonstrate that the cyber artists explore and take advantage of the Second Life media software modelling virtual installations and, at the same time, build relationships with the connected world. Moreover, the avatars themselves acquire independent sociability, flying and travelling within the virtual artwork, as the case of Juria Yoshikawa demonstrates.

Metaplastic open metaspace interactive media is a methodology that unifies the user's interaction processes within mixed reality spaces as a system of living artwork. The multi-plasticity of multi-sensory and multi-directional communication properties are driven by their own dialogue system. The system includes whole body interaction through the production of multi-sensory feedback within both the metaplastic virtual spaces and physical interactive devices. The human haptic interaction in the shared virtual space produces the sensation of tele-presence within the system while the mediated physical feedback with objects enforces the feeling of extended bodily senses.

The user's results give important information about the conceptual expression of his artwork, the resulting knowledge map, and their dynamics within virtual environments. Interactions during performance produce aesthetic effects on the virtual environment by transforming the entire system into a new piece of art.

The user's immersive experience is produced by the metaplastic metaspace simultaneously in three ways: the absorption of the input device into the user's body image, the integration of the screen interface into the user's extended body boundaries, and the activation of surrounding space through multisensory and haptic feedback.

The fluid immersive multidimensional meta-plastic metaspace is a living artwork system, a landscape of knowledge where the user can make his abstract surrounding experience. The interactor or virtual performer redefines his role within an immersion within the abstract space. This enables him to interact with the environment and make new forms of data creations, also with other connected users. The user in his relation with the synthetic environment realizes different level of participation/inclusion within the system, which changes his role from spectator to interactor and at the end "immersant" becoming themselves living human-code of the system defined with Char Davies's words in her installation *Osmose* (Davies, 2001). The volume forms develop into a system map and have a route orientation function. The orientation in the system is possible through signs, which indicate to users their possible options. The remote presence of the user's body and its extended senses are indicated within the Klee's man as a virtual pointer of analogue/opposite field polarity in the immaterial-materiality of sound, light, form, and colour that produce various space aesthetic effects. The user in these new metaplastic spaces could explore and interact with the artwork and contribute to change, delete, or recreate it in different conceptual landscapes.

THE METAPLASTIC CODE ART

Continuing Dave Griffiths' thought, software development could be divided into three broad categories based on the intent, or the nature of the goals it is designed to fulfil. These categories are gross simplifications, as most software is comprised of a blend of the following:

1. **Classical Tool:** The conventional concept of a piece of software is that of a tool for achieving some clear goal. This is not a matter of software complexity—there may be many different competing goals, and very complex implementation required.

2. **An Environment for Working In:** When the nature of the goal is more complicated, and involves more human issues, software often ends up providing functionality through an environment. This is usually a text or graphical user interface. In software designed for artistic use, programs often have to go one-step further, enriching their environment with a scripting interpreter or a visual programming language.

3. **Artistic:** A lot of software is written in a situation where goals are difficult to define in any way. Someone may write a program to exercise the use of a new language or try out something new. The goals for game play code in computer games and software written to produce generative art are very difficult to pin down. Software art is strongly ambiguous, as it includes programs, which are written to express something by merely existing, it is not even required that they run, or do anything at all. Sometimes software is the only way to express something. At other times, the writing of software is an artistic process of exploration, such as sketching code or live coding (Floss+Art, 2008, p. 250). Thus, the user can subvert the "goals" of the programme with their own creative process.

The Metaplastic Software is the Message

According to Marshall McLuhan, "The new medium TV as an environment creates new occupations. As an environment, it is imperceptible except in terms of its content. That is, all that is seen or noticed is the old environment, the movie. However, even the effects of the TV environment in altering the entire character of human sensibility and sensory ratios are completely ignored. The content of any system or organization naturally consists of the preceding system or organization, and in that, degree acts as a control on the new environment. It is useful to notice all of the arts and sciences as acting in the role of anti-environments that enable us to perceive the environment" (McLuhan, 1967).

However, according to the media theorists Manovich (2001) and Arjen Mulder (2004), whilst computers are indeed often also said to re-mediate the preceding media, they actually are a "Meta-Medium," a combination of all previous media: "Only in this case, it is not so much a matter of remediation of all old and new media, as it is a hybridation, a melting of unequal media to a new unity" (Mulder, 2004). This poses an interesting question: is it not true that the "user" is actualising a potential form generated by the software developer's algorithm? What a user/consumer of software is actually doing is placing his idea in a present environment. This works both ways, so he is (unconsciously) also conforming his idea to this set environment. The resulting physical shape becomes far from universal and it is, as mentioned, sometimes very specific to the software used. In this instance, we might even wonder who the actual producer of the work is. Software always, to a certain extent, influences our thinking; analogous to "the medium is the message," the software has become the medium and thus, the message. Metaplastic languages or symbolic code systems are methodologies based on abstract art language rules applied to digital symbolic systems needed for the construction of the metaplastic virtual media. Nowadays, the free software community collectively reflects on the meaning of art, code and their reciprocal relations. They aim to create open and shared systems associated with the defence of freedom and in opposition of closed information systems. To that end, the following paragraphs report the first metaplastic manifesto announcing some basic statements, in this first version, agreeing with the worldwide free software community philosophy (Floss, 2008).

Software Code as Art Creation

Statement 1: The product is a result of different levels of interactions. The relationships between developer/user constitute an alternative to the unilateral producer/consumer or provider/client relationships. This process can be defined as a cumulative feedback cycle based on the sharing of information as the driving force behind technological innovations.

Artwork as a Process

Statement 2: The old media introduced the material constraints to see art objects as completed works of art. Instead, software sees art as a process because the digital artwork, within its code, is immaterial, infinite, changeable, and replicable in different versions.

Coding as a Conceptual Practice

Statement 3: "Art can be highly formal, mathematical, or scientific. Programming as a mean of formalising one's thoughts, externalising them and testing their performance using a logical machine is therefore, a tempting method of writing for many artists" (Floss, 2008, p. 238).

Creating the Tool for Originality

Statement 4: "The modernist demand of originality in our art is still with us and many people consider the highest form of creativity to be artistic creativity where the artist transforms the cultural space in which he or she works (Boden, 1990). For many, it is by necessity that they build their own tools, as using other people's tools might lead to less thought and original design solutions to both aesthetic, formal and technological problems" (Floss, 2008, p. 239).

Coding as an Artistic Practice

Coding is an artistic practice in itself. In fact, many artists see it as a performative act and live-code in front of the audience with their screens projected on the wall (Toplap, 2007; Nilson, 2007).

Statement 5: "Coding is here seen as a way of externalising thoughts, in a manner similar to sketching by drawing or model building. When programming is seen as a performative action, a choreography of thought, it ceases to be a means to an end and becomes an end in itself" (Floss, 2008, p. 239).

Programming as Meta-Art

Statement 6: Like the Metaplastic design processes, creating something that creates something else is on the meta-dimension. Many software artists, such as Adrian Ward, see themselves as creating meta-art. "Art that is used by artists to create more art. It varies how the programmers see their role, from being a participant in the creation of the end object to rejecting all co-authorship and clearly separating the software as meta-art and the product that it creates when the artist uses it" (Floss, 2008, p. 239).

Coding as Craft

The programmer learns to think in the language that he or she works in and formulate the problems in the terms of that language often conceptualising the world through the means of programmatic paradigms (Floss, 2008, p. 240).

Statement 7: "...Coding is not only a craft: it is a performance as well, as the case of live-coding exemplifies. Live-coding requires that the practitioners are good at their trade, which involves fast thinking, fast typing, practised algorithms, and good knowledge of the material (programming environment) they are working with" (Nilson, 2007; Sorensen & Brown, 2007).

The threshold of the metaplastic dialogue system defines the liminarity between the real and the virtual spaces through the cyber-performer's body and psychological sensory extensions. It also activates the state transitions of the metaspace elements by proximity and defines, in this way, its own interactive zone with the cyber-performer. The computed visual metaplastic symbolic system codifies the interactor's emotional state variations into five new sensory de-fuzzified sequence values that can be used as an expression of the cyber-performer's coded stimulation caused by external environmental input and output system values. The sensory result is a fuzzy truth value that activates the decision making process of the metaplastic space. During his own cyber performance, the artist varies his emotional states with the virtual environment, which change continuously from "sensing" to "feeling" states through recursive cycles of feedback.

The Red and Black weights, which are the first units of the visual codification in metaplastic language, are non-binary or fuzzy values that should be considered as their very first "atomic" code level. The RB sememe is the atomic element of the metaplastic metaspace. It has a fuzzy value within the range of 0 and 1 (see Table 1).

The qualitative relations among every group of RB values create an RB sequence configuration that determines a particular characteristic of the metaspace. These RB code sequences form basic ring structures, which, by linking them together, create the entire metaplastic structure. The behaviours of the metaspace environment system can be seen in its processes of the visual rules matrix of relations between dynamic elements. The interaction within the dynamic cycles unifies

Table 1. The red and black sememe

RB sememe	RB value
● ●	+1 .....0 .... . -1

sensory states of the virtual environment, creating complex behaviours between itself and its own elements by assigning meaning through movement codification of interactive forms in the "Red and Black" semantic metaspace (Mura, 2010).

$$\text{Cyber Act}_i = 1 - f(\text{interp}(S_i(w)\text{vision}, S_i(w)\text{hearing}, S_i(w)\text{touch}, S_i(w)\text{body mov.}))_t; \quad (1)$$

$$\text{Metaspace RhytmForm} = \Sigma_i(f\text{Act}_i * f(\text{interp}(\text{Entity}_k \text{ state}_i, \text{Entity}_{k+1} \text{ state}_i))_t; \quad (2)$$

where: Act = Interaction state graduation; S = Senses function; w = Emotional state weight [0..1]; i = dialogue state; t = action time; interp = interpolation function; Entity state = Metaspace Entity state.

The resulting "w" value from the previous function is used to obtain "final Act state graduation" for different output channels, and interaction process results (vision, body, hearing, touch) (Table 2).

The metaplastic cyber-performer creates the live-metaplastic code on the fly doing his own virtual art. He codifies his human-states in conversation with the machine, playing with visual-sensory signs while the computer follows them. There is no distinction between creating and running a piece of the metaplastic code. The software runs while it is being created, gaining complexity via visual code inputs. The metaplastic live-coding environment makes it possible to execute code in order to generate its virtual synesthetic performance in real-time without having to restart any of the machine processes. It is not only the direct relationship between the cyber-performer and the metaplastic code that define live-coding acts, but also that which is between the performer and the audience. Metaplastic art as performance art, where a connected audience watches the virtual performance, contributing to the modification of metaplastic live coding, and enjoying the outputs (see Figure 1).

THE METAPLASTIC OPEN CODE PLATFORM

Starting with these notes:

The concept of open source is derived from computer software development. Open source software is a software that everyone can recreate and modify. This requires public access to the software's source code. The source code for a piece of software is equivalent to the score or preparatory work for a piece of music, drama or art, and it is similarly required to recreate or modify the finished work. Differently, Closed Source, as sold by corporations as Microsoft, does not make its source code publicly available and trying to recreate or modify it is prohibited by law (Floss, 2008, p. 294).

The Metaplastic framework system is accomplished with the open source philosophy in its current 1998's definition given by the hackers Bruce Perens and Eric Raymond.

Table 2. Emotional states results from the rules of the CyberAct function

Rule	CyberAct State	w	Emotional State
Rule 1	if sign value - and intensity -100	0.0	Relaxed emotional state
Rule 2	if sign value +/- and intensity 0	0.20	Mildly interested emotional state
Rule 3	if sign value + and intensity 50	0.50	Interested emotional state
Rule 4	if sign value + and intensity 100	0.75	Involved emotional state
Rule 5	if sign value + and intensity 150	0.85	High involved emotional state

Figure 1. The metaspace multi-realities schema

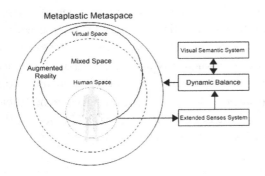

Figure 2. Two metaspace virtual artworks examples

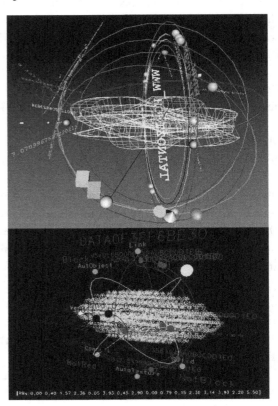

Raymond argues that open source software can create better products faster than the closed source method of writing software. Many of the most successful software programs in use today, particularly on the Internet, have been produced in this way.

Actually, the concept of open source continue to inspire artists, but it is an intentionally vague concept that reveals strategies that are of relevance to contemporary artistic practice and can place artists at the heart of current issues relating to free speech and the laws and technologies of censorship. The metaplastic model can be easily implemented within the Opencode Platform system. It could be also used differently into digital environments, for example: Web3D, interactive games, virtual heritage, digital archives, interface systems, information and visualization, mobile applications, virtual art platform and installations and many other fields. It is an open source software development environment for creating and deploying deeply collaborative virtual worlds on multiple operating systems and devices.

It is, in fact, a multi-platform system that is available for Windows and Java locally, online and mobile uses. The Metaplastic Platform shares its virtual worlds with different typologies for any kind of application through its own SDK. The complete system is available with different configurations for Personal Computers, PDAs, Mobile Phones, and other mobile devices. The Platform is shared with the public in an open format in order to use all of their own features. It is easy to configure with its 3D interface functions or within simple XML configuration files. Some user's interaction choices or environment settings are also possible to be modified with textual scripts during the software running. The user interacts with the system's different external devices as mouse, keyboard, gloves, touch-screens, GPR satellite world localization functions, and environmental sensors. The metaplastic system enhances the performance and it offers a multi-server architecture with containing the network of all its own connected entities.

Entities send their messages to the server regarding their state evaluations. The server computes every network interaction state and it decides what message should be sent and to which entity. This process continues from and to every connected server in the network. The network system cooperates online for the simultaneous execution process and its information distribution to all of its connected metaplastic machines. It acts between the client and the server through their own software applications. It runs with the following process steps:

1. The scene control begins with the user sensory input analyzes through the proximity function of the fuzzy dialog control system;
2. The Fuzzy state machine makes the evaluations, previously defined from membership sets and fuzzy rules;
3. The Balance function makes its evaluation with previously calculated values. The balance results activate all interaction processes and behaviors of the entire system;
4. The resulting values compose the semantic codification of virtual space;
5. This step provides the 3D calculations to build up the virtual space model;
6. The virtual space scene is visualized with the system drawing functions. Within this phase, the system communicates with the Web server to update the system states and it gives the resulting feedback to the fuzzy sensorial decision-making process (A phase). Finally, all the output results are combined with the user inputs into a new interaction cycle (see Figure 2).

CONCLUSION

The metaplastic discipline introduces new media, interdisciplinary practices and methodologies of Design and Cyber Arts between reality and virtual realities.

The metaplastic theoretical model within the MetaPlastic Design discipline leads to the definition of a fuzzy dynamic modeling system, developed through a visual formal language and puts into effect the composition rules of abstract languages to create artworks and design artefacts.

Metaplastic design is a new computational system modality suitable for designers, artists, and practitioners in order to create interactive media, which use their own metaplastic visual code directly from virtuality to reality, from software to hardware and vice versa through the Metaplastic Opencode Platform. The metaplastic design research field offers a basis for describing the multiplicities of technological, cultural, social, and economic domains and its physical and imaginary properties; it combines the emergent mediated communication environment with renewed CyberArt creative artworks and practices, moving from the known to the unknown with new ways of thinking and seeing the real world through virtuality.

REFERENCES

AA/VV. (2008). *Floos+art*. Paris, France: GOTO10.

Arts Machine. (2012). *The virtual metaplasticity platform project*. Retrieved June 2012, from http://www.artsmachine.com

Bru, C. (1955). *L'estetique de l'abstraction*. Paris, France: Presses Universitaries de France.

Chomsky, N. (1959). Three models for the description of language in information and control, on certain formal properties of grammars. *I.R.E. Transactions on Information Theory*, 2.

Davies, C. (2001a). *Website*. Retrieved May, 2010 from http://www.immersence.com

Davies, C. (2001b). *Multimedia: from Wagner to virtual reality*. New York, NY: W.W. Norton & Company.

Goodman, N. (1976). *Languages of art: An approach to a theory of symbols*. Indianapolis, IN: Hackett.

Grau, O. (2003). *Virtual art.* Cambridge, MA: MIT Press.

Greimas, A. J., & Courtés, J. (1982). *Semiotics and language: An analytical dictionary.* Bloomington, IN: Indiana University Press.

Laurel, B. (1990). *The art of human-computer interface design.* Reading, MA: AddisonWesley.

Levy, P. (1992). *Le tecnologie dell'intelligenza.* Milano, Italy: Ed. Traverso.

Manovich, L. (2001). *The language of new media.* Cambridge, MA: MIT Press.

McLuhan, M., & Fiore, Q. (1967). *The medium is the message: An inventory of effects.* New York, NY: Bantam Books.

Moles, A. (1990). *Art et ordinateur.* Paris, France: Blusson.

Mulder, A. (2004). *Understanding media theory.* Dordrecht, The Netherlands: V2 Publishing.

Mura, G. (2008). The metaplastic constructor. In *CAC 2 Computer Art.* Paris, France: Ed. Europia.

Mura, G. (2010). *Metaplasticity in virtual worlds: Aesthetics and semantic concepts.* Hershey, PA: IGI Global. doi:10.4018/978-1-60960-077-8

Mura, G. (2011). Multiplasticity of new media. In Ghinea, G., Ghinea, S. R., Gulliver, S. R., & Andres, F. (Eds.), *Multiple Sensorial Media Advances and Applications: New Development in MulSe-Media.* Hershey, PA: IGI Global. doi:10.4018/978-1-60960-821-7.ch013

Nilson, C. (2007). Live coding practice. In *Proceedings of NIME 2007.* NIME.

Rodowick, D. N. (2007). *The virtual life of film.* Boston, MA: Harvard University Press.

Sorensen, A., & Brown, A. (2007). AA-cell in practice: An approach to musical live coding. In *Proceedings of ICMC 2007.* ICMC.

Thürlemann, F. (1982). *Paul Klee: Analyse sémiotique de trois peintures.* Lausanne, France: L'Age d'Homme.

Tribe, M., & Reena, J. (2003). *New media art.* New York, NY: Taschen.

Wiener, N. (1988). *The human use of human beings: Cybernetics and society.* Cambridge, MA: Da Capo Press.

Zadeh, L. (1969). *Biological application of the theory of fuzzy sets and systems in the proceedings of an international symposium on BioCybernetics of the central nervous system.* Boston, MA: Little Brown.

KEY TERMS AND DEFINITIONS

Dialog System: Artificial cognitive system of the Metaplastic virtual world.

Digital Metaplasticity: Defined also within the neuroscience, but in digital terms is intended as an algorithmic plasticity which provides a new media aesthetics and logics, which is the definition that would be given in the Metaplastic discipline.

Form_Rhytm: The structural equilibrium composed with dynamic relations of form_weights to describe the metaplastic virtual world.

FSM: A fuzzy dynamic system model called "Finite State Machine" (FSM).

MetaPlastic Design: It is the specific trans-disciplinary research area that includes Art, Design, Architecture, Cybernetics, Cognitive Psychology, Artificial Intelligence, and Computer Sciences. From a point of view of technical-scientific studies, it describes plastic qualities of digital media high configurations and their conceptual expressions through the applications of abstract art languages and methodologies onto computational symbolic systems (new media).

MetaPlastic Language: Conceptual models based on abstract art language rules applied to digital symbolic systems.

Multiplasticity: It extends the metaplastic new media qualities to the multi-directional communication properties of the new media.

Red and Black Semantics: The Metaplastic virtual world semantic model.

Synaesthesia: (Psychology) The condition in which a sensory experience normally associated with one sensory system occurs when another sensory system is stimulated (McGraw-Hill Dictionary of Scientific & Technical Terms, 2002).

Metaplastic Metaspace: A conceptual cyberspace composed by a network of Web metaobjects (Metaplastic Virtual Worlds). The dynamic relationship between each knot of the network and the user, establishes the meaning of the metaplastic representation through its shapes and behaviours.

Metaplastic Open Metaspace: Interactive media that unifies the user's interaction processes within the spaces of mixed realities as living artwork systems.

Chapter 16
Virtual Communitas, "Digital Place–Making," and the Process of *"Becoming"*

Anita McKeown
University College Dublin, Ireland

ABSTRACT

In Aristotelian philosophy, the process of change from a lower level of "potentiality" to the higher level of "actuality" is known as "becoming," or to become more and more of what one is, or capable of "becoming." For this process to take place, the dissolution of the normative values or understanding of one's self and context is necessary (Turner, 1968). Such dissolution, although initially destabilising, can create an environment conducive to the values and normal modes of behaviour being reflected upon and transformed. The chapter considers how selected context-responsive projects that use the Internet, develop and harness "communitas" (Turner, 1967) and function as "liminoid" (Turner, 1974) space, facilitating new understandings of place. The virtual manifestations of place highlighted are then reflected upon for their potential in the process of "place-making" to enable the process of "becoming," for people and the specific location.

INTRODUCTION

Informed by ideas and theories from anthropology, deep ecology, and psychotherapy, the chapter explores how virtual communities and online interventions into offline realities are conducive to the production of a form of communitas. It is proposed that an experience of virtual communitas when related to physical locations rather than an event can enable re-presentations that lead to new understandings of place through the dissemination of situated knowledge. This new knowledge could be harnessed to contribute to a regenerative ecology, through developing more intimate less abstract relationships with our locations and co inhabitants, potentially repairing any fragmentation from the physical world. The chapter makes the argument that mindful interventions in the

DOI: 10.4018/978-1-4666-2961-5.ch016

virtual could transfer to our physical reality and be considered as a process of 'becoming', moving from 'potentiality' to 'actuality' or to become more and more of what one is capable of becoming.

'Communitas' refers to 'an unstructured community in which people are equal' or 'the sense of sharing and intimacy that develops among persons who experience liminality as a group' (dictionary.com). Stemming from the Latin communis, common or public, communitas is often used to denote a sense of community, public spirit, or a willingness to serve one's community. Communitas is the condition of equitable relationships, or comradeship, which Van Gennep and Victor Turner argued occurs within the liminal phases of rituals. The term Liminal derives from the Latin limen, or threshold coined by Arnold Van Gennep in *Les Rites de Passage, 1909*. Van Gennep discusses three stages that accompany movement from one 'cosmic or social world to another' (Madge & O'Connor, 2005, p. 93), separation (pre-liminal), transition (liminal), and reintegration (post-liminal). Victor Turner (1967) in his often-cited text 'The forest of symbols' picked up on Van Gennep's ideas, re-defining them within the context of 1960s counter culture to develop a new anthropological perspective on liminality. A more secular understanding of the liminal within Turner's work, which referred to as liminoid (1974) is applied to the spaces created online within the projects discussed.

The projects, *Deptford 45s*, *Live from Memphis*, and *Yellow Arrow* which utilise social media and the Internet, "a natural environment for liminality" (Waskul, 2004, p. 40) are considered for their potential in the creation of a liminoid space and communitas, producing what Guattari refers to as a 'rift or rupture.' It is argued that such interventions afford an opportunity for the deconstruction of given understandings of place by offering an interruption to a dominant narrative, which can aid reflection and contribute to the transformation of place through challenging existing narratives. These projects in conjunction with the ethos of open source software/culture can be harnessed

to undo given understandings of place. Through the deconstruction and consequently the co/re-authoring of place, a making and remaking of place that can extend from the virtual into the physical, is potentially a process of "becoming" both for the participants and place involved. The process of change from a lower level of 'potentiality' to the higher level of 'actuality' could be considered as a process of individuation for people and place.

This co-authoring could make a valuable contribution to the practice of 'place-making' through an opportunity of community and place-based blended learning that utilises various learning modalities e.g. auditory, visual and potentially kinaesthetic. Regeneration practices, development, and planning policies have impacted on the nature of public art works that have been commissioned, historically manifesting in monumental objects, as well as the commissioning process. The development of extended practices that are more holistic and context responsive, are being more regularly supported, with a move away from the monumental. Perhaps such practices have a more vital role to play with monumental objects being an unsuitable response to 21st Century global concerns, with contributions to the practice of 'place-making' the creation of legacies not monuments having valuable consequences.

'Place-making' potentially emerges as a process of 'becoming', both through a 'bottom-up' approach and the inclusion of a diverse expression of a place's personality. The place's personality becomes more fully understood, integrating the contributors to the projects ideas, values and resultant discussions and the re-presentations of the physical location. Connoll (1985) defined personality as the distinguishing characteristics of an individual, which differentiate him/her from others when displayed in a wide variety of situations and circumstances especially social ones. Through facilitating a reflective and transformative process by and for residents, social media art interventions could manifest the personality of a location, the collective understanding of that place. Conversely when the image of a 'place' is manipulated in relation to tourism and branding, similar processes used to sell an image of a place, become static through the creation of nostalgia, holding places to ransom with their history.

Positively, the constant re-presentation of multiple identities possible through the use of digital technology, ultimately offers processual re-tellings of the story of that place. This could constitute the creation of what Gergen (1991) refers to as a multiphrenic self, an identity that reflects the 'multiple identities pieced together from the multiplicity of mediated messages in our environments.' Through the constant re-presentation, more voices and experiences expand the understandings of place, forming a feedback system. Through this feedback system, the understanding of place is perpetually in motion, simultaneously challenging and increases the understanding, while disseminating awareness of its unique persona.

Digital interventions and their participant's interactions collectively co-author the unique personality of the location and offer an opportunity for 'individuation' (Jung, 1962) or to become more and more of what the location is capable off 'becoming'. The importance of connectivity for this process and to the participants and location is reflected upon and how such interventions facilitate more sustainable approaches to 'place-making' and what the benefits of this approach could be.

In conclusion, the chapter outlines and argues for practices and process that could contribute to how our places are made and constructed and the role social media art interventions that uses technology to further engage the public within that process. The chapter considers social media art interventions that use the Internet/social media as tools within the process of 'place-making,' the liminoid spaces created through the projects and how this could facilitate 'becoming'.

BACKGROUND

Aristotle understood humans to be a mix of matter and form, with matter being constant and form constantly developing and understanding that humans have an 'innate capacity for action: to change the world to his or her whim (techne), the ability to move from sheer possibility to actuality' (Brommage, 2005, p. 11). For Aristotle 'techne,' a way of knowing the world, makes use of art and craft skills and tools. With this in mind, we can begin to consider technology as the making, usage, and knowledge of tools that we use to make and re-make our world, from 'possibility to actuality' (Brommage, 2005) identifying contemporary technologies as logical tools for 'place-making.' Aristotelian philosophy, *has* defined this transformation as moving from a lower level of 'potentiality' to the higher level of 'actuality' as 'becoming'.

Both Robert Hahn (2001) and Indra McEwen (1993) have proposed the relationship between making and speculative thought in Greek thinking. Thinking through doing and the tacit knowledge developed through 'knowing ones craft develops an awareness of not only what is probable, but also what is possible' (Sullivan, 2005, p. 44). This lays the foundation for a consideration of the process of 'place-making,' a processual, dynamic event, in which we can contribute to the making and remaking of our locations/places as a process of 'becoming'. It is worth noting that within Greek understanding there was an 'indissolubility of craft and community' (McEwen, 1993). Arnold Borgman refers to technology as an activity that forms or changes culture claiming the application of math, science and the arts are beneficial for life. In this sense technology as a tool offering more than the opportunity 'to build' (Sherry, 2000, p. 7).

The transformational process of 'becoming' or to 'become more and more of what is capable of becoming, moving from potential to actuality'

(Brommage, 2005), is also referred to by Maslow (1954) as 'self-actualisation.' Jung proposed that for self-actualisation, to occur the integration of the conscious with the personal and collective unconscious is required (Jung, 1962, p. 301). Within Jungian psychoanalysis, a period of reflection and transformation is undertaken during which, the essential personality of the person, their individuality can emerge. Jung perceived this process of 'individuation,' as having a profound healing effect on the person (Jung, 1962, p. 433). The process of individuation is the creation of wholeness from fragmentation usually applied in relation to the human psyche within therapeutic practices of psychoanalysis or psychiatry. The projects are considered as a context, potentially conducive to individuation, a setting distinguished from but parallel with the mundane, everyday life of the individual. This context, the project's existence on line, related to a physical location and populated by residents of both realities, functions as a liminal phase or occurring in liminoid space.

For both Van Gennep and Turner the liminal state signifies a time of transition, a 'time out of time' where one is 'betwixt and between' (Turner, 1967, p. 97) both social status, social mores and beliefs. In order for the process of 'becoming'/ self-actualisation to take place 'the dissolution of the normative values or understanding of one's self and context is necessary' (Turner, 1969, p. 95). This dissolution, usually occurring in ritual during the liminal phase, although initially destabilising, creates an environment conducive to the individual's values and normal modes of behaviour being reflected upon and transformed.

The liminal phase represents a 'threshold' space that held the potential for communitas given the intimacy and commonality of shared experience that evolves through the liminal phase of an initiation or rite of passage (Turner, 1967). Turner understood communitas to be characterised by what Madge and O'Connor refer to:

As an equality of relations, a comradeship that transcends age, rank, kinship etc. and displays an intense community spirit. Thus people from all social groups may form strong bonds, free from structures that normally separate them (2005, p. 93).

Within the shared space of communitas, participants are considered to be in a transitional, mutable state in which the participant, being removed from the mundane, questions and challenges such social mores and beliefs. Turner identified that this part of the ritual process occurs also within secular societies through bringing the concept into contemporary alignment, through what he defines as liminoid space. Turner argued that liminal spaces could not be applied to 'modern societies,' however liminoid spaces have similar qualities and functions but are not part of a spiritual or initiatory journey with no rite of passage.

The importance of the liminal phases is that the 'time out of time' is offered therefore Turner's 'betwixt and between' of the liminoid space allows the status quo to appear to dissolve. This dissolution, whether real or perceived is essential for questioning one's self and context and the reflection necessary for the transformation sought after whether in a ritual, on a pilgrimage or participating in an event. The liminal phase or liminoid spaces created and the consequent process of reflection undertaken can then be considered as a learning process through which new understandings of a society, culture, or location are born. I will return to the concept of the liminoid phase and the potential it holds for transformation within the main section of the chapter and the tools and projects discussed.

Projections for 2050 suggest a global population of nine billion people. Limited resources, peak oil, climate change and the resultant economic impacts will play a significant role that in our lives. This will lead to the increasing importance utilising local assets, drawing on the power and knowledge held within local communities. Local development frameworks e.g. Transition Towns Networks, and national political agendas are beginning to address these matters. 'place-making' is experiencing a renaissance both conceptually and practically despite its demise in the 1970s and early eighties. However, any practices that facilitate the process must involve multiple voices, perspectives, and agendas beyond an economic bottom line. Place-making is a community-driven process of people making a place and 'strikes a balance between the physical, the social and what could even be considered spiritual qualities of a place' (PPS, 2011). It is important to introduce the theories of Gregory Bateson and Felix Guattari, in relation to the liminoid space's facilitation of new understandings of a society or culture, borne out of reflection. The following section will outline the key aspects of their work that have relevance for the potential for social media art interventions to contribute to a process of 'becoming' within 'place-making.'

Returning to Aristotle's understanding, 'place-making' could be re-considered as a process of 'becoming', with the current need for places to thrive in (not just survive in), can be interpreted as similar to the process of self-actualisation, places that become more and more of what they are capable of 'becoming'. Aristotle's suggestion, to move from sheer potentiality' to actuality' is reflected in Guattari's call for a 'permanent recreation of the world,' 'the shifting unfolding, processual, dynamic dimensions of cultural change: the shifting relations among liminality, communitas, and structure' (Weber, 1995, p. 527) is a process not dissimilar to holistic and sustainable 'place-making.'

In his book *The Three Ecologies*, Guattari sets out the foundations for a trans-disciplinary practice that stems from his psychoanalytical experience and political leanings. For Guattari, the three ecologies are the environment, social relations and human subjectivity. This approach brings all three into an intimate connectivity, an approach encapsulated within the practice of 'place-making.'

For this intimate connection between the three, Guattari coins the term Ecosophy, blending his activist philosophy with a political agenda that is a sustainable and integrated consideration of all living systems. Ecology is not only about nature and environmental practice but is actually the point of exchange and interchange of closely related elements and suggests that ecology serves two purposes. Firstly as "an example of how to pose the question of trans-disciplinarity on a large and stratified scale" (Genosko, 2009, p. 103) and secondly, functioning as a means by which to intervene in the production of subjectivity. This second function, is described as:

...emergent and processual, the subject emerges as it finds a certain existential consistency, without getting tied down to an identity once and for all... Open and full of potential, the subject is truly a work in progress/process (Herzongenrath, 2009, p. 107).

This progress/process is emergent and mutable although initially referring to Guattari's therapeutic work this approach could be viewed as equally applicable to the practice of place-making. In this sense, the construction of a place's unique personality is seen as a co-authored, processual, and evolving process and an important 'place-making' aim. This co-authoring process can exist within the mundane, everyday life of the individuals and the places involved, yet happens in parallel with lived experience, similar to the conditions Jung deems necessary for individuation.

For Guattari, the arts ability to 'rupture,' or produce a rift, which in turn affirms a way of seeing things differently, is the key value of the arts. Through his rehabilitation work with schizophrenics, Guattari recognized the importance of the creation of counter-factual representations that challenged the dominant narrative of their condition. Guattari, in his work with Deleuze, argued that the majority of the developed world (with particular relevance to a capitalist system) was a schizophrenic system, causing amongst other things an existential dis-ease. If the majority of the developed world is experiencing an existential dis-ease, could a targeted social media art intervention, creating a counterfactual representation initiate a process of reflection and heal the dis-ease?

If planners, artists or community developers initiated a process of reflection specific to a location challenge as a strategic activity, the intervention could function as the 'rift or rupture' Guattari deems necessary to enable a way of seeing things differently. The project, a liminoid space, could lead to a transformation or new understanding of that location and challenge the dominant narrative. Any resultant action manifesting within the physical location, could be argued for the project's function as a catalyst, initiating a process of 'becoming', that arise from the communitas developed through participation within the project.

'Dis-ease,' is a theme prevalent in the work of Guattari, Jung, and Maslow with regards to the importance of self-actualisation/individuation, a theme also arising in the work of Gregory Bateson. Originally trained as an anthropologist, Bateson's career spanned many disciplines including psychiatry, genetics, and communication theory. During the 1960s, he began to focus his theories within ecology, providing academic weight to the emerging environmental movement aligning with other scientists and academics of the time, e.g. James Lovelock.

Bateson considered environmental demise as a dis-ease equated with insanity, illustrated through using the 1969 environmental disaster in Lake Erie, as an analogy to highlight the relationship between nature and humans. In *The Death of Lake Erie*, Bateson (1972) conveys his idea of an eco-mental system being driven insane and how that affects us, the public/world inhabitants conveying importance of a healthy environment for our well-being.

You decide that you want to get rid of the by-products of human life and that Lake Erie will be a good place to put them. You forget that the eco-mental system called Lake Erie is part of your wider eco-mental system—and that if Lake Erie is driven insane its insanity is incorporated in the larger system of your thought and experience (Bateson, 1972, p. 492).

This spotlight on the feedback system and inter-relatedness of human environment interactions has importance for online interventions through their ability to connect, a form of communitas. Bateson (1972) argued that the "public" needed to develop an understanding of the concept of interconnectivity and how their actions would feedback into the system and affect change, both positively and negatively. Pushing the issue of connectivity, the call for a 'whole' ecology is based on his key argument; ecosystems would self-organise and develop new dynamics in response to change. Bateson argued that unless there was a radical consideration of the impact of human activity on the earth's ecology, its life systems would begin to deteriorate based on its self-organisational abilities. Any such re-consideration requires the development of new methodologies within professional disciplines including how we plan and develop the places we live. Bateson's view of nature "as a field of meaning in which human beings are participants" (1972, p. 492) underpins his concept of a regenerative ecology making holistic sustainable 'place-making' crucially important.

Both Bateson and Guattari recognised the need for change and considered the potential of the arts as agents of change that could contribute to the restructuring or reform that they both felt necessary. Bateson and Guattari held different view of the arts, for Bateson their importance was in their power of communication and ability to engage numerous disciplines and cross boundaries of thought extending into different levels of the mind. For Guattari, the rift or rupture in order to see things differently was important; however, despite this difference in relation to the purpose of the arts, we can see the trajectory from Bateson's ideas to Guattari's evolution of them, almost twenty years later and the potential of the arts to heal 'dis-ease' and lead to the self-actualisation of people and place. Both Bateson and Guattari were writing in advance of the current developments of social media and the Internet both of which facilitate interaction and exchange. Artists, in the creation of bespoke projects and regeneration practices could facilitate the potential of place-making as a core existential activity, necessary for our well-being in the short and long term.

Similarly, Ian Wright (2005) highlights the need for the integration of nature/culture and a more consciously global consciousness. The case for a 'whole' approach within planning is argued for including 'a more evolved collective mind charged with ecological wisdom (Wilber in Wright, 2005, p. 127). Within this framework, place-making, considered as a perpetual participatory event, becomes a crucial existential activity we are all collectively involved in, whether we are conscious of this or not. Like Bateson and Guattari this is an activist approach that is not single issue and could begin to develop the interconnectivity that Bateson argued for further initiated through the virtual communitas created online.

Planning is often conceptualised as an integrated process and so seems a natural candidate for the integration Wilber and Wright hope to achieve. Wright (2005) suggests, reframing planning as 'place-making.' This he sees as a potential solution, with the integration of the 'it,' the 'we' and the 'I,' deeming it an 'integral practice' (Healey, 1997; Sandercock, 1998). For the completion of self-actualisation/'becoming', an integral practice such as 'place-making' is required in order to produce the 'whole' necessary to transform from 'potential to actual': mind, culture and nature must all be addressed equally. Wright considers

the practical aspects of 'place-making' as comprising a mix of 'opening up spaces for dialogue, conversation and inter-relating: mediating between shared meanings and understandings: interrogating points of difference and framing action,' an intervention as necessary as Guattari's rift or rupture. Often characterized as 'human' art, the arts offer inspiration for the practice and process of place-making, being at home with the subjective, 'expressing essences or essential meaning' (Wright, 2005, p 134).

Planning in this sense would become 'communication centered,' a process, encouraging collaborative practices, an 'intervention-orientated enterprise,' defined as 'action with vision' (Wright, 2005, p. 136). These interventions or openings, potentially create an encounter facilitating a process of self-actualisation and 'becoming' in conjunction with the environment, thus an act of 'regenerative ecology.' If collectively we self-organise through a practice of 'place-making' that acknowledges the interconnectedness of the system, with ourselves integrated within the same system, then in essence this becomes the self-organising ability of the planet. The process of self-actualisation/'becoming' is initiated and thus place-making functions as a therapeutic process.

Continuing with this logic, the process of repairing the breakdown of Bateson's eco-mental system could be initiated through a process of place-based learning. This process could, in actuality be a process of individuation for the system, bridging the relationship between the inhabitants and their place of habitation. If we are 'connected,' as Bateson and others suggest, then a process of 'reparation of the self' could be applied to an eco-mental system where 'self' is the inhabitant and 'other' is the location/habitat.

Finally, 'place-making' could also contribute to a process of 'becoming' if considered by engaging with humanistic or dialectic theories and not just a phenomenological perspective. Being-in-the-world implies an interconnection between ourselves and a physical world, were our existence is realised. For Marx, we exist in a dialectical relationship with the physical world, shaping and reshaping it and ourselves. This could be considered as a socialist/Marxist interpretation of Aristotle's 'techne,' acting on our 'innate capacity for action: to change the world to his or her whim (techne), the ability to move from sheer possibility to actuality' (Brommage, 2005, p. 11). Marx, like Guattari, saw capitalism as inhibiting our potential to self-actualise and like both Guattari and Bateson understands us as integrated/part of our physical world. Often linked to Communism, I understand Marx to be more interested in how through our activities (often communal and collective) we continually make and remake the physical world and ourselves. For an integrated holistic approach to 'place-making' the social, political, economical, and environmental must all be taken into consideration as part of the ecosystem.

This background serves to introduce the key perspectives that informing the understanding of the rich potential which digital arts hold for developments in 'place-making as a process of 'becoming'.

Virtual Communitas and Liminoid Space

Since the mid-nineties, the Internet has had an immense impact on culture, and utilize as a tool within the project, an intervention into the dominant narrative or understanding of the locations to which they are responding. The term intervention has been in use since the fifteenth century, *interventionem* (Latin), 'an interposing' (The Oxford Online Dictionary of Etymology, 2010). As a dynamic noun, the root of the word '*intervenire*' directly relates to the use of intervention within a contemporary sense, translating as 'to come between' (The Oxford Online Dictionary of Etymology, 2010) and often used within health or social contexts.

Within the context of liminality, this could offer challenges to the mores and values of a society, culture or even a local community. The use of the social media as an art intervention has the potential to integrate multiple voices, perspectives, and understandings through a re-presentation of the collective knowledge of a location. Within the context of a social media art intervention, the projects *Deptford 45s, Live From Memphis* and *Yellow Arrow* can be considered as a hack or circuit bending that gets alternative information out into the world challenging the dominant narrative of location branding or reputation.

Social media supports social interaction, through accessible, often open source technologies and techniques, publishing content that enables a relationship between users and content. Web 2.0 and user generated content, has facilitated the mainstreaming through enabling 'non-techies' to participate in a wide variety of public platforms. The tools, platforms and infrastructures of Web 2.0, allows for the sharing of information through publishing and the creation of communities through online networks of people. This and the accessibility of mobile phones in particular smart phones and high bandwidth make social media readily available and allow users to not only passively consume content but be active content publishers or broadcasters. Blogs, wikis, podcasts, and content sharing sites e.g. Flickr, enable self-expression, and are further manipulated and incorporated into the projects discussed to encourage participation.

Turner understood communitas to be characterised by what Madge and O'Connor (2005) refer to 'as an equality of relations, a comradeship that transcends age, rank, kinship etc. and displays an intense community spirit.' The liminal qualities of the virtual space the project's produce may form the conditions conducive to creating a public spiritedness or a willingness to contribute to ones community that could be manifest within the physical community of the location, from potentiality to actuality. The projects discussed facilitate the dissemination of overlooked knowledge, about the community, which could challenge dominant narratives. Whilst such challenges will not change locations overnight they provide additional information that enable 'place-making' processes to be dynamic rather than static and enable a location to become more and more of what it is capable of 'becoming'. This agency while potentially inspired in the virtual spaces of the projects actualises in the material, physical locations.

Such projects allow open-ended conversations, a relational mode of production, often criticized for its idealistic and utopian approach. These are similar criticisms leveled at projects coming under the banner of relational aesthetics now with the additional complications of media platforms. Granted this is not necessarily a guaranteed positive outcome as the same tools can equally be used to create negative interventions, e.g. gang Web presence, equally intimately related to a location. However, the intention behind the projects is motivated towards a healthy positive contribution to the location both through their representation of the location and any impact on the physical aspects of the community. All the projects have in built securities to minimise negative outcomes where possible.

An additional key aspect for the production of communitas reflected in the projects is the nature of the unstructured gathering a focused period of shared experience, usually understood to occur within pilgrimage or ritual. Participants in the virtual spaces created by the projects discussed are for the most part unstructured; being there is no formal organisation beyond than the parameters of the project or its mode of contribution. Through the relationships evolved within the virtual space of the project, the shared experience can be considered as a form of communitas. As each project is connected by

a shared location providing a common interest and shared experience for the participants, the opportunity for communitas is increased.

New, digital and social media, including the Internet, as defined by Flew (2008), is characterised as being, easily 'manipulated, are networkable, dense, compressible, interactive' and we often perceive them as immaterial, further adding to our experience of the in-between or threshold. Whilst the activity undertaken cannot be separated from our pre-liminal understandings and connection to our embodied experiences and practices, we can transcend the physical limitations of time and space momentarily. There are concerns around negating the physical due to the lure of the virtual or online communities, however currently we cannot escape the physical world, even though our consciousness maybe perceived albeit momentarily, as disembodied.

Although there are discussions within cyber theory as to whether consciousness requires a body, for the moment as Stone states, "no matter how virtual the subject may become there is still a body attached" (Stone, 1994, p. 111). Pratt (2002) and Walmsley (2000) confirms 'communities and forums that exist online are still rooted in place and space whether that is a physical location or a space of shared interest, being human they can be rooted no other way.' This constant connection to a physical location is I propose the quality of the medium and the projects discussed that can be exploited as a liminoid space, a 'betwixt and between,' further utilised for their contribution to 'place-making' and the process of 'becoming'.

Whether as the creation of bits, the use of the Internet, through social media, virtual worlds, or simply searching for information, the virtual and corporeal are parts of the dualistic experience. This 'betwixt and between' exerts qualities of both realities and this dual nature has social, cultural and political implications. Geographers are increasingly examining what Kitchin refers to as 'the role of space and place in a distributed social space that lacks physicality' (1998a, p. 393). It is this very lack of a fixed physicality and the momentary transcendence or disruption of physical limitations within the virtual space of the project that can be exploited for the deconstruction or undoing of understandings of place that can occur in liminoid space. Indeed being able to juxtapose space and place simultaneously within the projects is a useful condition present in this 'natural environment for liminality' (Waskul, 2004, p. 40) a space related but distinguished from one's place, reminiscent of the Cartesian understanding of the mind's relation to the body.

Cyber disembodiment tends to align itself with the Cartesian mind/body split as Michael Heim, states "in cyberspace minds are connected to minds, existing in perfect concord without the limitations or necessities of the physical body" (Heim, 1993, p. 34). However, within Cartesian understanding the mind although distinguishable, was contained within a body and accessing virtual spaces online necessitates a body. Jaron Lanier claims: "[cyberspace] is just an open world where your mind is the only limitation" (Woolley, 1992, p. 14) yet access to cyberspace is limited by physicality and access to technology. However, the opportunity for the mind to create or imagine things not yet possible in the physical world is a useful perception.

Heidegger and Merleau-Ponty both assert how our lived phenomenological experience enables us to experience and perceive virtual reality a challenge to the mind/body split of Cartesian metaphysics often re-iterated through cyber theory, as in the work of Larnier and Heim. Merleau-Ponty's ideas on the production of knowledge supports the project's potential for creative digital 'place-making' as a process of 'becoming through transforming new knowledge and understanding of place into actual physical interventions. Ponty proposed that we experi-

ence things through our bodies; therefore, the corporeal position held by the participants of a virtual community is an essential condition for the production of knowledge. As the projects only exist in response to a physical location, then the knowledge produced and the experience of communitas would impact on some level on the location.

Bateson regarding knowing as a 'whole' process that involves the senses and the intellect, challenging what had become an accepted idea of knowledge since Descartes and reinforced through the Enlightenment. The Enlightenment focused on reason and logic as a way of producing knowledge, an important progression from superstition, and the power of the church. Yet The Age of Reason initiated a bias towards science as the only means of producing knowledge that despite Romanticism created a deep fragmentation favouring the intellect over, sensing or embodied ways of producing knowledge. Bateson's whole process involves the intellect, the senses and our tacit knowledge gained over time an aspect of the knowing that could be developed through the projects discussed.

As An Xiao (2010), social media artist and founder of Platea, notes:

The most striking aspect of social media art is that it contains facets of net.art, by being digital; visual art, by existing on a two-dimensional surface; public art, by existing in spaces used habitually by hundreds of millions of people; and performance art, by being inherently social. Whether the aggregate is greater than its sum remains to be seen ...

The projects discussed highlight how the potential of this aggregate in conjunction with the connection to their physical locations holds fertile opportunities to contribute to 'place-making' as a process of 'becoming', for the individual participant and their physical world.

Social media art interventions that encourage multiple perspectives and self-organising strategies seem obvious candidates for tools of engagement within 'place-making' practices in light of current economic and environmental concerns. Through making abstract relationships and dynamics of place overt, the counter factual re-presentations that arise in the projects discussed give them their liminal qualities and build on their ability to interrupt a dominant narrative.

Turner identified 'Ritual Liminars' or 'edgemen,' catalysts who 'possess the 'radical potential of cultural critique, or even deconstruction (Turner, 1969, p. 128) the questioning of accepted norms before re-integration into society. Indeed, it has been argued (Rosaldo, Ortner, et al.) that Turner's vision is somewhat Utopian and in fact that rather than being re-integrated into the status quo the individual may in fact seek to change it. Turner when explaining the essence of liminality stated it was " found in the release from normal constraints" adding that; liminars were individuals who had the power to "reveal the freedom, the indeterminacy underlying all culturally constructed worlds, the free play of mankind's cognitive and imaginative capacities" (1969, p. 161). Within a location or community, this could enable a community to represent itself through the voices of its residents, contributing to the creation of the personality of the place.

Weber considers the liminal phase to be simultaneously 'culturally dangerous but culturally creative' (1995, p. 526) a place of action. As the cultural beliefs are challenged and broken down any re-integration may include an inability to conform to the previous value system, yet this may in turn contribute to the creation of new systems. Social media art interventions functioning in a similar way to Turner's 'edgemen,' are harnessed to deconstruct an understanding of a location, through an 'indeterminacy,' which due to the relationship to the physical location could manifest in dynamic emergent practices.

The projects reviewed use open source and social media to showcase a location beyond nostalgic or conventionally commercial marketing approaches. The interventions initiated by artists, designers, and technologists, the projects were a way to express what they thought was important or exciting about their neighbourhoods. They felt sure others, not driven by commercial gain would want to see living breathing cities, not the usual tourist routes, but get insights from locals and a chance to really get under the skin and get to 'know' the locations, through an insider's perspective.

An Xiao, believes tools like Twitter and other social media platforms are giving us a rich new public landscape, with the 'tweets… are the new streets' (An Xiao, 2012) waiting to be explored with potential audiences or participants in excess of a billion. Connected by phones, tablets, laptops or desktops what potential does the crowd-sourced life hold for 'place-making' as a process of 'becoming'? The ubiquity of our digital technology particularly the Internet and consumer electronics has transformed the potential of technology 'a collective tool [to become] part of the fabric of culture' Sherry (2005). Our real-world lives could be re-defined through the use of technology and the users on the other end.

The first of the projects considered, *Live from Memphis (LFM)* (2001–ongoing), www.livefrommemphis.com currently describes itself as 'media, entertainment, and marketing for social good. By promoting an ethos of 'Connect. Collaborate. Create' (LFM, 2011) they are up front about supporting their city through 'producing social experiences, content, and resources to inspire, engage, and enrich cultural and economic growth to showcase the best of Music, Film and the Arts both to the local community and beyond. Their underlying belief is that in a local community connected to a wider context yet supportive, creative and imaginative, is not only a vibrant community but also a resilient community. To promote this LFM, produce a myriad of content and events e.g. an online magazine, broadcast programing, multiple Web series,' and live events. They also host a variety of community resources and manage the largest online archive of Memphis Music, Film, and Art.

Launched in 2001 by Christopher Reyes and Sam Lee, their first content was from local bands gigging in and around Memphis. They had an agenda to promote Memphis in a contemporary way, beyond its musical heritage of Blues, Soul, and Rock n Roll. Many of the local bands felt that they were not supported by agencies that continued to capitalise on nostalgia. Reyes and Lee managed to document over 70 bands within the first 5 months of existence, aiming to be as comprehensive as possible showcasing all the genres the city had to offer. They posted discographies, created mailing lists for the bands and enabled the audience to access live recordings, album recordings and artist's lists where the bands could post their own tracks and info. As the technology evolved so did *LFM*, using open source content management systems such as Joomla. The site goes from strength to strength and has fought an uphill battle with local agencies and authorities.

LFM is an example of how digital interventions can contribute to a process of 'becoming' when harnessed for the practice of 'place-making,' through developing and promoting a unique and attractive personality of a place. Paul O'Connor Executive Director of World Business Chicago, spoke to *SMARTcity Memphis* in 2007 affirming that the hardest audience, yet most important audience to convince for any city brand is its own people, who are often the most negative. This was supported in the conclusions of the 2006 *Talent Magnet Report* (SMARTcity Memphis, 2006), which showed that 'current marketing of Memphis reinforced an image among young people that it was frozen in time, a city of Elvis, riverboats and a languid, slow-moving culture.'

This highlights the need for places, which have as much need for a healthy self-image and that this is somewhat reflective of inhabitants' own self-image and knowledge of the location. One of *LFM's* most widely distributed projects; My Memphis interviewed about 40 Memphians involved in a range of creative professions to talk about their Memphis. This anecdotal approach not only encourages trust but also provides the community and opportunity to define itself differently. The project exists online at My Memphis TV and as a promotional DVD that was picked up by the local chamber of commerce and used to send to human resource departments and college campuses. Christopher Reyes, who shot and edited the film, sees it as a 'visual love letter to Memphis from Memphians.' When he began the interviews, he felt people were telling the same story he felt, and hoped the film would "make people aware of the fact that here is something special about Memphis under the surface." (Reyes, 2006).

There is something reminiscent of Turner's 'edgemen' in this statement, those 'liminars' that Turner believed 'possess the 'radical potential of cultural critique, indeed of deconstruction' (Turner, 1969, p. 128). Although not meant to be overtly radical or critical Reyes's My Memphis does deconstruct the prevailing image of Memphis, over riding the historical branding of the city and re-presenting a more relevant contemporary image, which for some maybe radical.

SMARTcity Memphis (2006) described it the My Memphis as a "good first-date strategy, having your friends talk you up and showing off your best assets. This sort of strategy is not only useful for outreach but helps to win over that hard to impress home crowd referred to by Peter O'Connor. Feedback at the launch of My Memphis from a woman who was planning to move at the supported this opinion as after watching the film, decided to stay in Memphis (Memphis Flyer, 2006), others stated 'I want to move to Memphis, but I already live here,'" SMARTcity Memphis, 2006). This challenging of an understanding of place, even our own experience of place highlights the potential of the digital intervention as a liminoid space, deconstructing our perceptions and knowledge.

Projects like *LFM*, self-organising and self managed, created by artists in an open, engaging, and collaborative fashion, using social media and the Web can contribute to a location's unique identity. This identity is co-created by the multiple knowledge and understanding held within the community as well as the sharing of the communities non-commercial assets. Through creating the opportunity to engage others in the process of creating an identity, this generates a healthy self-image and local investment of social capital through stake-holding and civic pride. The communitas created online within the *LFM* community develops relationships and knowledge that spill over into Memphis's physical landscape through the collaborative production of culture.

Yellow Arrow began in 2004 in NYC as a street art project, eventually existing in thirty-five countries and three hundred and eighty cities. Combining stickers, mobile phones and an international community connected via the Internet, *Yellow Arrow* was a public art project that transformed the urban landscape with local experiences. Yellow Arrow manifested as a "deep map" that 'expresses the personal histories and hidden secrets that live within our everyday spaces' (Yellow Arrow, 2012). In *Yellow Arrow*, we can see Aristotle's 'techne,' a way of knowing the world, that makes use of art/craft skills and tools, creating what McEwen referred to as the 'indissolubility of craft and community' (1993). The knowledge produced, created through personal narrative, lived experience and engaging multiple perspectives, moves closer to Bateson's understanding of knowing and Guattari's 'recreation of the world' (2005), through the ever evolving location, mapped by 'Yellow arrow.'

Yellow Arrow promoted the belief that every place is distinct and can be engaging if presented from a unique perspective, similar to the strategy employed by LFM. Using coded yellow arrow stickers to signpost different locations or objects, the project drew attention to the idiosyncratic or the overlooked. Through using SMS to send a message to the *Yellow Arrow* service number beginning with the arrows unique code, the author attaches a 'story' to the arrow. These ranged from poetic fragments, factual information, personal stories or provocations. When a yellow arrow was encountered its code was sent to the *Yellow Arrow* number and the caller receives the story on their phone, participants could also annotate their arrows using photos or maps online.

The project integrated mobile technology, the Internet, and the physical world building on the physical network of the service provider and the accessibility across social classes of the mobile phone and the Internet. The project capitalised on the notion of a network 'inherently a combination of physical, social, and technological' elements and evolved to create content that was organised around locally relevant themes.

Produced by Counts media, an arts and gaming company it was conceived by artists in New York, Berlin and Gothenberg, *Yellow Arrow* incorporated the playful interactive activities of gaming into the city and created a platform 'where people can contribute collectively to the places they live' (Shapins, 2005, col. 1) an example of digital creative 'place-making.' The project drew on theories from The Situationists and Baudrillard and the importance of the streets as 'the alternative and subversive form of the mass media' (Baudrillard, 1968).

Yellow Arrow sought to transform how we looked and related to our environments again changing our relationship to them by providing knowledge about a location, in particular personal or previously unpublished knowledge. This drew on The Situationist's concept of psycho-geography, concerned with the effects of the environment on our emotions and behavior, linking our inner landscape with the outer physical world. The inter-subjective approach taken by Yellow Arrow enabled a new understanding of place, which could then be used to contribute to changing a location if inclined as recognised by Rheingold,

There are two separate but connected issues here... One using the cyberworld to connect people's opinions, information and places in the physical world. The other is the bottom-up part: People making things happen, and even changing policies from the bottom up (Rheingold, 2005).

For any lasting change to occur it is necessary for there to be transference into action, this is the same whether the reflection, which advances the change, is manifest in the virtual or physical world. It is unclear in what areas the policy changes that Rheingold refers to occurred however it can be argued that this shows the potential of such interventions for 'place-making.' Furthermore Rheingold's observation confirms Yellow Arrow's ability to contribute to a process of 'becoming' from potentiality to actuality through the changes to policy that occurred as a direct result from engagement with the project. However, Rheingold appreciated the collective voices that were involved in the project despite taking issue with the physicality of the stickers, hoping they would eventually become completely virtual. The project concluded in October 2008, with all the content generated internationally by hundreds of contributors archived in the public domain at Flickr.

The final project discussed is the *45s series* 2005-2009, an on-going series of audio-visual projects, that exists both on and offline offering opportunities for continuous remixing and the creation of multiple understandings of a place. The format was influenced initially by pop culture during a residency in Memphis, TN. The core of the project is the 7x3 min format of audio-visual

mixes of specific locations, referencing the 7 inch single and the three minute pop song, collectively known as a '45'.

The films are made in a number of ways working with local residents to gather places of importance with in a location, a form of crowd sourcing that documents the places using found audio and video. These are often separately edited and mixed and re-mixed to create a psycho-geographic portrait of a location. Once this aspect of the project is complete the projects evolves to include motion sensor installations, films, psycho-geographic workshops to create audio-visual content and public projection events. The films and audio mixes are archived online including all the original samples, available for re-mixing and uploading. These common lands of digital data enable the contributors to create an on-going co-construction of the area through the virtual galleries and submitted portraits after the initial stage of the project is completed. This continues to encourage idiosyncratic, subjective re-presentations by a multitude of voices. Through the visual and audio "posing of possibilities beyond what is assumed to be the case," Macleod 2005, the on-going project activities lead to a conscious re-fashioning of 'place.'

The 45s series enables the process of place-based learning and re-learning evolving an intimate relationship with place and in turn the location's other residents. Enough compatibility is generated to enable communication and a more expanded experience of place and ultimately learning. Through the intimacy created within the shared experience (communitas) of the various aspects of the project and the de-construction/reconstruction that Turner refers to occurring during liminal phases/liminoid space, new understandings of place arise.

The project enables a virtual communitas through enabling diverse groups of strangers, to interact with people whose opinions, values, and culture are different. The participants are informally organized through the commonality of the location of the specific 45 project and their personal relationship or understanding of the place, their unique perspective shared with other participants. These multiple perspectives, collectively held in an online representation of the place, not only represent the place but also document the location's continual evolution, resisting nostalgia, the blight of many regeneration and development practices. These emerging relationships can then be capitalised to develop and evolve the places we live, conducive to our well-being with the legacies of the 45s projects including networking activities, campaigning forums and sustainable community activity.

The 'legacy' of the 45s, reflects and enshrines the community's self-directed, heterogeneous self-image, a healthy necessity for the process of 'becoming'. One of the locations in the series, Deptford, underwent extensive development with eight-ten major residential developments within two years. Bought off plan, the marketing for each development drew on the areas Maritime heritage and its commutability to other areas. Low percentages of the developments where ring-fenced for social housing, yet these where furthest away from the river (a key aspect of Deptford's history and culture) with the rest of the development 'becoming' 'dormer' residences with minimal contribution to the evolution of the location. Local residents are continuing to utilising the Internet and social media, e.g. deptfordis.org to campaign against future proposed development and create a more sustainable and imaginative vision for the future of Deptford.

CONCLUSION

Within this chapter, I wanted to outline the potential of virtual communitas for digital digital place-making and make the argument that this is a process of becoming, integrating us as co-authors of place that transform that 'potentiality' into 'actuality.' While considering the potential

of this to repair the process of fragmentation and separation that has occurred between us and our physical environment.

Turner's notion of liminoid space and its importance for establishing communitas provides a useful perspective from which to consider the projects discussed. The projects function as liminoid spaces, Turner's secular expression of the liminal, through enabling interactions that may not be possible in the physical location due to lack of leisure time, geographic distance and other obstacles to interaction. This does not ignore issues such as bias, social status or other issues we encounter as obstacles to interaction, as we bring those into any interaction we undertake. Rather it is more that the virtual spaces created afford further opportunities for communitas to evolve beyond the daily physical reality.

Existing online, using social media tools and a relationship to a physical location, their inherent condition of being 'betwixt and between,' qualifies them as liminoid spaces for the production of a virtual communitas. Their qualities contribute to their ability to cultivate communitas through the provision of threshold space within which residents gather and continually re-present and remake their location, through their contributions. Employing the Internet as a social medium, allows the audience/participants to be involved in the co-production of the virtual space as it evolves and any activities that transition from the online space into the offline physical locations. The shared experience of the project, focused around a location, results in a new, shared experiences of their common location.

It is important to stress that the relationship to the physical location is what provides the fertile ground for the projects to contribute to 'place-making' and the process of 'becoming'. The virtual expressions within the projects are actual expressions of the physical location consolidated into the liminoid space of the project. Returning to the classical Greek outlook and its recognition of the relationship between making and speculative thought, digital creative 'place-making' becomes a feedback system that involves interconnected situated and tacit knowledge from a range of disciplines, experiences, and perspectives. The Greek perspective of the 'indissolubility of craft and community' (McEwen, 1993) is integrated within a twenty-first century context.

Environment is an important factor in forming personality and includes cultural, racial, socioeconomic, educational, social guidance and health conditions. This being the case, place-making becomes an opportunity to develop a unique personality, through the reciprocal process of receiving and transmission between people and place and all the dynamics that involves. Returning to Bateson, the projects combine 'many levels of mind—unconscious, conscious, and external—to make a statement of their combination" (Bateson, 1972, p. 470) in this case a unique personality of place. Developments in technology such as augmented reality with the increasing accessibility of physical computing and sensing technology could increase the potential of for 'many levels of mind' to make unique 'statement[s] of their combination. When linked to a location such interventions or 'ruptures' into our physical world could serve to facilitate a more integrated relationship, with our position as distinguishable but not separate, creating a more symbiotic, sustainable connection.

Harnessing art/tech interventions, developed with their potentiality as liminoid spaces in mind, that challenge and deconstruct understanding of place, offers an encounter synonymous to the conditions necessary self-actualisation and 'becoming'. If undertaken in conjunction with the environment, an act of regenerative ecology, mindful interventions could facilitate the process of place based learning and re-learning that begins to address the eco-mental breakdown, the psychotic split between our 'selves' and the physical world as discussed by Bateson.

Through counterfactual re-presentations facilitated by the project's interventions and their virtual communitas affecting the physical location to which they are bound, perhaps

the issues of connectivity that Bateson felt the 'public' needed to know, could be initially addressed. Embedding such an agenda within public art, planning and regeneration practices could lead to a more holistic process. Utilised within the construction of our physical locations, this could then become a process of 'becoming'/self-actualisation for both the place and its residents. This could potentially initiate a process of reparation within place, addressing its eco-mental breakdown and further leading to the idea of co-authored place-making being an existential activity crucial to our well-being a process of 'becoming'.

A process towards the creation of wholeness from fragmentation, more usually applied in relation to the human psyche within therapeutic practices of psychoanalysis or psychiatry if applied to the relationship between ourselves and the environment could manifest as a process of individuation. If we are 'inter-connected' as Bateson and others suggest then a process of reparation of the self could be applied to the eco-mental breakdown of a system that is made up of self and other, other being the location/place and its residents. If as epigenetics suggests, change in gene expression can be caused by mechanisms other than within the DNA sequence, environmental factors become increasingly important not only for our well-being but our evolution.

REFERENCES

Arrow, Y. (2012a). *Website*. Retrieved from http://yellowarrow.net/v3/

Arrow, Y. (2012b). *About*. Retrieved from http://yellowarrow.net/v3/about.html#

Bateson, G. (1979). *Steps to an ecology of the mind*. Chicago, IL: University of Chicago Press.

Borgman, A. (2006). Technology as a cultural force: For Alena and Griffin. *Canadian Journal of Sociology*, *31*(3), 351–360.

Brommage, T. J. (2005). *Being as becoming: Aristotle's metaphysics and its contemporary implications*. Tampa, FL: University of South Florida.

Brommage, T. J., Jr. (2005). *Being as 'becoming': Aristotle's metaphysics and its contemporary implications*. (Unpublished Masters Thesis).

City Memphis, S. M. A. R. T. (2006). *Website*. Retrieved from http://smartcitymemphis.blogspot.com/2006/03/who-says-memphis-has-no-creative-class.html

City Memphis, S. M. A. R. T. (2007). *Website*. Retrieved from http://smartcitymemphis.blogspot.com/2007/07/week-in-memphis-branding-city-from.html

Communitas. (2011). *Dictionary*. Retrieved from http://dictionary.reference.com/browse/communitas

Connoll, H. M. (1985). *Essentials of child psychiatry* (2nd ed.). London, UK: Blackwell Scientific Publications.

Davis, B. (2010). *Website*. Retrieved from http://www.artnet.com/magazineus/reviews/davis/art-and-social-media8-4-10.asp

Deptfordis. (2012). *Website*. Retrieved from http://www.deptfordis.org.uk/

Etymonline. (2012). *Website*. Retrieved from http://www.etymonline.com/index.php?term=oxford

Flew, T. (2008). *New media: An introduction* (2nd ed.). Oxford, UK: Oxford University Press.

Flyer, M. (2002). *Website*. Retrieved from http://www.memphisflyer.com/memphis/livefrom-memphis/Content?oid=1108714

Flyer, M. (2006). *Website*. Retrieved from http://www.memphisflyer.com/memphis/love-at-first-sight/Content?oid=1125543

Genosko, G. (2009). *Felix Guattari: A critical introduction*. London, UK: Pluto Press Ltd.

Guattari, F. (2000). *The three ecologies*. London, UK: The Athlone Press.

Hahn, R. (2001). *Anaximander and the architects: The contributions of Egyptian and Greek architectural technologies to the origins of Greek philosophy*. Albany, NY: State University of New York Press.

Heim, M. (1993). *The metaphysics of virtual reality*. Oxford, UK: Oxford University Press.

Herzogenrath, B. (2009). *Deleuze/Guattari & ecology*. Basingstoke, UK: Palgrave Macmillan.

Jung, C. G. (1962). *Symbols of transformation: An analysis of the prelude to a case of schizophrenia (Vol. 2)*. (Hull, R. F. C., Trans.). New York, NY: Harper & Brothers.

Kitchin, R. M. (1998). Towards geographies of cyberspace. *Progress in Human Geography, 22*(3), 385–406. doi:10.1191/030913298668331585

Madge, C., & O'Connor, H. (2005). Mothers in the making? Exploring liminality in cyber/space. *Transactions of the Institute of British Geographers, 30*(1), 83-97. Retrieved 10/05/2011 from http://www.jstor.org/stable/3804531

Maslow, A. (1954). *Motivation and personality*. New York, NY: Harper.

McEwen, I. K. (1993). *Socrates' ancestor: An essay on architectural beginnings*. Cambridge, MA: MIT Press.

Platea. (2011). *Website*. Retrieved from http://plateastweets.blogspot.com/

Pollack, B. (2011, June 1). The social revolution. *ARTnews*. Retrieved: 30/11/2011 from http://www.artnews.com/2011/06/01/the-social-revolution/

Pred, A. (1984). Place as historically contingent process: Structuration and the time-geography of 'becoming' places. *Annals of the Association of American Geographers, 74*(2), 279-297. Retrieved 10/05/2011 from http://www.jstor.org/stable/2569284

Sherry, J. F., Jr. (2000). Place, technology, and representation. *The Journal of Consumer Research, 27*(2), 273-278. Retrieved 10/12/2009 from http://www.jstor.org/stable/254317

Stone, A. R. (1994). Will the real body please stand up? Boundary stories about virtual cultures. In Benedickt, M. (Ed.), *Cyberspace: First Steps* (pp. 81–118). Cambridge, MA: MIT Press.

Sullivan, G. (2005). *Art practice as research, inquiry in the visual arts*. London, UK: Sage Publications Ltd.

Turner, V. (1967). *The forest of symbols aspects of Ndembu rituals*. Ithaca, NY: Cornell University.

Turner, V. (1969). *The ritual process: Structure and anti-structure*. Hoboken, NJ: Rutgers University.

Turner, V. (1974). Liminal to liminoid in play, flow, and ritual: An essay in comparative symbology. *Rice University Studies, 60*(3), 53-92. Retrieved 10/05/2011 from http://www.jstor.org/stable/2713299

Walmsley, D. (2000). Community, place, cyberspace. *The Australian Geographer, 31*(1), 5–19. doi:10.1080/00049180093501

Waskul, D. D. (2004). *Net.seXXX: Readings on sex pornography and the internet*. New York, NY: Peter Lang Publishing.

Weber, D. (1995). From limen to border: A meditation on the legacy of Victor Turner for American cultural studies. *American Quarterly, 47*(3), 525-536. Retrieved 10/05/2011 from http://www.jstor.org/stable/2713299

Woolley, B. (1992). *Virtual worlds*. Oxford, UK: Blackwell.

Wright, I. (2005). 'Place-making' as applied integral ecology: Evolving an ecologically wise planning ethic. *World Futures, 61*, 127–137. doi:10.1080/02604020590902407

Xiao, A. (2010). *Always social: Getting noticed (2008-2010), part two*. Retrieved from http://hyperallergic.com/6700/social-media-art-pt-2/

ADDITIONAL READING

Bateson, G. (1979). *Mind and nature: A necessary unity*. New York, NY: Dutton.

Bateson, G., & Bateson, M. C. (1987). *Angels fear: Toward an epistemology of the sacred*. New York, NY: Macmillan.

Coverley, M. (2006). *Psycho-geography*. Harpenden, UK: Pocket Essentials.

Cresswell, T. (2004). *Place: A short introduction*. Oxford, UK: Blackwell Publishing.

Danto, A. (1997). *After the end of art*. Princeton, NJ: Princeton University.

De Certeau, M. (1984). *The practice of everyday life*. Berkley, CA: University of California Press.

Dean, T. A. (2005). *Place (artworks)*. London, UK: Thames and Hudson.

Ed Lacy, S. (Ed.). (1995). *Mapping the terrain: New genre public art*. San Francisco, CA: Bay Area Press.

Findley, L., Lukez, P., & Wampler, J. (1993). *The space between places*. Retrieved from http://places.designobserver.com/feature/the-space-between-portfolio-the-space-between/201/

Hall, T. (2012). *Art creativity and urban change in cultural agency and urban social change*. London, UK: Routledge Press Ltd.

Hall, T. A. (2005). *Public art in the city: Meanings, values attitudes and roles in interventions: Art and urban futures*. Bristol, UK: Intellect.

Ixia. (2004). *Desirable places: The contribution of artists to creating spaces for public life*. Birmingham, UK: ARTicle Press.

Jung, C. G. (1989a). *Memories, dreams, reflections*. New York, NY: Random House, Inc.

Jung, C. G. (1989b). *Psychology and religion: West and east* (2nd ed.). Princeton, NJ: Princeton University Press.

Kester, G. (2004). *Conversation pieces: Community and communication in modern art*. Berkley, CA: University of California Press.

Kwon, M. (2004). *One place after another*. Cambridge, MA: MIT Press.

Lefevre, H. (1991). *The production of space*. Liphook, UK: Blackwell Publishing.

Miles, M. (1997). *Art space and the city*. London, UK: Routledge Press.

Miles, M. (2005). *Interventions: Art and urban futures*. Bristol, UK: Intellect.

Moffat, D. (2007). *The coming ecologic epoch*: *Sim Van der Ryn at EDRA*. Retrieved from http://places.designobserver.com/feature/the-coming-ecological-epoch--sim-van-der-ryn-at-edra-----dispatches/469/

Rodman, M. (1992). *Empowering place: Multi-locality and multi-vocality*. London, UK: Blackwell Publishing.

Stocchetti, M. A.-S. (Ed.). (2007). *Images and communities: The visual construction of the social*. Helsinki, Finland: Gaudeamus-Helsinki University Press.

Turner, V. (1977). Process, system, and symbol: A new anthropological synthesis. *Daedalus*, *106*(3), 61–80.

KEY TERMS AND DEFINITIONS

Becoming: The process of coming into being, or developing from potential to actual. Originates from the Old English word *becuman*, which meant 'come to a place, come (to be or do something)'.

Communitas: The condition of shared experience. Often referred to within a religious or ritual context however has been used within a secular context since the late 1960s.

Community: Often community is used ideologically, denoting what should be rather than what actually is. Within the text, community is used to define a communitiy of interest, which in this case also refers to but is not bounded by a physical location.

Individuation: To distinguish oneself from others of the same kind, to develop unique and whole identity. Stems from the medieval Latin *individuat-* 'singled out,' from the verb *individuare*, from Latin *individuus*, from *in-* 'into' + *dividuus* 'divisible' (from *dividere* 'to divide').

Interventions: The action or process of intervening, to come between or to take part in something in order to affect change through either preventing or altering a result or course of events: Late Middle English: from Latin *interventio(n-)*, from the verb *intervenire*.

Liminoid Space: An in-between space that exists in a secular context considered within the text as a space that evolves within on and offline relationships in relation to a particular location.

Place-Making: The process of coming together to make place as a dynamic, processual activity.

Compilation of References

3 MDST. (2009). *Technology comparison: Surface acoustic wave, optical and bending wave technology.* Methuen, MA: 3M Touch Systems.

3ʳᵈ Woman. (2012). Website. *Retrieved from* http://third-woman.com/index.html

AA/VV. (2008). *Floos+art*. Paris, France: GOTO10.

Abel, R., & Altman, R. (2002). *The sounds of early cinema.* Bloomington, IN: Indiana University Press.

Adamson, G. (2007). *Thinking through craft*. London, UK: Berg Publishers.

Adorno, T. W. (2007). *Aesthetic theory*. London, UK: Continuum.

Adorno, T. W., Benjamin, W., Bloch, E., Brecht, B., Lukacs, G., & Jameson, F. (Eds.). (2007). *Aesthetics and politics*. London, UK: Verso.

Alac, M. (2008). Working with brain scans: Digital images and gestural interaction in fMRI laboratory. *Social Studies of Science, 38*(4), 483–508. doi:10.1177/0306312708089715

Albury, W. R., & Oldroyd, D. R. (1977). From renaissance mineral studies to historical geology, in the light of Michel Foucault's "The Order of Things". *British Journal for the History of Science, 10*(3), 187–215. doi:10.1017/S000708740001565X

Allen, P. (2008). Framing the body in augmented public space. In de Cindio & de Cindio (Eds.), *Augmented Urban Spaces*. Farnham, UK: Ashgate.

Altman, R. (2004). *Silent film sound*. New York, NY: Columbia University Press.

Altman, R. (Ed.). (1992). *Sound theory sound practice*. New York, NY: Routledge.

Anderson, N. (2009). Eye and image: Looking at a visual studies of science. *Historical Studies in the Natural Sciences, 39*(1), 115. doi:10.1525/hsns.2009.39.1.115

Anders, P. (1999). *Envisioning cyberspace*. New York, NY: McGraw-Hill.

Andrew, D. (2002). *Concepts in film theory: An introduction*. Oxford, UK: Oxford University Press.

Ansell Pearson, K. (2002). *Philosophy and the adventure of the virtual: Bergson and the time of life*. London, UK: Routledge.

Arrow, Y. (2012). *Website*. Retrieved from http://yellowarrow.net/v3/

Arte. (2009). *Gaza-sderot: Life in spite of everything*. Retrieved June 24ᵗʰ from http://gaza-sderot.arte.tv/

Arts Machine. (2012). *The virtual metaplasticity platform project*. Retrieved June 2012, from http://www.artsmachine.com

Ascott, R. (2005). Distance makes the art grow further: Distributed authorship and telematic textuality in la plissure du texte. In Chandler & N. Neumark (Eds.), *At a Distance: Precursors to Art and Activism on the Internet*, (pp. 282-297). Cambridge, MA: MIT Press.

Ascott, R., & Shanken, E. (Eds.). (2003). *Telematic embrace: Visionary theories of art, technology, and consciousness* (pp. 109–126, 191–208). Berkeley, CA: University of California Press.

Aston, J. (2010). Spatial montage and multimedia ethnography: Using computers to visualise aspects of migration and social division among a displaced community. *Forum: Qualitative Social Research, 11*(2). Retrieved June 24, 2012, from http://www.qualitativeresearch.net/index.php/fqs/article/view/1479

Aston, J., & James, W. (2007). *Voices from the blue nile: A portait of a refugee community*. Retrieved June 24, 2012, from http://voicesfromthebluenile.org

Aston, J., & James, W. (2012). Memories of a blue nile home: The photographic moment and multimedia linkage. In Vokes, R. (Ed.), *Photography in Africa: Ethnographic Perspectives* (pp. 104–126). Woodbridge, NY: James Currey.

Atkinson, T., & Baldwin, M. (2003). Air show. In C. Harrison & P. Wood (Eds.), *1900-2000: An Anthology of Changing Ideas*, (pp. 868-873). Oxford, UK: Wiley-Blackwell.

Augé, M. (1995). *Non-places: Introduction to an anthropology of supermodernity*. Paris, France: Verso.

Bachelard, G. (1994). *The poetics of space*. Boston, MA: Beacon Press.

Bakhtin, M. (1981). *The dialogic imagination*. Austin, TX: University of Texas Press.

Bakhtin, M. (1984). *Rabelais and his world* (Iswolsky, H., Trans.). Bloomington, IN: Indiana University Press.

Barker, M., & Munster, A. (2010). *The brainwave of a monk meditating on unconditional loving-kindness and compassion*. Retrieved April 20, 2011, from http://www.insideoutexhibition.com/

Barthes, R. (1977). *Musica practica, in image, music, text*. London, UK: Flamingo.

Barthes, R., & Heath, S. (Eds.). (1977). *Music, image, text*. London, UK: Harper Collins.

Bartram, A. (2006). *Futurist typography and the liberated text*. New Haven, CT: Yale University Press.

Bateson, G. (1979). *Steps to an ecology of the mind*. Chicago, IL: University of Chicago Press.

Baudrillard, J. (1981). *Simulacra and simulation*. Ann Arbor, MI: University of Michigan Press.

Baudrillard, J. (1983). *Simulations*. New York, NY: Semiotext. [e]

Bazin, A. (1995). *What is cinema? Volume one*. Berkeley, CA: University of California Press.

Beech, D. (2009). *Words and objects after conceptualism*. Retrieved from http://www.art-omma.org/NEW/issue%2011/pages/dave_beech.pdf

Benjamin, A. (2004). *Disclosing spaces: On painting*. Manchester, UK: Clinamen Press.

Benjamin, W. (1968). *Illuminations: The work of art in the age of mechanical reproduction*. New York, NY: Schocken Books.

Benjamin, W. (1973). The work of art in the age of mechanical reproduction. In Arendt, H., & Benjamin, W. (Eds.), *Illuminations* (pp. 219–253). London, UK: Fontana.

Benjamin, W. (1978). The author as producer. In *Reflections*. New York, NY: Harcourt Brace Jovanovich.

Benjamin, W., Eiland, H., & Mc Laughlin, K. (1999). *The arcades project*. Cambridge, MA: Harvard University Press.

Benjamin, W., & Mitchell, S. (1973). *Understanding Brecht*. London, UK: NLB.

Bergson, H. (1920). *Creative evolution*. London, UK: Macmillan and Co. Ltd.

Bergson, H. (1991). *Matter and memory*. New York, NY: Zone Books.

Berman, M. (1982). *All that is solid melts into air: The experience of modernity*. New York, NY: Simon and Schuster.

Biocca, F. (1997). The cyborg's dilemma: Progressive embodiment in virtual environments. *Journal of Computer-Mediated Communication*, *3*(2). Retrieved from http://jcmc.indiana.edu/vol3/issue2/biocca2.html

Biocca, F. (1999). The cyborg's dilemma: Progressive embodiment in virtual environments. *Human Factors in Information Technology*, *13*, 113–144. doi:10.1016/S0923-8433(99)80011-2

Blau, I., & Caspi, A. (2009). *What type of collaboration helps? Psychological ownership, perceived learning and outcome quality of collaboration*. Paper presented at the Chais Conference on Instructional Technologies Research 2009: Learning in the Technological Era. Raanana, Israel.

Boellstorff, T. (2008). *Coming of age in Second Life: An anthropologist explores the virtually human.* Princeton, NJ: Princeton University Press.

Bolter, J. D., & Grusin, R. (1999). *Remediation: Understanding new media.* Cambridge, MA: MIT Press.

Borgman, A. (2006). Technology as a cultural force: For Alena and Griffin. *Canadian Journal of Sociology, 31*(3), 351–360.

Bosnak, R. (2007). *Embodiment: Creative imagination in medicine, art and travel.* Hove, UK: Routledge.

Bourriaud, N. (1998). *Relational aesthetics.* Paris, France: Les Presses du Réel.

Bourriaud, N. (2009). *Altermodern.* London, UK: Tate Publishing.

Brenda May Gallery. (2011). *Al Munro.* Retrieved 1 February, 2012, from http://www.brendamaygallery.com.au/pages/artists_works.php?artistID=90

Bringsjord, S., & Shilliday, A. Taylor. J., Werner, D., Clark, M., Charpentier, E., Bringsjord, A. (2008). Toward logic-based cognitively robust synthetic characters in digital environments. In *Proceedings of the 2008 Conference on Artificial General Intelligence Conference,* (pp. 87-98). Amsterdam, The Netherlands: IOS Press.

Brody, R. (2008). *Everything is cinema: The working life of Jean Luc Godard.* New York, NY: Metropolitan Books.

Broeckmann, A. (2009). Intimate publics: Memory, performance and spectacle in urban environments. In McQuire, S., Martin, M., & Niederer, S. (Eds.), *Urban Screens Reader* (pp. 109–120). Amsterdam, The Netherlands: Institute of Network Cultures.

Brommage, T. J., Jr. (2005). *Being as 'becoming': Aristotle's metaphysics and its contemporary implications.* (Unpublished Masters Thesis).

Bru, C. (1955). *L'estetique de l'abstraction.* Paris, France: Presses Universitaries de France.

Bulhak, A. C. (2000). *On the simulation of postmodernism and mental debility using recursive transition networks. Dept Computer Science Technical Reports.* Melbourne, Australia: Monash University.

Bunkley, B. (2009). *Displaced animals 2004 - 2006.* Retrieved April 30, 2011, from http://www.britbunkley.com/

Burcaw, G. E. (1997). *Introduction to museum work* (3rd ed.). New York, NY: Altamira Press.

Bürger, P. (1972). *Theory of the avant-garde* (Shaw, M., Trans.). Minneapolis, MN: University of Minnesota Press.

Bush, V. (1945). As we may think. *Atlantic Magazine, 176,* 641–649.

Buszek, M. E. (2011). *Extra/ordinary: Craft and contemporary art.* Chapel Hill, NC: Duke University Press.

Cache, B. (2001). *Earth moves: The furnishing of territories.* Cambridge, MA: The MIT Press.

Caffentzis, G. (2007). Crystals and analytic engines: Historical and conceptual preliminaries to a new theory of machines. *Ephemera, 7*(1), 24-45. Retrieved from http://www.ephemeraweb.org/journal/7-1/71caffentzis.pdf

Cahalan, J. M. (1994). The guilty forgiving the innocent: Stanislaus, Shaun, and Shem in Finnegans Wake. *Notes on Modern Irish Literature, 6,* 5–11.

Callinicos, A. (1989). *Against postmodernism.* Oxford, UK: Polity Press.

Calvino, I. (1997). *Invisible cities.* London, UK: Vintage.

Canton, M., & Barnett, S. (Producers), & Synder, Z. (Director). (2009). *300* [Motion picture]. United States: Warner Brothers Pictures.

Card, S., Mackinlay, J., & Shneiderman, B. (1999). *Readings in information visualization: Using vision to think.* San Francisco, CA: Morgan Kaufmann Publishers.

Carson, D., McClave, B., & Millward, D. (ProducerS). (1996). *Geoderma 3D video.* Retrieved from http://www.youtube.com/watch?v=M0XPM_CrsAU

Casey, E. (2000). *Imagining: A phenomenological study.* Bloomington, IN: Indiana University Press.

Chandler, J., & Lippard, L. (1968). The dematerialization of art. *Art International, 12*(2), 31–36.

Charlton, J. (2010). *iForm.* Retrieved April 20, 2011, from http://www.mic.org.nz/artists/james-charlton/

Cheetham, M. A. (2010). The crystal interface in contemporary art: Metaphors of the organic and inorganic. *Leonardo*, *43*(3), 250–255. doi:10.1162/leon.2010.43.3.250

Chion, M. (1990). *Audio-vision: Sound on screen* (Gorman, C., Trans.). New York, NY: Columbia University Press.

Chion, M. (1999). *The voice in cinema* (Gorbman, C., Trans.). New York, NY: Columbia University Press.

Ch'ng, E. (2011). *IBM visual and spatial technology centre open day*. Retrieved 21 December 2011, from http://www.youtube.com/watch?v=A8yDEMhEkdg

Ch'ng, E. (2007). Modelling the adaptability of biological systems. *The Open Cybernetics and Systemics Journal*, *1*, 13–20.

Ch'ng, E. (2009). An artificial life-based vegetation modelling approach for biodiversity research. In Chiong, R. (Ed.), *Nature-Inspired Informatics for Intelligent Applications and Knowledge Discovery: Implications in Business, Science and Engineering*. Hershey, PA: IGI Global. doi:10.4018/978-1-60566-705-8.ch004

Ch'ng, E. (2011). Spatially realistic positioning of plants for virtual environments: Simple biotic and abiotic interaction for populating terrains. *IEEE Computer Graphics and Applications*, 99.

Cholodenko, A. (Ed.). (1991). *The illusion of life*. Sydney, Australia: Power Publications.

Chomsky, N. (1959). Three models for the description of language in information and control, on certain formal properties of grammars. *I.R.E. Transactions on Information Theory*, 2.

Ciocca, G., Olivo, P., & Schettini, R. (2012). Browsing museum image collections on a multi-touch table. *Information Systems*, *37*(2), 169–182. doi:10.1016/j.is.2011.09.009

City Memphis, S. M. A. R. T. (2006). *Website*. Retrieved from http://smartcitymemphis.blogspot.com/2006/03/who-says-memphis-has-no-creative-class.html

City Memphis, S. M. A. R. T. (2007). *Website*. Retrieved from http://smartcitymemphis.blogspot.com/2007/07/week-in-memphis-branding-city-from.html

Codes of Disobedience and Disfunctionality. *(2012).* Website. *Retrieved from* http://empedia.info/maps/41

Collins, K. (2008). *Game sound: An introduction to the history, theory and practice of video game music and sound design*. Cambridge, MA: The MIT Press.

Colman, F. (2011). *Deleuze and cinema: The film concepts*. Oxford, UK: Berg.

Communitas. (2011). *Dictionary*. Retrieved from http://dictionary.reference.com/browse/communitas

Connoll, H. M. (1985). *Essentials of child psychiatry* (2nd ed.). London, UK: Blackwell Scientific Publications.

Cook, P. (Ed.). (2007). *The cinema book*. London, UK: BFI Publishing.

Coote, J., & Edwards, E. (2006). *Recovering the material and visual cultures of the southern Sudan: A museological resource*. Retrieved June 24, 2012, from http://southern-sudan.prm.ox.ac.uk/index.php

Corby, T. (2008). Landscapes of feeling, arenas of action: Information visualization as art practice. *Leonardo*, *41*(5), 460–467. doi:10.1162/leon.2008.41.5.460

Correia, N., Mota, T., Nóbrega, R., Silva, L., & Almeida, A. (2010). A multi-touch tabletop for robust multimedia interaction in museums. In *Proceedings of the ACM International Conference on Interactive Tabletops and Surfaces*. ACM Press.

Courschesne, L. (1997). *Landscape one: Interactive film installation*. Retrieved from http://courchel.net/

Coyle, R. (Ed.). (2010). *Drawn to sound: Animation, film music and sonicity*. London, UK: Equinox Publishing.

Craft, A. C. T. (2010). *Crystallography - Al Munro*. Retrieved 26 October, 2010, from http://craftact.org.au/crystallography

Cubitt, S. (2005). *The cinema effect*. Cambridge, MA: MIT Press.

Cundy, D. (1981). Marinetti and Italian futurist typography. *Art Journal*, *41*(4), 349–352. doi:10.2307/776445

Curtiss, S. (1992). The sound of early Warner Bros. cartoons. In Altman, R. (Ed.), *Sound Theory Sound Practice* (pp. 191–203). New York, NY: Routledge.

Czarniawska, B., & Mazza, C. (2003). Consulting as a liminal space. *Human Relations*, 56.

Damer, B. (1998). *Avatars! Exploring and building virtual worlds on the internet*. Berkeley, CA: Peachpit Press.

Daston, L., & Galison, P. (2007). *Objectivity*. New York, NY: Zone Books.

Davies, C. (1995). *Osmose: Virtual reality environment*. Retrieved from http://www.immersence.com/osmose/index.php

Davies, C. (1998). *Ephémère: Virtual reality environment*. Retrieved from http://www.immersence.com/

Davies, C. (2001). *Website*. Retrieved May, 2010 from http://www.immersence.com

Davies, C. (2003). Landscape, earth, body, being, space, and time in the immersive virtual environments osmose and ephemere. In J. Malloy (Ed.), *Women, Art, and Technology*. Cambridge, MA: MIT Press. Retrieved from http:///www.immersence.com

Davies, C. (1998). Changing space: Virtual reality as an arena of embodied being. In Beckman, J. (Ed.), *The Virtual Dimension: Architecture, Representation, and Crash Culture* (pp. 144–155). New York, NY: Princeton Architectural Press.

Davies, C. (2001). *Multimedia: from Wagner to virtual reality*. New York, NY: W.W. Norton & Company.

Davis, B. (2010). *Website*. Retrieved from http://www.artnet.com/magazineus/reviews/davis/art-and-social-media8-4-10.asp

De Landa, M. (1999). Deleuze, diagrams, and the open-ended becoming. In Grosz, E. (Ed.), *Becomings; Explorations in Time, Memory and Future*. Ithaca, NY: Cornell University Press.

de Saussure, F. (2011). *Course in general linguistics*. New York, NY: Columbia University Press.

De Wolf, T., & Holvoet, T. (2005). Emergence versus self-organisation: Different concepts but promising when combined. *Lecture Notes in Computer Science*, 3464, 1–15. doi:10.1007/11494676_1

Dekeyser, S., & Watson, R. (2006). *Extending Google docs to collaborate on research papers*. Toowoomba, Australia: The University of Southern Queensland.

Deleuze, G. (1983). Plato and the simulacrum. *October*, 27, 45-56.

Deleuze, G., & Guattari, F. (1983). *On the line*. New York, NY: Semiotext(e).

Deleuze, G. (1999). *Foucault*. New York, NY: The Athlone Press.

Deleuze, G. (2001). *Bergsonism*. New York, NY: Zone Books.

Deleuze, G. (2001). *Difference and repetition*. London, UK: Continuum Books.

Deleuze, G. (2002). *Cinema I*. New York, NY: The Athlone Press.

Deleuze, G., & Guattari, F. (2002). *A thousand plateaus*. London, UK: Continuum.

Deleuze, G., & Tomlinson, H. (1989). *Cinema 2: The time-image*. London, UK: Athlone Press.

Deleuze, G., Tomlinson, H., & Haberjam, B. (1986). *Cinema 1: The movement-image*. London, UK: Athlone Press.

Deloitte. (2008). *The economic case for the visitor economy*. New York, NY: Deloitte.

Deptfordis. (2012). *Website*. Retrieved from http://www.deptfordis.org.uk/

Dietz, P., & Leigh, D. (2001). *DiamondTouch: A multi-user touch technology*. Paper presented at the 14th Annual ACM Symposium on User Interface Software and Technology. Orlando, FL.

Dixon, S. (2007). *Digital performance: A history of new media in theater, dance, performance art, and installation*. Cambridge, MA: MIT Press.

Douglas, M. (2002). *Purity and danger: An analysis of concept [sic] of pollution and taboo*. Oxford, UK: Routledge Classics.

Douglas, M. (2003). *Natural symbols: Explorations in cosmology*. London, UK: Routledge.

Dove, T. (2005). *Spectropia: Interactive feature film.* Retrieved from http://tonidove.com/

Dove, T., & Mackenzie, M. (1993). *Archaeology of the mother tongue: Virtual reality installation.* Alberta, Canada: Banff Centre for the Arts. Retrieved from http://www.banffcentre.ca/bnmi/coproduction/archives/a.asp

Dove, T. (2002). The space between: Telepresence, re-animation and the re-casting of the invisible. In Rieser, M., & Zapp, A. (Eds.), *New Screen Media: Cinema/Art/Narrative.* London, UK: BFI.

Dove, T. (2006). Swimming in time: Performing pro-grammes, mutable movies - Notes on a process in progress. In Hill, L., & Paris, H. (Eds.), *Performance and Place.* Basingstoke, UK: Palgrave Macmillan.

Downs, R. (2005). *Using resistive touch screens for human/machine interface.* Dallas, TX: Texas Instruments Incorporated.

Doyle, D. (2000). *Wandering fictions 2.0: Eleni's journey.* (MA Thesis). Coventry University. Coventry, UK.

Doyle, D. (2008). *Kritical works in SL.* Morrisville, NC: Lulu Publishing.

Doyle, D. (2009). *Kritical works in SL ii. Exhibition Catalogue.* Wolverhampton, UK: CADRE Publications.

Doyle, D., & Kim, T. (2007). Embodied narrative: The virtual nomad and the meta dreamer. *The International Journal of Performance Arts and Digital Media, 3*(2&3), 209–222. doi:10.1386/padm.3.2-3.209_1

Duchamp, M. (1917). The Richard Mutt case. *The Blind Man, 2*(5).

Duchamp, M. (1934). *Green box.* Paris, France: Rrose Sélavy.

Duchamp, M. (1957). The creative act. *ARTnews, 56,* 28–29.

Duchamp, M. (1966). *L'infinitif.* New York, NY: Cordier & Ekstrom.

Durkheim, É. (1984). *The division of labour in society* (Halls, W. D., Trans.). Basingstoke, UK: Palgrave.

Durkheim, É. (1995). *The elementary forms of religious life* (Fields, K. E., Trans.). New York, NY: The Free Press.

Ebron, P. (2006). Contingent stories of anthropology race and feminism. In Lewin, E. (Ed.), *Feminist Anthropology: A Reader.* Oxford, UK: Blackwell Publishing.

Economics, O. (2010). *Economic impact of heritage tourism.* Oxford, UK: Oxford Economics.

Eco, U. (1986). *Travels In hyperreality.* New York, NY: Pan Books Ltd.

Eden, M. (2012). *Website.* Retrieved from http://www.edenceramics.co.uk/diary.html

Eisenstein, S. (Producer and Director). (1947). *Ivan the terrible part one* [Motion picture]. Soviet Union: Mosfilm.

Eisenstein, S., & Marshall, H. (1987). *Nonindifferent nature.* Cambridge, UK: Cambridge University Press.

Eisenstein, S., & Taylor, R. (Eds.). (1996). *Selected works volume one: Writings 1922-1934.* London, UK: BFI Publishing.

Eisenstein, S., Taylor, R., & Glenny, M. (Eds.). (1991). *Selected works volume two: Written circa 1937-1938: Towards a theory of montage.* London, UK: BFI Publishing.

Eisensten, S. (1986). *The film sense.* London, UK: Faber and Faber.

Elkins, J. (2001). Art history as the history of crystallography. In *The Domain of Images* (pp. 13–31). Ithaca, NY: Cornell University Press.

Engelbart, D. (1962). *Augmenting human intellect: A conceptual framework.* Palo Alto, CA: Stanford Research Institute.

English National Opera. (2011). *Mike Figgis on Lucretia Borgia.* Retrieved 28/5/2012 from http://www.englishnationalopera.com

Eseryel, D., Ganesan, R., & Edmonds, G. S. (2002). Review of computer-supported collaborative work systems. *Education Technology & Society, 5*(2).

Ettlinger, O. (2009). *The architecture of virtual space.* Ljubljana, Slovenia: University of Ljubljana.

Etymonline. (2012). *Website.* Retrieved from http://www.etymonline.com/index.php?term=oxford

Feldman, J. (2006). Ruskin's minerals. *Field Notes, 1*(4).

Figgis, M. (Producer and Director). (1980). *Redheugh* [Motion picture]. United Kingdom: Artsadmin.

Figgis, M. (Producer and Director). (1988). *Miss Julie* [Motion picture]. United Kingdom: Metro-Goldwyn Mayer.

Figgis, M. (Producer and Director). (1996). *Leaving Las Vegas* [Motion picture]. France: Lumiere Pictures.

Figgis, M. (Producer and Director). (2000). *Timecode* [Motion picture]. United Kingdom: Screen Gems.

Figgis, M. (Producer and Director). (2002). *Hotel* [Motion picture]. United Kingdom: Moonstone Entertainment.

Figgis, M. (Producer and Director). (2011). *Lucretia borgia* [Motion picture]. United Kingdom: Sosho Productions.

Figgis. (2005). *Wikipaedia*. Retrieved 23/5/2012 from http://Wikipaedia.comMikeFiggis

Figgis, M. (2007). *Digital filmmaking*. London, UK: Macmillan.

Filmbug. (2012). *Website*. Retrieved 2/6/2012 from http://filmbug.com/dictionary/dogme95.php

Fleishman, G. (2011). Book transubstantiation. *The Economist*. Retrieved from http://www.economist.com/blogs/babbage/2011/10/media-digitisation

Flew, T. (2008). *New media: An introduction* (2nd ed.). Oxford, UK: Oxford University Press.

Flyer, M. (2002). *Website*. Retrieved from http://www.memphisflyer.com/memphis/livefrom-memphis/Content?oid=1108714

Flyer, M. (2006). *Website*. Retrieved from http://www.memphisflyer.com/memphis/love-at-first-sight/Content?oid=1125543

Forgan, S. (2000). Festivals of science and the two cultures: Science, design and display in the Festival of Britain, 1951. *British Journal for the History of Science*, *31*(2), 217–240. doi:10.1017/S0007087498003264

Forman, P. (2007). The primacy of science in modernity, of technology in postmodernity, and of ideology in the history of technology. *History and Technology*, *23*(1-2), 1–152. doi:10.1080/07341510601092191

Foucault, M. (2003). *The birth of the clinic: An archaeology of medical perception* (Sheridan, A. M., Trans.). London, UK: Routledge Classics.

Frampton, K. (1980). *Modern architecture: A critical history*. London, UK: Thames and Hudson.

Frodeman, R. (2006). Nanotechnology: The visible and the invisible. *Science as Culture*, *15*(4), 383–389. doi:10.1080/09505430601022700

Gance, A. (Producer and Director). (1927). *Napoleon* [Motion picture]. United States. MGM. de Beauregard, G., Rassam, J.-P. (Producers), & Godard, J. L. (Director). (1975). *Numero deux* [Motion picture]. France: Motion Picture.

Gaut, B. (2007). *A philosophy of cinematic art*. Cambridge, UK: Cambridge University Press.

Genosko, G. (2009). *Felix Guattari: A critical introduction*. London, UK: Pluto Press Ltd.

Geoscience Australia. (2012). *History of Australia's minerals industry*. Retrieved 15 February, 2012, from http://www.australianminesatlas.gov.au/history/index.html

Gibbs, J., & Pye, D. (2005). *Style and meaning: Studies in the detailed analysis of film*. Manchester, UK: Manchester University Press.

Gilbert-Rolfe, J. (1999). *Beauty and the contemporary sublime*. New York, NY: Allworth Press.

Gimzewski, J., & Vesna, V. (2003). The nanoneme syndrome: Blurring of fact and fiction in the construction of a new science. *Technoetic Arts: A Journal of Speculative Research*, *1*(1), 7-24.

GMTM. (2011). *Global multi touch market, by product (smartphones, tablets, laptops, televisions/LCD, tables, floors), applications (entertainment, infotainment, enterprises, others) & geography, 2011-2016*. Dallas, TX: Markets and Markets. Retrieved from http://www.marketsandmarkets.com

Godard, J. L. (Producer and Director). (1960). *A bout de Soufflé* [Motion picture]. France: Les Productions Georges des Bureaugardes.

Godard, J. L. (Producer and Director). (1961). *Une femme est une femme* [Motion picture]. France: Euro International Films.

Godard, J. L. (Producer and Director). (1962). *Vivre sa vie* [Motion picture]. France: Les Films de la Pleiade.

Godard, J. L. (Producer and Director). (1963). *Le Mepris* [Motion picture]. France: Les Films Concordia.

Godard, J. L. (Producer and Director). (1967). *Deux or trois choses que je Sais d'elle* [Motion picture]. France: Argus Films/Nouveaux Pictures.

Godard, J. L. (Producer and Director). (1967). *La Chinoise* [Motion picture]. France: Anouchka films.

Godard, J. L. (Producer and Director). (1967). *Le weekend* [Motion picture]. France: Ascot Cineraid.

Godard, J. L. (Producer and Director). (1969). *British sounds* [Motion picture]. Unreleased.

Godard, J. L. (Producer and Director). (1975). *Numero deux* [Motion picture]. France: Bela Productions.

Godard, J. L., & Gorin, J. P. (Producer and Director). (1972). *Letter to Jane: An investigation of a film still* [Motion picture]. France: Son Image.

Godard, J. L., & Gorin, J. P. (Producers and Directors). (1972). *Tout va bien* [Motion picture]. Italy: Anouchka Films.

Godard, J. L., & Milne, T. (Eds.). (1972). *Godard on Godard*. New York, NY: Da Capo Press.

Goldmark, D. (2002). *The cartoon music book*. Chicago, IL: Chicago Review Press.

Goldmark, D. (2005). *Tunes for toons: Music and the Hollywood cartoon*. Berkeley, CA: UCP. doi:10.1525/california/9780520236172.001.0001

Goodman, N. (1976). *Languages of art: An approach to a theory of symbols*. Indianapolis, IN: Hackett.

Graham, S. (2004). The software-sorted city: Rethinking the digital divide. In Graham, S. (Ed.), *The Cybercities Reader* (pp. 324–331). London, UK: Routledge.

Grau, O. (2003). *Virtual art*. Cambridge, MA: MIT Press.

Grau, O. (2003). *Virtual art: From illusion to immersion*. Cambridge, MA: MIT Press.

Greenberg, C. (1965). Modernist painting. *Art & Literature, 4*.

Greenberg, C. (1971). Counter avant-garde. *Art International, 15*(5), 16–19.

Greenberg, C. (1995). *The collected essays and criticism: Modernism with a vengeance, 1957-69 (Vol. 4)*. Chicago, IL: University of Chicago Press.

Greffe, X. (2004). Is heritage an asset or a liability? *Journal of Cultural Heritage, 5*, 1–309. doi:10.1016/j.culher.2004.05.001

Gregory, R. L., & Wallace, J. (1974). Recovery from early blindness: A case study. In Gregory, R. L. (Ed.), *Concepts and Mechanisms of Perception*. London, UK: Duckworth.

Greimas, A. J., & Courtés, J. (1982). *Semiotics and language: An analytical dictionary*. Bloomington, IN: Indiana University Press.

Grimshaw, M., & Schott, G. (2007). *Situating gaming as a sonic experience: The acoustic ecology of first-person shooters*. Paper presented at Situated Play. Tokyo, Japan.

Gromala, D., & Sharir, Y. (1994). *Dancing with the virtual dervish: Virtual bodies, virtual reality installation*. Alberta, Canada: Banff Centre for the Arts. Retrieved from http://www.banffcentre.ca/bnmi/coproduction/archives/d.asp#dancing

Grosz, E. (1999). *Becomings: Explorations in time, memory and futures*. Ithaca, NY: Cornell University Press.

Grosz, E. (2000). Deleuze's bergson: Duration, the virtual and a politics of the future. In Buchanan, I., & Colebrook, C. (Eds.), *Deleuze and Feminist Theory*. Edinburgh, UK: Edinburgh University Press.

Grosz, E. (2002). *Architecture from the outside: Essays on virtual and real space*. Cambridge, MA: The MIT Press.

Guattari, F. (2000). *The three ecologies*. London, UK: The Athlone Press.

Gwilt, I. (2010). Compumorphic art - The computer as muse. In S. Baker & P. Thomas (Ed.), *The First International Conference on Transdisciplinary Imaging at the Intersections between Art, Science and Culture: New Imaging: Transdisciplinary Strategies for Art beyond the New Media,* (pp. 72-76). Sydney, Australia: Artspace. Retrieved from http://blogs.unsw.edu.au/tiic/

Hahn, R. (2001). *Anaximander and the architects: The contributions of Egyptian and Greek architectural technologies to the origins of Greek philosophy.* Albany, NY: State University of New York Press.

Haidary, N. (2009). *In-formed.* Retrieved April 23, 2011, from http://nadeemhaidary.com/informed.html#Lima, M. (2009). *Information visualization manifesto.* Retrieved April 11, 2011, from http://www.visualcomplexity.com/vc/blog/?p=644

Hansen, M. (2004). *New philosophy for new media.* Cambridge, MA: MIT Press.

Hansen, M. (2006). *Bodies in code: Interfaces with digital media.* New York, NY: Routledge.

Hanson, V. L. (2012). Amidst nanotechnology's molecular landscapes. *Science Communication, 34*(1), 57–83. doi:10.1177/1075547011401630

Hardt, M., & Negri, A. (2000). *Empire.* Cambridge, MA: Harvard University Press.

Harrison, D. (2011). Crossing over: Oscillations between the virtual and the real. In *Proceedings of the Cyberworlds 2011 Conference.* Cyberworlds.

Harrison, D. (1997). Hypermedia as art system. *Art Journal, 56*(3), 55–59. doi:10.2307/777837

Harris, P. (2005). Deleuze, folding architecture. In Buchanan, I., & Lambert, G. (Eds.), *Deleuze and Space.* Edinburgh, UK: Edinburgh University Press.

Hart, M. (1992). *The history and philosophy of Project Gutenberg.* Retrieved from http://www.gutenberg.org/wiki/Gutenberg:The_History_and_Philosophy_of_Project_Gutenberg_by_Michael_Hart

Heim, M. (1993). *The metaphysics of virtual reality.* Oxford, UK: Oxford University Press.

Herzogenrath, B. (2009). *Deleuze/Guattari & ecology.* Basingstoke, UK: Palgrave Macmillan.

Heudin, J. C. (Ed.). (1999). *Virtual worlds: Synthetic universes, digital life and complexity.* Reading, MA: Perseus Books.

Hillis, K. (1999). *Digital sensations: Space, identity, and embodiment in virtual reality.* Minneapolis, MN: University of Minnesota Press.

Hodges, S., Izadi, S., Butler, A., Rrustemi, A., & Buxton, B. (2007). ThinSight: Versatile multi-touch sensing for thin form-factor displays. In *Proceedings of the 20th Annual ACM Symposium on User Interface Software and Technology.* ACM Press.

Hooper-Greenhill, E. (Ed.). (1999). *The educational role of the museum.* London, UK: Routledge.

Hornecker, E. (2008). I don't understand it either, but it is cool: Visitor Interactions with a multi-touch table in a museum. In *Proceedings of IEEE Tabletop.* IEEE Press.

Howes, D. (2003). *Sensual relations: Engaging the senses in culture and social theory.* Ann Arbor, MI: University of Michigan Press.

Icewaterpictures. (2008). *Mike Figgis.* Retrieved 1/6/2012 from http://www.youtube.com

Ihde, D. (2002). *Bodies in technology.* Minneapolis, MN: University of Minnesota Press.

InnovationNow. (2011). *Multitouch market research.* Kuala Lumpur, Malaysia: Innovation Now Sdn Bhd.

Inside Out. (2012). Website. *Retrieved from* http://inside-out.digitalalchemist.com.au/artists/

Inside Out. (2012). Website. *Retrieved from* http://www.insideoutexhibition.com/

Jackson, P. (Producer and Director). (2001). *The fellowship of the* ring [Motion picture]. New Zealand: Entertainment Film Distribution.

Jackson, P. (Producer and Director). (2002). *The two towers* [Motion picture]. New Zealand: Entertainment Film Distribution.

Jackson, P. (Producer and Director). (2003). *The return of the king* [Motion picture]. New Zealand: Entertainment Film Distribution.

Jackson, P. (Producer and Director). (2005). *King kong* [Motion picture]. New Zealand: Universal Pictures.

Jackson, L. (2008). *From atoms to patterns: Crystal structure designs fromthe 1951 Festival of Britain.* Shepton Beauchamp, UK: Richard Dennis and Wellcome Collection.

Jameson, F. (1999). *Brecht and method.* New York, NY: Verso.

James, W. (1997). The names of fear: Memory, history, and the ethnography of feeling among Uduk refugees. *The Journal of the Royal Anthropological Institute, 3,* 115–131. doi:10.2307/3034368

James, W. (1999). *The listening ebony: Moral knowledge, religion and power among the Uduk of Sudan.* Oxford, UK: Oxford University Press.

James, W. (2007). *War and survival in Sudan's frontierlands: Voices from the Blue Nile.* Oxford, UK: Oxford University Press.

Jensen, J. L. (2010). Augmentation of space: Four dimensions of spatial experiences of Google Earth. *Space and Culture, 13*(1), 121–133. doi:10.1177/1206331209353693

Jokilehto, J. (2005). *Definition of cultural heritage: References to documents in history.* ICCROM Working Group 'Heritage and Society'.

Jones, D. E. (2006). I, avatar: Constructions of self and place in second life and the technological imagination. *Gnovis, Journal of Communication, Culture and Technology.* Retrieved from http://gnovis.georgetown.edu

Jones, A. (1994). *Postmodernism and the engendering of Marcel Duchamp.* Cambridge, UK: Cambridge University Press.

Jung, C. G. (1962). *Symbols of transformation: An analysis of the prelude to a case of schizophrenia (Vol. 2).* (Hull, R. F. C., Trans.). New York, NY: Harper & Brothers.

Kehr, D. (2011). *When movies mattered: Reviews from a transformative decade.* Chicago, IL: University of Chicago Press.

Kinder, M. (2002). Hot spots, avatars, and narrative fields forever: Buñuel's legacy for new digital media and interactive database narrative. *Film Quarterly, 55*(4). doi:10.1525/fq.2002.55.4.2

Kitchin, R. M. (1998). Towards geographies of cyberspace. *Progress in Human Geography, 22*(3), 385–406. doi:10.1191/030913298668331585

Klanten, R., Ehmann, S., Tissot, T., & Bourquin, N. (Eds.). (2010). *Data flow 2: Visualizing information in graphic design.* Berlin, Germany: Gestalten.

Klein, N. M. (1996). *Seven minutes: The life and death of the American animated cartoon.* London, UK: Verso.

Klotz, H. (1997). *Contemporary art: The collection of the ZKM/center for art and media, Karlsruhe.* New York, NY: Prestel.

Knuuttila, T., & Voutilainen, A. (2003). A parser as an epistemic artifact: A material view on models. *Philosophy of Science, 70*(5), 1484. doi:10.1086/377424

Kozel, S. (1994). *Spacemaking: Experiences of a virtual body.* Retrieved from http://art.net/~dtz/kozel.html

Kozel, S. (2006). Virtual/virtuality. *Performance Research, 11*(3), 136–139.

Kozin, A. (2009). The appearing memory: Gilles Deleuze and Andrey Tarkovsky on `crystal-image'. *Memory Studies, 2*(1), 103–117. doi:10.1177/1750698008097398

Krauss, R. (2002). *The originality of the avant-garde and other modernist myths.* Cambridge, MA: MIT Press.

Kwon, M. (1997). Notes on site specificity. *October, 80.*

Lacan, J. (2007). *Ecrits: The first complete edition in English.* London, UK: W. W. Norton.

Lakoff, G., & Johnson, M. (1980). *Metaphors we live by.* Chicago, IL: University of Chicago Press.

Latour, B. (2008). *What is the style of matters of concern? Two lectures in empirical philosophy.* Dordrecht, The Netherlands: Uitgeverij Van Gorcum.

Latour, B., & Weibel, P. (2002). *Iconoclash: Beyond the image wars in science, religion and art.* Cambridge, MA: MIT Press.

Laurel, B., & Strickland, R. (1993). *Placeholder: Virtual reality installation*. Alberta, Canada: Banff Centre for the Arts. Retrieved from http://www.banffcentre.ca/bnmi/coproduction/archives/p.asp#placeholder

Laurel, B. (1990). *The art of human-computer interface design*. Reading, MA: AddisonWesley.

Lefebvre, H. (1991). *The production of space*. Oxford, UK: Blackwell Publishing.

Lem, S., Kilmartin, J., & Cox, S. (1970). *Solaris*. New York, NY: Harcourt Brace Jovanovich.

Levi-Strauss, C. (1968). The structural study of myth. In Levi-Strauss, C. (Ed.), *Structural Anthropology*. London, UK: Penguin Press.

Levy, P. (1992). *Le tecnologie dell'intelligenza*. Milano, Italy: Ed. Traverso.

Levy, P. (1998). *Becoming virtual: Reality in the digital age*. New York, NY: Plenum Trade.

Lichty, P. (2009). The translation of art in virtual worlds. *Leonardo Electronic Almanac, 18*(12). Retrieved from http://www.leonardo.info/LEA/DispersiveAnatomies/DA_lichty.pdf

Lindstrand, T. (2007). Viva pinata: Architecture of the everyday. In Borries, V. F., Bottger, M., & Walz, S. P. (Eds.), *Space Time Play: Computer Games, Architecture and Urbanism - The Next Level*. Basel, Switzerland: Birkhauser Verlag AG.

Lippard, L. (1997). *Six Years: The dematerialization of the art object from 1966 to 1972: A cross-reference book of information on some esthetic boundaries: consisting of a bibliography into which are inserted a fragmented text, art works, documents, interviews, and symposia, arranged chronologically and focused on so-called conceptual or information or idea art with mentions of a such vaguely designated areas as minimal, anti-form, systems, earth, or process art, occurring now in the Americas, Europe, England, Australia, and Asia (with occasional political overtones)*. Berkeley, CA: University of California Press.

Lister, M. (2003). *New media: A critical introduction*. London, UK: Routledge.

Lupton, E. (1994). A post-mortem on deconstruction? *AIGA Journal of Graphic Design, 12*(2), 45–47.

Luu, R., Mitchell, D., & Blyth, J. (2004). *Thrombolites (stromatolite-like microbialite) community of a coastal brackish lake (Lake Clifton)*. Wannero, Australia: Western Australian Threatened Species and Communities Unit (WATSCU).

Lynn, G. (1998). *Folds, bodies and blobs*. New York, NY: Books-by-Architects.

Lyotard, J. (1991). *The inhuman: Reflections on time*. Palo Alto, CA: Stanford University Press.

Mac Cabe, C. (1980). *Godard: Images, sounds, politics*. London, UK: BFI Publishing.

Mac Cabe, C. (2003). *Godard: A portrait of the artist at seventy*. London, UK: Bloomsbury Press.

MacDougall, D. (2008). *The corporeai image: Film, ethnography and the senses*. Princeton, NJ: Princeton University Press.

Madge, C., & O'Connor, H. (2005). Mothers in the making? Exploring liminality in cyber/space. *Transactions of the Institute of British Geographers, 30*(1), 83-97. Retrieved 10/05/2011 from http://www.jstor.org/stable/3804531

Maguire, S. (2009). Mobility, cosmopolitanism and public space. In McQuire, S., Martin, M., & Niederer, S. (Eds.), *Urban Screens Reader* (pp. 45–64). Amsterdam, The Netherlands: Institute of Network Cultures.

Mann, S., Nolan, J., & Wellman, B. (2003). Sousveillance: Inventing and using wearable computing devices for data collection in surveillance environments. *Surveillance & Society, 1*(3), 331–355.

Manovich, L. (2012). *On totalitarian interactivity*. Retrieved 2/6/2012 from manovich.net/TEXT/totalitarian.html

Manovich, L. (2001). *The language of new media*. Cambridge, MA: MIT Press.

Manovich, L., & Kratky, A. (2005). *Soft cinema: Navigating the database*. Cambridge, MA: The MIT Press.

Marinetti, F. T. (1913). *Destruction of syntax—Imagination without strings—Words-in-freedom*. Retrieved from http://www.unknown.nu/futurism/destruction.html

Martin Reiser. (2012). Wikipedia. *Retrieved from* http://en.wikipedia.org/wiki/Martin_Rieser

Maslow, A. (1954). *Motivation and personality*. New York, NY: Harper.

Massey, D. (2003). Some times of space. In May, S. (Ed.), *Olafur Eliasson: The Weather Report*. London, UK: Tate Publishing.

Massumi, B. (2002). *Parables for the virtual*. Durham, NC: Duke University Press.

Matthews, P., & Aston, J. (forthcoming). Interactive multimedia ethnography: Archiving, workflow, interface aesthetics and metadata. [forthcoming]. *ACM Journal for Computing and Cultural Heritage*.

McEwen, I. K. (1993). *Socrates' ancestor: An essay on architectural beginnings*. Cambridge, MA: MIT Press.

McLuhan, M., & Fiore, Q. (1967). *The medium is the message: An inventory of effects*. New York, NY: Bantam Books.

Meadows, M. S. (2008). *I, avatar: The culture and consequences of having a second life*. Berkeley, CA: New Riders.

Melville, S. (2001). *As painting: Division and displacement*. Cambridge, MA: MIT Press.

Merleau Ponty, M. (1969). *The visible and the invisible*. Evanston, IL: North Western University Press.

Meyer, J., & Bochner, M. (2001). How can you defend making paintings now? In *As Painting: Division and Displacement*. Cambridge, MA: MIT Press.

Miller, D. (2010). *Stuff*. Cambridge, UK: Polity.

Moffat, I. (2000). A horror of abstract thought: Postwar Britain and Hamilton's 1951 "growth and form" exhibition. *October, 94*, 89-112.

Moles, A. (1990). *Art et ordinateur*. Paris, France: Blusson.

Moos, D. (1996). Architecture of the mind: Machine intelligence and abstract painting. In Moos, D. (Ed.), *Painting in the Age of Artificial Intelligence*. London, UK: Academy Editions.

Morie, J. (2007). Performing in (virtual) spaces: Embodiment and being in virtual environments. *International Journal of Performance Arts and Digital Media, 3*(2&3), 123–138. doi:10.1386/padm.3.2-3.123_1

Morrey, D. (2010). *Jean Luc Godard*. Manchester, UK: Manchester University Press.

Moser, M. A. (Ed.). (1996). *Immersed in technology: Art and virtual environments*. Cambridge, MA: MIT Press. doi:10.2307/1576254

MSR. (2011). *Tablet demand and disruption: Mobile users come of age*. New York, NY: Morgan Stanley Research Global.

Mulder, A. (2004). *Understanding media theory*. Dordrecht, The Netherlands: V2 Publishing.

Mura, G. (2008). The metaplastic constructor. In *CAC 2 Computer Art*. Paris, France: Ed. Europia.

Mura, G. (2010). *Metaplasticity in virtual worlds: Aesthetics and semantic concepts*. Hershey, PA: IGI Global. doi:10.4018/978-1-60960-077-8

Mura, G. (2011). Multiplasticity of new media. In Ghinea, G., Ghinea, S. R., Gulliver, S. R., & Andres, F. (Eds.), *Multiple Sensorial Media Advances and Applications: New Development in MulSe-Media*. Hershey, PA: IGI Global. doi:10.4018/978-1-60960-821-7.ch013

Myers, N. (2008). Molecular embodiments and the body-work of modeling in protein crystallography. *Social Studies of Science, 38*(2), 163–199. doi:10.1177/0306312707082969

Nelson, T. (1987). *Computer lib/dream machines* (revised ed.). Redmond, WA: Tempus Books.

NHM. (2011). *New horned dinosaur hidden for 90 years in museum*. Retrieved 21 December, 2011, from http://www.nhm.ac.uk/about-us/news/2011/december/new-horneddinosaur-hidden-for-90-years-in-museum106428.html

Nilson, C. (2007). Live coding practice. In *Proceedings of NIME 2007*. NIME.

Nobel Media. (2012). *The Nobel Prize in Physics 1915*. Retrieved 20 February, 2012, from http://www.nobelprize.org/nobel_prizes/physics/laureates/1915/wh-bragg.html

Noorani, R. (2006). *Rapid prototyping principles and applications*. Hoboken, NJ: John Wiley and Sons.

North, C., Dwyer, T., Lee, B., Fisher, D., Isenberg, P., & Robertson, G. (2009). Understanding multi-touch manipulation for surface computing human-computer interaction – INTERACT 2009. *Lecture Notes in Computer Science, 5727*, 236–249. doi:10.1007/978-3-642-03658-3_31

Ocular. (2008). *Projected capacitive technology enhances clarity, durability and performance of touch screens*. Dallas, TX: Ocular.

Packer, R., & Jordan, K. (Eds.). *Multimedia: From Wagner to virtual reality*. New York, NY: W.W. Norton & Company. Retrieved from http:///www.immersence.com

Pallasmaa, J. (2005). *The eyes of the skin: Architecture and the senses*. Chichester, UK: John Wiley & Sons.

Patton, P. (1997). *Deleuze: A critical reader*. Oxford, UK: Blackwell Publishers Ltd.

Pauwels, L. (2008). An integrated model for conceptualising visual competence in scientific research and communication. *Visual Studies, 23*(2), 147–161. doi:10.1080/14725860802276305

Peltonen, P., Kurvinen, E., Salovaara, A., Jacucci, G., Ilmonen, T., Evans, J., et al. (2008). It's mine, don't touch! Interactions at a large multi-touch display in a city centre. In *Proceedings of the Twenty-Sixth Annual SIGCHI Conference on Human Factors in Computing Systems*. ACM Press.

Phillips, P. (2012). *The sixth shore details*. Retrieved 28 January 2012, now available at http://www.perditaphillips. com/portfolio/the-sixth-shore-2009-2012/

Phillips, P. (2009). Clotted life and brittle waters. *Landscapes, 3*(2), 1–20.

Pink, S., Hubbard, P., O'Neill, M., & Radley, A. (2010). Walking across disciplines: from ethnography to arts practice. *Visual Studies, 25*(1), 1–7. doi:10.1080/14725861003606670

Platea. (2011). *Website*. Retrieved from http://plateastweets.blogspot.com/

Plato. (360BCE). *The republic: Book X.*

Pollack, B. (2011, June 1). The social revolution. *ARTnews*. Retrieved: 30/11/2011 from http://www.artnews. com/2011/06/01/the-social-revolution/

Pred, A. (1984). Place as historically contingent process: Structuration and the time-geography of 'becoming' places. *Annals of the Association of American Geographers, 74*(2), 279-297. Retrieved 10/05/2011 from http:// www.jstor.org/stable/2569284

Quarrier, I. (Producer), & Godard, J. L. (Director). (1968). *One plus one is one* [Motion picture]. United Kingdom: Pro Cupid Productions.

Rajchman, J. (2000). *Constructions*. Cambridge, MA: Massachusetts Institute of Technology.

Rajchman, J. (2001). *The Deleuze connections*. Cambridge, MA: Massachusetts Institute of Technology.

Reiser, M. (2012). Website. Retrieved from http://www. martinrieser.com

Rekimoto, J. (2002). Smartskin: An infrastructure for freehand manipulation on interactive surfaces. In *Proceedings of the SIGCHI Conference on Human Factors in Computing Systems*. ACM Press.

Reynolds, A. (2002). *Mount fear: Statistics for crimes with offensive weapon South London 2001-2002*. Retrieved April 20, 2011, from http://www.abigailreynolds.com/ mntF/mntFSth.html

Reynolds, C. (1987). Flocks, herds, and schools: A distributed behavioral model. In *Proceedings of the Computer Graphics, SIGGRAPH 1987 Conference*. ACM Press.

Rheingold, H. (1991). *Virtual reality*. New York, NY: Summit Books.

Riggins, S. (Ed.). (1994). *The socialness of things: Essays on the socio-semiotics of objects*. Berlin, Germany: Mouton de Gruyter. doi:10.1515/9783110882469

Rodowick, D. N. (2007). *The virtual life of film*. Boston, MA: Harvard University Press.

Rost, M. (2001). *Teaching and researching listening*. London, UK: Pearson Education.

Ruskin at Walkley. (2012). *Reconstructing the St George's Museum*. Retrieved 4 February, 2012, from http://www.ruskinatwalkley.org/index.php?hotspots=off

Russett, R., & Starr, C. (1976). *Experimental animation: An illustrated anthology*. New York, NY: Van Nostrand.

Ryall, K., Morris, M. R., Everitt, K., Forlines, C., & Shen, C. (2006). Experiences with and observations of direct-touch tabletops. In *Proceedings of the First IEEE International Workshop on Horizontal Interactive Human-Computer Systems, TABLETOP 2006*. IEEE Press.

Ryu, B. H. (2010). Your mobile is tomorrow museum. In *Exhibition Catalog of Incheon International Digital Art Festival 2010* (pp. 29, 31, 38–39). Korea: Nabi Press.

Sassen, S. (2009). Reading the city in a global digital age. In McQuire, S., Martin, M., & Niederer, S. (Eds.), *Urban Screens Reader* (pp. 29–44). Amsterdam, The Netherlands: Institute of Network Cultures. doi:10.1016/j.sbspro.2010.05.057

Schafer, R. M. (1994). *The soundscape: Our sonic environment and the tuning of the world*. Rochester, VT: Destiny Books.

Schöning, J., Brandl, P., Daiber, F., Echtler, F., Hilliges, O., & Hook, J. (2007). *Multi touch surfaces: A technical guide*. Münster, Germany: University of Münster.

Schöning, J., Hook, J., Bartindale, J., Schmidt, D., Olivier, P., & Echtler, F. (2010). Building interactive multi-touch surfaces. In Muller-Tomfelde, C. (Ed.), *Tabletops - Horizontal interactive displays* (pp. 27–49). Münster, Germany: University of Münster. doi:10.1007/978-1-84996-113-4_2

Schroeder, R. (Ed.). (2002). *The social life of avatars: Presence and interaction in shared virtual environments*. London, UK: Springer.

Selin, C. (2007). Expectations and the emergence of nanotechnology. *Science, Technology & Human Values*, *32*(2), 196–220. doi:10.1177/0162243906296918

Sennett, R. (2002). *The fall of public man: On the social psychology of capitalism*. London, UK: Penguin Books.

Seow, S. C., Wixon, D., Mackenzie, S., Jacucci, G., Morrison, A., & Wilson, A. (2009). Multitouch and surface computing. In *Proceedings of the 27th International Conference Extended Abstracts on Human Factors in Computing Systems*. ACM Press.

Sermon, P. (1992). *Telematic dreaming: Performance installation*. Retrieved from http://creativetechnology.salford.ac.uk/paulsermon/dream/

Sermon, P. (2005). *Unheimlich: Multi-user performance installation*. Retrieved from http://creativetechnology.salford.ac.uk/unheimlich/

Sermon, P., & Gould, C. (2009). *Picnic on the screen: Interactive public video installation*. Retrieved from http://creativetechnology.salford.ac.uk/paulsermon/picnic/

Shannon, C. (1948). A mathematical theory of communication. *The Bell System Technical Journal*, *27*, 379–423.

Sherry, J. F., Jr. (2000). Place, technology, and representation. *The Journal of Consumer Research*, *27*(2), 273-278. Retrieved 10/12/2009 from http://www.jstor.org/stable/254317

Ship of Fools. (2012). Website. *Retrieved from* http://www.shipoffools.pwp.blueyonder.co.uk/artists/martin_home.htm

Shove, E., Watson, M., Hand, M., & Ingram, J. (2007). *The design of everyday life*. Oxford, UK: Berg.

Sider, L., Sider, J., & Freeman, D. (2003). *Soundscape: The school of sound lectures 1998-2001*. New York, NY: Wallflower Press.

Smith, C., & Rieser, M. (2010). *Inside out rapid prototype exhibition*. Retrieved April 20, 2011, from http://www.insideoutexhibition.com/

Sobchack, V. (1992). *The address of the eye: A phenomenology of film experience*. Princeton, NJ: Princeton University Press.

Soja, E. W. (1996). *Thirdspace: Journeys to Los Angeles and other real-and-imagined places*. Malden, MA: Blackwell Publishers. doi:10.1177/030981689806400112

Songlines. (2012). Website. *Retrieved from*http://www.hollandalexander.com/?attachment_id=615

Sorensen, A., & Brown, A. (2007). AA-cell in practice: An approach to musical live coding. In *Proceedings of ICMC 2007*. ICMC.

South West Catchments Council & Department of Environment and Conservation. (2011). *Glimses into disappearing landscapes*. Wannero, Australia: South West Catchments Council & Department of Environment and Conservation.

Southern, J., & Hamilton, J. (2003, October). Unfeasible symmetry. *Artists Newsletter Magazine*. Retrieved from http://www.theportable.tv/dmg/index.html

Sovereign Hill. (2012). *Google Earth - 3D model of Sovereign Hill*. Retrieved 18 February, 2012, from http://www.sovereignhill.com.au/sovereign-hill/

Sreedharan, S., Zurita, E. S., & Plimmer, B. (2007). 3D input for 3D worlds. In *Proceedings of the 19th Australasian Conference on Computer-Human Interaction: Entertaining User Interfaces*, (pp. 227–230). New York, NY: ACM Press.

Stail, R. (2007). *British film directors: A critical guide*. Carbondale, IL: Southern Illinois University Press.

Starshed. (2012). Website. *Retrieved from*http://www.electricpavilion.com/starshed.html

Steeves, J. B. (2007). *Imagining bodies: Merleau-Ponty's philosophy of imagination*. Pittsburgh, PA: Duquesne University Press.

Stephenson, N. (2000). *Snow crash*. New York, NY: Spectra.

Sterling, B. (2007). *Ascendancies: The best of Bruce Sterling*. Burton, MI: Subterranean Press.

Stockburger, A. (2007). Playing the third place: Spatial modalities in contemporary game environments. *International Journal of Performance Arts and Digital Media*, *3*(2&3), 223–236. doi:10.1386/padm.3.2-3.223_1

Stone, A. R. (1994). Will the real body please stand up? Boundary stories about virtual cultures. In Benedickt, M. (Ed.), *Cyberspace: First Steps* (pp. 81–118). Cambridge, MA: MIT Press.

Struppek, M. (2006). Urban screens - The urbane potential of public screens for interaction. *Intelligent Agent, 6*(2).

Sullivan, G. (2005). *Art practice as research, inquiry in the visual arts*. London, UK: Sage Publications Ltd.

Thomas, P. (2007). *Boundaryless nanomorphologies*. Paper presented at the MutaMorphosis: Challenging Art and Sciences. Prague, Czech Republic.

Thomas, P. (2009). Midas: A nanotechnological exploration of touch. *Leonardo, 42*(3), 186–192. doi:10.1162/leon.2009.42.3.186

Thürlemann, F. (1982). *Paul Klee: Analyse sémiotique de trois peintures*. Lausanne, France: L'Age d'Homme.

Tikka, P. (2008). *Enactive cinema—Simulatorium eisensteinense*. Helsinki, Finland: University of Art and Design Helsinki.

Tomkins, C. (1980). *Off the wall: Robert Rauschenberg and the art world of our times*. Harmondsworth, UK: Penguin.

Tönnies, F., & Harris, J. (Eds.). (2001). *Community and civil society*Harris, J., & Hollis, M., Trans.). Cambridge, UK: Cambridge University Press. doi:10.1017/CBO9780511816260

Tribe, M., & Reena, J. (2003). *New media art*. New York, NY: Taschen.

Trigg, R. (1983). *A network-based approach to text handling for the online scientific community*. College Park, MD: University of Maryland.

Trowbridge, C. (2006). Speakers concerning the Earth: Ruskin's geology after 1860. In Clifford, D., Wadge, E., Warwick, A., & Willis, M. (Eds.), *Repositioning Victorian Sciences: Shifting Centres in Nineteenth-Century Thinking* (pp. 17–30). New York, NY: Anthem Press. doi:10.7135/UPO9781843317517.002

Truffaut, F. (Producer and Director). (1959). *The 400 blows aka les quatre cent coups* [Motion picture]. France: Les Films du Carrosse.

Tufte, E. (1993). *The visual display of quantitative information*. Cheshire, CT: Graphics Press.

Tufte, E. (1997). *Visual explanations: Images and quantities, evidence and narrative.* Cheshire, CT: Graphics Press. doi:10.1063/1.168637

Turkle, S. (1995). *Life on the screen: Identity in the age of the internet.* New York, NY: Simon Schuster.

Turner, V. (1974). Liminal to liminoid in play, flow, and ritual: An essay in comparative symbology. *Rice University Studies, 60*(3), 53-92. Retrieved 10/05/2011 from http://www.jstor.org/stable/2713299

Turner, V. (1967). *The forest of symbols: Aspects of Ndembu ritual.* Ithaca, NY: Cornell University Press.

Turner, V. (1969). *The ritual process: Structure and anti-structure.* Berlin, Germany: Walter De Gruyter Inc.

Tuters, M., & Varnelis, K. (2006). Beyond locative media. *Leonardo, 39*(4), 357–363. doi:10.1162/leon.2006.39.4.357

Tversky, B., Kim, J., & Cohen, A. (1999). *Mental models of spatial relations and transformations from language.* Palo Alto, CA: Stanford University/Indiana University. doi:10.1016/S0166-4115(99)80055-7

Tylor, E. B. (1871). *Primitive culture: Researches into the development of mythology, philosophy, religion, art, and custom.* London, UK: John Murray. doi:10.1037/13484-000

Van Gennep, A. (1961). *The rites of passage.* Chicago, IL: Chicago University Press.

Veiteberg, J. (2005). *Craft in transition.* Bergen, Norway: National Academy of the Arts.

Vertov, D. (Producer and Director). (1929). *Man with a movie camera* [Motion picture]. Soviet Union: VKUFU.

Vertov, D., Michelson, A., & O'Brien, K. (Eds.). (1984). *The writings of Dziga Vertov.* London, UK: Pluto Press.

Vesna, V. (2012). *Zero@wavefunction.* Retrieved from http://notime.arts.ucla.edu/zerowave/zerowave.html

Vesna, V. (2012). *Nanomandala.* Retrieved 20 February, 2012, from http://nano.arts.ucla.edu/mandala/mandala.php

Virilio, P. (1989). *War and cinema: The logistics of perception* (Miller, P., Trans.). London, UK: Verso.

Virilo, P. (1997). The third interval. In Graham, S. (Ed.), *Cibercities Reader* (pp. 78–81). Oxford, UK: Routledge.

Von Trier, L. (Producer and Director). (2003). *Dogville* [Motion picture]. Denmark: Lions Gate Films.

Waldburger, R. (Producer), & Godard, J. L. (Director). (2010). *Film socialism* [Motion picture]. United States: Vega Films.

Walker Bynum, C. (2001). *Metamorphosis and identity.* New York, NY: Zone Books.

Walmsley, D. (2000). Community, place, cyberspace. *The Australian Geographer, 31*(1), 5–19. doi:10.1080/00049180093501

Ware, C. (2004). *Information visualization: Perception for design.* San Francisco, CA: Morgan Kaufmann.

Waskul, D. (2005). Ekstasis and the internet: Liminality and computer-mediated communication. *New Media & Society, 7*(1), 48–63. doi:10.1177/1461444805049144

Waskul, D. D. (2004). *Net.seXXX: Readings on sex pornography and the internet.* New York, NY: Peter Lang Publishing.

Weber, D. (1995). From limen to border: A meditation on the legacy of Victor Turner for American cultural studies. *American Quarterly, 47*(3), 525-536. Retrieved 10/05/2011 from http://www.jstor.org/stable/2713299

Webster, J., & Gibbons, B. (Eds.). (2001). *The duchess of malfi.* London, UK: AC&Black.

Weiss, E., & Belton, J. (1985). *Film sound theory and practice.* New York, NY: Columbia University Press.

Wells, P. (1998). *Understanding animation.* London, UK: Routledge.

Wheeler-Dixon, W. (1997). *The films of Jean Luc Godard.* Albany, NY: State University of New York Press.

Whitelaw, M. (2010). *Measuring cup (Sydney, 1859-2009).* Retrieved April 20, 2011, from http://www.insideoutexhibition.com/

Whitney, L. (2010). Nearly 1 in 10 using e-readers, poll says. *TeleRead.com.* Retrieved from http://www.teleread.com/ebooks/survey-shows-nearly-1-in-10-using-e-readers-and-e-readerusers-buy-more-books/

Wiener, N. (1988). *The human use of human beings: Cybernetics and society*. Cambridge, MA: Da Capo Press.

Wigdor, D., Fletcher, J., & Morrison, G. (2009). Designing user interfaces for multi-touch and gesture devices. In *Proceedings of the 27th International Conference Extended Abstracts on Human Factors in Computing Systems*. New York, NY: ACM Press.

Willis, H. (2005). *New digital cinema: Reinventing the moving image*. New York, NY: Wallflower Press.

Willocquet-Maricondi, P., & Alemony-Galway, M. (2008). *Peter Greenaway's postmodern/poststructuralist cinema*. Blue Ridge Mountain, PA: Scarecrow Press.

Wlatl, M., Timmerer, C., & Hellwagner, H. (2010). Increasing the user experience of multimedia presentations with sensory effects. In *Proceedings of the Quality of Multimedia Experience (QoMEX), Second International Workshop*, (pp. 124-129). IEEE Press.

Wobbrock, J. O., Morris, M. R., & Wilson, A. D. (2009). User-defined gestures for surface computing. In *Proceedings of the 27th International Conference on Human Factors in Computing Systems*. ACM Press.

Woolley, B. (1992). *Virtual worlds*. Oxford, UK: Blackwell.

Wright, I. (2005). 'Place-making' as applied integral ecology: Evolving an ecologically wise planning ethic. *World Futures*, *61*, 127–137. doi:10.1080/02604020590902407

Xiao, A. (2010). *Always social: Getting noticed (2008-2010), part two*. Retrieved from http://hyperallergic.com/6700/social-media-art-pt-2/

Yarow, J., & Goldman, L. (2011). How people really use their iPad: Our exclusive survey results. *Business Insider*. Retrieved from http://www.businessinsider.com/how-people-really-use-the-ipad-our-exclusive-survey-results2011-5

Yue, A. (2009). Urban screens, spatial regeneration and cultural citizenship. In McQuire, S., Martin, M., & Niederer, S. (Eds.), *Urban Screens Reader* (pp. 261–275). Amsterdam, The Netherlands: Institute of Network Cultures.

Zadeh, L. (1969). *Biological application of the theory of fuzzy sets and systems in the proceedings of an international symposium on BioCybernetics of the central nervous system*. Boston, MA: Little Brown.

Zapp, A. (2002). *The imaginary hotel: Networked installation*. Retrieved from http://www.azapp.de/ha_01.html

Zapp, A. (2005). *Human avatars: Interactive installation*. Retrieved from http://www.storyrooms.net

Zellweger, C. (2007). *Journal of modern craft review*. Retrieved April 20, 2011, from http://www.christoph-zellweger.com/about/

Zielinski, S. (1996). Thinking the border and the boundary. In Druckrey, T. (Ed.), *Electronic Culture: Technology and Visual Representation*. New York, NY: Aperture Foundation.

Zizek, S. (2004). *The true Hollywood left*. Retrieved 25/5/12 from http://www.lacan.com/zizhollywood.htm

Zizek, S. (2004). *Organs without bodies: Deleuze and consequences*. London, UK: Routledge.

About the Contributors

Dew Harrison is a Professor of Digital Media Art and works as the Associate Dean for Research and Postgraduate Study at the University of Wolverhampton, School of Art and Design, where she is also the Director of CADRE, Centre for Art, Design, Research, and Experimentation. She is a researcher and practitioner with a BA in Fine Art, an MA in Contemporary Art Theory, an MSc in Computer Science, and a PhD from the Planetary Collegium, CAiiA, in Interactive Art. Her practice undertakes a critical exploration of conceptual art, semantic media, and intuitive interfaces where she often works collaboratively and considers virtual curation a form of art practice. She continues to show her work internationally; most recently, two of her Digital Action Painting series were exhibited at the Centre for Contemporary Art in Poland, and has over 50 publications to date spanning digital art, consciousness studies, interactive games, art history, and museology.

* * *

Rina Arya is the Reader in Visual Communication at the University of Wolverhampton. Her research interests are interdisciplinary and include art theory and cultural studies. Her most recent monograph is *Francis Bacon: Painting in a Godless World* (Farnham, 2012). Forthcoming publications include *Chila Kumari Burman: A Celebration of Shakti* (KT Press) and *Abjection and Representation* (Palgrave Macmillan).

Judith Aston was a pioneer in the emergent multimedia industry of the mid-1980s, working on projects with Apple Computing, the BBC Interactive Television Unit, and Virgin Publishing. Holding an MA in Social Science from the University of Cambridge, she went on to study for a PhD in Visual Anthropology and Computer-Related Design at the Royal College of Art, which she completed in 2003. She now lectures at the University of the West of England, developing and leading her specialism in multiplatform documentary production and digitally expanded filmmaking. As co-founder of the i-Docs symposia (i-docs.org), her ongoing research interests are focused around developing innovative means through which to create polyphonic narratives and encourage intercultural dialogue.

Elif Ayiter is a designer and researcher specializing in the development of hybrid educational methodologies between art and design and computer science, teaching full time at Sabanci University, Istanbul, Turkey. She has published in journals such as JCS and *Technoetic Arts* and has presented creative as well as research output at conferences including Siggraph, Consciousness Reframed, Creativity and Cognition, ISEA, ICALT, Computational Aesthetics (Eurographics), and Cyberworlds. She is also the chief editor of the forthcoming journal *Metaverse Creativity* with Intellect Journals, UK, and is currently studying for a doctoral degree at the Planetary Collegium, CAiiA hub, at the University of Plymouth, with Roy Ascott.

Eugene Ch'ng is Senior Lecturer at the University of Birmingham. He is Innovations Director at the IBM Visual and Spatial Technology Centre and Do.Collaboration. He has formal education in a wide variety of fields (Fine Arts, Graphic Design, Interior Architecture, Computer Science, and Electronic, Electrical, and Computer Engineering). Dr Ch'ng's research has an overarching theme in Complexity Science. He specialises in advanced interactive systems, enhanced virtual environments, artificial life, and agent-based modelling for marine and terrestrial ecology that requires large computing clusters for processing of agent-interaction and computer graphics rendering, and digital heritage and culture. The fusion of 3D visualisation and agent-based modelling is a unique strength that is applicable to a wide variety of research. He is involved in editorial boards, grant review panels, technical and programme committees in international journals and conferences in his field. Dr Ch'ng is a member of the IEEE Computer Society.

Denise Doyle, with a background in Fine Art Painting and Digital Media, Denise is an Artist-Researcher and Senior Lecturer in Digital Media at the University of Wolverhampton, and PhD Co-Supervisor at SMARTlab Research Institute, University College Dublin. During her PhD research, she developed an art laboratory space in the virtual world, *Second Life*, to investigate creative practice in virtual world spaces. She continues to develop Kriti Island for that purpose. Denise has published widely on the subject of the virtual and the imaginary, the experience of the avatar body in virtual worlds and game spaces, and the use of virtual worlds for creative practice. She sits on two editorial boards, and her research interests include: virtual worlds, art-sci dialogues, interactive film, philosophies of the imagination, practice-based research methods, and digital narratives. She is currently working on a project entitled *Astronauts and Avatars* exploring bodies in real and virtual space.

Stefan Glasauer is a Professor of Neuroscience and the Director of the Center of Sensorimotor Research of the Ludwig-Maximilian University Munich. Glasauer uses computational and mathematical methods from systems and control theory to analyze and model physiological and psychophysical data to derive theories on behavior and perception. His research interests reach from spatial perception and navigation to human-robot interaction to navigation in real and virtual environments, vestibular and ocular-motor systems, posture, motor control, and grip force control.

Charlotte Gould has developed a number of interactive environments that explore user identity and the notion of a floating narrative. She teaches at the University of Salford, UK, and is currently developing location-specific work in which the user becomes an active participant in the narrative and explores methods of user-driven content. She has developed projects for the BBC Big Screen in Liverpool, the Glastonbury Festival, and the ISEA 2009 Belfast; she has presented at ISEA 2008 Singapore and at DAC09 in California.

Ian Gwilt is a Professor of Design and Visual Communication at Sheffield Hallam University. He has exhibited interactive installations and digitally informed artworks at a number of international new media events, galleries, and exhibitions, and holds a PhD from the College of Fine Arts at the University of New South Wales, examining the theory and practice of mixed-reality art. He also holds an MA in Interactive Multimedia (MAIMM), jointly conferred by the University of Balears (UIB) in Spain, and the Royal College of Art (RCA) London, and a BA Hons in Communication Design from Manchester Metropolitan University. Originally from the UK, he has lived and worked in Australia and New Zealand for a number of years, where he began to develop his research/practice around augmented reality and the graphical user interface as creative/cultural artifact. In his current role, he is also interested in exploring new contexts and applications for information design and 'post consumption' visual communication design forms.

Anita McKeown is director of the new CATALYST initiative at SMARTlab at University College Dublin. CATALYST is SMARTlab's Creative Arts Technology Access Lab for Youth Engagement, Social Inclusion, and Technology Transfer. Anita manages the artists and technologists in residence, who work with the lab and the wider community from CATALYST's Dublin studio base at UCD. Working with a number of organisations within the arts, e.g. ART.e @ the art of change, Lewisham Youth Theatre, Music in Prisons, Razor Edge, and Heart N Soul Theatre Company, she has developed extensive experience of project development and management within a range of contexts. This has informed her work as an interdisciplinary artist, producer, and researcher working in the public domain. In 2004, she won the prestigious Bravo Award, the only non-US citizen to do so, for a digital public art project in Memphis and was elected by invitation to the Royal Society of Arts in 2008.

Max Moswitzer lives and works in two cities: in Zurich, where he teaches at the Zurich University of Fine Arts, and in Vienna, where he teaches at the University of Applied Arts. Moswitzer's output is in the construction of playful situations, using dérive and détournement as methodology for transformation and reverse engineering of networked computer games and art systems. Since 1996, he provides his own server (http://www.konsum.net) and is a founding member of www.ludic-society.net. In 2007, Moswitzer moved some of his creative practice into the metaverse, i.e., Second Life, and more lately set up his own grid "New Genres Grid" in the open metaverse. His architectural installation "Whitenoise" was one of four winners for the first Annual Architecture and Design Competition in Second Life, an internationally juried event of Ars Electronica 2007. He is also the architect of "Ouvroir," a virtual museum in Second Life, and at New Genres Grid, created for Chris Marker with whom he collaborates extensively, both in and out of the metaverse.

Gianluca Mura is a transdisciplinary media researcher, architect, digital artist, and designer. His research area is within digital cultures interrelations among art, science, and technology. He holds a PhD in Industrial Design and Multimedia Communication from the Politecnico di Milano University. He is Founder and Editor-in-Chief of the *International Journal of Art, Culture, and Design Technologies* (IJACDT). He is a member of International Scientific Committees and Editorial boards on CYBERWORLDS, Computational Aesthetics (CAE, ARTECH), American Society of Cybernetics (ASC), Tools and Artificial Intelligence (ICTAI), Engineering Technological Innovations (IMETI), MIMOS

(Italian Movement on Modelling and Simulation). He is Chair of the CYBERWORLDS HCI and "Art and Design of Virtual Worlds" and CCCT "Interactive Communication Design Systems" international conference sessions. He organized the International Workshop "Virtuality in Arts and Design" between Politecnico di Milano and Ecole du Louvre, Paris, which has obtained a High Patronage of Italian Ministry of Foreign Affairs, Farnesina, Rome. His digital artworks have been exhibited internationally and are included in the Rhizome archive.

Alistair Payne received his Master of Fine Art from the University of Newcastle upon Tyne in 1998 and his PhD from Chelsea College of Art and Design in 2005. His thesis was titled, "Redefine and Reterritorialise: Painting as an Interdisciplinary Form." He was a Lecturer in Painting at Manchester Metropolitan University between 2002-2005 and at the University of Wolverhampton between 2006-2012, where he was the MA Fine Art Course Leader. Now working as the Programme Leader, BA (Hons) Fine Art, at Glasgow School of Art, he continues to publish writing on Gilles Deleuze and Painting, and to exhibit his work in both the UK and the US.

Martin Rieser is Research Professor at the Institute of Creative Technologies in the Faculty of Art, Design, and Humanities at De Montfort University, and has worked in the field of interactive arts since the early 1980s. As a pioneer curator of international exhibitions in electronic art, including *The Electronic Eye: European Electronic Art* at Watershed (1986), and the first international survey exhibition of Digital Printmaking: *The Electronic Print*, Arnolfini in Bristol (1989). He has recently co-curated the Inside Out exhibition of rapid prototyped miniature sculptures made as an artists' exchange between Australia and the UK, shown at venues in Australia and across the UK. His art practices in Internet and interactive narrative installation art have been seen around the world, including China, France, Holland, Austria, Greece, London, USA, Germany, Italy, and Australia. He has published numerous essays and books on digital art, including *New Screen Media: Cinema/Art/Narrative* (BFI/ZKM, 2002), and has recently edited *The Mobile Audience* (Rodopi, 2011).

Paul Sermon is a Professor of Creative Technology at the University of Salford. Since the early nineteen-nineties, Paul Sermon's practice-based research in the field of contemporary media arts has centred on the creative use of telecommunication technologies. Through his unique use of videoconference techniques in artistic telepresence applications, he has developed a series of celebrated telematic art installations and been awarded the Prix Ars Electronica "Golden Nica" for the hyper media installation "Think about the People Now," in 1991. He received the "Sparkey Award" from the Interactive Media Festival in Los Angeles for the telepresent video installation "Telematic Dreaming" in 1994.

Ian P. Stone has worked in the education sector since 2004. He graduated from the University of Brighton with a BA (Hons) in Humanities in 1998, and gained his MA in Cultural and Critical Studies from Birkbeck College, University of London, in 2011, where his dissertation was on the dialectics of the Jean Luc Godard films *La Chinoise* and *Tout Va Bien*. A heterodox post-fourth international Trotskyist, with research interests in mediation, Soviet and French film theory, and Marxist readings of culture from the 1960s onwards, he is a long-term member of the Socialist Workers Party. He is shortly to commence a PhD in the historiography of Brechtian form in film.

Ross Winning has developed long-time interests in film animation through further postgraduate study at the National Centre for Computer Animation at Bournemouth University. Subsequent projects have included freelance work for commercial broadcast TV. With a background in sculpture, he has also worked as a musician. These interests reflect in a current study that asks questions predicated on the specific function in animation of the relationship of sound and image. More recently, he is focusing on sound and prioritizing sonic phenomena as an avenue to undertake research in animation. This conjunction between two senses of sight and hearing are now informing that research, particularly its implementation and performance in animated media. Currently engaged in PhD study at the Animation Academy, LUSAD, Loughborough University. He also lectures in Animation and leads the Division of Digital Media at the School of Art + Design, University of Wolverhampton.

Suzette Worden is based in Perth, Western Australia. Her current research considers the materiality of design and the social implications of technology for design and new media. She is currently researching art/science relationships concerning astronomy and the development of the Square Kilometre Array (SKA), and geology and mineralogy as part of investigations of the history and cultural heritage of the mining industry in Western Australia. From 2002-2011, she was Professor of Design at Curtin University, in Perth, Western Australia, where previous projects included an Australian Research Council Linkage project 'Innovative Solutions for Wool Garment Comfort through Design' (2007-2010). She continues to supervise doctoral research projects in a part-time role. To date she has co-written three books, contributed chapters to seven, presented peer-reviewed research papers at many international conferences, and co-curated exhibitions on design.

Index